Finding Margaret

Finding Margaret

A case for Reincarnation

Margery Phelps

Cherokee Rose
Publishing, LLC

Canton, Georgia

Cherokee Rose Publishing, LLC, Canton, Ga.

Cover illustrations by Marcia Fajardo.

ISBN: 9780996890205

Printed in the United States of America

DEDICATION

To seekers everywhere –
may you find
Peace, Love and Joy.

INTRODUCTION

This is a true story. I have written it exactly the way it happened to me between January 1987 and December 1990. The descriptions of characters and names have been changed to protect their identity.

I originally wrote the story for my children – to share with them the lessons I learned on this incredible journey – and also as a personal catharsis. I needed to step back and take a look at all that had happened, which is why I wrote the story in third person and did not filter out the day-to-day family activities. It was important to me to be genuine (with exception of protecting certain identifies) and this is the Real Story.

An agent told me that this was not really a novel, that it was only a short story. It's my feeling, however, that to limit it to just the past-life portions would deny the reader the full understanding of how these events play out in daily activities. The trance sessions in the book are quoted from the actual transcripts of my work with my psychologist, Paul Schenk, Psy.D.

When the original manuscript was completed in 1992, my twin sister gave it to her friend and neighbor, who produces t.v. movies. She passed it along to a professional reviewer in Hollywood, who summarized it with the words: "This is a wonderful story." Because of the cost to produce the many period pieces in the book, the movie idea was abandoned; I still think it would make good film.

I hope you will not only enjoy reading about the journey I took to find Margaret, but will also see where there could be similarities in your own life – and that the lessons I learned will give you a deeper and more meaningful understanding of your own journey.

To learn more about the controversial subject of reincarnation please visit my website: www.Reincarnation-For-You.com. I am also available to do talks, so please contact me through the website.

Many years ago I read an inspiring book by Dr. Gerald Jampolsky and Diane Circincione titled *Love is the Answer*. It is my sincerest wish that after reading *Finding Margaret*, that you, too, will agree – Love really is the answer.

Margery Phelps
Waleska, Georgia
November 2015

CHAPTER ONE

"We shall be changed"
-1 Corinthians 15:51

N o, Philip! No, Baby. Please don't cry."

Emma's nightmare jerked her out of a sound sleep. Beads of sweat dripped off her forehead, her blue silk nightgown undulating with the vigorous beat of her heart.

"No, Baby, please don't cry," she called out, the troubling dream of her economics teacher, the handsome Philip Byrd, flashing through her mind again.

Mr. Byrd was kneeling in a muddy field; it was night; a looming shadow hung over him. He looked at his hands and cried.

Emma's body heaved in great sobs but she stifled the troubling emotion so as not to disturb the slumbering hulk next to her. Lying back on the pillow, she rolled over to look at the clock.

Two-thirty. God, two-thirty. Please let me get some sleep. I'm so tired.

Jim let out a long, rumbling snore and Emma poked him gently with a finger. He mumbled in his sleep and turned over, oblivious to his wife's distress.

Emma tossed and turned until five a.m. when she was finally rescued by sleep. She had thirty minutes of blessed peace before the alarm clock rudely awakened her. Reluctantly opening her eyes, she stretched and yawned.

"Come on, Honey. Time to rise and shine!"

The tall redhead was usually cheerful. This morning her pleasantries felt and sounded contrived. Emma was morose about dropping Mr. Byrd's eco-

1

nomics class but she assumed it was her only way out of the troubling nightmares about her teacher.

Jim's business is a mess; I'll have to work all weekend to get ready for taxes. The last thing I need is nightmares about a teacher.

Emma rose slowly from the king-size brass bed and shuffled toward the spacious bathroom she shared with her husband of twenty-two years. Jim was already dressed and passed her in the alcove between the closet and dressing room.

"Breakfast in thirty minutes, Baby," he said, patting her on the fanny. Jim's fat feet fell silently on plush carpet as he ambled through the bedroom and went downstairs to cook their morning meal.

Alone in their suite, Emma searched her mind for answers to puzzling questions about the teacher while brushing her teeth and washing her face. Staring into the mirror, she talked to the brown-eyed, fair skinned forty-two year old woman who gazed back at her.

I've never had such feelings.

A shiver ran down her spine.

—all those weird dreams and nightmares. If I'm away from Mr. Byrd, they'll go away. I'll be better off if I drop that class and never see him again.

Jim called her to breakfast. Emma put finishing touches on her makeup, highlighting cheekbones with rosy blush and coating eyelashes with rich, brown mascara. Emma was sensitive about her freckles and paid particular attention to her appearance. Her eyes were her best feature and she played them up, carefully defining brows and applying soft brown eye shadow. She outlined the heart-shaped lips of her small mouth with a russet colored lip pencil, filled in with matching lipstick, and patted powder on her little pug nose. Looking much younger than her years, Emma forced a smile at the face in the mirror while fussing with her thick mane of short, reddish blond curls.

Emma pulled pantyhose up each long leg and slipped a robe over her slender five foot seven inch frame before joining her husband and son at the breakfast table. The bacon was crisp and Jim's pancakes were yummy.

"Pancakes are delicious, honey" she said, sipping a cup of perfectly brewed coffee. *Jim's such a good cook,* Emma said to herself, remembering the first breakfast her husband made many years before. She was working until two and three every morning on the bookkeeping and inventory for his auto parts business and only had a few hours sleep before going to her full-time day job. After several months of this grueling routine, Jim volunteered to cook breakfast to let Emma could sleep an extra thirty minutes. He was useless when it came to accounting, the routine worked well and he had been cooking breakfast ever since.

Jim should be a house-husband.

At six feet two and weighing over two hundred and thirty pounds, he was an imposing figure. His short, dark auburn hair was always neat, even when the rest of his appearance was disheveled, which was most of the time. His dark brown eyes were framed with thick glasses that corrected his poor vision. Tanned, freckled skin reflected the out-door work he preferred. Jim's casual attitude and often-outlandish sense of humor did not lend themselves to the corporate America image Emma envisioned for him when they married.

She finished eating and ran upstairs to dress. Emma wanted to be on the road before seven o'clock to get a jump on the frantic Atlanta traffic. After the usual I love yous and good-byes, she put a bowl of milk in the garage for the cats and reminded Jim to fill the feeder in the dog pen before driving J.D. to school. Stopping briefly at the door to her mother's apartment, Emma called, "Good morning, Bee." Mrs. Browning was still in bed and returned her daughter's greeting. "I'll be in late tonight, Emma. Going to an opening at the High."

"Okay, Mama, have a good time and enjoy the exhibition," Emma answered, wishing she had time to go to gala openings of art exhibitions. Emma and her twin sister Rachel practically lived the first twenty years of their lives at the High Museum in mid-town Atlanta, and Emma missed those social events after her marriage to Jim. Although he was intelligent, he had not been raised with the fine arts and related activities. He had never been to the opening of an art exhibition and didn't know the difference between a Beethoven symphony and Mozart concerto.

Emma left the house and was serenaded with the morning recital of barking dogs and crowing roosters.

"Hush, pups," she called out. The dogs stopped barking when they recognized her voice and a rooster let loose with another splendid crow to welcome the new morning.

To her delight, Emma arrived at her office in Chamblee at seven-thirty; the perimeter highway traffic was lighter than usual and she made the twenty-five mile trip from Stone Mountain in forty minutes. She hung her coat in her bathroom and went to the kitchen to get coffee. At her desk Emma turned the page on the calendar. In the upper corner was a picture of a little bird and the quote for the day, "Change can begin with one person and one thought."

Emma was startled by the words. The night before she was standing in the cold February weather with Mr. Byrd, a light drizzle of rain falling on them while he told her, "Every one reaches a point in life where they must make some changes." The drawing of the little bird and Philip's words echoed in her mind.

That's strange.

She tore the page into little pieces and threw it away.

Good bye, Mr. Byrd. Please don't bother me anymore.

"I knew I shouldn't have taken that class. My feelings told me that I would regret it. Why didn't I listen to myself?" she mumbled.

Emma felt the new and strange emotions evoked by the teacher welling up again; she took out her journal and started writing. The first time she saw Mr. Byrd, four weeks earlier, she knew he would be an important person in her life. Why? In what way? Why did her silent voice tell her he was special, that she should protect him? From what? In spite of her life-long experiences with premonitions and foreboding dreams, she never had an episode such as this.

Philip Byrd had characteristics Emma admired in a man—he was tall and princely; his gray-blue eyes were deep set and penetrating. His black hair was thinning on the crown, exhibiting to Emma a sign of maturity and wisdom. His body was strong and athletic without being muscle-bound and watching his gestures she could sense strength in his hands. He had a brilliant mind and quick wit. His voice was deep and sonorous; when he talked she hung on every word. He was the epitome of manliness in every way except one—he easily blushed.

Although Emma admired Mr. Byrd, her attraction wasn't physical. His honesty and mental attitude were appealing and she felt he would never tell a lie. Like her mother, Mr. Byrd was honest to the core—unlike Emma's husband and his mother, whose lives were made up of pretense and deception. She longed for an open, candid, platonic relationship with him. He was special for some reason and Emma did not know what it was. In her dreams she saw him beside the aura of a woman and it was obvious they were in love. Was she his wife or girlfriend or someone from his past?

If I was infatuated with him, wouldn't I feel jealous of that woman? I care for her; he loves her; he's happy with her. They belong together but I don't know why. I do feel wonderful though when he smiles at me. I feel his happiness. I also feel such a terrible sadness. Why? Where does it come from?

A deep shiver shook her body.

Emma's strange feelings for Mr. Byrd intensified during the first few weeks of winter quarter and she wondered if the unusual emotions were mutual. Emma's sense of humor and interest in a wide variety of subjects made her popular with classmates and the teacher did seem to pay attention to her. Several students thought she was a teacher's pet because Emma was about the same age as the professor.

"When we walk to the parking lot after class we always chat for a few minutes," she wrote in her journal. "We talk about truth and honesty and how much lies hurt. He must have a family even though he won't talk about them; it seems to be a painful subject.

"I wonder if he can tell what I'm thinking; I always know what he's going to say. I feel safe with him; I trust him. When I told him last night I had to drop his course, he was kind and understanding; he seemed to be sorry I would not be there any longer. He said we all get to a point where we have to make changes; I wonder what kind of changes he has made.

"I feel sadness around him. When he looks at me, though, he smiles from the bottom of his soul. I hope he believed me when I told him I have an ulcer and my doctor ordered me to drop some activities. I'm glad I had the ulcer to use as an excuse. I know why I dropped the class. Being with him is too painful; I can't bear that grief. God, what's happening to me? In my forty-two years I've never felt this way!"

Emma was thankful the phones weren't busy while she wrote in her journal. She went to the kitchen for coffee, picked up her economics book and leafed through it while thinking about school and completing her accounting degree. When she started reading her mind wandered off; unable to concentrate, she returned to her journaling, recording her first encounter with Philip Byrd.

He ran into the classroom the opening night of winter quarter and slammed his book down on the desk. Emma was absorbed in the first chapter of the text book and did not stop reading to acknowledge his presence. She ignored him a few moments longer until she felt a stare and looked up into the most intriguing eyes she had ever seen. In that moment, Emma saw a vision that gave her a foreboding premonition.

He's special—protect him.

The words were spoken by a small woman with short gray hair and a sweet, very wrinkled face. Rimless glasses sat on her short, pointed nose and a depression era dress and shawl covered her frail body. She peered at the teacher

5

over the top of her spectacles and held her arms out in front of Mr. Byrd as if to shield him from some sort of danger.

Emma's *special feelings*, her label for mystifying dreams and visions, were always about someone she knew or loved. She was stunned. She did not know this man and she had no idea who the little woman was. She was scared; very, very scared.

What's happening to me?

She blinked her eyes to erase the vision. The little woman was still there, repeating her foreboding message. Looking down at her desk, Emma opened and closed her eyes. "Go away!" she demanded under her breath.

In a commanding voice, the teacher said, "My name is Philip Byrd. I'll be teaching this course."

He asked the students to introduce themselves. "Tell us something about yourself and why you're in school."

The class was a cross-section of America; there was a brilliant young man from Viet Nam who wanted to be an electrical engineer; a late-twenties lady who was a crime photographer for the Georgia Bureau of Investigation; the middle-age man who was a ceramics engineer; several college kids who were taking the class because it was required for their degrees. And there was Emma, the brown-eyed, middle-aged secretary.

When her turn came Emma told them she was a mother of two; her daughter was a sophomore at Georgia Tech and her son a freshman in high school.

"My name is Emma St. Claire. I'm a secretary. I've been in construction for seventeen years and done some contracting on my own; even built my own home. I was journalism major in college many years ago, I'm a Red Cross volunteer and," she happily stated, "I'm an identical twin!"

Emma also told her classmates she had been in college off and on for many years and decided she would never finish.

"Only fools complete their education—wise men never do. I hope someday to be very wise."

Her comment generated chuckles from classmates who must have been wondering why someone her age would be in college. The teacher made pleasant comments about each person's remarks. He showed a genuine knowledge of photography and asked the GBI lady several technical questions. Each student received a few minutes of the Prof's undivided attention. Emma was one of the last to speak. When she finished she was disappointed not to receive the same courtesy. She thought her comments were clearly as pertinent as the others and was hurt to be passed over.

In retaliation she blurted out, "We told you about us. Now we want to know something about you. What are your qualifications to teach?"

Mr. Byrd glared at her. He couldn't ignore Emma's question and was annoyed he should have to answer to a student—even if she was close to his age.

"I have an engineering degree and received my master's in economics. I've worked at Atlantic Air Lines for ten years and I've been teaching forever," he said, glaring at Emma condescendingly as if to say, "Does that qualify me to teach you?"

He hastily changed the subject and started his introductory remarks. "When was the Declaration of Independence signed?"

One loud mouth yelled out, "July Fourth, 1776."

Emma knew that was not the right answer to the question and kept her mouth shut.

"July Fourth was the day the Declaration was posted. It was signed on August second."

He went on to tell them that things are not always what they seem; that truth is often obscured; that you have to search your entire life for Truth—and the way to Truth is education.

"If you are not in this class to learn for the sake of learning, you don't have any business being here."

Now I know why he ignored my remarks about education and wisdom—I stole his thunder. Score one for the student.

The remaining class time he lectured them about honesty, truth and open-mindedness; and economics.

Economics? This guy should be teaching philosophy.

Class ended too soon for Emma; she was spellbound by the economics teacher. Younger students left but Emma lingered behind to bundle up for the twenty-degree weather on the cold January night. She put on her boots, heavy fur-lined leather coat and fur hat. Likewise, the teacher stood in a far corner, putting on his overcoat, hat and scarf.

How cute he looks.

Emma felt motherly as if watching her small son. While trying to ignore her maternal feelings for him an unexplained shiver ran down her spine. Her body trembled; she was freezing cold.

Such a handsome boy. And smart.

Emma wanted to put her arms around him, give him a hug and tell him she was proud of him, the way she would display her affection for J.D.

How did he grow up so fast?

She stared intently at him, feeling he was only a toddler; she wanted to pick him up and cradle him in her arms. Emma shivered again while trying to shake off the bizarre emotions.

"I bet he has never told a lie," she mumbled, remembering the hurt from her husband's most recent bout of deception.

"I'm looking forward to this class," Emma finally said to him. "I don't know anything about economics—this will be a challenge."

"I've been studying economics for years and I'm still learning."

They left the classroom together. Emma's heart was pounding like a hammer and the sensation alarmed her.

What is this man doing to me? Why do I feel this way? I have a dreadful feeling something bad is going to happen.

"I guess you're parked in the student parking lot, aren't you?" he asked, implying that she shouldn't be walking with him.

"No." She was half embarrassed and half delighted to have an excuse to walk and talk with him. "I have a permit for the teacher's lot; have a little neuritis in my leg—can't tolerate too much cold. I got these boots in Germany," she prattled on, "and get them out every winter. Don't know what I'd do without them. We don't make them the same way in this country and they would never last eighteen years the way these have. There ought to be some sort of economics lesson in that, don't you think?"

He grinned at her and chuckled.

"I think you're going to do okay in my class."

He turned toward his car; Emma was alone in the dark.

She climbed into her cherry red Chevy pickup truck, thankful for the time to be alone. Still puzzled by her maternal and protective feelings for a grown man who was a complete stranger, Emma was relieved when the road to home appeared and she turned off the freeway. A mile from her house she steered the truck onto a rock and gravel trail. The old road was in bad condition from winter weather and a storm the week before had been its undoing.

Reaching the driveway her truck started up the slight incline toward Fairfield, the grand home she and her family designed and built. Most of the lights were out but the rambling cedar house was clearly visible in the moonlight. Remnants of frozen rain were sprinkled on drooping junipers that lined the sidewalk to the porch, and lights in the breakfast room shone through the wide kitchen window. It was warm and inviting.

Emma thought about Mr. Byrd.

What kind of home does he have? Does a beautiful wife welcome him home? He's special; he should have a beautiful woman on his arm.

Even though Emma's love for Jim had been tarnished by his years of habitual lying and his over-bearing, interfering mother, she was pleased to be greeted by someone who loved her.

"How was your class?" Jim asked when she opened the back door off the garage. Because the garage was full of Jim's junk and possibilities Emma left her truck outside. For years Emma silently endured Jim's mess—every wrecked car he was going to rebuild and sell; every motor to be overhauled; every transmission to be repaired. None of the possibilities ever became realities; Jim's business debts soared and Emma became the person she dreaded most, a working mother.

"Class was wonderful. We have a terrific teacher this quarter."

Emma wished that Jim would teach as they had planned; she put him through his last two years of college and a year of graduate school and his refusal to work in education was a bitter disappointment.

Jim kissed her softly on the lips and Emma hugged her husband while he ran his rough hand down her backside.

Good old Jim. Always ready to jump in the hay and have a romp.

"Why don't you pour us a glass of wine?" she suggested.

Emma stuck her head in the door of Bee's studio apartment to check on her mother. "Whatcha up to now?" Emma asked. Bee was sitting at her drawing board, working on a botanical drawing. "This is for the Chattahoochee Nature Center," she said, without taking her eyes away from her work. Knowing that Bee did not tolerate interruptions while she was working, Emma silently slipped back out the door. Emma's mother had a distinguished career as a medical and scientific illustrator for the C.D.C. and her work impacted the lives of millions of people. With Bee's drawings, doctors in remote villages in the far reaches of the globe were able to make diagnoses of diseases and prescribe treatments and she was recognized as an expert on many parasitic afflictions.

After her retirement, Bee devoted herself to ecological and nature groups and did art work for their publications for free. As the sole support of her three children, Bee had been a tireless, high-energy person, self-sufficient and self-motivated. Now she was enjoying life with travel and friends, church and civic organizations.

Emma breezed through the kitchen and huge family room and walked down the long hall to J.D.'s room. His crutches were lying on the floor and he was propped up in bed with his leg in a full-length splint.

"How's your knee feeling tonight 'Punkin?" she asked. J.D. had a serious case of Osgood-Schlatter disease and the painful disorder frequently required the use of leg splints to hold his knee in place while the broken and chipped bone fragments healed. He had been in and out of knee braces and splints since he was ten, and always handled the painful disability without complaint.

"Okay, I guess," he mumbled.

She kissed her fifteen-year-old son on the cheek, brushing aside the swatch of curly red hair that hung on his forehead. He was already as tall as Jim and sporting activities gave him a defined musculature. Like his dad, he wore glasses but J.D. had beautiful, piercing blue eyes. His voice was deep yet quiet and in spite of his size, he was gentle, thoughtful and almost too sensitive. Emma's son was a masculine edition of her first born, a tall, slender, pretty redheaded daughter.

Slowly climbing the wide staircase to the master suite, Emma studied each spindle, each put in place by the hands of her family during the two years it took them to build the impressive home. At the top landing she paused before entering her retreat. Thick moss green carpet invited her to dig her toes into its plush pile. Sitting on the white sofa she unzipped her boots and leaned back, massaging her feet while gazing at portraits of her beautiful children.

In spite of warm clothes, Emma's leg ached. Hobbling to the bathroom she turned on the tub faucets and started to undress. Easing her tired body into the swirling Jacuzzi bubbles, Emma was soon mesmerized. Submerged to her chin, she thought about her reactions to the strange man.

Why do I feel this way? What am I supposed to protect him from? Why?

She thought she had achieved most of her life's goals; her children were nearly grown and their home was built. She was looking forward to having grandchildren some day. Now, for some reason, she was being drawn to a man she didn't even know and felt there was something important she had to do.

What? What am I supposed to do?

Her thoughts were interrupted by Jim presenting her with a glass of wine. He undressed and slipped into the tub although he had showered earlier in the evening. Jim St. Claire never passed up the opportunity to rub his naked body next to Emma's in the Jacuzzi.

***

"Emma. Emma, you out there?"

Her boss was calling again and Emma realized she had been totally absorbed in thoughts of Philip Byrd and everything that happened the day of her fateful meeting with him. She had written five pages.

I've got to get myself together.

She put her journal aside and rushed into Joe's office.

"Yes, Joe?"

Joe was seated at the imposing partner's desk in front of five tall windows in his handsome office. Afternoon sun filtered through sheer curtains and accentuated Joe's rich, brown hair. His almost leathery skin was deeply tanned, even in winter months, and his average build, five foot eleven inch body was clothed with a wine-colored turtleneck shirt beneath an expensive argyle sweater. Even when dressed casually, he was elegant. Joe was nine years older than Emma and if asked to describe him, she would say he was cute. He had a square face with a turned-up nose, full lips and half-rimless glasses brought attention to his hazel eyes.

"Didn't you say you were putting on a pot of coffee? I could use a shot!"

"Of course. Sorry it slipped my mind."

Emma went to the kitchen to put on the afternoon coffee—her duty since Joe made the morning coffee. Emma thought about her good fortune in landing a job with Joe. The atmosphere at home was frequently unpleasant, at best, and Emma's job was a breath of clean, fresh air on a hot, smothering polluted summer day. The coffee finished perking and Emma poured a mug for Joe and a cup for herself. When she set it on his desk, he asked her how school was going.

She started slowly, "My ulcer is acting up again and my doctor said to slow down." She chuckled, "I figured it would be better to drop school than to quit my job."

"That's for damn sure. Guess you do stay pretty busy, don't you, what with J.D.'s football and soccer and PTA and those other clubs you belong to."

Emma heard the bell on the door and looked around to see Jim entering the office. She tried to greet him warmly although she was irritated he interrupted her conversation with Joe. Jim didn't keep regular business hours and frequently dropped in on Emma to handle personal business, much to her chagrin.

"Whatcha need?" she whispered.

"We're going to put a second mortgage on the house," he said in a demanding voice, "you have to sign these papers."

11

He handed her a legal file folder full of mortgage deeds and loan commitments, legal descriptions and sundry pertinent papers. Emma was leafing through the file when the special feeling spoke to her: *Don't sign these; we will lose everything.*

"I can't sign these, Jim."

"What do you mean? My attorney approved them and the bank is waiting on them right now. Hurry up, would you. I need to get out there."

"I told you I can't sign them," she retorted, trying to keep her voice down.

"Why not?" Jim asked angrily.

"My feelings say we'll lose everything if I sign these papers."

"Oh, you and those feelings of yours. You're always conjuring up things. Why don't you ever think positive?"

"I do think positive, Jim. I also have to listen to my inner self. Right now it's telling me not to sign these stupid papers."

"Stupid? Is that what you call my business? It will be stupid for us not to take some money out of the house and use it. We have too much equity in it. Besides, my business needs some cash," Jim said pathetically with a change of tone. "If you don't sign these, I'll lose my company. That's what your silly feelings should be telling you, 'cause that's the truth." He was almost begging her now. "Please, Emma, this will be the last time. I promise."

Every time Jim manipulated their finances to draw out cash he promised it would be the last time. Emma's inner voice told her that this really would be the last time.

We'll lose everything.

She sat at her desk and reviewed the documents. Everything appeared to be in order for a second mortgage on their home. If for some reason Jim couldn't pay off the forty thousand dollars when it was due in twelve months, the bank promised to roll it into their first mortgage and give them a new loan. Emma did some calculations, including her income and rent from another house. Even with no money from Jim, the income ratio for the new mortgage was acceptable to her and the house was increasing in value yearly.

"Okay," she relented, "this is absolutely the last time, Jim. I don't know why you don't go to your mother for this. She's the one who wanted you to build houses to begin with. It was never my idea."

Emma signed the papers and went to the supply room to Xerox them for her personal files before returning them to Jim. She kissed her husband on the cheek.

"Be careful out there."

Jim smiled adoringly at his wife.

"You won't be sorry."

Emma watched him drive away in his old pick-up truck.

Yes, I will; we'll lose everything.

Larry, Emma's other boss, came in and handed her an envelope with information and forms on a new subcontractor.

"Emma, please open a new vendor file on this fellow. You'll have to send him our standard letter requesting his insurance certificate and employer identification number. Don't forget to enclose some of our subcontractor draw forms and the usual stuff."

"Okay."

Glad to have some work to keep her busy, Emma opened the envelope and pulled out the subcontract agreement. Her knees went limp and she sank into her chair when she read the name: Byrd Landscaping Service. Emma moaned.

Not again. What the hell is going on?

One of the awful nightmares about Philip Byrd came flooding into her mind. He was kneeling in a muddy field at night and was holding an object; Emma could not make out what it was. She thought he was planting something. Then he looked up and started crying. The bad dream always awakened Emma and sent shivers up and down her spine.

Such things don't happen.

She booted up her computer, ran forms for Byrd Landscaping, typed a letter and took it to Larry for his signature.

"Will you have more mail today? This is my Red Cross night and I need to get my uniform on and freshen up before I leave."

"That's fine, go ahead." He handed her the signed letter.

While she powdered her nose and brushed her teeth, Emma pondered again the day's distressing events.

My special feelings are getting the best of me. I'll have to try harder to ignore them.

Emma changed into her Red Cross uniform, gathered the mail and left. When she steered her truck into the hospital parking lot Emma realized she had made the entire trip in a fog, with no memory of the twenty-mile drive.

Got to get myself together; people are depending on me. Philip Byrd will have to protect himself. Once and forever and ever, good-bye, Mr. Byrd!

She slammed the heavy truck door.

Scurrying up the emergency door entrance ramp, Emma waved to the cheerful security guard and her friend on the desk.

"Busy tonight?"

"No, not too bad," the elderly lady answered. "I think CCU got a new admission from us, though. I sent the paperwork to the front desk; it should be on the census when you bring it up."

"Okay. I'll check for a new admission. Have a quiet evening."

"Thanks. See ya at the cafeteria."

Emma thought momentarily how nice it would be to sit down and have a pleasant meal with her fellow volunteers and friends on the admissions staff. She reached the Intensive Care Unit, put her coat and purse in the locker room and brought up the patient census on the computer. She wrote patients' names in the Red Cross visitation book and crossed the hall to CCU where she repeated the process, chatting happily with nurses while the printer put out a new census. Emma yanked it off and turned to the desk to enter names in the book.

Not again, no, no, not again.

"You okay, Emma?" one of the nurses asked.

"It's nothing."

Emma tried to brush off the surreal feelings. The name of the new patient in CCU, in bed number one, was Mr. William Byrd. Emma had a strange pain in her chest as another vision of the little gray-haired lady flashed through her mind; and a very strong chill shook her body.

CHAPTER TWO

"Gladness and joy are taken away..."
-Jeremiah 49:33

Emma was pleasant and compassionate while helping visitors in ICU and CCU but beneath her calm and cheerful demeanor lurked nagging premonitions about protecting Philip Byrd and losing everything. She hoped someone would sign up to visit the new patient in coronary care. By the time she left the hospital at nine o'clock, his only visitors had been doctors and nurses. She drove home in another fog, relieved to arrive safely at her refuge in the country on North Ridge Road; it was another world, far, far away from the chaotic pace of Atlanta.

Ignoring the negative feelings from her encounter with Jim earlier in the day, Emma cheerfully greeted her husband.

"Hi, Honey."

Jim was working on an engine in his workshop.

"Any interesting cases at the hospital?"

"No, nothing special. I need to call Rachel," she said, running into the house.

Rachel was the levelheaded twin. She always had solutions for Emma's problems. Although Rachel didn't have Emma's history of special feelings, she had enough episodes to know how frightening they could feel and she never lacked advice. Even though they were identical twins, Rachel frequently referred to Emma as "the lesser twin." Rachel was slightly heavier and Emma was taller and the minor differences magnified the disparity. Unlike her sister's usually long, full haircuts, Rachel opted for shorter styles with curls. They both had worn contact lenses but Rachel reverted to glasses after a cornea injury.

"Rachel." Emma snuffled.

"I knew you were going to call, Sweetie. What's the matter? You sound upset."

"Remember the economics teacher I told you about and the warning that he was special and I was to protect him?"

"Yes. Has something happened?"

"I dropped his class yesterday, Rachel. I couldn't stand those feelings."

"Good for you, Emma. You always worry about everyone else. I'm glad it's behind you."

"That's what I thought when I dropped the class. You won't believe what happened today."

Emma gave Rachel a blow-by-blow description of the day's events that kept bringing up Philip Byrd's name and launched into yet another discourse of the troubling dreams.

"The first one came only a couple days after I met him. He was kneeling in a field at night. There were puddles around him, and mud, and trees in the distance. For some reason there's a shadow behind him. How can there be a shadow at night? He's looking at something on the ground; I don't know what. Then he looks up and starts crying."

Emma sobbed while recounting the nightmare that plagued her.

"Please don't cry, Sweetie."

"Then there's a dream of him in an office. He's talking to people. There is a woman with him that I can't see."

"What do you mean, you can't see her."

"She's an aura. A light. Some sort of presence right next to him."

"Is that everything?" the younger twin asked.

"No, there's one more. I hear a loud noise while I'm sleeping and wake up in a panic, calling his name. The first time it happened I thought it was a thunderstorm. When I went to the window and looked out, it wasn't even raining. Besides, thunder storms are rare in winter."

"This is quite a puzzle, Emma. Try not to let it bother you. It must be something out of his past. Maybe he's grieving for someone and that's what you're feeling."

"Why? I've never had a special feeling about a stranger. Never. Why him? I've never had one about the past either. They're always in the future. I even had one about myself today."

"You did? What?"

"Jim showed up at the office and talked me into signing some papers for a second mortgage. We have quite a bit of equity and he needs more money for his damn business. My feelings told me we would lose everything. I didn't want to sign anything. Jim pressured me. He never has given my special feelings any credence. Anyway, the papers appeared to be in order and his attorney had checked them over. We have tons of insurance, too. I don't know why I feel terribly negative about it. Lose everything? Good Lord, I don't know how it could happen."

"It won't happen, Emma. We'll figure out what's going on and you'll know what to do. You've done that lots of times," Rachel consoled her sister. "You wouldn't be alive and I wouldn't have a beautiful redhead niece at Georgia Tech if her Mama didn't have e.s.p..."

Emma ignored Rachel's allusion to the fact that Emma would already be dead if she didn't have e.s.p.

"I hate that expression, Rachel." While trying to explain how uncomfortable those words were to her, memories of a day in 1967 floated before Emma's eyes.

She was standing in a crystal factory near Frankfurt, Germany with Shirley, the wife of a major. Against her feelings, Emma left eight-month old Allison in the care of Shirley's children—in the car. It was a cool, balmy day and the windows were down. In Germany, the children were frequently left outside unattended, even in trams on sidewalks. Being in a large, comfortable car would be safe.

About ten minutes later Emma's silent voice said, *check the baby*. She told Shirley she was going to look in on the children but her friend said, "They're fine; you can see them from this window over here."

Emma's voice said again, *check the baby*! Without hesitation Emma charged down a long aisle of expensive crystal, heeding the advice of her silent voice, oblivious of costly damage she would do if she banged into a shelf. Frantically opening the tailgate of the Chevy station wagon Emma retrieved a bundle of blanket.

"Move," she snapped at Shirley's two alarmed children. They had made a heavy Army blanket bedroll and wrapped it around Emma's precious baby, trapping Allison and completely cutting off air.

Jerk the blanket, the voice said. *Jerk the blanket.*

Emma feared her baby was dead; she hysterically pulled the blanket. The bundle unrolled, over and over. There was no indication of life within the folds. Emma jerked and pulled, again and again, tears streaming down her face. On the final yank, Allison rolled free and landed on her back with a flump, gasping as a breath of air was forced into her lungs by her fall against the carpeted floorboard. The baby's deathly whitish gray color disappeared before Emma's eyes and she thanked God for saving Allison's life while clutching the darling baby to her breast.

Shirley would never acknowledge the incident and Emma felt estranged from her new friend. This was one time Emma St. Claire was glad she had e.s.p.

***

"You have a gift, Emma; a God-given gift. The answers will come to you. They always do," Rachel said softly.

An hour later Jim came upstairs and found Emma curled up on the sofa, clutching pillows, crying in her sleep.

"Baby," Jim whispered to his slumbering wife, "I've got the water running for your bath. Please don't cry. My business will be okay—as soon as I sell another house. You'll see. Come on now and soak in the tub; you'll feel better," he said softly, pulling her up.

The tub was almost filled and Emma turned on the water jets before submerging herself in body massaging bubbles. She thought about her teacher. She had never been telepathic with anyone except Rachel and her uncanny ability to read Philip Byrd's mind was troubling. Emma did not know the first thing about economics but for some reason she always knew what her teacher was going to say before he said it. His lecture about opportunity cost was one that Emma would never forget.

He came into class, slammed his book on the desk to get the students' attention and started his lecture, as usual, with a question.

"What is opportunity cost?"

Emma thought about ice-cold beer.

We are in the middle of winter. Why would I be thinking about a beer now? I hardly ever drink beer anyway. If I was going to have a beer it would be on a hot summer afternoon after I mowed the lawn.

Even though Emma tried to concentrate on the lecture she missed much of the explanation of opportunity cost.

"Now you can see," Mr. Byrd said, "the opportunity cost for an ice cold beer on a hot summer afternoon when you've finished cutting the grass will be much higher—"

18

Emma was lost again. How did she know he was going to talk about a cold beer? On a hot summer afternoon? Why did she know what he was going to say? Emma did not understand her mind's attachment to this teacher and it scared her. No, it terrified her.

Why has he affected me this way?

Emma thought of his beautiful smile and icy cold shivers shuddered down her spine and violently shook her body.

***

The sun was up before Emma on Saturday and she awoke with a start when morning light hit the bedroom windows. She never closed the curtains because there was nothing behind their house except woods and it didn't bother Emma that a deer or rabbit might see her naked in the bedroom. She loved being close to nature. After a breakfast of sausage, fried eggs fresh from the yard and homemade biscuits, Emma enjoyed a leisurely second cup of coffee while she and Jim discussed the day's activities.

"Whatcha up to today, Honey?"

"I'm going out to the subdivision to set the grade stakes for another house. The bank gave me the go ahead yesterday. Said the more I build the better."

"Jim, you're only one man. You can't possibly start another house. You don't even have contracts on the other three yet. You think you're making money because you get construction draws. Don't forget, you have to pay your vendors and subcontractors with that money first. I wish you had a better grasp on accounting. You'd realize what your business is doing to us. You work sixty hours a week and you're killing yourself. The bank loves for you to build houses because you have to pay them huge amounts of interest. They are the only ones making any money. Can't you see that?"

"I can't do anything right, can I?" Jim yelled and stormed out of the house.

Emma was remorseful over her words even though she was right. Everything they had was invested in Jim's business; only the bank was making money. By the time Jim finished a house and sold it, interest had eaten away their profit. Emma thought it would be more sensible for Jim to work directly for the bank if they wanted to be in the home building business. Because the loan officer was disorganized and slack, characteristics of Jim, Emma worried about the deals they conjured up; she wrote to Jim's vendors and told them she was not an officer of his company and was in no way responsible for his bills.

Emma did the bookkeeping only, refusing to sign checks, contracts or construction loan commitments.

She cleaned the kitchen and went upstairs to dress for morning errands. The previous night's crying was cathartic and Emma felt calm, though her eyes were swollen and red. She put on a favorite pair of snug old jeans, one of Jim's T-shirts, a warm silk turtleneck shirt and the heavy wool cream-colored cable-knit sweater Jim gave her for Christmas. She pulled on her German boots and marched down the stairs. The temperature was in the low thirties when Emma stepped outdoors into the cheerful sunlight.

"What a glorious morning." She took in a deep breath and stretched. "What a wonderful day to be alive!"

Emma hummed a tune while walking down the path behind the house to the dog pen.

"Morning, pups, Mama's here," she called out to her motley crew of canine friends. Alex was taking his morning romp in the fifty-gallon water pan he used for a pool while the other seven dogs were still in their heated doghouse. Emma gave them each a handful of dog biscuits, emptied and cleaned their drinking water pail and left the fresh water running to refill it while she fed the chickens, clucking softly at them as they gathered around her when she entered their pen.

I do love it out here. Please, Lord, don't let anything happen to my little corner of the world.

She returned to the dog pen and turned off the water after running the hose in Alex's swimming pool. The small black water spaniel jumped into the fresh, icy cold water. "Don't know why you don't freeze to death, Alex."

"I've got a busy day, folks." Emma gave each of her pets a pat before heading up the path to her truck. The canine chorus was in fine voice by the time she was out of sight, the rooster pitched in with his morning crow and Emma drove down the long driveway to the dirt road.

Emma enjoyed the freedom of Saturday mornings; the sparkling sun and crisp February air put roses in her cheeks. She steered her truck to the east when she reached the freeway and savored the warmth of sun on her face. Feeling guilty about her husband's angry departure, she decided to swing by the new subdivision and make amends with Jim. One of his houses was nearing completion and she wanted to see how he had decorated it. Although Emma would be the first to admit that her opinion was biased, she thought Jim had a remarkable flair for decorating; his homes were lovely.

"Howdy," she called to Ray when she saw the rotund developer leaning against his truck, sipping on a cup of coffee, "have you seen Jim this morning?"

"He was here earlier; said he was going to set the grade stakes on Lot Nine," the affable man replied.

When Emma could not find Jim at Lot Nine she drove down to the cul de sac next to the lake where the first houses were nearing completion. She was annoyed when she arrived at Jim's new house and found his truck parked on the freshly poured concrete driveway.

"Jim, are you here?"

She pushed open the unlocked door.

"Yeah, I'm in the kitchen."

He was laying tile around the Jenn-Aire range mounted in an island cabinet in the center of the kitchen.

"Honey, this is beautiful."

The kitchen was light and airy and decorated in shades of pale gray and white with rose-colored accents. The wall covering in the breakfast room was stylish and sophisticated and not the typical kitchen motif the other builders used. Jim learned from his wife that kitchens should be both beautiful and functional and he spared no expense to achieve these ideals. Solid oak cabinets were carefully stained and varnished inside and out and were as smooth as a baby's bottom.

"I thought you were going to set the grade stakes on Lot Nine."

"I forgot. I'll do it later."

Emma was concerned that Jim had forgotten what he planned to do and changed the subject.

"This house should move quickly, Honey, you've outdone yourself this time."

He smiled adoringly at his wife, appreciating her acceptance of his efforts. "Have you seen the master bath?"

"Not yet. Have you set the Jacuzzi the way you planned?"

"Yep, I did. You'll love it; go take a look."

Emma leisurely toured the ample two-story house. Jim ought to be a decorator, she thought, looking out the dining room window at his truck parked on the driveway. The red Georgia clay embedded in the tires left tread marks on the three-day old concrete and she knew it would be next to impossible to remove the stains.

Will he ever learn?

Emma couldn't understand why Jim was meticulous about some details and blatantly careless about others.

What difference does it make how beautiful the house is decorated if it doesn't have curb appeal?

After checking over the rest of the house and admiring the master bath, Emma returned to the kitchen and kissed Jim on the cheek.

"Don't let me stop you; think I'll look at your Tudor house across the street before I leave."

"I'll go with you. I'm at a good stopping place."

Although Emma bit her tongue when they walked past Jim's truck, she could contain her annoyance no longer.

"Why did you park your truck on the fresh concrete?" she quietly asked.

Jim looked down in dismay at the red stains.

"I didn't think about it."

"You ought to," Emma said in rebuttal, trying to hide her irritation.

"You always find something to criticize, don't you," Jim snapped.

"Please, Honey. I'm not criticizing. I'm trying to help. Who's going to look inside a house if the new drive is already stained? First impressions are important to home buyers."

They arrived at the front door of the Tudor house.

"Haven't you already set the plumbing fixtures in this house?" she inquired when they stepped onto the porch.

"I guess," Jim blankly responded.

"Honey, you have already drawn the money for the dry-in on this house; the insulation and sheet rock. Don't you remember?"

"No, I don't."

He looked as if he was lost in a fog. He unlocked the door and pushed it open; Emma's jaw dropped to her chest.

Following payout schedules on contractor draw sheets from the bank, she expected to see this house nearing completion. Instead, she stared at stud walls. Not only was sheetrock missing, hardly any insulation had been hung.

"My lord, Jim," she said, completely dismayed. "What in the world is going on? How did you draw more funds on this house?"

"I don't know. The inspector approved it and gave it to me. Insulation and sheetrock subs were supposed to be finished," he explained apologetically.

"Why didn't you come over here and look for yourself?" Emma retorted, trying to keep her voice below a yell.

"I guess I forgot."

"Forgot? How could you forget about a house? A house that's costing over a hundred thousand dollars. How in the world could you forget? What the hell is the matter with the bank's inspector? Why did he approve a fifty percent draw on a house that's only thirty five percent complete?"

Jim was completely unable to comprehend the seriousness of the situation and meekly said, "I don't know."

"Jim," Emma explained carefully, lowering her voice, "fifteen percent of one hundred thousand dollars is fifteen thousand dollars. That's a lot of money. Where is it? What did you do with it?"

"I don't remember." He looked blankly at his wife.

"Shit. Wait 'til I get my hands on that loan officer. He's gonna get a piece of my mind first thing Monday morning."

She stomped out the door in a huff, mumbling, "How the hell will I ever straighten out this mess?"

Emma stopped at the construction shack and spoke briefly with Ray.

"Have you noticed anything strange about Jim? I feel something's wrong. He seems out of it."

"I wasn't going to mention it, Emma; Jim hasn't been himself lately. I've found him sleeping in his truck a couple of times and one day he was asleep in a bathtub. Subs are always looking for him and when he shows up he can't remember where he's been."

"I've suspected as much, Ray" Emma said meekly. "He told me plumbing fixtures were set in the Tudor and insulation isn't even installed, much less sheetrock and fixtures. He's drawn fifteen thousand dollars he can't account for."

"I hate to hear that, Emma. You better get him to a doctor. He's probably a little anemic or something."

"Yeah, maybe he's a little run down. Thanks, Ray," she said sincerely, "I appreciate your help."

"Sure thing, Emma. Let me know if I can do anything."

Emma started the truck and put on a classical music tape to calm her nerves. Something was wrong with her robust husband and at the back of her mind the premonition played its wicked words again.

We're going to lose everything.

∾

CHAPTER THREE

"Do not throw away your confidence...
for you have need of endurance"
-Hebrews 11:35, 36

Monday morning Emma was hot on the phone to Jim's banker. After a few pleasantries, Emma let fly with her real feelings.

"Why the hell did you people let Jim draw fifteen thousand dollars ahead of his construction?"

The banker did not reply.

"Don't give me the silent treatment, Mr. Crumbley. You know exactly what I mean. It is not good business to let a contractor draw ahead of progress. Jim advanced funds to his subs and it will be worse than pulling hen's teeth to get that house finished."

The banker hemmed and hawed for a minute and made some feeble excuses about helping contractors when they got in a jam.

"You're the reason Jim's in a jam, Mr. Crumbley. If you had any business sense you wouldn't loan exorbitant amounts of money to a relative newcomer to the construction business. Jim's barely got his feet wet and you people have him committed to build six huge houses in a very weak market. I think you're irresponsible and negligent and I want to go on record as opposing the entire situation."

"Thank you, Mrs. St. Claire," the banker said smugly. "I believe Jim will work it out."

"I don't think so, Mr. Crumbley. I think you have created a mess and I don't know how I'm supposed to clean it up."

"The loans are Jim's business, Mrs. St. Claire. We never expected you to be involved."

"For your information, Mr. Crumbley, I've been in construction for seventeen years. I know what I'm talking about. Jim's in a financial mess and I want you to know it. If he doesn't work things out I don't want First Federated to come crying to me for the money. Do you understand?"

"Perfectly, Mrs. St. Claire. You're not responsible for Jim's business debts. Thank you for bringing his situation to our attention."

Emma steamed the entire morning.

The next week passed slowly for Emma and she looked forward to her sister's visit the following weekend. Rachel and Jack arrived at three o'clock Saturday afternoon and the twins retreated to Emma and Jim's bedroom where they could be alone. Rachel sat on the white sofa, slipped off her shoes and settled into a pile of throw pillows.

"This is a gorgeous room, Emma; what a place to relax!"

"Wish I had time," Emma replied with a pause, making herself comfortable at the opposite end of the eight-foot sofa, "kinda hard when I have a lot on my mind. Everything has been hectic lately. Mother stays on J.D. constantly. I never imagined how nasty she would treat him. After feeling what I did during her surgery, I couldn't say no when she said she wanted to come live with us."

The morning of Bee's open-heart surgery, the twins and their older brother were sitting in the waiting room when Emma turned to Rachel with a painful expression on her face.

"They've started Mother's heart."

"What do you mean?" Rachel had asked.

"They defibrillated her heart. I could feel it. Look at the clock; its eleven twenty. Her heart is beating again. I know it is."

Shortly after noon, the surgeon came into the waiting room.

"Your mother is doing fine. She'll be in cardiac intensive care in a couple of hours and you can see her."

"What time did you defibrillate?" Rachel asked.

The doctor looked puzzled, wondering why she would ask such a question.

"We started closing at eleven thirty and after we defibrillate, we usually watch the heart and do some routine clean-up work for about ten minutes before we close. Why do you ask?"

"Oh, curiosity."

Now, three years later, Rachel's twin sister was caught in the middle of a family dilemma that was tearing her apart.

"I'm sorry, Emma. Everyone was happy when you moved here. Mother was thrilled; every time I called her she told me how wonderful it was to be living in the country. She loved her long walks with J.D. and the dogs. They were always talking about things they found in the woods together—the unusual plants that only grow on Stone Mountain granite. She went to J.D.'s soccer games, and football games at the high school. Why did it go wrong? What happened to change it?"

"I don't know, Rachel. It started while we were building Jim's mother's house next door. After Janice and David moved in, it got much worse. Much, much worse."

"Didn't it occur to you that Satan's Daughter had something to do with it?" Rachel asked, referring to Jim's mother.

"I don't know. Will her tormenting me ever end? Why would she do anything to hurt my little boy? What could she possibly have done?"

"Emma, we're talking about a person who told you from the start of your marriage that she would always be in control of everything. That she was Jim's mother, that she would always be first in his life, that you would shut up, sit down, and stay out of her way. Honestly, Emma, I don't understand how you have put up with her evil, conniving schemes all these years; how you moved beyond what she did the week you were married is totally beyond me. She wanted you to die, you know she did. She would stop at nothing to hurt you and you are sitting there like some little innocent child, letting her beat up on you, and not only you, now your son, too!"

Rachel was angry.

"Mother is the one who yells at J.D., not Janice."

"You can bet my bottom dollar, Emma. Janice said something to Bee that set her off."

Emma chuckled. "Bee, what a name for Mother. She spends most of her life spreading honey; when something gets her ticked off, though, she stings the devil out of you."

"That's exactly right and this time something has ticked her off. If you don't believe Satan's Daughter put her up to it, you're either blind or too kind-hearted for your own good."

Emma started to cry and Rachel changed the subject. "Are you still having dreams about that teacher?"

"Yes, almost every night. For weeks I was afraid to go to sleep because I couldn't face that dreadful nightmare again. I'd lie there and cry. It was brutal. I have it behind me now."

Emma tried to sound optimistic. Deep inside she knew it was not over.

Bee returned from her D.A.R. meeting late in the afternoon and the three women sipped Chablis while having a mother-daughter chat.

"Where do you find the energy to work full time, go to night school, do Jim's bookkeeping and take care of this huge house?" Rachel asked. "You could make a fortune if you could bottle it up and sell it."

"I run super charged on adrenaline," Emma laughed.

"Oh, she's an organizer," Bee chimed in, using a caustic tone she reserved for comments about the older twin. Emma shook her head and smiled, blowing off the burning, bitter words while wondering why her mother and husband couldn't be a little organized, too. It would make her life easier if she didn't have to constantly pick up after them. Bee left trails of cookie crumbs from the pantry to her studio where she watched television, and Jim had a perpetual track of grease from the garage door to the kitchen sink where he washed his hands under the high-rise faucet even though there was a bathroom next to the back door.

I'll spend the rest of my life picking up after slobs.

When Bee started her tales of woe about every illness and death that had recently befallen her aged friends, the sisters excused themselves.

"We have to get ready for our evening on the town," they said in unison.

"Did you get the recent morbidity and mortality report?" Jim asked with a chuckle when the twins breezed through the family room.

"Of course," Rachel said, "what do you expect from someone retired from C.D.C."

Together the twins climbed the stairs to the master suite and Emma collapsed on the sofa.

"What's the matter, Sweetie?" Rachel asked.

"Have one of those darned headaches. How 'bout bringing me my migraine pills."

Rachel scurried off to the kitchen. She promptly returned with a glass of orange juice and Emma's prescription.

"Boy, that came on fast. Here. Take these."

Emma downed pills and juice while Rachel closed curtains to darken the room. Lost in pain, Emma drifted back to the year before Bee's open-heart surgery, when she herself almost died from a rare form of meningitis. It was another example of Emma St. Claire ignoring her e.s.p. and regretting it.

She was admitted to the hospital with severe headaches, vomiting and paralyzing neuritis in her pelvis and leg. The doctor suspected meningitis and said a spinal tap would be necessary to make the diagnosis.

"While we're doing the spinal tap, we'll do a myelogram, Emma. You could have a tumor causing the neuritis."

Emma peered up at the little man agreeably from her sickbed and her doctor explained the procedure.

"Because you're allergic to iodine, we'll have to use a different contrast medium for the spinal x-rays, Emma. After we puncture your spinal column with a needle, we'll draw out some spinal fluid for study and then we'll inject a chemical which will enable us to see your spinal cord on the films."

As soon as the doctor said *chemical* the alarms sounded in Emma's head. "Don't do this," her silent voice demanded.

Emma reprimanded herself.

For heaven's sake, it's a little spinal tap. What could it do to me? I'll be fine. I'm a volunteer at this hospital, and everyone knows me. They're not going to let anything bad happen.

She was put on a gurney and taken to the x-ray department. *Don't do this,* was repeated when Emma was moved onto the x-ray table. Emma was talking to the doctor and technician while silently telling her feelings to shut up and be quiet.

These are my friends. I'll be fine.

Emma breezed through the supposedly painful procedure without any complaints and returned to her room, smiling and talking with the orderly. Within an hour, she was retching violently as her sick body attempted to rid itself of the poison in its system and a few hours later Emma's brain stem was swollen to the size of a tennis ball and bulged out the back of her neck. Her body curled into a fetal position; she was paralyzed with pain and every cell in her body screamed in agony at the chemical assault.

Too sick to be scared, Emma thought she would never recover. Her only reprieve from the paralyzing illness came when she drifted off into a foggy dream. She did not understand the dream of the petite blond-haired woman and the dark haired man sailing on a merchant ship in the eighteenth century but somehow it took away her thoughts of death. During waking hours she would think of the couple, and the small boy sailing with them, and she knew she had nothing to worry about. Then Emma would tell herself to get better because her children needed her and she had something important to do with her life.

"You have chemical meningitis," her doctor finally admitted, shaking his head slowly. "I've never had a patient with this."

The doctor was clearly distressed and Emma thought he was probably worried about being sued. She was in the hospital for twelve days and survived in spite of her family's worst fears. However, the after-effects would be with her for the rest of her life because she developed migraines.

Emma St. Claire's special feelings had been right again and migraine headaches would be a life-long reminder of the power of her inner voice.

Thankful that the medicine had done its work quickly, within an hour Emma and Rachel were chattering incessantly while bathing and dressing. By mixing and matching apparel, they came up with nearly identical outfits. The middle-aged women enjoyed being twins and their antics were a source of amusement to both husbands. It wasn't unusual for Rachel and Emma to show up at family gatherings dressed alike, although one never told the other what she planned to wear. Many times one twin would get a new haircut to surprise her sister, only to find out that the other twin also had the same new style.

There was a great deal of telepathy between them and Emma's e.s.p. and strong empathy for her sister allowed her to feel what Rachel felt.

***

Rachel's first son was born while they lived in Germany, and when she went into labor, Emma paced the floor, taking cleansing breaths while her sympathetic labor kept pace with her twin's real labor, although they were sixty miles apart. When Rachel's hard labor started at eleven p.m., Emma's pain became intense and lasted until two-thirty in the morning. She awoke Jim from his sound sleep.

"Wake up, Honey, Rachel has a ten-pound boy!"

"How do you know that? Jack hasn't called."

"She has a ten-pound boy and I know that because my labor stopped. Wish I could have been with her. I did what I could to help. I'm exhausted."

Emma went to bed and was fast asleep when the phone rang at four o'clock.

"Hi, Jim," Jack said ecstatically, "we have a nine pound fifteen and one-half ounce boy and he was born at two thirty this morning."

"Yeah, I know," Jim responded sleepily, and hung up the phone.

Five years later when Rachel's second son was born, Emma sat by her sister's side.

"Please help me, Emma. My labor with John was easy 'cause you did half the work."

"I'm trying, Rachel, I am. Nothing's happening to me. Believe me, if I could help, I would."

Rachel's fever rose to one hundred and three degrees while she labored for two and a half days. Emma was frantic with worry; her body felt nothing. Rachel finally produced a healthy ten pound nine ounce boy on Sunday morning, only hours before Emma had to catch a plane back to Atlanta. Three days later, when Rachel took her new son Bobby home from the hospital, Emma called.

"I can help you with the baby, now, Rachel!"

"What do you mean?" her puzzled twin asked.

"I can nurse him. I've got milk, lots and lots of milk."

***

The two women stood in the closet while they dressed. "This is the grandest closet I've ever seen; must be nice to have this space," Rachel said.

"I enjoy it. I never gave up my dream for this house, Rachel; not once. People told me it was a pipe dream. Here it is. Some pipe, huh?"

The closet was under a dormer on the front side of the house and Jim built a window seat for Emma from which she had a view of the expansive yard below. In pre-dawn hours, when the moon was full, she watched deer grazing on the lawn. The seven-and-a-half-acre tract of land was Emma St. Claire's little piece of paradise, a longed-for dream that she turned into reality; she told everyone she would live there until they carried her out in a box to put her in her ground. She called the window seat her Prayer Place and routinely sat there late at night to commune with God and nature and watch the stars while contemplating life.

Why do I drive myself into the ground? What's the purpose of life? Is life just one crisis after another? I feel as though something is hanging over me, that there is always another problem right around the corner. Why? Why do I have the problems I have? Why is life challenging and complicated? Why do I feel that there is something extremely important I have to do?

It wasn't uncommon for Jim to find Emma asleep in the window seat, her retreat in her little corner of the world.

***

"Where are we going for dinner?" Rachel asked Emma while they descended staircase together to the family room, where their husbands were enjoying a cocktail.

"Our friend Frank Chung recently bought a bar called O'Malley's and changed the name to Frank's Place. There's a baby grand piano on a pedestal surrounded by the bar and the pianist does unbelievable impersonations—everyone from Elvis to Lou Rawls. Frank said he was keeping the entertainer for a while and I thought you'd enjoy seeing him."

"Sounds great, doesn't it, Honey?"

Rachel gave Jack a lovable squeeze. The men looked handsome, and Emma affectionately straightened Jim's tie. She enjoyed seeing him dressed in something besides grubby clothes.

He's handsome; why can't he look this good more often? she wondered.

They arrived at Frank's Place on Memorial Drive in Stone Mountain and were seated at a booth near the bar with a good view of the pianist. He played a few numbers Emma requested while they dined. The meal was excellent and Emma enjoyed every bite, feeling blessed the migraine had not been severe enough to ruin the evening. The two couples enjoyed their anniversary celebrations and the evening of laughter and dancing gave Emma a welcome reprieve from the veil of depression that fell on her when she met Philip Byrd.

During the next few weeks Emma finished tax returns for Jim's business, their personal return, her mother's and her grandmother's estate. Long nights of tedious work were punctuated with arguments with Jim over his business. For the third year he failed to make a profit and had reached the end of the rope. Jim withdrew from Emma more and more and work on his houses proceeded at a snail's pace. Although he said his two dump trucks were turning a profit, accounting records proved otherwise.

Emma's children were the source of happiness in her life and she looked forward to their weekly soccer games and myriad school activities. Her own teenage years had been unhappy and Emma readily admitted she was enjoying her youth vicariously through her children. She laughed with them at this idea and thanked them profusely for the happiness they brought her.

Emma was reviewing a class schedule for spring quarter one day at the office when her phone rang.

"Mrs. St. Claire?" a snippy sounding, high-pitched voice asked in a strong Southern drawl.

"Yes, this is Emma St. Claire."

"My name is Sheila Hilton. My husband and I bought one of Jim's houses and we are thoroughly disgusted with him. Since you are a party to the contract, we're holding you responsible."

"No, you're wrong, Mrs. Hilton, I didn't have anything to do with that house."

"Yeah? Don't give me that; your name was on the contract documents at the loan closing. There is something wrong with the carpet and we want it replaced or I'm going to sue you."

Emma was dumbstruck. Why was her name on contract documents? How could she be held accountable for a contract she didn't sign? What was wrong with the carpeting Jim installed? He complained of Mrs. Hilton's demands but said everything was fine when the sale closed. No escrow funds were held because the house passed every inspection without a hitch.

"What's wrong with your carpet?" Emma asked the high-strung woman.

"Seams are coming apart. Everywhere in the house. It looks awful. You better replace it or I'm going to sue you."

"It will be taken care of, Mrs. Hilton. I'll have my husband call you tonight."

"No, that won't do. You have to take care of it or you'll hear from my attorney." The woman slammed down the phone.

Emma called Jim at the construction shack and left a message for him to call a.s.a.p.

"That bitchy Sheila Hilton called me to gripe about her house. Who the hell does she think she is?" Emma demanded when Jim phoned back five minutes later. "That dumb bitch is threatening to sue me over the carpet in her damn house. Why haven't you taken care of it? Don't I do enough to help you? Do I have to put up with your miserable customers, too?"

Between the depression that dominated Emma's mind and the current threat of a lawsuit, she was too disturbed to even think about her name being on the contract.

Jim hemmed and hawed and finally told Emma he didn't know what was wrong with the carpet, that the installers had been back numerous times to repair it.

"Get the damn stuff fixed or I'm going to be sued!" It was Emma's turn to slam down the phone.

She was still steaming three hours later when she got home.

Why can't Jim get a job and work the way normal people do? Why in the world did I give up my education to put him through graduate school? He hasn't had a regular income in four years. We've put everything in that damn business and he walks around in a fog half the time.

Emma scanned the mail. There were two certified letter notifications from the post office.

What now? Somebody else must be mad at him.

Jim arrived shortly after Emma and she was still opening the stack of bills for his company when he walked up behind her and kissed her on the neck.

"Kinda hard to feel lovable when your husband's clients are suing you," Emma said sarcastically. "Why can't you get that bitch's carpet fixed? If the carpet installers can't do it, call a carpet repairman. I don't care what you do. Get Sheila Hilton off my back."

Emma was furious and Jim knew it.

"By the way," she said angrily, "here are some notifications from the post office. How many other people are threatening to sue us? Pick up these certified letters first thing in the morning and let me know what they are about."

She stomped off.

"Good grief," Emma moaned when she saw the kitchen. Her mother had obviously fried a hamburger for lunch; the stainless steel range was covered with a thick coat of dried grease, a half-burned frying pan was in the sink. Cookie crumbs were dissolved in tea spilled on the counter top and a can of her mother's chocolate syrup was turned over in the refrigerator.

Why can't she ever clean up after herself? I'm just a scullery maid to that woman.

Emma cleaned the stove with hot, soapy water, scrubbed the charred frying pan, and wiped up dirty counters before tackling the refrigerator. Sticky syrup was accumulated under a vegetable drawer.

What's the matter with the people in this house? Can't they ever do anything for themselves?

Emma was mad and hurt. She started to cry.

Why do I have to do everything?

She opened cabinet doors and drawers, removing pots and pans.

Damn, damn, damn.

She slammed each door as hard as she could.

Emma's habit of slamming doors started when she was in college. Her mother verbally abused Emma from the time she was five years old and by the time she was nineteen her ego was in shambles. Coupled with a dreadful premonition Emma had, that had been fulfilled with the death of more than a hundred people, Emma was angry and in such deep despair and depression that she ate a bottle of aspirin hoping to end her visions and her pain. Bee sent Emma to a psychiatrist who recommended that Bee have therapy, since she was the source of the verbal abuse.

"I don't intend to change," Bee angrily told the doctor, "you'll have to fix her so she can live with me."

Emma went into counseling for two years and slowly emerged a vivacious, self-sufficient extrovert with a great deal of empathy for anyone suffering any sort of pain. She also acknowledged her anger, would say, "I'm mad," and slam a door as a symbol of letting go of anger rather letting it destroy her. Emma learned a great deal about emotions and human relations from the counselor and even though changing herself was a painful process she was glad she had the experience. In those two long, challenging years, Emma and the doctor had never, not once, ever talked about her e.s.p.

***

J.D. came in with a mid-term report that brought a smile to his mother's face. Like his father, he had a sharp mind. In spite of his intelligence, though, Jim never succeeded at anything and Emma prayed her son would do something worthwhile with his life.

Jim was a sweet, lovable man and pleasant to live with when he wasn't lying, but he never used his master's degree to support his family, preferring instead to indulge in hare-brained business ventures that were always backed by his mother, Janice Crymes and his step-father, David. He never made any money in spite of hard work and Emma wished her mother-in-law would get out of their lives. Because Janice had frequently threatened her, Emma learned to stay out of Janice and Jim's way, painfully accepting that their marriage was by no means normal because there were always three people in it–Janice was in the driver's seat, Jim was in the front passenger seat, and alone, in the back, sat Emma.

Jim and Janice were unusually close for a mother and son and after their wedding Janice told Emma it was a funeral. Then she went on to tell Emma, in her sickening, soft spoken, voice, "You may be Jim's wife; I will always be his mother and I will always come first in his life."

Janice was good at destroying relationships. She had been married and divorced from Jim's dad three times, and after Big Jim's death she took up with her new boss, David Crymes. He was a wonderful man, and Emma adored him. It seemed as if David, too, was under the spell of Janice, and he, like Emma, went along to get along. More than anyone else, David recognized the hurtful things Janice said to Emma and there was an unspoken empathy between them. They both set aside their own feelings to keep peace in the family. They were both quiet, kind and considerate and knew the art of turning the other cheek. They each took the high road and set a good example for J.D. and Allison. At family dinners, it wasn't unusual for David to give Emma an understanding nod when Janice launched into one of her frequent narratives about the love of her life, Big Jim.

Janice's favorite story was about Big Jim's family and how they disowned Janice and her children after his death, how cruel they were to the widow and her fatherless children. Emma assumed David knew the truth about the situation although they had never discussed it. Emma satisfied her own curiosity with a phone call to Jim's cousin shortly after their wedding and she was told that Janice had done the same thing to Daddy St. Claire that she had done to Emma. "Jim's my husband now," she reportedly said, "you better get out of his life and leave us alone."

Of course, Big Jim's dad was broken hearted. How can a parent ever be expected to give up a child simply because they get married? A parent-child relationship is nothing like a man-woman marriage and in mentally healthy individuals there is certainly room for both. No one ever accused Jim's mother of being of sound mind. She carried on her destructive behavior from generation to generation.

Declaring she wasn't ready to "let him go" Janice demanded that Emma and Jim stay at her house the first week of their marriage. After a two-day honeymoon, Emma and Jim went home to Jim's mama. During dinner the next evening, Janice said she was worried about poor little Emma being in the apartment when Jim was not there, that she would need protection, and told Jim to teach Emma how to use 'the gun.' The gun was a .45 that belonged to Jim's father.

In their room that night Jim took the gun out of his nightstand drawer and showed Emma how to hold it, remove the safety, and aim. He taught her to remove the clip and empty the chamber before returning it to the nightstand.

The following night the indoctrination was repeated: Dinner at Janice and David's dining room table, with Jim's mother imploring him to teach Emma how to use the gun. Later, while cleaning up the kitchen, Janice said to Emma, "the most priceless gift we have is the privacy of our own thoughts." Janice raised one eyebrow and glared. Emma wondered what Janice meant.

If you have a pure heart and live an honest life, why would you ever have to hide your thoughts?

Later, in Jim's room, they had another firearms lesson. Emma sat to Jim's left, facing him catty-corner. He was holding the gun and clip when Emma's silent voice screamed, *Move!*

It startled Emma when she heard *move* and she spontaneously recoiled, falling into the pillow behind her.

At that same moment, Jim pushed the clip into the unloaded gun and it fired. A 45 caliber bullet whizzed right past Emma's nightgown, blew out a window, and headed for the trees in the back yard.

Jim looked at Emma and said, "Why the hell did you put a bullet in the chamber?"

She had never touched the gun.

Emma realized she had been spared for a reason but also had to question who had put the bullet in the gun. Someone wanted her dead. Was it Jim's mother? Had she not said everything to Emma in the few days prior that would indicate she might do such a thing? That was one thought Emma did hide in the privacy of her mind, sharing it only with her sister. It was Emma's private hell, being married to a man whose mother wanted her dead. She resolved to respond with love, to be kind and generous. Being bitter never solved anything.

"You can always buy more with honey than you can with vinegar," Emma's grandmother used to say.

Over the years Emma nicely said to Janice, "Please don't baby Jim. We'll never be self-sufficient if he can come to you whenever he wants something."

Each time Janice retorted, "You sit down and be quiet, Emma. This is between me and my son."

Emma finally gave up any effort to discuss finances with her over-bearing mother-in-law, knowing that when Mrs. Crymes gave Jim money, she was taking something away from him—his independence, his ability to support himself and his family, his desire to acquire gainful employment, his desire to succeed, his ability to rise above failure.

***

Emma could hardly wait for school to start the last week of March. She enrolled in cost accounting and looked forward to the challenge of a mentally demanding course. She thought of Philip Byrd and wondered if he would be teaching economics again.

Maybe I could engage him in a conversation and find out something about him. If he would only talk to me—

Emma's dreams of the teacher persisted in spite of nightly prayers begging God to take them away.

Why would I dream the same things over and over about this man? And who is that little lady who tells me he's special?

***

After several more harassing phone calls from Sheila Hilton, Jim's attorney wrote to the bothersome woman telling her to cease and desist or she would be facing a law suit herself. Jim finally found a carpet repair man who corrected the faulty carpet and reported that it was the personable Mrs. Hilton's fault as her precious little cocker spaniel was attracted to the carpet seam glue. When repairs were made, fresh glue was used; the glue attracted the dog, which immediately started gnawing on the carpet when her owner was out of sight. Jim paid more than four hundred dollars for carpet repairs, averting a costly, unjustified law suit against his wife. To Emma, it was money well spent.

Certified letters from vendors demanding payment of invoices became commonplace and every notification from the post office caused Emma to burst into tirades.

"Why don't you pay your bills, Jim?" she demanded. "If I ran our personal finances and this house the way you run that damn business of yours, we would be sleeping on the street and starving."

Emma's outbursts were met with a complacent non-rebuttal from Jim, who would shrug his shoulders, say, "I don't know," and wander off to destinations unknown. He would reappear hours later acting as if nothing had happened.

38

Because Jim advanced too much money to subcontractors on the Tudor house, he could not get them to complete their work. Emma told Jim time and again not to pay for work until it was done. Jim was a soft touch; everyone knew it and wheedled money out of him. Emma decided Jim and the Crymes would have to work it out. It was his business and his mess. She had more than enough to take care of. The awful premonition that they would lose everything continued to eat at her and Jim's lack of incentive to work out his business problems, coupled with his obvious withdrawal from her, only reinforced her angst.

How could we lose everything?

Their home represented twenty-two years of backbreaking work and satisfied dreams and housed the precious possessions acquired during their marriage.

It can't happen. It can't. It can't!

Emma got to school early and went by the bookstore before picking up her usual cup of vending machine decaf coffee. An earlier class ended and the hall was packed with students when Emma spied the tall, dark-haired man advancing towards her in the crowd.

I wonder if he'll remember me.

"Hi," Philip Byrd said to Emma in a very friendly tone, "how are you doing?"

He does remember me.

"Fine, I'm doing fine. How 'bout you?"

"Good," he said, smiling at her. They passed, and he was out of sight.

He's okay. He is okay. He looks wonderful. It was good to see him. That smile. I love that smile. Why does that man's smile affect me this way?

Emma felt warm and happy for the first time in weeks and she was grinning ear to ear when she entered the classroom.

I should have known he was okay. He is a big boy now. He's perfectly capable of taking care of himself.

Emma ignored the shivers running down her spine and unconsciously pulled a sweater around her shoulders when her body shook with head-to-toe chills.

The cost accounting class was every bit as hard as Emma had been told and the mental stimulation was satisfying to her. She could lose herself for hours at a time tackling homework problems—a welcome reprieve from Jim's business and her worries about losing everything and protecting a man she did not know from an unknown situation. Philip Byrd was teaching a class at the same hour and they frequently passed in the hall. He was always pleasant and smiling. He appeared to be a patient man and often stayed late after class to discuss problems with his students.

"Wish I could talk to him" Emma would say under her breath when she saw him with other students. "I have something more important to talk about than economics."

Emma tried to rationalize her feelings for Mr. Byrd. She worried about him and was always relieved to see his smiling face at school, telling herself again and again he was grown up now and could take care of himself. His beautiful smile warmed her soul.

Why do I feel there is a storm around him?

She shivered.

Maybe his wife or girlfriend is giving him a problem. I'm empathic. Maybe I'm feeling some sort of stress in his life. Why? Why a stranger?

Jim's business was deteriorating rapidly and, biting her tongue, Emma finally went to Janice and David.

"As long as you prop up Jim and his hair-brained schemes, he'll never learn to stand on his own two feet. He's going to have to sink or swim, and giving him more money is a waste."

Emma's pleas fell on deaf ears and Janice continued to run Jim's life. Had he not been such a sweet, pleasant man to live with, Emma would have left the mediocre, lie-filled marriage, controlled in every aspect by Janice. She chose, instead, to uphold her marriage vows, for better, for worse, for richer, for poorer. Emma was not a quitter; she stood by Jim and propped him up, though she refused to carry his financial baggage any further.

Jim's health was another concern. Over the winter he gained more than forty pounds and become increasingly lethargic. Emma begged and pleaded with him to get a checkup. "Honey, you need to have your thyroid checked. It might be acting up again. You haven't had a blood test in two years. Remember how bad you felt when you had thyroiditis when J.D. was a baby. You probably need to be taking more thyroid hormone. Please go to the doctor."

Jim had a ready excuse to cancel every appointment Emma made and it got to be a joke at their family doctor's office. "I'll get him there one day," Emma told the receptionist after Jim failed to appear the third time.

"We're not going to renew his prescription for thyroid medicine unless we see him again," Dr. Keller told Emma.

"That's fine with me. When he runs out of little blue pills he'll be in to see you right away."

Much to Emma's dismay, the prescription had been renewed in late February; Jim had enough pills to last until sometime in June.

***

One Saturday morning Emma straightened paperwork and surveyed Jim's checkbook.

Allison can help her dad this summer. When school lets out, I think I'll turn the books over to her. She's had more accounting classes than I have and the experience of full-charge bookkeeping will be good for her.

Spring quarter passed much too quickly for Emma. The accounting class was not only stimulating, it was fun. The affable teacher had been a student at Georgia State when Emma and Rachel were there in the mid-sixties and they always had something interesting to discuss.

Why can't I have a nice friendship with Mr. Byrd like I do with my other teachers? No special feelings, no worries, no dreams or nightmares—just a teacher and a student, both adults. Philip Byrd is a constant source of concern. And that smile. Why does his smile affect me the way it does?

By final exam time, Emma was addicted to her twice-a-week ration of Philip Byrd's smile. Jim's business problems and her mother's crude treatment of J.D. and sloppiness in the kitchen were never-ending sources of irritation. For some reason, and in spite of still frequent dreams and nightmares, the handsome Mr. Byrd's smile always made Emma feel wonderful. If she was depressed and saw him, she would be happy. If angry, his smile would calm her. If she felt weakened by the load she was carrying, he would give her strength. No matter what her problem, he would always erase it with his smile.

Whenever anything is wrong Philip Byrd can make it right with his smile.

At the end of the quarter she was no closer to solving the riddle of Philip Byrd and sank into a depression after he told her the last night of school that he was taking the summer off.

How in the world will I survive without him? What is this man's power over me? It's not lust; I can't even imagine going to bed with him. What is it? Who is that lovely aura I see with him in that office? Why can't I see her? Is she someone from his past? Why do I have such an affinity for her? I want to know who she is. I can't bear the thought of never seeing him again. I think I would rather die.

41

CHAPTER FOUR

"Find grace to help in time of need."
-Hebrews 4:16

The week after school ended, Emma and Jim took J.D. to Holden Beach. Emma looked forward to a complete rest—long walks on the beach at night, leisurely meals, and visiting friends at another beach house a block away.

The vacation did not turn out as planned. Jim collapsed the moment they arrived and slept twelve hours every day. His hands and feet were horribly swollen and strolls on the beach were only a memory from pleasant times in the past. Jim couldn't walk more than a few hundred feet before sitting down to rest.

"Jim, you are going to the doctor the minute we get home," Emma told him one morning in no uncertain terms. "There is something wrong and we're going to find out what it is."

"Aw, I'll shake it off," Jim said lethargically, "probably some sort of bug."

"I'll be damned if it's a bug," Emma retorted. She knew her husband was a very sick man. The words were no sooner out of her mouth when the premonition played its depraved refrain: *We're going to lose everything.*

Jim was sound asleep in the car when Emma drove up the long driveway to the house on Saturday night.

"Come on, Honey," she pleaded, awakening her hefty husband.

"He's sick, awfully sick," she said to J.D.

Emma and J.D. unloaded suitcases and Emma unpacked while J.D. checked on the chickens and dogs. He came back to the house, kissed his mother on the cheek and went to bed.

After Emma put away the suitcases she went to the long deck on the back of the house to inspect her flower boxes; much to her dismay, the plants were wilted and dying in dried, cracked dirt. Bee had not watered one time during Emma's vacation.

This is disgusting; beautiful plants withering and dying. What's the matter with that woman? Can't she ever do anything to help me? I can't even take off one damn week.

Emma was mad. She saturated each flower box while pulling off dead leaves and dried blossoms.

It was almost eleven o'clock; Emma was tired. Sitting on the porch she drank in the fragrance of the night air. She loved country living where air was fresh, roads were dirt, ice cold pure water came from deep wells, there was an ever-changing cornucopia of wild flowers to decorate fields and roadsides from March through November, horses grazed in pastures, and roosters crowed at sunrise every morning. North Ridge Road was Emma's heaven on earth. She gazed at the stars and talked to the moon.

What is this thing we call life all about, anyway? Work, work, work. Is that it? Why? Why am I here? What's going on? What's it about? Will I ever understand life? I can't believe we come here simply to eat and sleep and make love and work and then die. There has got to be more to life than that.

***

Emma and Jim were waiting by the door to the doctor's office on Monday morning when nurses arrived. Jim was depressed and mentally confused and his physical symptoms alarmed Dr. Keller.

Although young, Dr. Keller was the model family doctor. He knew medical histories of each family member without looking at charts and always had a joke to make them laugh and feel better. This particular morning there were no jokes, only a furrowed brow and look of deep concern.

"Jim's blood pressure is sky high," Dr. Keller told Emma after the examination. "His thyroid feels huge, which could account for the rapid weight gain and lethargy. I've ordered blood tests; we should have results in a couple of days. In the meantime, we're scheduling x-rays and scans. I'll call you as soon as we receive the reports."

While driving Jim home, Emma mulled over her decision to attend summer school. She was already registered for a psychology class.

Even though it's gonna to be a long, hot summer I still want to go to school. At the rate I'm going, I'll be fifty before I graduate.

She decided in favor of school.

Jim probably needs more thyroid hormone—in a couple of weeks he'll be good as new.

Classes started Tuesday night and Emma was delighted to see a long-time friend of Bee's sitting at the teacher's desk when she arrived.

"Dr. Horner," she said to the ample-size, smiling man, "what are you doing here?"

"Why, I've been teaching at this college for sixteen years, Emma. What are you doing here?"

"I've been in night school and I'm taking psychology this quarter."

"Have a seat," Dr. Horner said with a grin on his friendly face, "I'm teaching this class."

Emma took a seat on the front row.

This is wonderful. What a stroke of luck.

Dr. Horner, a retired clinical psychologist, was a highly respected member of Emma's church and he and his wife were long-time friends of Bee's. Emma had always admired Dr. Horner but did not know he taught college. His opening lecture was stimulating and she looked forward to many pleasant hours in his class.

"How is your family?" Dr. Horner asked Emma after class, "and how is your wonderful mother?"

"My husband is having some health problems," she answered, wondering why he would call Bee wonderful.

"I'm sorry to hear that; nothing serious I hope."

"We're waiting on test results now; my mother is fine."

"Your mother is some kind of character, Emma. I probably shouldn't say this. I don't know how anyone can live with that woman. Don't get me wrong, now. I love your mother. She's a wonderful person for twenty minutes at a time. I sure couldn't live with her."

"Living with her is akin to living with a manic depressive, Dr. Horner."

Emma's tone pleaded for help and advice.

"I know, Emma. She's not a true manic-depressive though she does exhibit some of those symptoms. She gets mad as hell and cusses out someone and then the next instant she's as sweet honey."

"A few weeks ago J.D. answered the telephone and the answering machine was still on. Mother started screaming at J.D. about something and we picked it up on the recorder."

Emma looked at the kindly man and touched him gently on the forearm. "You wouldn't believe the language that came out of her mouth, Dr. Horner.

There are times when I use an expletive but I don't cuss out people and demean them the way she does. She verbally abused me when I was a child."

"We've ignored verbal abuse for too long, Emma. Verbal abuse is every bit as damaging as physical abuse. Anyone who is abusive in any way is not acting in a normal manner. For years we have treated children for the damage caused by abuse. The only way to stop it is at the source."

Emma and Dr. Horner arrived at the parking lot.

"I'm glad I'm in your class this quarter. Say hello to your wife for me." Emma waved to the mild-mannered man and went to her truck.

Jim was sound asleep when Emma crawled into bed and cuddled up next to him. His breathing was labored; she rolled him onto his back and propped up his head with a pillow.

"Maybe we'll have the test results tomorrow," she mumbled, drifting off to sleep.

Several hours later Emma sat bolt upright, shaking uncontrollably, breathing rapid, short breaths.

"Mr. Byrd!" she wailed, "Mr. Byrd!"

It happened yet again. Emma heard the deafening noise and awakened in a panic.

"No," she moaned, "no, no. Please dear Lord—"

After a week of peaceful sleep at the beach Emma thought the dreams of Philip Byrd had finally ended. She started to cry.

Why, dear God, why does this go on? Will it ever end?

She tossed and turned while words of the troubling premonitions played incessantly.

We're going to lose everything.

He's special, protect him.

***

Emma was already dressed when her radio alarm clock turned on. Beethoven's Ninth Symphony was playing on WABE, and the last movement, *Ode to Joy*, soothed to her raw nerves.

There must be some purpose for this agony. What is it? Why do I get these messages in my poor ole brain? We're not going to lose everything are we? We can't. We've worked hard for years and years. No one handed us this place. We earned it ourselves. Even if it burns down we have plenty of insurance and we can rebuild.

Why am I having that awful nightmare about Philip Byrd again? Maybe I'm over-extended and my mind is telling me to slow down. But I feel great. I have tons energy. I'm not engineered sit and do nothing the way Jim does. Jim can turn off his problems. Maybe I should ignore my special feelings. Maybe they are getting the best of me.

J.D.'s rooster was crowing lustily when Emma left the house, praying in a whisper, "God, I love this place. Please don't let me lose it."

A flood of deep yellow Coreopsis blooms on the embankment across the driveway greeted Emma and led her down the narrow, winding dirt road. The cheerful plants were interspersed with hefty clumps of brilliant white, delicate Queen Anne's Lace, Emma's favorite wildflower. In a few days their season would end, they would wither and die. Next year, at the same time, in the same place, Coreopsis and Queen Anne's lace would bloom again, giving Emma a sense of continuity and peace. This was where she belonged.

Emma was anxiously awaiting a report from Dr. Keller when Joe called her into his office for dictation and she was happy for the diversion. Before they finished, the phone rang. Joe answered it on his speakerphone and Emma heard Dr. Keller's voice asking for her.

"Go ahead," Joe said. He knew Emma was worried about Jim and she went to her office to talk to the doctor.

"It doesn't look good," he started. "I've already had the blood test reports forwarded to Mayo for evaluation. Jim has a very rare thyroid condition and he's extremely toxic; it's a wonder he's alive. I don't know how he's even functioning. Has he been erratic?"

"Yes, he has Dr. Keller. Very erratic. For months. I first noticed it last Christmas. He started withdrawing. He hardly talks to anyone. Of course, you've heard his voice. He's constantly choking. I've begged him for months to get a check-up."

"We still have more tests to run; in the meantime we've got to get his blood pressure under control. I'm calling a specialist; we'll try to get him in for a visit this afternoon. Can you get him there?"

"Of course. J.D. is out of school; he can drive him. Let me know where he has to go."

"Oh, brother." Emma hung up the phone.

"What's the problem?" Joe asked.

Joe was the next best thing to a big brother and Emma easily talked to him about anything that bothered her. She cried on Joe's shoulder about Jim's business problems and he always had useful advice. The only thing Emma never discussed with Joe was her e.s.p. That was a topic reserved exclusively for Rachel, the only person Emma could trust with her special feelings.

"You take whatever time you need," Joe said.

"There's no use in me sitting in a doctor's office. J.D. can take Jim to the doctor. I'm sorry for the interruption. Let's finish our quote."

While Emma was typing the proposal, Dr. Keller called back with the name of the endocrinologist.

"I gave him Jim's test reports and they are very alarmed; they're working him in this afternoon. Jim should be there by two o'clock."

"He'll be there."

She called J.D. and gave him instructions.

"Please ask the doctor to call me after he sees Daddy, Punkin."

"Okay, Mom," J.D. said in his deep voice. "Don't worry, Mom. Dad's gonna be okay."

"I know he will, J.D., I know."

Emma was on pins and needles the rest of the day while waiting to hear from the endocrinologist. She finally decided he wasn't going to call and was cleaning up her desk when the phone rang.

"Mrs. St. Claire?" a pleasant, masculine voice asked.

"Yes, this is Emma St. Claire."

"Emma, this is Dr. Jander." Emma was pleased with the doctor's intimate style, using her first name.

"Your husband is a very sick man and he needs surgery. We'll have to stabilize his blood pressure first. Right now he's a poor candidate for a good outcome. The surgery itself can be risky under the best of conditions and his weight could complicate it even more. J.D. has taken him over to the surgeon's office. Jim should rest as much as possible; please see that he takes the medicines I prescribed."

"Yes, of course, Dr. Jander. I'll see that he does. Thank you very much for calling me."

"By the way, Emma, Dr. Keller tells me that Jim has been erratic for quite a while."

"Yes, he has. Is that one of the symptoms of this illness?"

"Yes indeed, it is. From the level of toxins in his blood I would estimate he's been ill for almost a year."

"A year!" Emma exclaimed. "That long? A year. How could he have been sick that long?"

"I don't know, Emma. Apparently he's been hiding the symptoms. Has he been confused, forgetful or absent-minded?"

"Yes, that's exactly how he's been acting. I frequently catch him in lies. A few weeks ago we were shopping at Market Square and he couldn't even get out of the parking lot. He kept driving up and down the aisles looking for the exit lane. I finally had to direct him."

"I'm not surprised, Emma. He's probably been mentally incompetent for most of the past year."

Emma thanked Dr. Jander again and hung up the phone. Her hand was trembling.

A year. Mentally incompetent for a year. My God; and he's trying to run a business. No wonder everything is such a mess. A year. Good Lord, no telling what he's bungled up in a year. How did this happen? How in the world did this happen to us? I knew he wasn't quite right. But incompetent? No wonder he's lied. He didn't know what he was doing or saying. A year. My God!

She got up from her desk and went to her bathroom; bottled up tears spilled out her eyes, ran down her cheeks and dripped into the sink.

***

Emma was starting dinner when J.D. came bounding in the back door followed by Jim, shuffling along with his head down, looking dejected.

"Hi, Honey," Emma said calmly, hugging the bear of a man. She put her head on his stocky chest and looked down to hide her grimace. Jim put his swollen hands on his wife's shoulders and pulled her closer to him, as if the embrace could erase the problem.

"The surgeon wants to operate as soon as possible." Jim choked out the words; he was scared and Emma knew it.

"You'll do fine, Honey; I know you will."

"That's easy for you to say. You're not the one who's getting their throat cut," Jim said angrily, changing his demeanor and pushing Emma away.

"No, I'm not, Jim. Have you forgotten I've had four operations myself? I know what pain is and I know what it's like to be scared before surgery. If you take your medicine and do what the doctors say, you'll be okay."

"Really?" He looked apologetic.

"Of course. You'll do fine. The thyroid gland is easy to get to; you won't have to be cut up the yazoo the way I was to get that tumor out of my pelvis."

"I still don't care for the idea of getting my throat cut." He shuffled off to the family room and stretched out on the sectional sofa.

Emma went back to the kitchen where she was frying chicken.

"Umm, my favorite." J.D. picked up the lid to the over-sized skillet to inspect the chicken. "Make the gravy real thick, Mom."

"J.D., the gravy will be nice and thick. How about setting the table while I finish dinner?"

While eating, the family talked about Jim's surgery and running his businesses while he was laid up. Allison volunteered to be superintendent on the houses and handle the checkbook for her dad and J.D. said he would call the asphalt plant for the morning dispatches for Jim's dump trucks. Emma had faith that her daughter could supervise construction of four houses although she was leery about Allison being involved in financial side of Jim's business, other than posting the books.

"Allison, Daddy has a lot of business problems right now. His vendors are sending him dunning notices for past-due invoices and the bank is after him for interest payments. I don't want you signing business checks," Emma said.

"Don't worry, Mama. I'll get the checkbook balanced and keep Daddy away from it. If he can't get his hands on it he can't mess it up."

"I still don't feel right about you being involved with the money, Darling. Doing the books and supervising subs is one thing. Signing checks is another. It doesn't feel right to me. Don't do it."

"Are you having one of your special feelings about it Mama?"

Allison respected her mother's e.s.p. and regularly sought her mother's opinion, knowing the advice would be sound. If she ever had any doubts as to the wisdom of her mother's feelings, they were erased when she was a senior in high school.

A few weeks before graduation Allison told Emma she wanted to go to Ft. Lauderdale with some classmates when school was out. Allison had traveled quite a lot by herself and with friends and generally Emma never worried about her daughter. This time her e.s.p. said, "It will be a bad trip."

"It will be a bad trip," Emma said calmly to her daughter.

"What do you mean? Does that mean I can't go? Will I get hurt or something?"

"No, you'll be fine," Emma assured her daughter. "Nothing will happen to you, or to your body, that is. However, it will be a bad trip and you'll wish you hadn't gone."

Taking her mother's advice into consideration for about half a minute, and realizing that she, herself, was in no danger, Allison eagerly called her friends to tell them she could go.

"It will be a bad trip," Emma's e.s.p. said again.

The morning after graduation Allison loaded her car, including a brand new two-hundred-dollar camera. Her wallet was stuffed with three hundred dollars in cash she earned at two part-time jobs.

"Don't you think you should take traveler's checks, Allison?" Emma asked.

Mother's advice went unheeded. Allison happily pulled out of the driveway in her sporty, maroon Oldsmobile Cutlass Brougham. Emma was not distressed about the trip because she knew her daughter would be alright. She also knew that for some reason it would be a bad trip. The next day she received a call from Allison.

"Mama," she bawled into the phone. "My new camera was stolen. I never even got to take it out of the case!"

"I'm sorry, Darling. Try to take care of your things. Be careful and stay alert."

"I will, Mama, but my camera is gone."

Allison was angry with herself for not heeding her mother's advice. Emma hoped that would be the end of Allison's woes for the trip. Two days later Allison called, again in distress.

"Mama, my wallet was stolen. I don't have any money," she cried into the phone.

"Didn't you get traveler's checks after you got there?" It was a foolish question; obviously Allison did not have traveler's checks. The premonition finally played itself out the following morning.

"Mama," came the loudest of wails over the phone, "my car was stolen."

Allison's perseverance the next two days paid off because her car was finally located on a distant beach where it had run out of gas and been abandoned. Allison returned from the trip educated in the wisdom of her mother's e.s.p. She was alright; she had never been in any sort of danger; but it was a bad trip.

CHAPTER FIVE

**"If no one knows what will happen,
who can tell him when it will happen?"**
-Ecclesiastes 8:7

June and July were unusually hot months for Atlanta and the extreme heat took a toll on Jim. He continued working on his houses and, with a great deal of assistance from Allison, construction activity picked up. Allison balanced the checkbook and was getting a handle on the bills. Some accounts were still running sixty days past due but it appeared that if they sold one of the houses, the company could survive. Scans showed numerous cysts in Jim's thyroid and his doctors said he would have surgery as soon as his condition was stabilized. Medication reduced his blood pressure and he practically lived at the offices of the endocrinologist and the surgeon.

Emma entertained the idea of dropping out of school but she enjoyed the psychology course and class hours were a welcome reprieve from Jim's illness and business and Bee, whose disposition alternated from thoughtful and considerate to spiteful and mean. Emma could never make sense of her mother's temperament and after-class discussions with Dr. Horner were a source of insight. Dr. Horner told Emma she was too sensitive to her mother's moods, not knowing that Emma was sensitive to everyone. For as long as she could remember, Emma had the capacity to put herself in the shoes of another and feel what they felt. When her brother had pleurisy as a teenager, Emma felt his pain in her chest; when Rachel was jabbed in the leg by a tree limb while playing in the woods when they were ten, Emma screamed in agony; feeling what others felt was common to Emma. She didn't understand why she was this way and analyzing it never gave her an answer.

Although Emma trusted Dr. Horner implicitly, she could not bring herself to discuss her special feelings with him. Long ago she locked them in a closet and gave the keys only to Rachel and Allison. To the rest of the world, the door was bolted. Jim called her a witch when Emma gave an opinion based on her e.s.p., J.D. had no opinion one way or the other, and her mother's verbal abuse cut off any meaningful communication. Emma never knew how Bee would react to anything she said. When things bothered her, she either kept them to herself or shared them only with Rachel.

Previous summers Emma and Jim enjoyed leisurely walks down the lower end of their road to a small, scenic lake. A huge boulder protruded into the water and they sat there while tossing sticks to Alex, who bounded in and out of the clear water of the two-acre lake that was water spaniel heaven. Emma adored the small black dog. He would stare into her face with his slightly impaired vision as if to say, "I understand you, Emma St. Claire. We are the very dearest of friends and I love you." Whenever Emma was blue she would take Alex on a long walk to renew her optimism. There was a compelling bond between them and although Emma had owned many, many dogs, Alex was the one she truly loved the most.

An even closer bond grew during the long, hot summer because Jim was unable to walk with them and Emma found herself talking to Alex about everything from mad vendors, disreputable bankers and building houses to e.s.p., nightmares and Philip Byrd. Although the dreams abated somewhat, Emma thought she could purge her soul by expressing her strange feelings and dreams in letters in her diary.

"Why do I feel this way?" she wrote. "Why do I miss a man I don't even know? Don't you see what your smile means to me? Who is that lovely soul with you? Why do I care for her?"

Emma asked herself every possible question, trying to sort out bewildering emotions about the mysterious man. "Why are you kneeling in the mud at night? You'll get your clothes dirty."

After several weeks she had a considerable stack of letters so one day Emma took them out to the granite outcropping in front of the house and burned them.

"There," she said emphatically to Alex. "I'm rid of each and every one—the feelings, the dreams, the nightmares. They've all gone up in smoke."

Then she sat on the rock, in the midst of the yellow sundrops that grow only on Stone Mountain granite, clutched Alex to her chest and cried.

Why? Why did this happen to me?

Finally, Emma gathered her wits, picked herself up and went into the dream home she built with her own hands.

The St. Claire household settled into a summer routine as best they could with everyone making allowances for Jim's health. Bee did the cooking; Emma was the scullery maid. Construction crews put in long hours in the summer and the workload at Joe's office kept pace with the increased production. Emma thrived on the activity and thanked God daily for blessing her with an exorbitant amount of energy. Between her job and school, Jim's business, maintaining the house on seven acres and caring for numerous animals, Emma was very busy.

One Friday afternoon the last week of June, Joe called Emma into his office. He was reading the Invitation to Bid list published in the county newspaper.

"What's a Transfer Station?" he asked.

"I have no idea. Why do you ask?"

"I see on this list that there's going to be a transfer station on North Ridge Road. Thought you might know about it."

"Beats me," Emma said "A transfer station? There's a new sewer line going in the creek basin. Maybe it has something to do with that."

"No, that doesn't sound right. Why don't you call the county and find out what it is."

"I'll be glad to." She took the paper from Joe's desk.

Emma spent the rest of the afternoon on the telephone, calling various offices at the county. Every department referred her to another. She began to feel there was some sort of conspiracy of silence. Finally, after ten phone calls and innumerable transfers, she was put in touch with a man in the Sanitation Department.

"Can you tell me anything about a transfer station on North Ridge Road?" she politely inquired.

"Yeah," came a somewhat crude reply. "We're gonna put our new garbage transfer station out there."

"A garbage transfer station?" Emma asked incredulously. "What's that?"

"When in full operation we'll have 'bout three hundred garbage trucks working outta there. They'll be haulin' in garbage from the south side of the county and we'll pour it into machines that will compact it and then it will be sent to the landfill."

"What!" Emma cried in a tone of complete shock. "You're going to be dumping garbage and smushing it up? Three hundred trucks? Are you mad?

North Ridge Road is a one-lane dirt road. You can't put that kind of business operation out there."

Emma was furious. She didn't want to intimidate the only information source she found and tried to calm down. Joe heard the loud exclamation and came into her office to see what was going on.

"What's the street address?" she asked the burly sounding voice.

"Seventeen Fifty," he replied and hung up the phone.

"It's not good, Joe." Emma looked at her boss as if he could do something. "My house is at Fourteen Eighty. They want to put a garbage dump less than a mile from my house. Can you imagine how that will smell? I can't believe this. I cannot believe this."

Joe shook his head and went back to his office. "You know how this county operates, Emma. They're going to do as they please. They could care less about your home. What about your neighbors? Maybe you can get the community together and fight it."

"I'll call Millie Reed. She's our Community Relations Rep. She should know what's going on."

"Millie?" Emma asked when the elderly neighbor answered her phone. "This is Emma St. Claire. Do you remember me? We live on North Ridge Road."

"Of course, Emma," the animated woman replied.

Emma met Millie when they successfully fought a landfill application ten years before Emma and Jim built their house. Millie was active in community affairs and was highly respected for her work.

"Do you have any information about a garbage transfer station on my road?"

"No, I don't. I'm glad you called though. I got notice that someone has applied for a landfill permit on North Ridge again and I was going to call you tonight."

"A landfill!" Emma exclaimed. "A landfill, too? I don't believe this. They're going to turn the most sacred, scenic part of the county into a garbage dump and landfill. They can't do that to us. They can't." Emma was almost hysterical.

The rest of the afternoon drifted by slowly for Emma; she was anxious to get home to check out the landfill and garbage dump sites.

Can't imagine how they can even think about doing these things to us. A one-lane dirt road, no public water or fire protection. Beautiful species of endangered plants that don't grow anywhere else in the world live on that rocky ridge. Surely, there must be some mistake.

At four o'clock Emma started cleaning up her desk. She picked up Joe's coffee cup, washed the coffee pot and freshened her makeup. At four-thirty Emma made a hasty retreat to the door.

"I'm going to check out this transfer station thing," she called to Joe over her shoulder, "I'll see ya on Monday."

Friday afternoon traffic was heavy. Emma had too much on her mind to listen to news and turned on a classical music tape. She took a deep breath and relaxed as Rimski-Korsakoff's *Scheherazade* came over the speakers. She thought how odd it was that she preferred driving a truck and listening to classical music.

By the time Emma arrived home it was too late to investigate the transfer station site so she called Millie, who came over right away with a copy of the landfill application.

"We scrimped and saved and did without extras for seven years to pay for this land before we built, Millie. The people at the county showed us the land use plan; in fact, I still have a copy. They said only office parks could be built out here if it didn't stay agricultural or residential."

"You'd better read this letter." Millie handed the paper to Emma.

Emma knew that landfills could pollute ground water, create fire hazards and attract insects and rodents. What in the world would a landfill do to her home? Would her children and grandchildren be able to drink their well water? Would the air be fouled by odors? Emma read the Zoning Board letter and to her horror learned the site was right across the road from her in-law's house, which faced another one lane trail that intersected North Ridge. The back property line of Emma and Jim's place was the northern boundary of the Crymes' domain.

"What in the world can we do?" Emma pleaded.

"I would suggest we hold a community meeting right away and get organized to oppose this," the sympathetic, white haired lady responded. Beneath Millie's placid demeanor lurked an intelligent and politically shrewd character who never backed down when her home turf was threatened.

"That's a great idea. We have two weeks before this proposal comes before the Board. Surely, we can arouse some community interest in that time. After your Community Council meeting on Monday we'll know what we're up against."

Emma was on the phone when Jim arrived a few minutes later.

"What's going on? I passed Millie Reed on the driveway?"

"Look at this." Emma handed him the notice while dialing another number. He read the zoning board letter and in typical Jim fashion shrugged his shoulders.

"Why get hot and bothered? We've already got a landfill out here anyway and it hasn't done any harm."

"What do you mean we already have a landfill out here?" Emma angrily retorted. "There's nothing out here except a few families who love living in the country with their children, horses and chickens. Landfill my eye."

Jim leaned back in one of the captain's chairs at the old round maple table in the breakfast room and sipped on a beer.

"Of course we do. You remember old Henry Marcus, don't you? He ran a landfill for Consolidated Container for years. It was shut down by the EPA in 1978 for some sort of violations—dumping ink and glue in the ground."

"Are you kidding, Jim? This is serious and I'm not in the mood to put up with another one of your lies!"

"I'm not lying, Emma. I wish you wouldn't say that," he said. With a dejected hurt look on his face he went into the family room to read his newspaper.

"Golly. The world could be coming to an end and Jim would sit down to read the funny papers and editorials."

"Why don't you and J.D. go get a pizza? I'm too busy to cook and I'm not hungry."

Emma hung up the phone and joined Jim in the family room.

"I'm sorry I snapped at you, Honey. I'm upset. I found out about a garbage transfer station down the road and now Millie has given me this letter about a landfill application. If these projects go through we could be ruined. Lord only knows what it would do to our property value. Not to mention the noise and traffic and pollution. Then you tell me we already have a landfill out here. Where is it? Are you positive it was closed for violations?"

"Yeah. It was closed while I was working for that cartage company. Don't you remember? They leased trucks to Consolidated. They were always breaking down over at the landfill and I went over there a lot of times to work on them. One time I was there and some EPA inspectors came by looking for Henry. Said they were gonna shut down the place. Not too long afterwards it was closed."

Emma was surprised that Jim remembered the details of something that had happened nine years ago although he couldn't remember where he had been the day before.

58

"Where is it? Could we get in there?"

"Definitely. The old road is on the other side of Hudson Creek. We wouldn't have any trouble walking in."

The old road to the abandoned landfill was overgrown and Emma had forgotten about it.

Emma dreaded unloading the news on her in-laws and dispatched J.D. and Jim with the notice from Millie; then she started cleaning the house. Jim and J.D. returned with pizza from Brick House and Janice and David's assurance they would do everything they could to help. Janice would prepare a petition and they would start collecting signatures the next day.

Emma hastily choked down a slice of pizza and tackled the housework. Her adrenaline was pumped up and she stayed up past midnight cleaning and washing clothes since she could not relax. Her mother arrived a little after eleven and gave Emma a ten-minute dissertation on the evening's theatrical performance, what she had eaten for dinner and the latest medical news from her aging friends. Emma finally got a word in edgewise and told her mother they had a slight community crisis. As usual, Bee went into a tirade and insinuated the entire mess was Emma's fault; she marched back to her apartment and slammed the door.

Emma soaked in her Jacuzzi for a long time and made a mental list of weekend activities before dropping into the brass bed. She would get Allison to make posters and her retired in-laws could circulate petitions. Emma assumed Millie would spearhead the campaign and felt confident they could stop the projects. Then she thought about her usual chores: grocery store, church, cooking, gardening. The list was endless. Jim rolled over and put his arm around her, pulling her next to him. She fell asleep in his embrace thinking about garbage trucks, landfills and Philip Byrd.

***

"Don't cry, Baby. Please don't cry."

Emma's dreaming voice awakened her from a sound sleep. Philip Byrd was kneeling in mud, at night, with the looming shadow hanging over him. He was cradling something in his lap. Then he looked at his hands and started to cry.

Why is he crying? What's the matter with him? Is that mud on his hands? Why would that make him cry? God, will it ever end?

Emma rolled over and looked at the clock. It was nearly four-thirty. Jim was snoring loudly and Emma propped him up on pillows, tilting his head back to clear his airway. The tumor was immense and pressure on his throat choked him, especially when he was sleeping.

Between Jim's snoring and nightmares of Philip Byrd, any further sleep was out of the question. Emma climbed into her prayer place in the closet and looked at the stars twinkling in the moonless sky. Crickets and katydids hummed their summer tunes, deer munched thick grass at the edge of the landscaped yard, and Emma St. Claire sat at her window and asked God over and over, "Why?"

CHAPTER SIX

**"I send my messenger...who will
prepare your way before you."**
-Matthew 11:10

Jim was still asleep when Emma left the house on Saturday morning. She visited her dogs, fed the chickens and collected eggs. Allison was eating cereal in the breakfast room and J.D. was sprawled on the family room floor, watching Nova, when Emma came in to wash the eggs.

"I thought I would go down the lane and tell those folks back there what's going on. They aren't as close as we are but they won't want a garbage dump and landfill out here anymore than we do. Who knows, maybe a bi-racial effort will help us. J.D., when Daddy gets up, tell him I'll be back around noon. He said he wanted to go to the old landfill with me."

"Okay, Mom."

J.D. poured a glass of orange juice and flopped back onto the floor to watch his favorite show. Emma smiled fondly at her son. Wasn't it only a few days ago he was a baby? Now he was over six feet tall. She gazed out the wide kitchen window while washing eggs and the memory of a long-ago episode of her extra sensory perception flooded her mind.

***

When Allison was seven years old she took ballet classes in Decatur on Friday afternoons. Because Emma was working full time, Bee drove Allison to the dance studio after school and Emma picked up her daughter on the way home from work. Jim would get J.D. from nursery school on Fridays and everyone would arrive home within a few minutes of each other.

One hot Friday afternoon in late spring Emma followed her usual routine. She stopped at the dance studio and picked up Allison. The moment they got in the car, Emma's e.s.p. said, "Go down Church Street."

I don't want to go down Church Street. That would get me in the Friday afternoon traffic in downtown Decatur. I always go down College Avenue.

"Go down Church Street."

I don't want to go down Church Street. That's a dumb idea. I'm going down College Avenue.

Emma fastened seat belts, turned on the ignition and drove down Church Street. She was literally drawn in the opposite direction from her usual route. The stagnant air was hot, traffic was heavy and Emma was mad at herself for going down Church Street. They were sitting several cars behind a red traffic light when Emma noticed a distinctive familiar green Jeep Gladiator pickup truck parked in a lot half a block away.

Surely, that's not Jim's truck. He was supposed to pick up the baby. Did he forget today is Friday?

Emma was irritated.

Here I am driving down Church Street in bumper-to-bumper traffic to find out that Jim forgot my baby. That idiot. How could he do such a thing?

The light turned green and Emma was slowly propelled toward the green Jeep. The closer she got, the faster her heart was beating; she felt as though it would jump out of her chest.

Calm down. You still have time to get to the nursery and get the baby.

They advanced toward the parking lot; Emma was in a mild state of panic.

What's the matter with me? Get a hold of yourself, Emma.

When they were parallel to the lot Emma got a close look at the truck. Yeah, it was Jim's truck. Then she nearly passed out. Bouncing up and down on the seat, alone, was her twenty-two-month-old baby. Her precious baby was sitting in a truck, by himself, in the middle of Decatur. The windows were rolled up and the baby was drenched with perspiration. His face was fiery red and he looked like he was on burning up. Emma moaned.

My God, My baby; my baby. Dear Lord, I could have lost my baby!

Emma St. Claire's e.s.p. was right; again.

***

62

"I'm going out to the subdivision, Mama," Allison said, snapping her mother out of the daydream. "The sheetrock sub promised me he'd start the stucco house yesterday but he didn't show up. I called him and said if doesn't have a crew there today I'd find someone else."

"Good for you, Allison. I knew you'd get a handle on it. If I have time I'll come by. I've got a lot to do today."

"Don't worry, Mama. I can handle it. The subs are learning that I won't pay them until the work is done and done right. They're griping 'cause Daddy gives advances and I won't."

"I wish you weren't signing checks, Allison."

Allison sighed.

"It's easier if I handle the checkbook, Mama. Daddy makes a mess of it."

"Yes, I realize that. I also know he will take a sheet of checks out of the back of the book; that way you won't know they're missing. If you insist on signing checks, Darlin', for goodness sake don't let your father near the checkbook. In his mental condition there's no telling what he'll do."

Emma gave her daughter a hug, kissed J.D. on the head and left the house. The summer heat was oppressive and the prevailing wind from the south felt hot on her fair skin.

The Coreopsis and Queen Anne's lace were wilted from the hot, dry weather and Emma made a mental note to pick one last bunch before they were gone for another year. At the intersection of two dirt roads she turned east toward the cluster of five homes a mile down the narrow lane, right beyond the entrance to an abandoned rock quarry.

"Mrs. Ames, are you here?" Emma called from the truck window. The old shanty sat adjacent to granite outcropping at the top of a long, steep rocky driveway. A mean looking old dog with a nasty growl rushed at her when she opened the door.

"Why hello, Miz St. Claire."

Emma cringed at the stereotypical attitude of servitude in her neighbor's voice. The elderly black lady caught the old dog by the collar and shut him in the house.

"What brings you down here? You needin' Rick to do some yard work?"

"No, thank you; not today Mrs. Ames—too hot to work in the yard. I wanted to pay a call to tell you what's going on. Have you heard anything about a landfill and garbage transfer station the county wants to put out here?"

"Gracious me, no." She leaned toward Emma, "What'd you say, a landfill?"

"Yes, that's what we've been told. They also want to build a station for three hundred garbage trucks. They'll dump garbage and compact it before they send it to the sanitary landfill in the south end of the county. Of course, we're opposed to these projects. I hope we can count on y'all to help us."

"Yes indeed. We'll do anything we can. You jes tell us what to do 'cuz we jes don't know. My family's been out here since the war," Mrs. Ames told Emma, referring to the War Between the States, "and it seems we is always havin' to run folks off that wants to take it away from us. I duz git sick of it. Why they's even started blastin' the rock agin."

"What? Blasting? At the old quarry? That quarry has been abandoned for at least ten years and this area has been rezoned since then. They can't quarry down here. This rock runs under our homes; it could crack our foundations. Do you know who's doing it?"

"No, ma'am, I doesn't. It duz shake da house when it go off. Ain't you heared it none over your way?"

"No, I haven't heard anything; I leave for work before seven and I don't get home until after six. I'll ask my family. Maybe some of them have heard something. We'll get to the bottom of it though. I know what they are doing is illegal."

"We 'preciate what you is doing, Miz St. Claire."

"We're in this together, Mrs. Ames. I'll be back in a few days with petitions to sign. If you could spread the news I would appreciate it. We need everyone to save our community."

"Thank you, Miz St. Claire," the sweet old lady said. "You jes lets us know what's to do."

Emma's truck crept along the narrow, meandering lane, past the rock quarry and curved south toward the village. When she reached Hudson Creek she pulled over to the side of the road. To her left lay a dense, beautiful forest, rich with wild flowers and a haven to deer, red fox, squirrels, rabbits, raccoons, opossums and no telling what other kinds of animal life. On the right were gently rolling hills leading to the high ridge that dissected that area of the county. The Board of Commissioners had chosen the bucolic land to Emma's left as the site for a garbage dump; the landfill would be on the right.

What's going on in my little corner of the world? My home. My dream. The place I was going to live until I die. The gathering place for friends; for the grandchildren I'll have some day. How could we possibly lose it? Even if it is de-valued, it's still ours. I don't care if it's not worth as much money. As long as it's mine. It's everything I ever wanted. Please, Dear God, don't let me lose everything.

Emma made short order of her errands and returned home before noon with fifty-pound bags of dog food, feed and corn scratch for the chickens, ten bags of groceries for her family and several bunches of Coreopsis and Queen Anne's lace for herself. J.D. unloaded the truck while Emma arranged flowers in an antique crystal vase.

"There's a message for you from Mrs. Reed," J.D. said when he brought in the last load of groceries, "something about a meeting this afternoon."

"Thanks, J.D. I'll call her right away."

Emma set the container of wildflowers on the end of the kitchen island and called her neighbor.

"What's up, Millie?"

"I talked to Rob Slater and Cheryl Johnson. They spearheaded the recent campaign to stop commercial development along Rockbridge and they're both available for a meeting this afternoon. Can you meet us at the construction shack at MacCormick's Cove at two o'clock?"

"Of course. I'm going down to the old landfill with Jim in a few minutes and I'll see you at two. Thanks for calling."

While Emma put away groceries, Jim literally choked down the sandwich she made for him.

"Take it easy, Jim. We're not in a hurry. You need to take smaller bites and eat slower."

Jim coughed violently and beat his enormous fist against his chest. Every meal was more difficult for him to swallow and each choking attack alarmed Emma more. His face would turn scarlet red as he gasped and she was concerned he would pass out.

"Here, Honey, sip some water."

She kissed her husband on the forehead and patted him gently on the back. Jim put his arm around Emma and pulled her to him. His eyes were watering from the choking spell and she watched her husband's heaving chest as the attack began to subside.

"You okay now, Honey?"

"Yeah, I'll be fine in a minute. I'm tired of this mess."

"I know you are. You only have a few more weeks and then it will be behind us. Dr. Keller says your blood pressure is a lot better; I'm sure getting out in this oppressive heat isn't helping you any. Maybe you better not go to the landfill with me. I can find it by myself."

"You're not going down there alone; I'm going with you," he said in an authoritative tone.

Although Jim was not a possessive or jealous husband, he was very protective of his wife. He always wanted to know where she was going and when she would be home and he was not about to let her wander around an abandoned landfill by herself.

They drove across the decrepit wooden slat bridge and parked at the side of the road. The entrance to the old landfill was littered with tires overgrown with thickets of blackberry bushes and honeysuckle vines. After they made it through the brambles the path was open to the top of mound.

"Look at this, Honey." Emma knelt down and brushed some loose dirt away from the edges of a small hole, about an inch in diameter. "These are test boring holes, Jim. There might be some more. You stay here while I go to the top of the ridge."

"I can make it up there," he said indignantly, huffing and puffing his way up the incline. Beads of sweat poured down his round face and the collar of his shirt was soaking wet.

"Jim, we'd better go back. The temperature is over one hundred degrees today and you shouldn't be out in this heat. I'm about to die and there's nothing wrong with my metabolism."

"Not much further," he protested. "We might find something important."

At the top of the hill they had an unobstructed view of Henry Marcus' landfill where dozens and dozens of acres of dense forest had been laid bare and unsystematically covered with every type of litter waste imaginable. Test boring holes were easily spotted and some were several inches in diameter. Emma forced her hand into one of them and felt layers of cardboard, newspapers, cellophane wrappers and other unidentifiable debris.

"I hate to think how deep this pile of trash is, Jim. There is hardly any covering. Aren't landfills supposed to be layered with dirt? No wonder this place was shut down. I don't know anything about landfills. This doesn't look right, does it?"

"Henry didn't seem to have any rhyme or reason to where stuff was dumped or what was dumped. Anyone could come in here and unload anything even though it supposedly belonged to Consolidated. A lot of this paper waste is from their plant on Industrial Boulevard."

From their vantage point Jim was able to point out three distinct mounds of refuse that ran like long fingers for hundreds of yards into distant trees. Some of them were forty to fifty feet deep. The heat was unbearable and Emma and Jim were sweating profusely by the time they returned to the truck.

"I've been thinking, Honey, we ought to get the house appraised again. Janice and David should do the same. If by any chance this damn landfill reopens and the county gets away with their wild-ass scheme to put a garbage dump out here too, we may be looking at some serious land devaluation."

For the first time since she could remember, Jim agreed with Emma. Of course, he didn't know that at the back of her mind the silent voice was saying again, *we're going to lose everything*.

Emma dropped Jim at the Crymes' house and ambled down the winding road to her two o'clock meeting. Rob and Cheryl were sitting on the floor and Millie was leaning against a drafting table when Emma opened the door to the construction trailer at the entrance to the new subdivision. Emma suddenly felt uneasy, as if she had intruded on a secret meeting of some sort. When she told them about the boring tests and Jim's revelation about the landfill being closed for violations, the other three acted somewhat pleased. Rob handed her a copy of the papers he had submitted to the Board of Commissioners opposing the Rockbridge commercial development and Cheryl gave her the name of a woman attorney who helped other neighborhood organizations with environmental issues.

After reviewing Rob's papers Emma asked, "Who's going to be our noble leader? You each have a lot of experience with this sort of thing; do you think we can win?"

Millie spoke up first.

"I've fought a lot of battles over the years and I'm getting too old for it. I'm going to have to depend on one of you."

"Don't look at me," Rob threw in quickly. "My job is too demanding right now and with my family and church activities, I don't have the time."

Cheryl wasted no time in putting in her two cents worth.

"I can't do it this time. Too much time is involved and I don't know anything about landfills. We need someone who can do the research and someone who is close to the problem, too. It doesn't concern me anyway. My house is right in the middle of a subdivision."

The three turned their eyes toward Emma.

"I can't do it," she protested. "I don't know anything about landfills and I've never done civic work, either. I wouldn't know where to start."

"We're available to give advice," Rob said cheerfully. "You can do it. Besides, you're the natural one for the job since you're on North Ridge. The rest of us are at least a mile away and we're not going to be affected the way you are. We'll help you, Emma; this is one fight we're not leading."

Emma was shaken. How could they say they wouldn't be affected? If the most prosperous neighborhood was devalued surely they would be hurt, too. Couldn't they see that?

Besides, none of them was any busier than she was. Where would she possibly find the time? She had never been before the Board of Commissioners. Organize a community fight against the Board? Gad. What a horrible thought.

Rob stood up and dusted off the seat of his pants.

"Call me if I can be of any help, Emma."

Emma shook her head slowly and gave him a wide, tight-lipped smile, saying to herself that she had no idea what to do. She felt lonely and abandoned.

"I will, Rob. Thanks for coming."

Emma wished she could be sarcastic because no one was willing to do anything constructive for her but she couldn't. Sarcasm was not part of her makeup. She thanked each of them sincerely and drove home in a daze.

Me? Why in the world did it fall on my shoulders? I haven't got the foggiest notion what I'm supposed to do. Where will I find the time? There is a tremendous amount of work and research to be done. Where will I start? I'll have to pray over this and trust God to show me the way.

Jim was pouring a glass of sun tea when Emma returned to the house.

"How'd the meeting go?" he asked.

"You're talking to the noble leader and she has no idea what's going on."

"What do you mean?

"Millie and Rob and Cheryl said they can't do it this time. They want me to spearhead the community drive against these projects."

"You can do it," he said nonchalantly, as if it was as easy as baking her family's favorite chocolate cake.

"Honestly, Jim. How can I do it? Where will I find the time? Someone needs to go to the county offices and round up information about these projects. Since every project in the county has to get a permit that would be the logical starting point. Someone needs to contact the State environmental agency. Aren't they part of the Department of Natural Resources? Then there's the E.P.A. We need to call them, too. We need to know what the rules and regulations are for these sorts of projects. Someone needs to call this attorney and find out our legal position in this situation. Someone should go to the library at Georgia Tech and research landfills. This will give us unbiased, factual information to present. Maybe the Civil Engineering department at Tech has someone who will help us. Someone needs to put up posters at every road intersection in this area to tell people what's going on. We'll need a slogan, maybe "stop the landfill and dump the dump." Something catchy. Flyers should be distributed to every house detailing the information about Board meetings, community meetings, and protest marches. Petitions have to be circulated, too. We'll need hundreds of signatures, not the few we have here on North Ridge. Someone needs to join environmental groups—Sierra Club and Georgia Conservancy. Those organizations could be a tremendous help. Someone needs to gather, compile and organize this information to make it effective and useable. Do you understand what I'm saying, Jim? There's a lot that needs to be done and I have no idea where to start."

Jim shrugged his shoulders and shook his head at his agitated wife.

"Sounds to me you know exactly what needs to be done. No wonder they elected you."

He went upstairs to take a nap and left his wife alone in the kitchen. Emma sat at the table and rested her chin on her tight fists, furrowing her brow and staring into the distance in her typical manner when contemplating a problem.

What did I say? Why did Jim say I know what to do? All I said was—

Emma sat in a trance, staring out across the lawn, trying to remember everything she said in her tirade.

When I was driving home after the meeting I said God would have to show me the way.

She took a note pad and pen off the kitchen counter and returned to the table, mulling over the words in her mind. Then she outlined her battle plan.

CHAPTER SEVEN

"The battle is the Lord's"
-1 Samuel 17:47

By Monday morning Emma felt more comfortable with her new vocation. Allison was making posters, J.D. volunteered to hang them, Janice and David were circulating petitions and Emma set up a network of friends to act as liaisons between her committee and each subdivision in the surrounding area. Taking advantage of the unusually quiet morning at the office, she typed a flyer and ran five hundred copies on lime green paper before making phone calls.

"This flyer should get the neighbors' attention," Emma said. She picked up the phone and called the Atlanta office of the Federal Environmental Protection Agency.

"We don't have any jurisdiction is this particular situation, Mrs. St. Claire," the water quality engineer said. "However, I can assure you the E.P.A. would never allow any sort of landfill activity where people are drinking well water. It is not a matter of if the wells will be polluted; it is only a matter of when. Furthermore, if we did close that old landfill as you believe, it would be illegal under our guidelines to reopen it for any reason unless it was cleaned up first."

"In other words, our water will be polluted and they can illegally reopen a hazardous landfill but you can't help us, is that right?"

"That's right. I wish we could. That is not our jurisdiction now. It was turned over to the states and Georgia took over some time in seventy-eight or seventy-nine. We don't even have the files."

"Can I quote you, Mr. Moore? We're making a presentation to the Board of Commissioners on August twenty-fourth and we need every bit of ammunition we can dig up."

"Yes ma'm, of course. I doubt it will do any good—our hands are tied behind our back. You can quote me, though, Mrs. St. Claire: It is only a matter of time until your water is polluted."

Emma transcribed shorthand notes she made during her conversation with Mr. Moore and put them in a notebook. Then she called the Civil Engineering Department at Georgia Tech and was connected to a professor who had extensive knowledge of landfills. After describing to Emma the geological formations in her area of the county and concurring with Mr. Moore about the water pollution, he suggested she visit the Tech library. Emma typed up this new information and added it to her notebook.

Emma repeated this process time and time again and within a few days she had a significant amount of data. Landfills were bad news and she became a one-woman-save-the-environment army, calling everyone she could think of at both the state and local government to voice her objections and spending many late hours in the Georgia Tech library researching what she considered her personal enemy. News of the environmental war spread and Emma found herself the community spokesman; most of her precious time at home was spent on telephone calls from worried neighbors. By the end of the week more than five hundred homeowners had signed the petition; Emma sent Jim to the Department of Natural Resources with one set of the protest petitions and another copy was delivered to the County Board of Commissioners.

When Emma got home from work on Friday night she found Jim sitting in the living room with a strange man.

"What's going on now?" she asked in an irritated manner, not knowing what Jim was up to.

"You told me to get the house appraised. This is Mike Jelks from the Smithfield Mortgage Company and he has a copy of the appraisal for us."

"Mortgage company? Why do we need a mortgage company?"

Mike looked embarrassed and Emma realized she had been rude.

"Jim told me about the landfill, Mrs. St. Claire. He also told me about the second mortgage you have on this beautiful home. He thought you should go ahead and refinance the house with Smithfield and pay off the second mortgage with First Federated in case there's a devaluation. With this current appraisal we won't have any problem qualifying you for a new mortgage."

Emma was quiet and contemplative for a few moments, rocking slowly in her favorite chair. Caught up in Jim's illness and the landfill she forgot about the balloon second mortgage. Shaking her head slowly, she tightened her lips and clenched her fists.

"We'll owe First Federated forty thousand dollars in February. Will there be any problem with that much cash?"

"Not right now, there won't. You have a lovely place here and its current value, according to the appraisal, is two hundred and forty thousand dollars. You have more than enough equity and income to justify a new mortgage. We just need to get something going before the landfill becomes official."

Emma leaned back in the rocker and sat motionless, going over the details in her mind. A wide smile slowly formed on her lips and she was almost giddy.

We won't lose everything; we won't; we won't; we won't. We'll pay off our mortgages with First Federated. Then, when Jim sells his houses, we'll be home free and I'll be shed of that damn bank. Eureka! Thank you, thank you Lord. Good-bye and good riddance, First Nasty Bank.

"Okay, where do I sign?"

A mortgage application for the Smithfield loan was filled out and signed and Emma wrote a check for the application fee.

"I can't wait to get the mortgage on this house away from First Federated, Mr. Jelks," she said, handing him the check. "How soon do you think we can close?"

"Not long since we already have the appraisal. I'll push it as hard as I can. By the time Jim gets out of the hospital we ought to be ready."

"What? Gets out of the hospital? His surgery isn't even scheduled yet."

"I meant to tell you," Jim said sheepishly. "Dr. Jander called today. My surgery is set for eleven o'clock on the twenty-fourth."

"The twenty-fourth? You're kidding. You can't have surgery on the twenty-fourth. That's the day we go before the Board of Commissioners. At ten in the morning."

"That's when I get my throat cut."

A sinking spell overcame Emma; she sank back into her chair. Her husband was facing major surgery and she was facing the Board of Commissioners. On the same day. Her glee at getting the house mortgage away from First Federated faded as the premonition played again.

We're going to lose everything.

***

Emma's only respite from landfills, garbage dumps and nightmares was the psychology class with Dr. Horner. Every spare minute of her time at the office was devoted to her war against the Board and making time to study was not easy. Somehow she managed to maintain a high 'A' in the course and was looking forward to completing the class and retaining her straight-A standing, until the night her beloved teacher announced final exams.

"The final will be on Tuesday, August twenty-fourth at seven thirty. It will be a two-hour exam. Bring a lot of sharp pencils."

Emma raised her hand with a look of chagrin on her face.

"You did say the twenty-fourth, didn't you, Dr. Horner?"

"That's right. Do you have a problem with that date, Emma? If you do, see me after class and we'll work out something."

Emma was mesmerized by her thoughts.

Why do these things happen? Why does my final exam have to be on the twenty-fourth? Is this for real? Good grief. What's next! How in the world can I prepare for a final exam, a presentation to the Board of Commissioners, and give Jim the moral support he needs all at the same time? I can't leave him alone right after he has major surgery. He was always there for me, after every operation. I can't let him down. I won't let him down; he's counting on me being there. Does God think I'm a three-ring circus? How in the world does He expect me to take care of this?

After class Emma told Dr. Horner her situation and they agreed she should take the exam the following week.

"You'll get an incomplete, Emma. I promise, as soon as you take the final I'll get the paperwork in and you'll get your grade. You're going to make an *A* anyway and if this exam didn't cover new material, I'd let you exempt it."

"Thank you, Dr. Horner. I don't know how I can manage otherwise. I hate the thought of having an incomplete on my record; I guess there's no other way."

"No problem, Emma. It will work out for the best. You'll see. Trust the Man Upstairs."

"I do. More than you can possibly imagine. Sometimes I wonder if I'm crazy because I talk to God; but He always helps me work things out; that can't be too wrong, can it?"

"No, Emma. It's never wrong to talk to God, no matter where you are or what you're doing. It seems to me that you've had some pretty rough times in your life and these trials and tribulations have made you what you are, independent and strong. I'd be willing to bet that the Almighty has made you strong for a purpose and as long as you look to Him for guidance, you'll never go wrong."

Dr. Horner's words ran around inside Emma's mind during her drive home.

God is making me strong for a purpose? What purpose? To have e.s.p. and dreams and nightmares I don't understand. How am I supposed to accomplish something for Him if I don't even understand what's going on in my own life?

Emma's mild mannered, intelligent, articulate father-in-law agreed to make the presentation to the Board and dozens of neighbors were expected to attend the meeting on the twenty-fourth. After much soul-searching, Emma decided to make a relentless verbal assault on the Board and included intimidating legal phrases such as dereliction of duty and malicious intent to cause bodily harm in her paper that would be submitted to the Commissioners.

Against doctor's orders, Jim continued working right up to the day of his surgery; before dawn that morning he went out to one of the houses to plant and mulch shrubs. Emma finally rounded him up, rushed him through a shower and they were sitting in his hospital room at ten o'clock when an orderly appeared with a stretcher.

"We're ahead of schedule, Mr. St. Claire. Your nurse will be right down to give you an injection and then I'll be taking you to surgery."

Jim looked nervously at Emma and reached for her hand.

"You're gonna do fine, Honey. I know you are. You'll be up and around in no time. Behave yourself and do what they say and I'll be sitting right here waiting for you."

"Why don't you go on over to the Board meeting? It wouldn't take you five minutes to get there."

"Janice and David and Bee and the kids are there with a large contingent of neighbors. The attorney who read over my presentation for me said it was excellent. We're hitting them hard, Jim. I can't do anything now except wait and see. I would rather be here close to you while I'm waiting."

A nurse gave Jim his final pre-op injection and he was taken away. Emma opened her psychology book to study for the final exam. It was a futile gesture. How could she study when her life was in the hands of a surgeon and the seven members of the County Board of Commissioners? She went to the cafeteria for coffee, speaking to familiar faces on the way. Then, before she returned to Jim's room, Emma went to the chapel and prayed for a long while.

Emma was standing in Jim's hospital room an hour and a half later gazing out the window when the phone rang.

Thank goodness. That must be the surgeon. He said the surgery should take less than two hours.

"Mrs. St. Claire?" a serious-sounding female voice asked.

"Yes."

"I'm calling for Dr. Beauregard. There have been some complications with your husband's surgery and he expects to be working on him at least two more hours, maybe three. The tumor has grown down into his chest. We'll keep you posted."

"I appreciate your calling. Thank you."

Emma had the weak-knee feeling and rapid pulse of one who has heard bad news. She was leaning on the edge of the bed when her children entered the room with Janice and David. Allison looked pale.

"We lost, Mama. The room was full of our neighbors and Grandpa made a great talk. The Board chairman jumped up shouting when he read your paper. The TV stations were there and everything. Those bastards can go ahead with the landfill."

"You wouldn't believe that idiot Board chairman, Maloof," J.D. interjected. "He says that dead trees won't make a methane problem because they're not organic. Can you believe that? How can anyone be that stupid?"

Everyone was talking at once, trying to get in their money's worth about the ordeal with the Board, about how they were sending the east end of the country down the tube. Two more landfill applications had already been filed and now the precedent had been set. Nothing could stop them.

Finally, Janice asked if Emma had heard anything about the surgery. After Emma explained the nurse's recent report the angry roar over the Board decision gave way to a quiet atmosphere of gloom. There was nothing to do but sit and wait, with the overriding feelings of being useless and helpless. She hugged J.D. tightly.

"Daddy's gonna be fine. We've had the bad news for today. Y'all go get some lunch. I'm too stressed out to eat."

Sensing Emma's need to be alone, Janice and David took the children to lunch, although Emma knew her mother-in-law would have preferred to stay. This time she would stand up to Janice and her control. No one could make her leave Jim's room. She wanted to be alone. She wanted to talk to God in her own quiet way and ask Him again for the strength to get through it.

What are we going to do now, Lord? Our beautiful home holds everything You have given us. Are we really going to lose it? Why? What have we done to deserve this?

Four and a half hours after Jim was taken to surgery the doctor called. He sounded very tired.

"This was an unusual case, Mrs. St. Claire. The tumor had grown down into Jim's chest cavity, behind the larynx. His vocal nerve was completely encapsulated; he would have lost his voice permanently within a few weeks. It was tedious work to free that nerve from the tumor. There will be a lot of irritation so don't be surprised if he can't talk. I believe we got it in time and in a few months his voice will return."

Emma thanked the doctor profusely for everything he had done for Jim and then she thanked God for everything He had done. The day had not been a complete bust. Jim was going to be alright.

Ten days after Jim was released from the hospital Mike Jelks called Emma at work.

"Smithfield Mortgage has approved your loan, Emma. As soon as we get the payoff figures from First Federated we'll be ready to close."

"Thank goodness. I've been scared there would be a snafu with this landfill and garbage dump business making the news. We had a spot on t.v. the other night and the reporter even interviewed me at my office. Did you see it?"

"No, I didn't. I'm sorry about everything you've been through. Even though your property will be devalued, once we close the loan you won't have to worry about it."

"What a relief it will be, Mike. That's my little corner of the world. It is everything I ever dreamed of having. Someday I hope my grandchildren will cherish it as much as I do. I don't know how to thank you enough, Mike. We're going to push the county for water and paved roads. We may have lost a battle. The war is still being fought. As long as this place is ours, Jim and I don't care what it is worth in dollars and cents. Our home is priceless to us."

"We should be able to close by the end of the week. I'll give you a call when I have a date."

"Great. Can't wait to get that call, Mike. Thank you again."

Emma heaved a sigh of relief. Jim was on the mend and she was going to get rid of First Nasty. The house would be financed with a reputable mortgage company and she would finally get a decent night's sleep. Long hours working on landfill research, studying, and caring for a sick husband took a toll on the usually vibrant redhead and dark circles formed below her eyes. She squeezed in enough time to study and take the final for Dr. Horner's class and was pleased to receive another *A*. Allison was looking forward to fall quarter at Georgia Tech and J.D. was now a high school sophomore; and Emma had all but forgotten Philip Byrd and the bizarre mishmash of dreams of nightmares.

We aren't going to lose everything. What a preposterous premonition. Philip Byrd is not special to me. There's no reason why I should protect him. Maybe my e.s.p. was playing itself out and I'll never have another episode. What a wonderful relief that would be.

Mike Jelks called again a few days later.

"Emma, I'm sorry to bother you again. We're having a little trouble getting loan payoff figures from First Federated. Do you think you could send them a letter today requesting the info?"

"Of course; I'll do it right away. Why won't they give the figures to you? Our mortgages state very clearly that we can pay off the loans at any time. What do you think those s.o.b.s are up to, Mike?"

"Have no idea. If you put it in writing I don't believe legally they can refuse to give you the figures."

Emma wrote a letter to the executive vice president of the bank politely requesting payoff figures and was shocked to receive a reply within three days. She expected them to drag their feet or come up with some lame excuse. In the past, they blamed their bookkeeping errors on their computers and she figured they would come up with some sort of stunt to milk a few more days of interest out of her. She tore into the envelope and almost passed out when she read the letter. Then she ran upstairs to her prayer place and bawled. By the time Jim found her thirty minutes later she was almost hysterical.

He could hardly talk and words squeaked out of him. "What's the matter, Baby? What's wrong now?"

"Read this letter from your damn bank, Jim. Those bastards want me to pay off three hundred thousand dollars in construction loans for your company before they'll give me the payoff figures on our home. What the hell is going on? I'm not responsible for your business loans. I've never signed a single damn paper for that bank except for our personal mortgage on this house. How can they do this to me, Jim? How? I told you those people were no good. I begged you not to do business with them. If you had stayed with Decatur Federal or Trust Company this never would have happened."

"Calm down, would you. We'll get to the bottom of it. I'll call Crumbley first thing in the morning and get it straightened out."

"You better. Do you realize what this is, Jim? Extortion. That's what it is. Plain and simple. They are trying to extort three hundred thousand dollars out of me for your damn business and they are using my home as leverage. They can't get away with this, Jim. They've screwed us for the last time."

The following morning, after Emma left for work, Jim picked up the checkbook and drove to the bank where he cashed a check for two thousand dollars; then he met his attorney, Douglas Griffin, in Stone Mountain. Doug called the loan officer at First Federated and scheduled an eleven o'clock meeting.

"You better let me drive, Jim. I don't want you over-taxing yourself."

"I appreciate that. Do you mind if we stop at the bank on the way? I need to cash a check."

"Be glad to. Any other stops you need to make while we're out?"

"No. A little pocket change will take care of me."

At a nearby branch of his bank Jim cashed another check for a thousand dollars before they drove to Loganville to meet Pete Crumbley at First Federated.

"What can I do for you Jim?" the bank officer said cheerfully, ushering Jim and his attorney into his office.

Doug took over the conversation. "My client's wife received a letter from you folks yesterday, Mr. Crumbley, insisting that she pay three hundred thousand dollars in construction loans Jim has with you. Can you explain that?"

"Jim has gotten behind on his interest payments and before we foreclose on his loans we thought we'd give Mrs. St. Claire the opportunity to pay them off. It was just a courtesy."

"Mrs. St. Claire doesn't consider it a courtesy, Mr. Crumbley. She has no obligation to you on these loans and we would appreciate it if you would provide her with the payoff figures on her house. Jim has come here out of his sickbed to ask you to give him a sixty day moratorium on the construction loans."

Crumbley leaned back in his leather executive chair and put his feet on the mahogany desk, crossing long arms over a broad chest.

"Don't know about that, now."

"Jim has done more than a million dollars of business with you in the last two years. That's a lot of money for one man to generate. It seems to me it would behoove you to extend a little good will toward him until he is recuperated. You've always gotten your money and there's no reason to think otherwise."

The sleazy banker took his feet off the desk and leaned forward on his elbows, clasping his hands beneath his wide jaw, curling his thin lips into a tight smile.

"Rules are rules, gentlemen. We can't extend your loans, Mr. St. Claire."

Jim was hardly following the conversation. Pete had always been his buddy, the man with the money. He would slap Jim on the back, tell him what a great job he was doing and Jim would sign another construction loan. Now Jim was laid up and his buddy had turned into a hard, cold, heartless banker.

"Come on, Doug. Let's get out of here," he squeaked.

"Tell your wife to pay us the three hundred thousand and we'll give her the payoffs."

Jim shot the banker a bird and Doug practically shoved him out of Crumbley's office.

"Calm down, Jim. We'll get it worked out. Making that asshole your enemy won't help you any."

On the drive back to Stone Mountain Doug gave Jim a Dutch Uncle talk.

"Legally they can foreclose your construction loans, Jim. There's no way around that fact. I don't understand why they think they can hold Emma responsible, or why she would have that kind of money. Do you?"

Jim shrugged his shoulders and shook his head.

"You better round up your loan documents and get them to my office. I wish you had let me in on this. Who reviewed the loan papers for you? Which attorney did you use?"

Jim choked out a response. "The bank had an attorney in house. He drew up everything."

"Jim, you're not telling me that you didn't have your own legal representation are you?"

"The guy's an attorney," he whispered. "I figured everything was okay. It was the same old stuff. I signed a bunch of papers and they gave me the construction loans."

Doug sat in the parked car outside his office shaking his head slowly.

"This is unbelievable Jim. I have no idea what you've signed. For Christ's sake, man. What possessed you to do such a thing?"

Jim stared blankly out the window and shrugged his shoulders again.

"I'll do the best I can Jim; I'm not promising anything. You better go on home and get back to bed. Ask Emma to round up the files and bring them to me."

"Okay, Doug. Thanks for driving."

Jim got in his old blue pickup truck and stopped at another branch of the bank, with the checkbook in tow, before driving home with five thousand dollars cash in his pocket. He laid the checkbook on Allison's desk and went upstairs to bed.

Allison returned from registration at Georgia Tech and picked up the checkbook and file folder of current invoices. She had met her boyfriend for lunch and was still smiling about their decision to give their families some exciting news the next weekend. Systematically she filled in each check stub and brought down the balance. Then she wrote and signed checks, filed the paid invoices and left the envelopes to be mailed on her mother's desk in the kitchen with a note:

"Mama, I am out of stamps. Please mail these checks for me tomorrow. The checkbook is balanced, the journals are posted and the filing is done. Having dinner with Steve tonight. Luv ya lots! Allison."

When Emma arrived she found Jim asleep in bed, J.D. watching television while working on his homework and Allison's note. She picked up the stack, stamped each envelope and put the mail in her car. Then Emma and J.D. ate soup and sandwiches in the family room while discussing weekend football games. Emma didn't care for the idea of her son playing football but he worked incredibly hard and she supported his efforts although she missed the colorful play-by-play commentary he used to give her when they sat together at games.

"Do you think you'll play in the game tomorrow night, J.D.?"

"I don't know, Mom. Everyone at school thinks I should be a football jock 'cause I'm big," he said forlornly.

"J.D., you have to do what's right for J.D., not the kids at school. They weren't born with defective hips and flat feet. They don't know the pain of Osgood Schlatter in both knees or the agony of a severe burn. If you want to play, play because you enjoy it. You have to do it for yourself, J.D. No one else. Not me or Daddy or Allison. You don't have to measure yourself against anyone else either. God only made one James David St. Claire and He loves you 'cause you're you. And I do, too."

Emma went to the kitchen to wash dishes, pondering J.D.'s various leg and knee ailments while standing at the sink. She always felt responsible for the severe burn even though she was not there when the accident occurred.

***

J.D. was only ten years old when they were finishing the house. Emma was hanging wallpaper in the breakfast room that Saturday morning. Jim was on his way to pick up J.D. at the soccer field and Emma asked him to bring her a thermos of hot water from home for instant coffee. Standing on her work stool a wave of nausea overcame her and she envisioned boiling water spilling, followed by a burning pain. She had no idea what it meant and ran down the driveway, yelling for Jim to stop. It was too late. Jim was out of hearing distance and Emma was left alone, without any transportation, feeling helpless.

Hot water. My God, please don't let anyone get hurt. It feels awful; painful and hot. Please, please Dear Lord.

She returned to her work. The ill feeling was distressing and pervasive.

An hour later Jim returned with J.D. and the thermos. Her son hobbled into the house and collapsed, looking strained and ash colored.

No, please no. Not my baby.

Jim had gone home and boiled water. Then he poured it into a pump-top thermos and closed the top without securing both latches. He carried it by the swinging handle, set it on the floorboard of the car, and drove to the soccer fields where he picked up J.D. A few minutes later, they rounded a sharp curve. The thermos tumbled over, the partially latched top came loose, and boiling water spilled onto the child's leg, ankle and foot.

The Emergency Room at the hospital immediately referred them to a burn specialist. A few days later when Emma was washing J.D.'s clothes she found the skin and flesh that had been boiled off her son's leg still clinging to the inside of his sock where Jim had yanked it off before applying a thick coating of greasy ointment which had further aggravated the burn. If only she had been there. Emma would have given her son proper first aid by submerging the injured limb into ice water; Jim's incompetence had only caused more distress and exacerbated the injury.

J.D. missed four weeks of school and bravely underwent tortuous debriding sessions. Although he was in agony, he never shed a tear and for the rest of his life he would carry the scars of an accident his mother had foreseen and was powerless to prevent.

***

For several weeks Emma was blessed with peaceful sleep and not one thought about Philip Byrd and the dreadful nightmares. Now, for some unknown reason, the memory of J.D.'s burn brought into her mind the image of the teacher kneeling in the muddy field at night.

Why, Dear God? Why do I see these things? What is the purpose of the feelings if I am not to use them wisely? Please, Dear Lord, please take them away from me.

The next few days gave Emma the escape she longed for. J.D. played for ten minutes of the last quarter on Friday night and Saturday she was thrilled to see her daughter running onto Grant Field, carrying clusters of white and gold balloons. Allison was a member of the elite Ramblin' Reck Club and had earned the privilege of escorting the football team into the stadium to the cheers of the crowd and the delight of her very proud mother. Saturday night Allison and Steve walked into the kitchen holding hands, looking happy and scared at the same time.

"We have something to tell you, Mama."

Allison was clinging to Steve's arm.

"Don't keep me waiting." Emma felt unusually happy, almost giddy.

"Mrs. St. Claire," Steve spoke hesitantly, "Allison and I want to get married."

Emma rushed around the island and embraced them both.

"I am very, very happy for you. This is wonderful. Do your folks know, Steve? What does your mom say? When? When is this wonderful event to take place?"

"My folks say it is fine with them if you and Mr. St. Claire approve. We haven't set the date yet—we're thinking about getting married next summer."

"Of course! I'm thrilled. Absolutely thrilled. Can we have a big wedding? Whatever you want is fine with me. It would be nice to have a big wedding at St. Martin's. Allison would be a second-generation bride there. This is wonderful. If you don't get married until next summer we'll have plenty of time for an engagement party. A real engagement party right here in our home. We'll invite everyone. This is going to be fun."

Allison and Steve were pleased with Emma's response.

"We were concerned you would want us to wait until we graduate."

"Why? You're mature people. You're both world travelers and you've each dated a lot. If you want to get married I don't see anything wrong with it. You'll have a lot on you to finish your last year of college but it will give you a sense of what's important—and that will be invaluable experience down the road."

"What do you think Daddy will say?"

"Don't worry about him. He'll go along with it. Besides, he's clearly outnumbered. He's resting upstairs. Why don't you go tell him now while I finish dinner?"

The young lovers went upstairs to share their happy news with Allison's father and Emma went back to her cooking.

The first time I saw that handsome young man I knew he was the right one for Allison. I know they're going to be very happy together for many, many years. Glad I don't feel the way I did when my two closest sorority sisters married.

83

Emma was at her best friend's house the week before Judy's wedding to an outstanding man at Georgia State where they attended college. Judy was happily opening a wedding gift when the message came clearly to Emma, *This marriage will never last.* It was a preposterous premonition. They were both intellectually gifted and had a promising future. Eighteen months later they were divorced.

The following summer Emma was attending a bridal tea for another sorority sister, a lovely young woman she had known since third grade. Charlotte was marrying into a prominent, supposedly high-class family. During the tea, when someone mentioned the fiancé's name, Emma's silent voice said, *this is a mistake.* It was only after the lavish wedding when Charlotte was on her honeymoon that she learned her new husband was gay. For the next several months Charlotte endured brutal beatings. A few months later she moved back to her parent's home. The marriage was annulled.

Emma was thrilled this time, though, because her very first impression of Steve played over and over, *He's the right man for Allison.*

***

Emma did not abandon her war against the garbage dump and landfill. She was determined to defeat them at the state level, the next stage in the approval process. Emma had finished an absorbing conversation with a helpful employee at the Department of Natural Resources when Jim's attorney called.

"Have you gotten the files together for me?" Doug asked.

"What do you mean? What files?"

"I drove Jim to the bank last Thursday for a meeting with that Crumbley creep. Seems Jim may have signed a number of documents at the bank that I've never seen and I asked him to get copies for me. Didn't he mention it to you?"

"No. I thought he was in bed. No wonder he was sleeping soundly when I got home. What exactly do you need?"

"Jim's construction loan documentation. Purchase contracts for the land, applications for loans, pay request and draw sheets, and anything else pertinent."

"That shouldn't be any problem. Allison has been working on files this summer and she got copies of a lot of stuff from the bank. Can I bring them to you tomorrow afternoon?"

"That would be great. I'm at a loss to understand why they think they can hold you responsible for Jim's loans, Emma. Maybe we'll find out when we read the contracts Jim signed."

"I hope so, Doug. I want to close our new loan and the appraisal is already seven weeks old. We've got to get moving on this before the mortgage company gets wind of the landfill. I don't want them to find some way to withdraw their commitment."

"They're locked in for sixty days, Emma. We should have it cleared up before then."

Emma slipped into her contemplative pose, leaning her elbows on the desk and resting her tightened jaw on her fists. Her eyes were focused on two squirrels playing in the old oak trees in the yard beyond the wide window wall in her office, her random thoughts scattered among fears of a dreadful premonition coming true. She slowly shook her head.

The doctor said Jim could have been incompetent for a year and Doug said he's never seen any of the contracts Jim signed. I hate to think about it. What in the world has Jim done?

CHAPTER EIGHT

**"The Lord heard our voice and saw our affliction
and our toil and our oppression."**
-Deuteronomy 26:7

As soon as Emma got home from work she put a roast in the oven then hurried to the attic where Jim's business records were kept in a row of filing cabinets. She retrieved the documents Douglas wanted, closed the drawer and was starting out the door when a small box, sitting on the top shelf of an old bookcase, caught her eye.

Wonder what's in this old box—there's a bunch of stuff in this attic; it would take me a month to sort through it.

Standing on her worse-for-wear workbench, Emma reached for the small tattered pink satin box of keepsakes. Sitting in her tired rocking chair Emma sifted through carefully wrapped treasures. To her delight she found the silk bonnet Bee gave to Allison when she was born and the embroidered lace handkerchief made into a Christening cap for J.D. There was Allison's mother-of-pearl and silver teething ring; J.D.'s first shoes.

Emma was thrilled with this unexpected pleasure and could hardly wait to share the mementos with Jim and the children. She browsed quickly through other contents of the box and found an envelope of papers from the V.A.

Wonder what this is?

The envelope held correspondence Emma had with the V.A. because Jim's G.I. Bill benefits were overpaid when he was in graduate school. For months Jim insisted he returned the checks because he knew his entitlement had expired and Emma adamantly told the federal agency her husband did not owe the money. When the V.A. finally supplied her with copies of cancelled checks, with Jim's endorsement, Emma had to eat a lot of crow and refund overpayments. She smiled, remembering they were short of cash at the time and it took her months to pay back the money.

I wish he only owed three hundred dollars now.

Emma dug to the bottom of the box and retrieved another envelope, this one holding appraisals of her wedding ring and a jade necklace from Janice. It was a choker and Emma chuckled at the irony – that her mother-in-law would give her a choker for a wedding present. As for the wedding ring, Emma had long ago abandoned it to the bottom on her jewelry box and replaced it with a gold band she bought for herself. She never attached importance to the ring that Janice told Jim to buy. Emma had no choice in the selection; nor did Jim. Janice Crymes had selected the wedding ring and Emma detested it.

There was also a stack of Jim's grade reports from Georgia State College. Emma had never seen them and surmised that Janice had given them to Jim when she went on a cleaning binge and burned up scores of old family documents, including letters Emma had written to her during Jim's Army days when they lived in Germany.

With a grin on her face she recalled Jim's story of the ancient history class and how the professor said no one deserved an *A* in history because no one could know enough to earn the highest grade. Jim told her proudly that he earned the first and only *A* that Prof ever gave and Emma relayed this story to many friends over the years. It was her way of reinforcing strong feelings that Jim should be a history teacher. She glanced over each report, looking for the much-cherished grade. Then she went pale.

He lied to me. When we were starting to date he lied to me. How many lies have there been over the years?

Emma gathered up the precious possessions of her children's infancies, not wanting them contaminated with the deceits contained in old V.A. documents and college report cards and stormed out of the attic, slamming the door. The grade report she left behind was caught by a breeze through the open dormer window and slithered to the floor where it laid open for anyone to clearly see the grade her husband made in ancient history. It was a *C.*

What had been a happy adventure into cherished old memories became a torrent of tears and fears of the future. Emma retreated to her prayer place in her closet, clutching the treasures to her chest.

How much more can I take? Jim has been lying to me for twenty-two years. I should be immune to it by now, but each lie hurts more than the one before. Each one is a knife twisting in my heart. His doctor says he's no longer toxic, that his lying is a psychological problem. He refuses to get help. He won't change. He's not strong enough to face the pain of change. Give me strength, Dear Lord. Give me patience and understanding to do what you would have me to do.

Emma carefully repacked the keepsakes in a clean shoebox and went downstairs to finish dinner. She didn't say a word to Jim about the V.A. papers or the old grade report. What good would it do, anyway? There would be another fight, more hurt feelings, more tears. Nothing good would come of it; it was better left unsaid. She called her family to the table and they sat down to another delicious meal. Conversation was happy and they ate leisurely; no one knew the pain in Emma's heart.

After dinner Emma went to see Janice and David, stopping at the dog pen on the way to play with Alex and the other dogs. The small black dog gave her the lift she needed.

"How's my Alex dog? You love your Mama, don't you Boy. I love you, too," she said, gently caressing his long silky ears. "You don't know what a lie is, do you Bubba. You love everyone; yes you do. Why can't people be more like dogs?"

Emma played fetch with the canine crowd for a few minutes and reluctantly left her friends. Her heart was beating rapidly when she arrived at the front door of the Crymes house.

"Hi," she forced herself to say cheerfully when Janice opened the door. Years of kowtowing to Janice made Emma's mission even more uncomfortable.

"Do you have a few minutes? I need to talk to you and David."

"Why come on in. Can I get you some pie?" There were times when Janice was sincere and agreeable, and her pastry was delicious. Emma resisted. Knowing the visit would not be pleasant she did not want to prolong the agony. She spoke softly.

"I'm thoroughly disgusted with Jim's business and his failure to get the psychological therapy his doctor says he desperately needs. He's been awfully sick, I know. Even though his surgeon released him, he still won't go back to work. The houses are sitting, waiting to be completed, interest charges are piling up and the bank has started foreclosure. I know first-hand how long a recovery can take but Jim has problems that can't be cured by surgery. His entrepreneurial exploits have created a tremendous financial and emotional burden on me.

"I want you to know that Allison and I will not do the bookkeeping for his business. We have more than enough to handle as it is. I've worked hard for twenty-two years and we're on the verge of losing everything. You said you would back his business because of my expertise in construction. Well, I was never included; he has never listened to me. He has always done it his way and only his way. Please look at this from my perspective for once. His houses are being foreclosed, we owe that damn bank forty thousand dollars and the county is burying us in landfills and garbage dumps. I'm getting out of Jim's business and hope it is not too late to salvage what's left of our marriage."

Janice and David were shocked; neither one gave Emma any hope, encouragement or support. She dried her eyes with her ever-available Kleenex and left the house quietly.

The cool evening air was pleasantly stimulating and Emma decided to take the long way home. She walked briskly down the long concrete driveway and turned to the north when she reached the dirt road. Horses across the lane were corralled for the night and she stopped to talk to them when they extended long heads over the fence for a scratch between the ears.

God, I do love it out here. Please don't let them take it away from me.

At the intersection of the two roads she turned right again and walked along the front of their property, admiring trees blowing gently in the wind. Emma spent six weeks one summer cleaning out tangles of honeysuckle, blackberry and poison ivy vines that grew over the giant trees and strangled them. Now they were free to grow and spread their limbs.

Emma stretched her arms toward the heavens.

Thank you, Lord, you have freed me from an onerous burden. My husband's business is behind me; at long last. I did my very best for him and I have no regrets. I tried. You know how much I tried. Thank you, Lord. Thank you.

***

Atlanta's fall weather was extraordinarily beautiful and Emma relished happy times spent with her children under clear blue skies surrounded by the russet red, burnished copper and lemon yellow trees that decorated her city with the finest autumn colors. Grant Field was the place to be on Saturday afternoons and Emma St. Claire was there for every game, dressed in her classy black jumper with tiny gold polka dots over a gold blouse with black dots. She wore a wide-rim black felt hat and straps of the jumper were adorned with stickers of the mascot Buzz and commemorative pins of various football games.

Fifth Street, adjacent to the stadium, was the site of the Georgia Tech Tailgate Party where hot dog, ice cream and popcorn vendors lined the street faithfully decorated with huge white and gold balloons. Fans adorned with hats and buttons extolling the virtues of the Yellow Jackets milled around the closed-

90

off street, partaking of the camaraderie of the occasion. A swarm of the loyal gathered around Kim King, John Dewberry and Al Ciraldo at the WCNN broadcast booth on the gymnasium plaza that overlooked the crowd while others flocked to the jazz band at the corner of Techwood Drive. Many, like Emma, wore headphones and listened to the pre-game show; when the Yellow Jacket marching band appeared, everyone clapped their hands in rhythm to the drum beat while heartily singing the Ramblin' Reck fight song.

Jim knew next to nothing about football and went to games as Emma's exofficio escort while J.D. entertained his mother with a running color commentary, explaining intricacies of play action passes and quarterback options, safety blitzes and three-men front.

Steve's fraternity house was the site of post-game get-togethers and Emma enjoyed visiting with the brothers. Allison had supervised painting and re-carpeting of the sprawling house during summer vacation and the front walk, laid with new red brick and refurbished landscaping, gave a handsome welcome to guests. The St. Claires hosted several wiener roasts and hay rides for the fraternity and it pleased Emma immensely to be greeted by many of the brothers with a warm, "Hi, Mom," and a hug.

Wonderfully happy Saturdays and planning a wedding were Emma's only reprieve from the oppressive premonition that she would lose everything, and during long weeks that beautiful autumn Emma and Douglas hassled back and forth with the bank officer with volumes of correspondence trying to get loan payoff figures. When the loan commitment expired the end of October, the mortgage company refused to accept another application from Emma and Jim; they had heard about the landfill and the garbage dump. Mike Jelks went to work for another firm and a new loan application was being processed at a painfully slow pace.

The premonition about Philip Byrd lingered quietly on the edges of Emma's consciousness and she was thankful that she wasn't plagued every night with troubling nightmares. Her decision to forego academic pursuits was upsetting but wedding plans and landfill fights filled every spare moment in her busy schedule.

The quarry mining company, operating under some obscure grandfather clause, which Emma believed to be illegal, also created havoc on North Ridge Road with gigantic blasts and drilling operations that shook houses to their foundations. The St. Claire's and their neighbors filed numerous nuisance complaints. County officials refused to shut down the mining operation. Emma was convinced that someone at the county had been paid off and this idea was reinforced when she received a call from Ned Dickson, the prominent real estate developer who owned six hundred acres across the lane from the St. Claire's.

"Something illegal is going on out there, Emma," he said to her in a late evening call. "I can't get involved because there could be repercussions against me and my company. You must get the Georgia Bureau of Investigation involved. There have been payoffs. This information comes from a reliable source and that's everything I can tell you. I must not be identified either."

Keeping her promise to Ned that he would remain anonymous, Emma wrote to the GBI soliciting their help and a few days later received a phone call from the local investigator.

"We've looked at the information you provided, Mrs. St. Claire," the man had said, "and we believe there is a very real possibility of illegal activities. Unfortunately, any requests for investigations must come from the County District Attorney. We can't do anything until we hear from him."

At the investigator's suggestion, Emma wrote to the D.A. and sent copies of the same info she gave to the G.B.I., including her requests for soil boring data, which were rejected by the Environmental Protection Division, her request for information under the Freedom of Information Act regarding the shutdown of the old landfill, also rejected, and a sworn statement from Lyndell Jackson, the owner of the property where the transfer station was to be built. Mr. Jackson insisted the county illegally seized his property and said he intended to sue them. Emma's suspicions there were illegal activities were confirmed by the D.A.'s silence. He never acknowledged her letter or requested an investigation.

It was another dead end for Emma and brought her one step closer to losing everything. In spite of research, publicity, petitioning and appearances before the Board of Corruption, as she called the DeKalb County commissioners, nothing Emma did could stop the incredible set of circumstances that were set in motion the day she signed the second mortgage.

Emma hired Goodson Accounting, a local firm, to handle Jim's bookkeeping and turned the books over to them the way Allison had left them, posted and balanced. She was relieved to have Allison out of Jim's business and when the bank statement came the first week of November Emma didn't even open it.

"Give this to Harvey Goodson first thing tomorrow, Jim. He should balance the checkbook immediately."

Emma hoped the shock of her resignation would jolt Jim into responsibility and it pleased her that he was responding in a positive manner, until she received a phone call a few days later.

"Emma, this is Harvey Goodson."

"Hello, Harvey. What can I do for you?"

"We were reconciling Jim's bank statement and came across something unusual. I can't locate Jim and I thought maybe you could explain it."

Emma was irritated to be bothered again at her job for her husband's business problems and forced herself to sound pleasant.

"I'll give it a try, Harvey. Reconciling Jim's checkbook has always been a time-consuming job. Allison kept it balanced to the penny while she was writing checks. What's the problem?"

"There are three checks written out of sequence. They were written on the same day, to cash; they total five thousand dollars."

"What! Are you kidding? Allison would never do something like that."

"No, not Allison. Jim. Jim wrote three checks and cashed them himself. Two were written for two thousand and one for one thousand. He must have taken them from the back of the checkbook because there is a gap of about two hundred checks between the ones Allison wrote and these."

"Harvey, Allison watched that check book like a hawk. Five thousand dollars in cash! I can't imagine what he could have done with it. I never saw it around the house."

"Until he produces receipts to account for it, I'll charge it off as a draw."

Good grief – five thousand dollars! What in the world did he do with that money?

Mired up in problems wrought by her husband, Emma found it tricky to be pleasant to clients on the phone and turn out construction proposals for her boss. Emma felt herself falling headfirst into a deep pit; it was very dark. She was alone.

Don't give up, Emma. Pull yourself together.

Emma's pep talk had the required effect and she breezed through the rest of the busy day. During the long drive home, however, she began to boil. By the time she arrived she was furious when she confronted Jim with the checkbook.

"How in the world can you be so deceitful and underhanded? Why did you take checks out of the back of the checkbook? Can't you understand what you've done? Your lies and your damn business are ruining us. I hate it, Jim. I hate what it has done to our family and what it has done to our marriage."

Jim stared blankly at his wife. He was caught; again. There were no excuses. He was an irresponsible liar. He hurt the people who loved him.

"What did you do with the five thousand dollars, Jim? Harvey says he doesn't have any receipts to cover it."

"I paid off some of my subs. I can get receipts."

"You mean you paid subs with cash and didn't get receipts? Haven't I told you a thousand times you have to leave a paper trail? You must have invoices from subs and pay them with checks. That way you have it documented; not only for us, for the subs and the IRS, too. If you ever get audited you'll end up paying taxes on money you didn't earn. Doesn't any of this make sense to you?"

Jim was dejected. Totally. There was no denial his wife was right. Damn it. She was always right about business matters. Thanks to Janice, Jim never wore the pants in the family; but he did work. God knows he worked hard; no one ever said Jim St. Claire was lazy. He was only human, with human faults. But he would never admit he was less than perfect; when he made a mistake he lied about it or make up some feeble excuse. Then Emma would find out about it and unleash her wild fury on him. Emma told him time after time that mistakes could be corrected, that they were learning tools.

"You have to admit you made a mistake, Jim, if you want to learn from it."

How many times had she patiently said this to him during their long marriage? Had he ever listened to her? Had he ever heard what she was saying? Mistakes were not the cause of her tirades; his lies were. Every lie was another brick on the thick wall he was building between them.

Emma despised that wall and tried to knock it down with sincere forgiveness and unwavering love.

"I know you didn't mean to hurt me, Honey," she would say with pain in her heart. "I forgive you. Please don't ever lie to me again."

They would have a long embrace, followed by a quiet discussion and peace would return. This time was different. Emma didn't forgive Jim. He had thrown away five thousand dollars.

Emma made one of J.D.'s favorite dinners, pork chops smothered with mushroom gravy. After a quick meal she left Jim to clean up the kitchen. Another neighborhood, five miles from North Ridge, was battling landfill developers and Emma hoped to form a coalition with her committee and hit the state DNR officials with a unified community outcry against the perpetrators.

She arrived at the old Bruce Street School in Lithonia shortly before eight o'clock and fifty or sixty people were already gathered for the meeting. Perched in front of the assemblage sat the local county commissioner, Olin Faulkner.

"What the hell is he doing here?" Emma muttered to herself. She harbored a hearty disdain for the squatty little man who did nothing to help her and, in fact, had voted for the landfill on North Ridge. When she confronted him with this fact he stated in a rather nasty tone that Emma's vote did not count.

"There aren't enough of you on North Ridge to make any difference," he said.

"You mean, because there are only fourteen families on North Ridge, we're not strong enough to swing an election and that gives you the right to vote for something that will hurt us and you don't care?" she yelled.

"That's right," he said smugly. "You don't count."

After that encounter Emma adopted a line from her favorite prayer as her battle cry and whenever she felt overwhelmed she said, *I am but one, but I am one.*

The neighborhood spokeswoman opened the meeting with a long and flowery introduction of Olin Faulkner, who then talked for thirty minutes about everything he was doing to stop the landfill. Emma was nauseated by the arrogant politician who wisely left the meeting before she took the floor.

"Did you know," Emma asked the homeowners, "that we throw away enough aluminum in this country to rebuild our entire fleet of commercial airliners every three months?"

"Did you know that it takes twenty-nine trees and four hundred and ten gallons of fuel to produce one ton of paper and then it takes eight cubic yards of landfill space to bury it?"

Emma caught their attention and rattled off more facts.

"Did you know we spend eight months of our lives dealing with junk mail? That one day's worth of junk mail could heat 250,000 American homes? That junk mail uses 100 million trees a year?"

"Current landfills in Atlanta will be full in two to seven years and seventy percent of the landfills in Georgia will be full by the fall of 1994. Creating more landfills is not the solution to our waste problem.

"It is a proven fact that landfills pollute ground water, which leads to pollution of streams that run through them, which leads to pollution of our rivers. Ninety-seven percent of Georgia's rivers are polluted," she said forcefully. The audience gasped.

"That's right. Only three percent of the rivers in Georgia meet federal Clean Water Act standards. Yet these landfills that we oppose both feed the Yellow River basin."

"In addition, Georgia industries and businesses produce forty billion tons of hazardous waste each year," she went on, "and, on this beautiful planet we call home, forty-nine million acres of rain forest are destroyed each year. That's about one and a half football fields a second. We are creating waste and destroying vital natural resources and then we bury it in our ground. If we condone one landfill, we are condemning the earth we live on, the water we drink, the air we breathe.

"If this great nation can put a man on the moon we can figure out a way to reduce, recycle and dispose of waste. Many people have said to me that they are only one, that their effort won't amount to much. If we are united, we can make a difference. We are each accountable to our fellow man and to our unborn children and grandchildren. Each one of you is important.

"We must start recycling our paper, glass, plastic and metals," she urged them.

Then she concluded with a few lines from her favorite prayer.

"I am but one, but I am one. I cannot do everything, but I can do something. What I can do, I ought to do. I pray that you each will do something to help us save our community."

Emma thought she made a good presentation and she answered a number of technical questions, giving them facts about landfills they had not even considered; their decision not to form a coalition was a complete shock to her.

"We don't care what happens to y'all," the tall brunette spokeswoman said arrogantly. "We're gonna get a Bill through the Legislature that will prohibit landfills within a mile of the county line. Since we're only a half-mile that will take care of our problem. If there has to be a landfill out here, we're better off if it's in your backyard, not ours."

"Diane, don't you realize that the Board of Commissioners is sending this entire community down the environmental tube? If the landfill and garbage dump go on North Ridge the precedent will be set. Anyone can come out here and dump anything. You may be within a mile of the county line and be protected. The rest of this community will become an environmental disaster and you'll pay for it. Mark my word."

After the meeting broke up, Emma packed her books and research reports in the grocery store carton she used for a tote and walked dejectedly to the door. Several people thanked her for the informative talk and one of the men offered to carry the heavy box to her car.

"I'm losing the war, Mr. Biggers. My own community won't even help. They're going to be sorry. In a couple of years when there are three or four landfills, garbage dumps and incinerators in Lithonia, they'll want to do something. Then it will be too late. This whole area will be covered with refuse. It will get dumped, buried or burned out here. Out here where there are endangered plants and a delicate eco system. It will be destroyed. United we could have made a stand against it. Divided we will fall."

"I think you're right, Mrs. St. Claire. Diane is very shortsighted. Your talk opened my eyes about landfills and I'm going to start some recycling at my house."

"That's wonderful, Mr. Biggers. Every little bit helps. Remember what I said. I am but one, but I am one."

"I won't forget that, Mrs. St. Claire. Some of us are on your side."

"It is not a matter of being on my side. What matters is doing what's right; what's best for everyone."

Emma drove home slowly. Without a unified effort there was little hope for success with the DNR. The landfill and garbage dump would be approved and the St. Claire's beautiful home, Emma's lifelong dream, would be worthless.

CHAPTER NINE

**"If you wish to be complete, go and sell your possessions
...and you shall have treasure in heaven."**
-Matthew 19:21

Emma was in a deep sleep, curled up snug under the covers. Suddenly, with an abrupt jerk, she sat bolt upright in bed and covered her ears with her hands to blot out the crashing sound that roared through her head.

Not again. Please, Lord, no more, no more.

Rudely awakened, her heart pounded; sweat ran down her face. She started to cry.

What is that awful noise?

She wept, cupping her hands over her ears. Tears streamed down her face while the nightmare of Philip Byrd raced through her mind. He was kneeling in a muddy field, crying. An enormous shadow made the scene even more ominous. Emma was almost frantic. For weeks she was spared the terror of the troubling dream and assumed it was behind her.

Dear God, no. Not again. Please, please take it away from me.

Holding her head in her hands, she rocked back and forth in the bed.

No, no, no.

Emma collapsed against the pillow, tears running down her cheeks, across her ear lobes and onto the lace-trimmed pillowcase. When her cheeks and ears were thoroughly drenched, she turned over on her stomach and buried her face in the pillow, kicking her feet against the mattress. Finally, worn out with extreme fatigue, both mental and physical, she fell into a fitful sleep.

The alarm went off at its usual time and Emma dragged her weary body into the bathroom, fumbled for the light switch, and squinted into the mirror. Her eyes were swollen and red and dark circles reflected the strain of her restless sleep.

Shit.

Emma detested that word but there were times it felt appropriate. She poured Visine liberally into each eye before washing her face and brushing her teeth; she peered into the mirror again. Itching, burning, aching eyes squinted back at her.

I look awful. This is hell. Damn nightmares about a man I don't know and the man I've been married to for twenty-two years is killing our marriage and everything we've worked for.

She sat at the vanity and tried in vain to cover the damage done by hot tears.

Wish I could understand Jim—wish I could read his mind.

Emma could not cope with the dreams that readily unveiled a disturbing future to her and once again pushed to the deepest recesses of her mind the nightmares and warnings about her teacher. And the troubling visons of the little gray-haired lady. Who was she?

The on-going environmental battle with DNR over the landfill and garbage dump and persistent threats from Jim's bank were more than enough for Emma to handle. First Nasty foreclosed on Jim's loans and held Emma responsible for the deficiencies between funds Jim drew and the money they received from the sale of the houses. She adamantly denied responsibility for Jim's obligations and Douglas scheduled a number of meetings with bank officials only to have each conference canceled for one lame excuse after another.

"They want to force a foreclosure on my home, Douglas," she said to the attorney one day. "Our place is worth much more than what Jim owes on his loans. When the landfill and garbage dump start operating I know it will be devalued, and then I won't get one blessed dime out of it. If we don't get the payoff figures from that damn bank and refinance before the first of February, I'll have to sell to satisfy that cursed second mortgage those bastards hold. Have you ever seen a more complicated mess?"

Emma's entanglement with First Federated gave her a victim's view of the savings and loan scandal that was sweeping the country and she cringed at every television news broadcast that mentioned the bailout.

"We're bailing out crooks," she said to J.D. one evening as she passed through the family room on her way to the kitchen to fix dinner. "If the savings and loan associations had any sense of fiscal responsibility this never would have happened. Every one of those money grubbing institutions is in trouble because they are selfish and shortsighted. They only cared about getting loan commitments and fattening their own pockets."

J.D. pulled his long body up off the floor where he was sprawled in front of the t.v. and followed his mother.

"I don't understand, Mom. How are they doing that?" he asked while rummaging through the refrigerator.

Emma put on her apron and started chopping vegetables for salad.

"They claim interest income on construction loans as they disburse the funds, J.D., sort of the way a farmer might claim income from his orchard based on the number of blossoms on his trees in the spring, although he doesn't earn anything until the fruit ripens and he harvests his crop. The banks put out inflated earnings statements based on the funds when loaned, not on the funds plus interest earned when repaid."

"When the bank said Daddy completed that house eighty-five percent, they claimed income on eighty-five percent of the loan, even though the house was only fifty percent finished and he hadn't paid them back what he borrowed."

He chomped down on a carrot.

"Very good, J.D. Their financial statements showed income that wasn't there. If a late spring blizzard hits the farmer's orchard and ruins the crop, he would have been wrong to say that he had made a profit; and the bank was wrong to show a profit on funds they loaned Daddy on a house that was never completed because he got sick."

The vegetable chopping became more deliberate, the sharp blade of the knife tapping loudly against the cutting board.

"They didn't care about the borrowers' ability to re-pay and they sure as hell didn't care about their investors. They let any warm body borrow money. No one in their right mind would loan that much money to a sick man with an unsuccessful track record. They didn't care about the Jim St. Claire's."

Emma was angry.

Chop! Chop! Chop!

"They were only interested in making money for themselves."

Chop! Chop! Chop!

"How's that, Mom?"

J.D. ate the carrot and picked up a stalk of celery.

"More than likely the loan officers at First Nasty got some sort of incentive to make loans. The more they loaned and the quicker they did it, the more interest income they showed on their books."

The hungry teenager dipped a celery stick into the Ranch dressing and took a bite.

"The more money the bank made, the more they paid their officers, huh?" he asked.

"Yep, that's right. Of course, that would be okay if everyone they loaned money to paid them back. When houses stopped selling, or people got sick, or there were other extenuating circumstances, the bank didn't get paid back and they didn't have the money they said they had.

"That's when it started to collapse. There were similar situations going on across the good old U. S. of A."

Emma mixed the chopped celery, carrots, tomatoes, onions and mushrooms in a wooden bowl and added lettuce.

"Now the whole country is paying for it. We're going to suffer because of the wicked greediness of crooked bankers. Every one of them ought to burn in hell for what they've done."

As usual, Emma's frustration about First Nasty released a flood of weeping sobs and she fled to her prayer place in the closet and cried profusely; and prayed.

Why, Dear Lord. Why must I lose everything?

The nightmare was playing itself out in spite of Emma's efforts; it was inevitable, for whatever the reason. She always believed in God and His place in her life and refused to abandon her faith in Him simply because, again, another nightmare was becoming reality.

Maybe someday it will make sense. Please give me strength to get through one more day, Dear Lord, one more day.

Emma dried her eyes, powdered her nose, put on lipstick and went downstairs to finish making dinner for her family.

***

The third week in January, almost a year to the day after Emma received the warning they would lose everything, she sat in the lobby of Douglas' office on a cold, rainy, Wednesday afternoon and thumbed through files stacked in a cardboard carton while the attorney rehearsed testimony with her husband in a nearby conference room. The long-awaited confrontation with the vice president of First Federated was at hand and Emma relished the idea of seeing him squirm. Jim told her it would not be necessary for her to meet with the bank officials, that he could handle it. Emma angrily retorted.

"Pete Crumbley told me last summer that I wasn't liable for your construction loans, Jim. Then when I went to pay off our home mortgage, they tried to extort three hundred thousand dollars out of me. This afternoon we're gonna get to the bottom of it and they'll be eating crow."

Douglas agreed Emma's testimony might prove beneficial even though she had no contractual agreements with the bank, other than the mortgages on their home. She sat patiently in the lobby, thinking optimistically about the outcome of the meeting.

I'll have the payoff figures tomorrow. Then when we get the new appraisal, we can close my new loan and we won't lose our home. The home we dreamed of and planned for years. The home we built with our own hands for our children and grandchildren.

The lobby door swung open and a well-dressed man stepped in, followed by a younger, bashful looking fellow and a court reporter carrying his equipment.

Emma inspected the trio.

That man in the Brooks Brothers suit is the V.P. and the young wimpy one is his attorney.

The V.P. cast a condescending glare at Emma, which he tried to cover with a smile when she returned his piercing stare.

Douglas ushered the men into the conference room without making introductions and left Emma alone in the lobby with Jim's files. An hour and a half later Douglas returned.

"This is the worst deposition I've ever seen, Emma. Jim says one thing and then contradicts himself five minutes later."

"He can't take that kind of pressure, Douglas. His doctor said he was incompetent for at least a year. He probably has no idea what he did last summer."

Emma knew in her heart that Jim was a pathological liar, but everything they owned and cared about was resting on the outcome of the meeting; she was determined to defend her mate.

"I'm getting ready to call a halt to it, Emma. Now that I've seen their files, I don't think you and Jim have a defensible position."

Emma was shocked.

"I must talk to those people, Douglas. Please don't deny me this one chance," she pleaded.

"Okay, Emma, okay. At this point, though, I don't know what good it will do."

A few minutes later Jim returned to the lobby. He was wet with perspiration; his face was pale. His appearance alarmed Emma. She was scared. Taking a deep breath and then sighing, she picked up the box of files and pranced into the conference room with a prayer on her lips that God would guide her.

Emma glared at the V.P. again and dropped the box onto the floor with a loud thud.

"You shouldn't have brought those files in here, Emma," Douglas whispered, somewhat miffed.

"I'll need them," she replied meekly.

"I don't know why." He was irritated.

Douglas made cursory introductions and Emma settled into a chair, took another deep breath and relaxed.

Give me strength to get through this, Lord.

"Mrs. St. Claire, do you have any objection to giving a sworn testimony?" the attorney asked.

"Absolutely not," Emma said enthusiastically.

She raised her right hand, was sworn in and Douglas made a statement for the record that the others giving testimony had already been sworn in. Proceeding with the deposition, preliminary questions and answers about Emma's age and occupation were dealt with quickly. Then the bank's attorney said, "We are going to ask you a few questions about these construction loans, Mrs. St. Claire."

The wimpy man gently patted a stack of papers lying on the table as if they were a sacred treasure.

"May I see them, please?" Emma asked.

The wimp looked at the V.P. for approval and then pushed the stack across the high gloss table.

Emma laid them in her lap, relaxing against the back of the chair with her elbows on the armrests. There were fourteen packets of documents, one for each of Jim's construction loans. Although ten of the houses were sold, and construction loans paid off, Emma took her time and carefully examined the file on the first loan, then compared it to the file in her box. Douglas moaned. The atmosphere in the room, already tense, was heavy with hostility and anticipation. Emma began to slowly shake her head. The further she got into the stack, the more her heart began to beat; she felt lightheaded and took a sip of water. Then she resumed the examination, shaking her head and sighing.

Let them squirm for a while.

She put another file on the table. Douglas leaned toward her, wondering what she was up to. He had already gone through the documents during Jim's deposition and nothing had been accomplished. He was anxious to end the entire unpleasant episode. Jim had defaulted on four construction loans and the bank had produced evidence proving Jim's legal obligations as well as Emma's.

After her tedious scrutiny of the first few loan packages, Emma picked up the pace, quickly flipping through them, making mental notes while eyeing specific portions of each document. Her light-headedness slowly faded and the corners of her mouth turned up as a giddy feeling swelled inside her. Stacking the papers neatly, she paused to take another sip of water before standing. Her face broke into a grin, her eyes sparkling; the pounding in her chest subsided.

"Thank you, gentlemen," she said sweetly. "I do appreciate this."

Emma handed the papers to the vice president and sat down. Then she turned to Douglas and whispered.

"Can I ask them a question?"

Douglas reluctantly nodded and Emma addressed the bank officer in a firm voice. Her smile was gone and she looked very serious.

"I notice that every one of these loan packages refers to something called the Builder's File. May I see that file, please?"

The vice president cleared his throat and turned his back to the conference table while conferring with his attorney. The two men whispered, nodding and shaking their heads while considering Emma's request. What could she be looking for? What was she questioning in the file that Jim and Douglas had overlooked? Surely she didn't think she was smarter than her husband's attorney. She was only a secretary.

They thumbed through volumes of correspondence from Emma which she had sent certified mail. There was no way they could deny that she had asked for the loan payoff; that didn't matter though. She and her husband owed First Federated for the defaulted loans and they had every right to hold her to the commitment. Still—what was she up to?

"The builder's file does not pertain to this matter, Mrs. St. Claire."

"I believe it does, gentlemen. May I see it, please?"

"I don't know if we brought it with us."

Douglas spoke up.

"One moment please. I want to confer with my client."

Emma pushed her chair away from the table and turned toward Douglas. He whispered into her ear.

"What are you up to, Emma? Jim and I have both been through the construction loan files. In spite of your objections, I don't think you have a leg to stand on."

Emma's eyes twinkled; a grin lit up her face.

"Douglas, I realize you're Jim's attorney and you've evaluated the evidence presented. I told Jim two years ago when he began doing business with First Federated that I didn't feel right about these people. I knew they would do something bad; something that would hurt us. They have done something bad; real bad, and I have the proof. Give me another moment. Please?"

Douglas was incredulous and shook his head. What in the world was this fiery redheaded secretary up to?

"My client has asked to see the builder's file, gentlemen. Do you want to produce it or do we get a court order?"

Faced with the inevitable, the vice president pulled a legal size file folder from his brief case and handed it to Emma. Inside was Jim's resume, with descriptions of his past construction experience. Emma glanced at it. All lies. He had never done those things. She wished she could have blamed those falsehoods on his illness but he had been fine two years before when he started building houses and financing them with First Nasty. It was typical Jim. Make something appear to be what it wasn't.

A resume with Emma's name on it was also in the file. Someone had re-typed it and changed the content.

He had no right to give them my resume and change it, too! How dare he!

The next document in the file was the "Builder's Loan Application and Financial Statement."

Here it was. The last document Emma needed to prove her case. She glanced over it quickly, noting inflated assets and understated liabilities. Again, she shook her head slowly.

She turned the document over and examined the last section, then slowly, methodically, neatly stacked the papers in the file and returned it to the vice president.

"Thank you, again, gentlemen. I do appreciate your patience. I have looked at what you call 'evidence' and I still see no reason for you to hold me liable for my husband's loans with your bank."

"Mrs. St. Claire," the vice president stammered. He sensed that something was out of order and squirmed again in his chair. "I believe we have produced more than enough evidence to prove your liability in this matter. You not only signed the Builder's Loan Application and Financial Statement, you also personally guaranteed every one of your husband's construction loans."

"No, gentlemen," Emma said meekly, with a slow shake of her head. "Not only is my resume wrong, I have never seen these documents before; I never signed them. Every one of them is a forgery."

Douglas collapsed against the back of his chair, his hand covering his eyes. "Ohhhh—my gaaa—sssshhhh," he moaned.

"In addition, gentlemen, it appears that the guarantees I supposedly signed were added to the documents after my husband signed them. Not only does his file copy not contain the guarantee you claim I made, my name is not even mentioned in his files. It appears to me gentlemen that you have attempted to deceive my husband."

The bank officer went pale, his arrogant demeanor melting like a snowflake on a Bunsen burner. His hands quivered and, feeling hot around his collar, he struggled to loosen his tie. Beads of sweat poured off his brow. He dabbed at his forehead with a linen handkerchief. The attorney sat by quietly, taking slow deep breathes to regain his composure. If what this woman was saying was true, his client, the V.P. and First Federated Bank were guilty not only of forgery, but fraud and extortion, too.

The room was silent except for the heart hammering each man was hearing in his own ears. The court reporter took advantage of the break and quickly downed a glass of water, looking at Emma with a sense of appreciation.

She's got them by the balls.

The bank's attorney finally got himself together.

"Mrs. St. Claire, please write your name several times on this piece of paper."

"Of course. I'll be glad to."

The vice president and his attorney compared Emma's signature to the signature on several of the documents. After a few moments the attorney addressed Douglas.

"We will conclude this deposition at this time, if you have no objections."

"None whatsoever," Douglas replied, smiling. "No doubt Mrs. St. Claire will want me to get back in touch with you."

The vice president and his attorney flinched. Emma St. Claire was the last person they ever wanted to hear from again.

"By the way, Mrs. St. Claire would appreciate it if you would release the loan balance figures on her home."

"Why, of course," the vice president said, clearing his throat. "I'll do it first thing in the morning."

The vice president and attorney from First Nasty made a rapid retreat, wondering how long it would take Emma to file the lawsuit. They left Douglas' office looking the same way Emma's husband appeared after his ordeal with them—thoroughly beaten and totally dejected.

***

Emma had another restless, sleepless night. This time the cause was not Philip Byrd. Who could have changed her resume? Who could have forged her signature? Was it another attempt by her mother-in-law to destroy her? Had her husband been a party to the fraud? Would the gates to hell ever close?

***

Monday morning Emma called the loan officer.

"Hi, Mike," she said eagerly. "I got the loan payoff figures from First Nasty."

"That's good, Emma." Mike did not sound very pleased and Emma was puzzled.

"The vice president sent me a letter; I got it in the Saturday mail."

Mike cleared his throat.

"We can close our new loan now, Mike. As soon as you get the appraisal. You can't imagine how scared I've been that I'd have to sell my home to pay off that stupid second mortgage of Jim's. I am so relieved. This is wonderful!" Emma bubbled into the phone.

"Emma," Mike started slowly. "I got the new appraisal."

Gad, how he hated to tell her the news.

"That's terrific, Mike! Can we schedule the closing date now?"

Mike tried again to explain the situation to his client.

"Emma, the appraisal is too low."

"What? What do you mean too low? How can it be too low? The house was valued at two hundred and forty thousand dollars six months ago. I only need to borrow is a hundred and sixty. I realize we can only get eighty percent on a re-fi first mortgage. The number is not that low, is it?" she pleaded, as if Mike had some control over the appraised value of her home.

"Emma, the house only appraised for a hundred and sixty."

Emma gasped. No, it couldn't be that low; it couldn't. Eighty percent of a hundred and sixty was only a hundred and twenty-eight thousand dollars; it wasn't nearly enough.

There was a deathly silence on the phone and the wicked premonition played again:

We're going to lose everything.

Mike tried to explain.

"There has been a great deal of publicity about the landfill and the garbage dump, Emma. The appraiser knew about them. While he was at your house, he heard the blasting from the quarry and investigated it. He had to take everything into consideration. You're looking at noise pollution from the quarry, water pollution from the landfill and traffic problems from the garbage dump. From a marketing standpoint, your beautiful place is not appealing and that has affected the value."

Mike continued while Emma stifled her emotions.

"I tried shopping a new second mortgage for you, Emma, in hopes you could pay off your second with First Federated. No one will touch it. Land values are falling out there and that makes the deal too risky. If you defaulted on your loan, the first mortgage holder would have a prior claim. The second mortgage holder could be left high and dry.

"I am sorry, Emma. Maybe you can sue the county for damages, or at least some sort of compensation."

"I talked to Jim's attorney last week, Mike. To prove a loss we'll have to sell the house. Don't you understand? No matter what recourse I might have after I lose my home, nothing can ever replace it. Nothing. Our home is gone. Everything we worked for is gone. We've lost everything."

Emma hung up the phone choking back tears. Her dream had been right again.

Damn, damn, damn.

In the next forty-eight hours she listed her home for sale and mailed invitations to Allison and Steve's engagement party to be held the Saturday before Valentine's. Caught up in preparations for the buffet dinner party for eighty-plus guests, Emma finally put to rest her premonition about losing everything. She felt the house would be sold within two weeks and, as her grandmother would have said, there was no use crying over spilled milk. What was done was done; and what was done was torture.

The following week Emma received an offer for the house at its appraised value and the next day a back-up contract arrived. The real estate agent carefully explained the circumstances to the purchasers and they knew they were buying a house down the street from a garbage dump and landfill and across the road from a quarry. The low appraisal made the property attractive anyway and the worst prognostications about pollution were met with bland acceptance.

"We need the space," the vibrant, blue-eyed blonde mother of three told Emma. The rambling ranch house was ideal for her elderly parents who could not negotiate stairs and a similar house in the prominent Dunwoody area, north of Atlanta, on less than an acre of land, was selling for a hundred and fifty thousand more.

"Surely the house won't lose more value," the husband said optimistically.

"We feel bad to take advantage of your misfortune," the wife said.

"Please don't," Emma responded. "I'm glad that something good is coming out of this. I hope you all will be very happy here for many, many years. I thought I would be here forever. I called it my little corner of the world. It was everything I ever dreamed of."

She bit into her lip to stop the trembling while signing the contract. In her heart Emma knew something good would come out of her despair, that something great would come out of the home she built with love. In a month it would no longer be her little corner of the world.

***

Emma was happily singing love songs in the kitchen the morning of the engagement party when the vision of the little gray-haired woman appeared.

"He's special," she said. "Protect him."

Shivers ran up and down Emma's spine; she shook with fright and cold, extreme cold.

How in the world could this be happening?

She wanted to retreat to her prayer place but preparing for the enormous party kept her in the kitchen. Happy tunes she was merrily humming moments before the vision were lost in a deep abyss of despair.

God, will I ever get though it? Will it ever end? I need you more than ever. Lord, please get me through tonight.

Jim arrived with cases of champagne and started to ice it down. He was completely oblivious to his wife's distress.

First things, first, Emma said firmly, repeating her mother's advice. *Prioritize. Take one step at a time. No matter how far down you are, you can always take that first step. Then the next step comes easier, the path less rocky, the view more clear. Yes. One thing at a time. First things, first.*

Emma had an engagement party to prepare and she threw herself into it like a fine tuned engine. Things started to fall into place: the smoker was ready for hams and tenderloins of beef, cheese was sliced and stacked in spirals on silver trays, various hot and cold hors d'oeuvres were ready to set out, flowers were arranged on tables, Rachel's homemade crescent rolls were brushed with butter, curried fruit was placed in baking dishes, broccoli and mushrooms were chopped, carrots were ready to be glazed, and simmering on the stove were ten quarts of Emma's special rice. In a few hours, eighty-five guests would be arriving at her home.

She put a smile on her face and at seven o'clock that night Emma St. Claire greeted friends, relatives and neighbors. Allison and Steve were showered with unexpected engagement gifts and everyone enjoyed a delicious meal, lovingly prepared by Emma with Rachel's help. Even Jim did yeoman's duty. After dinner, their wedding priest toasted the young couple while they stood on the staircase landing, overlooking the guests in the gaily-decorated family room. Red and white balloons, bouquets of flowers, flickering candles and a throng of family and friends all belied the anguish in Emma St. Claire's heart.

CHAPTER TEN

**"But if you do not forgive, neither will your Father
who is in Heaven forgive your transgressions."**
-Mark 12:26

Monday evening Emma met Allison at the Food Court at Lenox Square, a shopping mall in the Buckhead area, north of Atlanta. Over a baked potato, they had happy talk about the wedding but Jim's financial problems soon invaded the conversation.

"Daddy's sick, Mama. There's no way someone in their right mind would do the things he's done. I don't know how you put up with. I can't imagine that Steve would ever lie to me. If he did, boy, hell would break loose!" Allison laughed.

"You'll never have to worry about Steve, Darlin'. He'd never lie. You couldn't have found a man more opposite from your father. The first time you brought him home and walked into the kitchen with him, my e.s.p. told me that he was the right man for you."

Allison beamed at her mother. "You felt that way from the start?"

"Right from the start. Scouts honor." Emma held up her right hand.

Allison was pleased to learn that her mother had special feelings about Steve.

"Now that we're back on a pleasant subject, I have something good to tell you. I made the last payment on your car and the bank sent me the title. Here it is, Darlin'. The Cutlass is yours."

Emma laid the title to Allison's maroon Oldsmobile on the table, remembering how hard her daughter worked to make the down payment.

"I'll keep the car in my name and it will be fully insured under the policy Daddy and I have until you and Steve are married. Then I'll sign it over and you can get your own policy. How does that sound?"

"Sounds great to me!" Allison smiled, then leaned across the table and kissed Emma on the cheek. "Thank you, Mama."

"You're a wonderful daughter, Allison. You've been a terrific student at Tech. You've earned it!"

Emma squeezed Allison's hand, again admiring the beautiful custom-made engagement ring. Years ago, Emma longed for diamonds of her own; her hopes faded with each investment Jim made in his company, or in another truck. There was never anything left over for Emma. Now Allison, her precious daughter, had as handsome a ring as any girl could desire, and that made Emma happier than if it had been her own.

"Come on, Allison, let's go shopping for that new dress for the fraternity formal," Emma said, pulling her daughter to her feet.

The two women window-shopped their way down the mall, with Allison frequently taking her mother's arm to escort her to another wish window.

"Mama. Look at that suit. Wish I could buy it for Steve. Wouldn't he look great in it?"

"Look at this dress, Allison. Only four hundred and fifty dollars. Don't you wish you could afford it?"

It went this way at each enticing display window, the two laughing and wishing down the mall, until they reached Rich's, where Allison led her mother to the Regency Room.

"I've been naughty, Mama," she said sheepishly.

"Okay, Allison," Emma teased. "Let's see what you've done."

Allison spoke to a saleslady, who left the two women sitting on the brocade sofa, laughing and whispering, while she went to the back to retrieve a dress Allison had already picked out. She returned a few minutes later with a long, shimmering, pink sequin gown.

"It's gorgeous, Allison. Absolutely gorgeous."

Turning to the saleslady, Emma continued her bubbly approval of Allison's dress.

"She's going to be crowned sweetheart of her fiancé's fraternity on Saturday night. Won't she look wonderful?"

The astonished saleslady agreed. It wasn't typical for Emma to make public pronouncements about her special feelings. This was different, though. The feeling was about something good. If it did not come about as Emma foresaw,

114

there was no harm done. Allison knew her mother could be a real tease and took Emma's exclamations about the huge honor of being a fraternity sweetheart as merely another of her mother's wishful thoughts. Emma knew otherwise. Allison would be the sweetheart.

Allison insisted on paying for the dress herself with the money she earned working part time in the domestics department at the J. C. Penney store at Northlake Mall.

"You had to sell a lot of towels and sheets to purchase this dress, Darlin'. I wish you'd let me pay for it."

"Did it ever occur to you, Mama, how many letters you had to type to earn the money for the wedding?" Allison jokingly retaliated. She cocked her head to one side and gave her mother a cute, lopsided grin.

"Allison, you always have a way of putting things into perspective. I know there's no use arguing. You are grown up."

"I am? I wonder if Steve knows." She threw back her head and laughed.

The two women left Rich's arm in arm, laughing and talking until they got to the parking lot. After hugging good-bye, Allison got into her Cutlass and headed for the house near the Tech campus that she shared with three other students. Emma had bought the house the year before, with the understanding that Allison would manage it, collect rent from her boarders and pay the utilities. As a business venture it worked fine and Allison and Steve were building an addition to the back of the house, which they planned to occupy after the wedding.

During Emma's long drive home she mulled over wedding plans while listening to Beethoven's Ninth on WABE and she decided to use the last movement of the symphony for the postlude after the ceremony.

Ode to Joy; how lovely for a wedding.

Jim's continuing financial problems and talk of bankruptcy were overwhelming concerns for Emma and having Allison's car paid off was little comfort, making the shopping trip to Lenox Square with Allison that much more precious, giving her a few cherished moments of happiness.

Thursday night Emma's weary body was drifting off to sleep when Allison called in a panic.

"Mama, my car has been totaled. It's absolutely ruined."

"Are you okay, Allison?" Emma quickly asked. "You're not hurt are you?"

"No, Mama. I was standing at the door of the fraternity house after the meeting tonight. I had the car keys in my hand and Steve was helping me with my coat. Then out of nowhere some idiot came careening down Fowler Street in a brand new Buick. He sideswiped one car, hit the rear of Saundra's Honda, which rammed the end of my car and pushed it into a tree on the side of the road and the car parked in front. He went into a spin and hit the driver side of my car and finally crashed into another. It's the most awful mess you ever saw."

"Allison, calm down. You weren't hurt. That's what's important. We have plenty of insurance on the car, Darlin'. Please don't cry."

"Mama, if I had been crossing the street, that wild drunk would have run over me," she wailed.

"Thank the Good Lord you're okay. What a blessing. Do you need me to come down there?"

"No, Mama. The Atlanta Police arrested the dumb jerk. Would you believe he borrowed a friend's brand new car? That car is totaled, too. The guy wasn't even a student. He turned into the campus from Tenth Street to get away from police chasing him. There are police cars everywhere."

"I'll call the insurance company first thing in the morning, Darlin'. Are you sure you don't you need me down there?"

"I'll be okay. Steve will drive me back to the house."

Emma reassured Allison that everything would work out, that the car would be replaced and reminded her to be thankful that she was not hurt.

Jim rolled over in the bed and asked Emma what was going on. He was not disturbed when Emma gave him the news; he shrugged his shoulders, turned over and went back to sleep. The next morning Emma called the insurance company to report the accident and file a claim for the car.

"What did you say? Did I hear you right?" Emma exclaimed.

"I said, Mrs. St. Claire," the soft-spoken female account manager repeated, "your Oldsmobile is not covered. Your husband called us Monday and removed the collision insurance. The only coverage you have is liability. If your daughter had hit someone else, the damage she did to them would be taken care of. I'm sorry. Your only recourse is against the man who hit you. Hopefully, he's got enough coverage."

"I doubt it. He totaled four cars and damaged a couple others."

"Let us know if we can help you," the woman said in a sweet singsong voice.

Emma was incredulous. Why in the world would Jim cancel the collision insurance? She was furious and called him at the house.

"Jim," she shrieked into the phone. "Why the hell did you cancel the insurance on Allison's car? I just finished paying for it. Now it's gone. It is totaled and there's no insurance!"

There was a long silence before Jim spoke.

"I figured we would save some money on the insurance since the car was paid off."

"You idiot!" Emma yelled. "How could you be that simple-minded? What the hell difference does it make whether or not there's a loan on the car? The car was in my name. I made every note payment. Allison made the down payment. Now you've gone and canceled the insurance and everything we had invested in it is gone! Do you understand, Jim? Gone!"

Emma was crying.

"I figured that if anything happened to it that I could fix it. What's the big deal?"

"Jim, the car is totaled. This is not a little fender-bender. There is nothing salvageable except maybe the tires. The front, rear and both sides were hit. Why did you think you could fix it?"

Emma slammed down the phone.

I can't believe it. That guy's not going to have enough insurance to replace Allison's pretty car. Now her car is gone. Just like the house. Gone. How much more will I lose before this ordeal is over? How much more?

Larry returned from the post office and handed Emma the morning mail.

There were times, such as this, when Larry's fanatic devotion to the Georgia Bulldogs was transcended by his compassion for his loyal secretary whose daughter was a Ramblin 'Reck from Georgia Tech.

"What's the matter?" he asked in a brotherly manner. Larry was a devoted husband and father and over the years Emma worked for him she came to depend on him the way she would a family member. Although they moved in different social circles and their contact was restricted to office hours, Emma never hesitated to ask Larry for advice. They shared the mutual respect that develops between a boss and his secretary. Unloading her story made Emma feel better.

"That's unbelievable," he said, shaking his head. "Whatever possessed Jim to cancel the insurance?"

"He thought he'd save us a little money. Can you imagine? Because he wanted to save a few dollars, I've lost thousands. I don't know how I'll replace that car."

"That's a shame, Emma," Larry said sympathetically, leaving his secretary alone with her musings.

My marriage is not what it seems. No one knows the heartache and pain. If it wasn't for the children I would have left Jim years ago. Now is not the time, though. I'll have to put up with it. Allison deserves the wedding of her dreams. No one knows what he's done to us. No one knows what Janice has done to me. What would people say?

And that awful premonition. Dear Lord, what else is going to happen? How much more can I stand? Am I going to lose everything? What does that mean, 'everything'? Everything I own and care about? Surely nothing will happen to my children. No, I know I won't lose my children. In some sort of way, I am gradually being stripped of everything I own? Why? Why is this happening to me? Whatever happens, Dear Lord, please guide me through it.

The next day Emma apologized to Jim for yelling about the car insurance. As usual, he was the one at fault and Emma made amends to keep the peace. Once again, she forgave him.

Restless with anticipation, Emma arose early on Saturday morning. This would be a big day in her daughter's life but Emma would not be a part of it. Her little girl was grown up now, walking her own path. Emma smiled into the mirror while envisioning Allison in the pink sequin gown. Leisurely applying her makeup, Emma mulled over the previous night's dream.

Emma was driving a full-size car with velour seats. Sun shining through the windshield reflected silver rays off the dashboard. Emma was wearing a party dress that had a ruffle around the low cut neckline. The waist was gathered and a full skirt, darker than the ecru top, was neatly spread out on the seat. She was in the midtown area of Atlanta, across from the Memorial Arts Center. Turning into Ansley Park, she drove around for a while, finally turned onto Piedmont Road, then drove back through the lovely old neighborhood of stately homes and turned right onto Peachtree, in front of White Columns, the home of WSB radio and television. She was lost and she'd be late getting to the party.

Jim called her to breakfast.

"I'm pouring the coffee, Baby," he hollered up the stairwell.

Emma ran a brush through red curls, put on lipstick and pranced down the stairs. Happy thoughts about her daughter and the dream about going to a party put her in a jovial mood.

"Morning, Punkin," Emma said to her son, running her long fingers through his red hair.

"Morning, Mom," he replied, looking up from the sports pages of the morning newspaper.

After a relaxed breakfast with Jim and J.D., Emma took Alex for long walk down the shady trail north of the house. It wound around thickets of idle blackberry bushes, through open fields where the little dog flushed a covey of quail and meandered up a long, steep hill to the dense woods that crawled down the far side of the knoll that surrounded the lake, nestled in the shallow valley.

Emma stopped to catch her breath at the hilltop, the sunlight through the giant trees casting long shadows on the heavy carpet of dried leaves beneath her feet. The air was fresh and invigorating and the sound of Alex splashing in the water beckoned her.

Making her way carefully down the steep path that wound through the trees, Emma reached the boulder that protruded into the lake. Alex swam toward her, climbed onto the rock, wiggled and shook cold water off his wet, shiny black body.

Emma faked a cringe.

"Alex, you little devil, you!"

He looked into her eyes in his understanding canine manner. There was a bond between them and they communicated through silence.

"What are you thinking about, this morning?" he looked at her quizzically.

"Tonight is a big night for Allison. She's going to look fabulous."

Emma laid back on the rock, soaking in warmth from the sun. Alex licked her in the face.

"Alex," she exclaimed, wiping her mouth with the back of her hand.

She picked up a twig and threw it into the lake, Alex standing by her, watching intently. When it hit the water with a splash, he dove in, swam to the floating object, retrieved it in his mouth and returned to Emma, wiggling and wagging his way up the rock.

"Good, dog!"

She took the twig out of his mouth and threw it again. They continued for several rounds, until the little animal got winded.

"That's enough for today, Alex. Mama's got things to do."

The black spaniel reluctantly followed Emma up the path, then returned to pick up the twig Emma left on the rock. When he finally caught up with her, he laid the stick at her feet.

"One more, time, Mama. Throw the stick for Alex one more time."

"Okay, Alex. We'll take this stick home."

Emma picked up Alex's new toy and the two companions leisurely walked home. To see Emma with her dog one would never imagine that she was losing everything. For the time being, she had her dog and that was enough.

At eleven thirty Saturday night the phone rang and Emma jumped to answer it.

"Mama, I've been serenaded by sixty-five college men. They sang their fraternity song after crowning me Sweetheart!"

"How wonderful! I knew it would be you. I'm absolutely thrilled."

After exchanging "I love yous" Allison returned to the fraternity festivities and Emma called Rachel. No matter what time of day or night, there was never an inappropriate time to call Rachel to share the happy news.

"That was some kind of party you gave the kids last weekend, Emma," Rachel said, changing the subject.

"Yes, it was fun, wasn't it? I couldn't have done it without you, though."

The sisters talked about the engagement party for a few minutes and then Rachel asked about the economics teacher.

"You haven't had more dreams about that man, have you?"

"Yes," Emma gave a long, low sigh. "I must be out of my mind. Last night I had a different dream, though, and it was nice. Thank the Good Lord, it didn't have anything to do with that man."

Emma told Rachel about the car and the party dress.

"I don't have that dress, Rachel. I don't have that car either. What do you suppose it means?"

"For heaven's sake, Emma, think. In a few months you'll be dressed up and going to parties for Allison and Steve."

"Why, of course. How senseless of me. Sometimes I think this depression that looms over me has affected my mind. I can't remember trivial things. If I didn't make lists, I would probably cease to function altogether."

"It's not that bad, is it? You were happy at the party last week."

"I'm glad to hear you say that. I guess I put on quite a good show if I fooled you."

"Emma, you should have told me if you were stressed out. Maybe it would have helped to talk about it."

"How would you have felt if I had told you I was having visions of that little old lady while I was cooking; and I was so cold I was shivering, in spite of all the heat from the stove and ovens?"

There was a loud gasp on the other end of the phone. When Rachel regained her composure, Emma explained.

"I don't know how much more I can take, Rachel," Emma said, choking back the emotions that flooded her voice. "I feel as though I'm caving in. I feel as though I have something terribly important to do. I—I—I can't figure out what it is."

"You are planning a wedding, Emma. You're also selling a house. Those are two big items on your agenda."

"No, it's not the wedding or the house. Taking care of my son and planning the wedding are the only things that keep me going. When I get down about Jim's lying, or his failing business, or the landfill, or garbage dump, or that damn bank, or losing the house, or mother yelling at J.D, I think of my children. My handsome son and my smart and pretty daughter. I picture a beautiful day, and how happy I'll be when my daughter marries that wonderful young man."

"Mother always said she wanted to live long enough to see Allison walk down the aisle at St. Martin's. Now she will, Emma. I wish that she and J.D. could get along better."

"Me, too. I don't know what their problem is; they have done a job on each other. I've told J.D. to stand up to her and he does. It's a miserable situation—my child being estranged from my mother. When Bee moves to her apartment next month, I can't imagine that J.D. will ever go visit her."

"You couldn't blame him. I still feel Janice has something to do with it."

"I'll never forget the look on Bee's face the first time she saw J.D. when he was only fifteen minutes old. She was absolutely ecstatic. She always adored him. She took him to his first symphony performance when he was four years old and he loved it. Sat on the edge of his seat the entire performance, quiet as a mouse. She took him to the Circus for years. They went to church together. She always supported him in his athletic endeavors; she bought baseball bats and soccer balls, and lord only knows how many uniforms and team fees she paid so he could play sports. Janice never did any of those things. Never. And he adores her."

"He adores her pies, Emma. Wait until he takes a bite of one of her lies. One of the days he'll know the truth about his other grandmother."

"Don't say that, Rachel. I've protected my children from the awful side of Janice's character their entire lives. They think she's wonderful. I can't begin to imagine how bad it would be if I ever said anything against her. They might hate me."

"Emma, it has always puzzled me why people think Janice is such a great person. She doesn't come from a background worthy of such praise. Yes, her mother was as close to sainthood as a living soul could be, but her father and brother were both drunks. Janice's son is a pathological liar and her daughter is a drug addict. That's some resume."

"I have considered the fact that she is probably jealous of Bee. I mean, Bee is quite accomplished. She did something important with her life; she made the world a better place with her work in science and medicine and her beautiful botanical drawings. Janice bakes pies and types memos."

"That's what I'm talking about Emma. Listen to me," Rachel said firmly. "Ignoring the things Janice has done to you is equal to ignoring cancer; it won't go away or get better until you fight it. If you don't, it will eat at you, and you will suffer the pain of it. Eventually, those you love will suffer right along with you."

"My world is falling apart, Rachel. I'm not taking on Janice Crymes right now. I don't know what caused the problems with Bee and J.D. I'm lost. Totally lost. I don't know what to do about anything."

"Emma, until you met that teacher, you were one of the happiest people in the world. You've always faced problems with a smile on your face. Look what you've gone through with Jim's business the last fifteen years and his wicked mother your entire marriage; and you've been looking after Bee for years, checking on her every day since she retired and then moving her into your home. Even when you were curled up in a fetal position with meningitis, you smiled."

"That's 'cause my mouth was about the only thing I could control," Emma laughed.

"See? That's what I mean. No matter how bad things are you always have a smile or a laugh."

"You make me feel good, Rachel. I don't know how I'd ever manage without you. You're strong and wise."

"I don't know about that. If I'd been having nightmares for a year about someone I don't know, I'd probably go crazy."

"Maybe I am insane, Rachel. Maybe that's what's wrong with me."

"Emma St. Claire!" Rachel ardently protested, "How dare you talk that way about my twin sister. You're not insane! Do you hear me? You're not! You have e.s.p. and you're working on something important. That's it. You are not insane. Never say that again!"

"Who is that little old lady, Rachel? Why is she doing this to me?"

Without resolving Emma's dilemmas, the twins said good-bye and Emma fell into another restless sleep.

The following weekend channeled another meaningful event into Emma St. Claire's life. Allison injured her knee playing soccer and follow-up x-rays and an MRI showed a torn meniscus, the cartilage in the knee. Surgery was ruled out because a degenerative disease was also diagnosed.

Emma was devastated; as usual, she put up a positive front.

"You're going to be fine," she reassured Allison. In the back of her mind was the inexpressible alarm: Would her beautiful, lithesome daughter be bent and deformed the way Emma's father had been during his youth? Was there some sort of inherited disease working on Allison?

122

Emma had to know. She had not seen her father since she was twenty years old. Where was he? Was he still alive? Would he care to hear from her if she found him? Would he be able to offer her any insight into Allison's condition?

Emma resented growing up without a father. It was not easy for her to tell friends that she didn't know where her father was, or what he did. She had neither seen nor heard from him in more than twenty years. She knew nothing about him, except that he probably lived somewhere in Texas.

"I'll write to Uncle Ed. Maybe he'll know where Daddy is."

A long letter to her beloved uncle, explaining Allison's condition and requesting any information he might have on her father, brought a quick reply. Uncle Ed gave Emma her father's address and an update on his medical condition and life-long struggle with disabling disease.

When Bee saw the envelope from Ed and asked Emma about it, Emma realized she would have to contact her father on the sly, and future correspondence would have to come to her at Joe's office. Any open contact with her father would only enrage Bee, and that was a battle Emma could not take on. Not right now. Emma's father was a taboo subject and his name was never mentioned. As a child she adored him; now he was a ghost from her past.

"You're my twin," he had told her. "Rachel is your mother's twin and you are mine."

He would hold Emma on his knee and sing a song about Barney Google while drawing a comical picture of the fish and his "goo-goo-googly eyes."

The reminiscence of an adoring father brought a smile to Emma's face.

"He still cares; I know he does."

Emma sat at the typewriter, her brow furrowed. She enjoyed writing; this time words would not come.

"What do you say to a father you haven't seen in twenty-three years?"

Slowly, deliberately, her fingers touched the keyboard. Two words appeared on the paper: Dear Daddy.

"What if I open old wounds? He might hate me. Why should he care about me, anyway, after all these years?"

She thought of things he had missed—birthday celebrations, Thanksgiving feasts, Christmas festivities; his children's weddings; and the births of his grandchildren. Did he even care?

"I don't know if he's rich or poor; I don't know anything about him. I know that I need him."

Her mind wandered back to the dark days following her parent's divorce.

Why did he leave me? Why?

Bee moved to an apartment with her children and shortly afterwards Emma had her first asthma attack. Years later, during therapy with Dr. Clements, she learned the correlation between the loss of her father and asthma. The stress was unbearable for the five-year-old and it literally left her gasping for breath. That was not Emma's only response to the painful separation.

Emma's mother hired a teenage girl, who lived in the adjacent apartment building, to watch the twins after school. The first day they arrived at the sitter's, an eerie thought flashed through Emma's mind.

We won't be here for long.

The five year old was scared. A very explicit message crossed through her mind, as if someone hidden in the recesses of her brain had turned on a ticker tape.

We won't be here for long.

The child's immature mind was incapable of understanding either the message or the source. She was terrified.

Several days later the teenage baby-sitter looked Emma straight in the eyes; with her face very close to the child's, she said, "You're a very strange little girl."

The next day the baby-sitter told Bee that she would no longer be able to watch the twins.

"You'll have to find someone else to take care of them," she said without further explanation.

This was Emma's first experience with extra sensory perception and her e.s.p. told the truth. The baby-sitter had taken care of them for only two weeks. They had not been there for very long.

Emma pulled her mind out of the past and typed a letter to her father, telling him about her husband and children. She told him about Allison's knee and the painful back condition that came about as a result of being immobilized by the knee injury.

I know in my heart my Daddy has tried to contact me. He didn't completely abandon me. I know he didn't. Somehow, he got close to me. I know he did.

CHAPTER ELEVEN

"My soul has become troubled."
-John 12:27

Saturday evening Emma put on a happy face and walked down the back path to the Crymes' house. Humming *Ode to Joy*, she stopped at the dog pen and played fetch with Alex before catching up with her husband and son who had gone ahead, carrying Emma's famous chocolate cake. Since Bee was at an Atlanta Symphony performance with her friends, it was an ideal time for Emma, Jim and J.D. to have a meal with Janice and David. It had taken Emma twenty-two years to stand up to her mother-in law and she realized her outburst about Jim's business permanently altered their relationship. She hoped for the sake of her children that things would be acceptably pleasant again.

Emma's hopes were shattered after the pleasant meal when Mrs. Crymes made another one of her assertive and demanding pronouncements.

"Grandpa and I don't want to live next to a landfill. We've bought a new house near Conyers. We're moving next week. Y'all will move into this house and pay us rent for the next two years until J.D. is out of high school. Then you can do whatever you want."

Emma was in shock.

How could they expect her to live next to her dream house? Wasn't it bad enough that she had lost it because of her husband's business shenanigans? Why couldn't her family move to the nice subdivision house she had found? It would be torture to live here. Didn't they know that? Didn't her feelings matter?

Jim's mother prattled on.

"This house has plenty of space and your things will fit in. You can build a little pen for the dogs and a hen house for J.D.'s chickens. He'll only be two miles from his school."

Emma was still in shock. Wasn't it enough to endure Jim's sorry business ventures for twenty years—underwritten by Janice under the guise of 'helping' them? If Mrs. Crymes would stay out of their lives, maybe Jim would learn to be responsible. She never let go. If her son stumbled, she'd pick him up, usually at considerable expense, dust him off and then back him in another wild-ass scheme. Now she was demanding that Emma and Jim and J.D. move into this house, this awful house that Emma despised.

Through the heavy mist that was forming in her eyes Emma could see her son smiling. J.D. obviously thought it was a grand idea. He had no idea how his grandmother had always controlled and manipulated Emma. He had no idea that this was another nail in the coffin of his parent's marriage.

It wouldn't work! She would be miserable there.

Emma tried to express her feelings without offending her in-laws again.

"I don't know—" she sputtered. "It might be hard to live next door to—"

"Oh, pooh!" Janice retorted. "You have to put that house behind you and get on with your life."

Emma retreated into the silence of her own thoughts.

It will be behind me. It will be right behind me and I'll have to look at it every day.

Mrs. Crymes finally said, "You can do anything you want to this house. I know it is plain. You can fix it up."

Emma couldn't believe her ears. She was in a stupor. She felt drugged and helpless, the way one feels in the recovery room after major surgery. Things were happening around her; she had no control; the sounds of voices were far, far away—

***

Emma's despair over her family's living arrangements lasted until the following Friday morning when Larry tossed the mail onto her desk. A small envelope on top of the stack was hand-addressed to her; the post-mark was Salado, Texas.

She tried to stay calm and set it aside, then quickly opened Joe's mail and carried it into his office. Returning to her desk, she picked up the light blue envelope and studied it carefully, turning it over in her hands as if it was an ancient treasure, before carefully slicing it with her monogrammed, silver letter opener.

It had been a long, long time, almost twenty-three years; what could her father possibly say to her?

"My dearest Daughter," it began.

The letter was everything Emma hoped for and more. Her father's obvious love and concern for his daughter emanated from every word on every page. She read it three times. With each reading Emma felt a happiness she had not known in a long time. His words were comforting and revealed to her the spirit of a loving and devoted father; a father she had not known since her pre-school years. The agony of losing her home was insignificant when compared to the joy of being re-united with her dad.

He gave her the name of the disease he had and a detailed description of his battle with arthritis of the spine when he was nineteen, how the doctors had put him in bed for more than a year and when he was finally allowed to resume a normal life, his back had become fused in a twisted and bent position; his six-foot three inch athletic body was emaciated and had shrunk to less than six feet. He implored Emma to keep Allison active.

"Exercise is the best medicine for this condition," he wrote.

Enclosed with the letter were several newspaper articles about treatments for ankylosing spondylitis being done in Texas and he invited Emma to bring Allison to Dallas for a definitive diagnosis.

Emma had heard several versions of her father's illness from her uncle and her late grandmother. Now she had the right story and she was amazed at the similarity to Allison's condition.

Mr. Browning was very active and athletic as a young man. He received a basketball scholarship to Georgia Tech and during a game his sophomore year, he fell and injured his hip. It was during his sedentary recuperation that he first experienced back pain and was sentenced to a year in bed for healing.

Allison was athletic and never had back problems either—until the bad knee injury sidelined her. For the first time in her life she was not physically busy. She started ballet school when she was three and danced until she was fourteen, when she took up running track and playing soccer.

There were many similarities in the two medical histories. Emma knew she had done the right thing by contacting her father. If Bee ever found out Emma had written to her dad, hell would break loose. Emma tossed off the brief worry about Bee because she had justification for getting in touch with him. The fact that she had the thrill of knowing her father again was a bonus.

After reading the letter one more time, Emma reluctantly put it away. She picked up the phone and dialed Allison's doctor.

"That's very interesting," he said. "I think we ought to do a gene study right away. Ankylosing spondylitis is inherited. If Allison carries the gene there's a one in four chance she'll develop this very serious arthritic disease."

Emma mumbled into the phone, "Will she be disfigured the way my father is?"

"I can't guarantee you she won't be but arthritis treatment has advanced significantly since the mid-thirties. With proper exercise, diet and medication, we should be able to control it. Knowing what to look for now is a tremendous help. You were very wise to contact your father."

"What does the gene study involve?"

"A blood test. It takes at least a week, maybe even ten days, to get the results; the sooner you can bring her in, the better. I'm curious to know if she carries that gene."

"Yes, I am, too, Dr. Keller," Emma said, almost in a whisper. "I'll have Steve bring her to your office this afternoon after classes."

"Great. I'll be in touch as soon as I know something."

***

Emma's anxiety over the gene study was tempered by the arrival of Allison's wedding gown a few days later. She scheduled a fitting with their consultant at the bridal shop and met Allison there after work. The candlelight satin gown with cathedral length train, encrusted with seed pearls nested on hand-made lace, had been custom made in Korea to Allison's measurements. It fit almost perfectly. Emma was thrilled.

"Darlin'! Your dress is beautiful. You look absolutely gorgeous! How in the world can I wait until the end of July?"

"The next few months will fly by, Mrs. St. Claire," the pretty brunette bridal consultant replied while helping Allison out of the elegant gown.

"We still have to select a florist, Mama," Allison said eagerly, "and my friends are giving me a couple of showers. Some of the folks in Thomson want to entertain, too."

Allison chatted on enthusiastically, not realizing that the word 'Thomson' had triggered a vision in her mother's mind. Emma's thoughts were flooded with pleasant, loving sensations she did not understand and the vision of the little gray-haired lady standing in front of Mr. Byrd saying, "He's special—"

Emma blinked her eyes slowly with deliberate exaggeration.

"Are you okay, Mama?" Allison asked, gently touching her mother on the shoulder.

"Yes; fine. I had something in my eye and it was irritating my contact lens."

Allison turned back to the consultant to go over a few details about the fitting while Emma stayed in the dressing room, seated on the white satin bench. Visions of the little gray-haired lady again flowed through her mind, her heart was beating very loudly; and a strong shiver ran up and down her spine.

***

The next few months flew by and Emma found herself caught up in a whirlwind of activities. By the end of March she finished tax returns and closed the sale on her home. Bee was moved into an apartment in northeast Atlanta, where she would be close to her church and civic activities, and Emma, Jim and J.D. moved into Janice and David's house.

Acknowledging that her husband and son were happy about the move, Emma tried to be optimistic, even telling them it was a relief to be out of the huge house. The real cause for Emma's good spirits was something entirely different—nightmares of Mr. Byrd would not be moved into their new home.

Emma's resolution was repeated over and over, silently to herself. Each time she made the trip from one house to the other, carrying prized belongings she did not want moved on the pickup truck, she would repeat the mantra:

It is over. I won't have those dreams. I won't; I won't. They are behind me, now. Good-bye, Mr. Byrd. Don't ever bother me again!

As fast as Jim and J.D. moved in furniture, Emma directed the arrangement of each room and quickly made order out of chaos. She set up J.D.'s room first, wanting her son to feel comfortable in his new bedroom even though she knew that she herself could never be happy in the Crymes' house. She made his bed and unpacked a huge box of stuff from his room at Fairfield, moaning at the sight of five different sets of crutches and leg splints her son had been in and out of for years. Maybe the worst was finally behind him, too. That's what Dr. Keller said and Emma held on to the hope that her son would no longer have the awful pain.

His pain his behind him; mine is behind me.

After setting out toiletries in J.D.'s bathroom, Emma tackled the kitchen, living room and upstairs bedroom she would share with Jim. She hung pictures, carefully situated her many house plants and within twenty-four hours the five bedroom house was comfortably settled and looked as if they had been living there for years. The first night they were exhausted from the hard work of the move and Emma slept soundly for eight hours. The next night she was awakened by thunder that jolted her out of a deep sleep. She sat bolt upright in bed, Mr. Byrd's name being formed silently by her trembling lips.

No, no, God, I thought I had left it behind me. Please, please. Take it away from me.

Emma rolled over, away from Jim's snoring, and cried until the early morning hours, when she heard the rooster crowing.

The following night she had another dream about the car and party dress. This time she arrived at a Tudor style house. Emma did not get a clear impression of the exterior, as her mind transported her quickly from the car to the hallway off the kitchen, where she found herself in a crowd of people at a party.

***

Dr. Keller called a few days later with the result of Allison's test.

"I'm sorry to tell you that Allison does carry that gene, Emma. It means she has a one in four chance of developing the disease," he said, repeating his previous opinion. "We'll need to watch her closely. I'm going to put her on a new medication; it should cut down on her inflammation. Let me know how she does."

"I will, Dr. Keller. Is there anything else I can do?"

"No. Not now. At this time we can't predict what will happen. Remember, even though she carries that gene it does not mean she will get the disease."

"I know. Thank you very much, Dr. Keller."

Emma hung up the phone and stared out the window. The trees were budding out and daffodils in the yard were in full bloom. Squirrels played chase up and down the oak tree near the door and birds chirped merrily in the warm sunshine; and Emma St. Claire's beautiful, statuesque daughter carried the gene for a crippling, disfiguring disease.

"She's in your hands, God," Emma prayed aloud in the empty office. "Please watch over her; keep her always in your loving care."

***

Jim's business could not be salvaged; during his illness the interest on construction loans created an unbearable debt and when the bank could not

130

recover their funds by foreclosing on Emma's house, they turned to her husband for the deficiencies. Janice refused to bail him out again. The only escape he had was bankruptcy.

After dinner one evening the second week in April, Emma found Jim at the desk in the office, a room off the kitchen at the back of the house. He was writing out a list of his assets to turn into the bankruptcy court and Emma glanced over his shoulder, noting the various items: his dump trucks; his construction and mechanical tools; and his personal vehicle. After that was a list of other assets.

Her face became taut and a scowl crossed her brow. She barked at him, "What the hell have you listed my truck for, Jim? You have no right to put my personal property on that damn list!"

Jim looked defensive and sheepish.

"Yes, I do. I have to sell everything I possibly can to reduce my debt and that red truck is worth a lot."

"Are you out of your mind, Jim? That truck is mine, not yours! What the hell do you think you're doing?"

He reached in the drawer and handed her the title he had hidden.

It was the title to Emma's red Chevrolet pick-up truck; and imprinted on the front was the name 'James D. St. Claire.'

Emma was furious.

"That's wrong, Jim! That's wrong! How could you let such a thing happen? Why did you hide that title from me?"

The truck note was in Emma's name, her married name, Mrs. James D. St. Claire. The title office had obviously made a mistake and issued it in the name of her husband. Legally, the truck was Jim's.

"I'm not letting you get away with it, Jim. You're going to sign my truck over to me. That truck is mine! I've made every payment! You can't do this to me!"

"I could get in trouble if the court finds out. My attorney said I had to list my assets; and that truck is one of them."

"The hell you say. I'll be damned if you're going to use my truck to pay off your damn business debts. I've lost enough because of you and your mother and First Nasty. You're not getting one blessed dime out of me. Do you understand? Not one damn dime!"

She marched out of the room and slammed the door as hard as she could.

J.D. had a hurt look on his face when she rushed through the living room and out the front door. His parents had another argument. He hated to hear it.

131

He hated what had happened to his family. The teenager went into his room, closed the door and turned his stereo up to its loudest setting.

Emma hoped the move would be a new beginning for them; instead, it was more of the same old s-h-i-t. Outside, alone with her thoughts, she rounded up Alex and went for a walk. It was too late in the evening to go to the lake; instead she turned toward the east, to check out the quarry. The granite outcropping sloped down a long, steep hill and terminated at a small creek. Surface quarrying had scared the face of the rock and remnants of precious wild flowers, lichen and miniature wild cactus lay dying amongst the debris.

"This is sickening," Emma said to Alex. "Look at these little flowers. They never had a chance. We're losing our precious wildlife, Alex. When they finish blasting the hell out of this rock, it will be covered up with garbage. Garbage, Alex. The garbage will rot, and stink, and create methane gas. Then the rainwater will wash down through it and carry bad chemicals into the ground. That's called leachate, Alex."

The little dog cocked his head and looked quizzically at his mistress.

"They're a bunch of assholes, Alex. Every damn one of them. Come on. Let's go home before I get sick."

Emma and Alex climbed up the rock and turned west, toward home. In the distance they heard a loud rumbling sound and the ever-alert spaniel growled although he couldn't see what lay ahead, around the bend.

"What is it boy?" Emma asked. "What's that awful sound?"

Emma's question was answered when they reached the curve; her heart started beating rapidly and she grabbed Alex by the scruff of the neck and started running.

The sound was coming from a huge tracked vehicle controlled by a driver perched inside a cage at least fifteen feet atop the behemoth. Emma had heard that the quarry operators were bringing in more equipment but this was outrageous. This machine—this quarry monster—in her backyard.

The monster took up the entire roadbed, obliterating everything in its path as it rumbled and roared down the narrow, winding lane. The gargantuan rock hauler approached Emma and her dog, blocking their only escape route. It was moving much faster than she could run and it would have been lethal to turn back. The operator could not hear her screams over the belching clamor of the monster. Thickets of blackberry brambles on one side of the road covered the edge of a sheer drop-off and Emma had no choice. She had to run toward the embankment on the other side, crossing the path of the monster. Emma held

Alex tightly in her arms and ran. The little dog wriggled frantically, wanting to attack the quarry monster headed toward his mistress.

Emma scrambled up the embankment, stumbling, then falling. Alex was still in her arms, beneath her. The machine rumbled closer and closer, tree branches twenty feet in the air snapping as easily as match sticks while the gigantic monster crushed everything in its path. The operator did not see Emma, struggling to regain her footing on the side of the road. The monster came closer and closer.

"God, help us," she cried out.

She clutched Alex more tightly, rolled onto her back, then slowly, painfully pushed herself, and her beloved dog, up the slope, out of harm's way. The quarry monster rumbled by them and disappeared around the curve.

***

The evening after Emma's encounter with the quarry monster she went car shopping with Jim. Emma was not particular when it came to cars; she wanted one that was clean and comfortable and any color except black.

A new car was not even an option. Jim always insisted that low-mileage used cars gave good service without the up-front depreciation. At one lot she found a beautiful white Oldsmobile with a white interior. Jim rejected it.

"It will be too hard to keep clean."

"The seats are leather, Jim. I can keep it clean," she retorted. "I'm not the one who works in grease. This car is exactly what I want."

He resented the comment and pushed her toward a dark blue Pontiac with a dark blue interior. The four-door car was handsome, Emma had to admit, even though it was not what she had in mind. She wanted something smaller.

"This is a good car," he insisted. "We'll get a lot of service out of it."

"I don't know," Emma mumbled, slowly shaking her head. The dark blue car with velour seats was luxurious.

"Come on; let's drive it," he said persuasively.

Emma slid behind the wheel and the salesman handed her the keys. She was giddy while playing with the power seat, radio and tape deck. This car might work out. They took a test drive on Peachtree Industrial Boulevard, turning onto Broad Street in Chamblee, and returned to the lot. Jim signed over the title to Emma's truck for trade in. There was no way in hell he was going to put her vehicle into his bankruptcy assets.

Because they bought the car at night, and Emma only drove it at night, it wasn't until she picked it up the next afternoon and drove it in daylight that she saw the sunshine reflecting off the dash. An eerie feeling came over her. The car was large; it had velour seats; and the reflected sun on the dashboard was silver.

Emma wanted the small, white car with leather seats. Her husband talked her into buying this car—this car that was an exact duplicate of the car she was driving in her dream about going to the party.

Good Lord, she moaned quietly while driving back to the office. *What in the world have I done?*

***

Emma was singing in the kitchen on Saturday morning while washing breakfast dishes when Jim's mother sailed into the kitchen, holding up a hanger from which hung a new party dress.

Emma stared blankly at the garment.

"Isn't it lovely?" Janice asked in her sing-song tone.

"Yes, lovely—" Emma could hardly talk.

"I thought you could use a new dress for Allison's shower in Thomson," she said. Over the years Janice had thrown Emma a number of bones in the form of stylish dresses, which Emma appreciated since Jim seldom bought her anything and she did not have the money to buy nice clothes for herself.

Emma forced a smile and took the hanger from Janice.

"I'll try it on right now," she said, retreating to her closet in the room off the kitchen. Emma had been spoiled by the spacious closet with the window seat. To retaliate when they moved into the Crymes house, she put her clothes in the walk-in closet in the room she used for an office. Without realizing it, it was her first step in separating herself from her husband.

Now she stood in the closet, staring at a dress that Jim's mother had given her. Her heart pounded. A tear formed in the corner of each eye.

Why, Dear Lord? Why do these things keep happening to me?

She slipped the dress over her head. The ruffled neckline and gathered waist flattered her figure and the ecru bodice was a good color for Emma.

Sighing deeply, she put on a smile and pranced into the living room to model the dress—the dress that was already familiar to her—the dress that was an exact duplicate of the dress in her dreams. Unwittingly, Emma St. Claire acquired both the car and the dress she dreamed about.

This should have been a pleasant e.s.p. for Emma; but a few nights before Jim talked her into buying the blue Pontiac, Emma had another dream about the car, the dress and the party. In this dream, when she arrived at the Tudor house, she was met at the door by Mr. Byrd and the aura of the beautiful woman. Emma was even more puzzled.

Why, Dear Lord? Why?

***

After church on Sunday, Jim drove Emma and J.D. out to the Crymes' new home. Although Emma did not look forward to the visit, she went along pleasantly, doing her best to be a good wife and daughter-in-law. She had faked it for years and it was pointless to change now. Jim parked on the street and Emma gazed down at the A-frame house sitting mid-way on a long lot that sloped toward a lake. The driveway was quite steep. Emma wondered why Janice and David would want to live in a house on such a precipitous site.

"This is a bad place," her silent voice said.

A bad place? Why? What will happen here? What should I do? A bad place. What does that mean?

Jim opened Emma's car door and they walked carefully down the long drive holding hands, Emma teetering on high heels, feeling as though she were tumbling forward.

"Not a very good lot," she said.

"I don't see anything wrong with it," Jim answered defensively.

"Not safe—" Emma almost whispered.

What good would it do to tell Jim about her premonition? Anyway, she didn't even know what it meant. For years Mrs. Crymes told Emma to, "Sit down, be quiet and stay out of it."

And that's exactly what Emma did.

After the twenty-five cent tour of the new house, Janice served hot apple pie on the spacious deck, overlooking the lake.

"I can see why you enjoy this place, Janice," Emma said, taking in the peaceful view.

Conversation was light, though somewhat strained, and Emma was thankful for an early departure. Hugs and cheek kisses were passed around and Emma, Jim and J.D. left. While driving away, Emma glanced back at the house.

This is a bad place.

By the first week in June final arrangements were made for the wedding and Emma was looking forward to upcoming bridal showers and parties in Allison's honor. She was disappointed that the party dream was about Mr. Byrd. She tried to put it out of her mind even though she had a very vivid impression of the Tudor house and its occupants.

The flat yard was bordered on one side by ornamental trees and azalea bushes; there was no visible driveway in the front and Emma thought that was rather strange. Where would the occupants park their cars? The brick steps led up to a wide stoop and an arched doorway.

The interior was spacious and Emma thought there should be an upper floor although there was no staircase. The wood floors had been refinished in the front of the house. The butler's pantry and breakfast room floors were dark, old and stained. A line of demarcation was clearly visible between the old and newly finished wood.

Sunlight shone through long windows in the living room, diffused by white sheer curtains. Most of the sparse furniture was casual. An antique sideboard stood in stark contrast along one wall. Through a doorway Emma could see a small computer sitting atop a roll-top desk. It looked to Emma that someone had recently moved in; boxes were stacked and scattered throughout the rooms.

The kitchen, though roomy, was dingy and in bad need of a good cleaning and paint job. Sunlight poured in through the double windows over the sink. She could not see the view to the backyard from the window.

Wall covering in the bedroom was dark and Emma could not make out the pattern on the paper. Wide base and crown moldings, painted white, made a striking contrast to the navy blue walls. A king-size, unmade bed was on the wall adjacent to the door from the hall.

Emma St. Claire could not imagine why she would be dreaming about a party for her teacher. She was deeply troubled by her thoughts and feelings for the aura of the woman with Philip Byrd.

I have a real affinity for that lady. They are happy together and I am happy for them. I must be going mad. None of this makes any sense. My mind has snapped.

During a phone conversation with Rachel one evening Emma bubbled with enthusiasm about the party to be held in Thomson.

"I wish I could explain my feelings about that little town," Rachel. "I love to go there. I feel as if I'm at home. I mean—I don't know; I'm terribly confused."

"What, Emma? Tell me."

"The first time Jim and I drove over to Thomson to meet Steve's parents and his sister, Cynthia, I told him I could understand why Allison loved it. I felt as if I had been there before and everything was familiar to me. When we drove by the school, I said to myself, *Look, the old school is still there.* Then I wondered why I had such a thought."

"That's strange. You'd never been to Thomson before."

"I know that. Get this—I recognized everything. In fact, when we went to Cynthia's senior piano recital a few months later, I directed Jim to the old railroad station. It has been restored and is used for parties and receptions. That's where the recital was. I knew how to get there. When Louise was giving me directions, I thought, I know how to get there. I don't need instructions."

"How odd, Emma; I don't know. Your e.s.p. is getting more and more complex. I can't figure out what's going on in that mind of yours."

Emma laughed.

"You can't figure out what's going on. How do you think I feel? When we were driving to Clark's Hill Reservoir to visit the Kings at their lakeside cottage, we followed Louise's directions. It was eerily familiar to me and then we turned off and I thought this isn't the way we usually go home."

"What does that mean, Emma? This isn't the way we usually go home. Who's *we* and what is *home?*"

"I have no idea."

"It's a mystery, Emma. A very troubling mystery."

***

J.D.'s sixteenth birthday was two weeks before the wedding. Although it was not always easy to round up his friends during the summer for suitable birthday parties, Emma always made the day special for him. They had trips to the beach, or parties at Atlanta-Fulton County Stadium where the Braves played, or went on camp-outs. Each birthday celebration was different and fun, embellished by a special cake and lots of presents.

Emma did not want J.D.'s special day to be overshadowed by wedding festivities and planned to take her son to an elegant dinner at his favorite restaurant. Those festive plans were thwarted the night before his birthday when J.D. told Emma he wanted her to make him a fried chicken dinner and have a celebration at home.

Later, in bed, Emma told Jim about the change in plans.

"J.D. wants a fried chicken dinner at home tomorrow night. That means I'll have to stop at the grocery store on my way home; you'll have to do the birthday shopping. I ordered a new pair of shoes for him; Rich's is holding them; Macy's is having a sale of summer clothes. Please go by there and get one of the sales people to help you select some new shirts and shorts. You can also go by the video store and pick up that new game he wants. Okay?"

Jim was reading a book and grunted.

"Jim, are you listening to me? Tomorrow is J.D.'s sixteenth birthday. You'll have to pick up the presents and have them wrapped because I have to buy the groceries. I couldn't go tonight because I had to bake the cake he asked for."

"Huh—"

"Jim, I can't do everything. Will you please listen to me?

"Yeah, yeah, I heard you. Go by the mall and pick up the kid's birthday."

"You better not let him down, Jim. I mean it."

Emma rushed through the grocery store after work and made a mad dash for the house. She wanted to have decorations hung before J.D. got home from football practice. A bunch of colorful balloons was hanging from the chandelier and the chicken was browning in the iron skillet when Jim and J.D. arrived.

"Smells great, Mom," the teenager said, lifting the lid on the heavy pan and inspecting his dinner. He went to his bathroom to shower.

"Where are the presents, Jim? Did you get them wrapped pretty?"

"Huh? The presents. I didn't have time to get them."

"What. You didn't have time. You mean you didn't make the time. You didn't make time to get presents for our son's sixteenth birthday. How can you be so callous? How can we celebrate with no presents? He'll be crushed. Thank goodness I have a card."

Jim shrugged his shoulders.

"Why didn't you get the presents if you wanted him to have presents?"

"Jim, you know that J.D. wears a size fourteen shoe and they have to be special ordered. I planned to pick them up after work, along with the other things he wanted. I would have had plenty of time before we met for dinner at Petit Auberge. When he asked me to make dinner here, there wasn't enough time. Did it ever occur to you that I can't do everything?"

Emma was angry.

J.D. reappeared, scrubbed and smelling good. He gave his mother a hug and peeked again at the simmering chicken.

"Make the gravy real thick, Mom."

"It will be, J.D."

Dinner was delicious and J.D. devoured his favorite foods. He pretended he wasn't hurt because there were no presents. His mother knew otherwise. He was crest-fallen and Emma could feel his pain.

Emma hastily made up 'Birthday Coupons' redeemable for a shopping trip and shoes and put them in the card. It was no better than putting mild salve on a gunshot wound. Although the thought was there, it didn't stop the ache in his heart.

Damn, Jim. Damn, damn, damn. Is there no end to the heartbreak he'll inflict on his family?

CHAPTER TWELVE

"For God has not given us a spirit of fear,
but of power and of love and a sound mind."
-2 Timothy 1:7

How many folks you expecting at the wedding?" Joe asked Emma two days before the nuptials.

"About three hundred. Steve's cousin, Dr. Eugene Odum, the famous environmentalist is coming! My mom is elated she's going to meet him. And two of my favorite people in the whole world—Bruce and Suzie Hall—are coming, too. He's a correspondent for CBS. He's been on assignment at Cape Canaveral for the shuttle launch. Suzie called and said he's flying home for the weekend and he can come to the wedding. Of course, my mom is thrilled out of her mind about that, too. She adores Bruce."

"Sounds as if your mother is primed for the main event."

"She certainly is. Ever since Allison's birth Mom's said she wanted to live long enough to see Allison get married at St. Martin's. Now her wish is coming true. I even bought her a dress to wear 'cause I knew she'd never spend the money, even though she's got plenty. She says it's the most beautiful dress she's ever had and she started crying when I gave it to her. I've never seen my Mom cry about anything material. I think she recognized the love behind the gift."

"Mothers have a way of doing that, don't they?"

"She's something else. She's been a different person since she moved into her apartment. We go to dinner and symphonies together with two of her lady friends. She even got me season tickets to the Alliance Theater. We have more fun. I never imagined that our relationship could be this good. If only she hadn't been verbally abusive of J.D."

Emma's happiness waned momentarily thinking about the hurts inflicted upon her son by her mother. The phone rang and she rushed to her desk to answer it.

"Good morning, Johnson Construction," she sang into the phone.

"Mr. Johnson, please. This is Leo Satterfield with the County Sanitation Department."

"One moment please." The song was gone from Emma's voice.

It was obvious she was not pleased that someone from the County Sanitation Department was calling her boss. She pushed the hold button.

"Joe, there's a Leo Satterfield on the phone. Says he's with DeKalb County."

"I wonder what the hell that bastard wants," Emma mumbled to herself. In her opinion anyone who worked for the sanitation department was responsible for her losing her home and she cringed at the mention of anything to do with the county or the Board of Corruption.

Emma wanted to listen to the conversation but the phone rang again. It was the florist with one final question. Her thoughts returned to the wedding and then she went into the kitchen to get coffee. She never gave Leo Satterfield's call another thought.

***

Emma arose at five o'clock the morning of the wedding and cleaned the house. She was too nervous and euphoric to sleep and at that hour of the day there was little else to do. Allison and Grace, her maid of honor, awoke at nine and Emma fixed them French toast, Allison's favorite breakfast.

The next few hours the girls kept Emma jumping.

"Mom, where's—" Grace called out. It gave Emma a special thrill when Grace called her Mom.

"Mama, have you seen—?" Allison asked. Emma would retrieve whatever it was the girls needed; it was delightful fun and she enjoyed every moment.

At noon the bride and her maid of honor left for the beauty shop and Emma got herself ready for the wedding. The skies were clear, not a cloud in sight. It would be a beautiful day for Allison and Steve to start their life together.

When Emma arrived at the church she got a glimpse of Louise and Steve's aunt running toward the parish hall with big bunches of multicolored balloons.

Wonder what Louise and Linda are up to now?

Emma laughed. She glided down the outside stairway to the bride's room where she was greeted by Rachel and the brides' maids. They looked radiant in their fuchsia pink satin gowns. What a glorious day.

The bouquets and floral arrangements from Weinstock's Florist were prettier than anything Emma had imagined; everything and everybody looked festive and elegant. Majestic music from the organ accompanied the trumpet solo that played during Allison's walk down the aisle and the Nuptial Mass was conducted without a single glitch. After the recessional, *Horn Pipe* from Handel's *Water Music*, the organist played *Ode to Joy*. Emma's little girl was married. Guests spilled out into the hot July afternoon to the melodic pealing tones of bells in the carillon and crossed the walkway to Gable Hall, where champagne was poured and an elaborate array of food awaited.

After the reception, Allison and Steve were showered with birdseed while dashing through the well-wishers toward the Rolls Royce limousine. Allison's satin gown billowed by the breeze that caught the long veil and enveloped the handsome couple with swirls of white netting. The chauffeur opened the door and watched in amusement while the newlyweds maneuvered their way into the vehicle through a dazzling array of balloons packed into the passenger compartment of the finely-appointed car.

"That's what you were doing those balloons!" Emma said gleefully to Louise.

Louise beamed.

Once inside, Steve opened the sunroof and the balloons slowly floated upward, dancing around Allison and Steve, who waved to their families and friends from the open top of the limo.

"How beautiful!" Emma said excitedly.

"Does that suit you?" Louise asked with a twinkle in her eyes.

"Of course! What a beautiful send-off!"

"I thought it would be fun!" Steve's mother said, waving to her son and new daughter.

The limousine started to pull away from the curb.

"Wait," Emma said, grabbing the door handle. "Wait. I want a picture."

She knocked on the opaque window with the palm of her hand.

"One more picture!"

The door swung open and the happy, smiling couple leaned forward, surrounded by the red, green, blue, orange and yellow balloons, lilies and exquisite Princess Di roses of Allison's bouquet framing their faces. The photographer hit the shutter button.

"What a wonderful shot. That will be a picture to cherish."

Steve closed the door and the chauffeur drove away with Emma's daughter and her new son.

They're on their way to a new life.

The guests waved and clapped and called out felicitations: "Congratulations!" "Best wishes!" "Good luck!"

The pleasant noise rose in volume to become a cheerful roar as the newlyweds departed. Above them one voice rang out in a most joyful song.

"Have a beautiful, happy life, Darlin."

***

The week after the wedding J.D. went to football camp at Georgia Tech. Emma drove to town every afternoon to watch him practice in Rosebowl Field. When he came home, he had his camp photo, taken with Bobby Ross, the head coach of the Yellow Jackets.

"J.D. I love this picture. Imagine. You and Bobby Ross. He's going to be famous some day. Georgia Tech is going to have a terrific season real soon. You'll see."

J.D. shook his head as if to say, "Yeah, right Mom."

***

The hot, dry summer of Allison's wedding was followed by a beautiful, crisp autumn, Georgia Tech football games on pleasant Saturday afternoons, and Emma's thrill at seeing her son dressed out in a varsity football uniform for his high school. Weekdays were busy at the construction company and Emma relished the activities.

She enrolled in the Certified Professional Secretary review course at DeKalb College and enjoyed the stimulating round of courses in economics, accounting, business law, behavioral science, business communications and office technology.

The horrible kitchen Emma despised was remodeled and she finally felt comfortable preparing meals for her family. With the sink now located in the island, Emma could look outside while working on dinner. She was thankful to be out of the claustrophobic corner where the sink had originally been set next to the stove.

Jim and J.D. built a new run for the dogs, much to the chagrin of Alex, who resented the small confines after the full acre spaciousness of the other pen. He was often found outside, wandering free, having either dug under the fence or climbed it. Out of concern for Emma's dog, Jim ran an electrical wire around the fence and the low-voltage charge it carried would mildly shock Alex when he touched it. Emma hated the drastic measure for her dog's safety. It was only done as a last recourse.

Work, evening classes, J.D.'s activities, Friday night high school football, Saturday afternoon college games and Sunday morning church took most of Emma's time. Occasionally Emma's mother treated her to an evening at the Atlanta Symphony, preceded by dinner at Houlihan's or Country Place, across Peachtree Street in Colony Square. Emma's duty on these outings was to be the chauffeur and escort for Bee and her friends. These were pleasant events for Emma; she dearly loved her mother's friends and it gave her time to visit with her mother unencumbered by the stifling atmosphere of Jim's presence.

Jim purchased a Kenworth road tractor and was hauling goods and commodities between Atlanta and Charleston or Jacksonville. Even though Emma considered it a gross waste of his mind and his education, she set up a simple bookkeeping system for him and helped him keep up with his paperwork.

Occasional thoughts of Mr. Byrd puzzled Emma but the dreadful nightmares finally ceased and she was, at long last, able to return to a regular sleeping routine. That early autumn of 1988, Emma St. Claire felt better than she had in a long time. She was optimistic about the future until the September afternoon when Jim's mother called in a panic.

"Emma," Janice choked out, "I'm at the hospital with David. There's been a bad accident."

Emma's heart raced. She knew that house was a bad place. Emma's e.s.p. had been right again. *Damn, damn, damn.* Now David was hurt. Emma knew that he'd had an accident in the awful yard.

"What happened?"

"He was riding his lawn mower up that steep hill and it turned over on him."

"How bad is he hurt?"

"Real bad. They've taken him into surgery."

"What sort of injury—" Emma could hardly talk. Something bad had happened to the sweet, wonderful man she loved. Why did it have to happen?

"The blade—" Janice finally choked out, "the blade cut him on the back. Awful."

"The blade. Didn't that mower have a dead man's pedal? The blade should have stopped turning the minute his foot came off of it."

"No, the mower is old. The blade kept turning. It cut him to pieces. I was in the house and never heard anything. He laid in the yard crying for help. Finally one of the neighbors came over. It was ghastly." She was crying.

"Where are you? I'll come out right away."

Emma left the office and drove to the hospital to be with her in-laws, berating herself on the way for not having done something to prevent the accident.

What could I have done? I knew it was a bad place. It never occurred to me that such a horrendous accident would happen. If I had to know that it was a bad place, why couldn't I foresee this? Damn my e.s.p. Damn, damn, damn.

After several hours of surgery the doctors told Mrs. Crymes her husband would recover although there was much damage and it would take months to heal. Emma felt it was her fault and carried agonizing guilt over the accident and began to feel she was falling backwards into a bottomless pit.

Why, dear God. Why do I have to live this way?

A few nights later, while deep in slumber, Emma had another dream about Mr. Byrd and the aura. The radiating light started to take on the shape of a woman and Emma strained in her sleep to get a close look. Mr. Byrd was standing in an office full of people working at computer desks, when a man came out of a side office and handed Mr. Byrd an envelope. He opened it, looked at a paper inside, and put it in his coat pocket.

There was nothing foreboding or frightening about the dream and the next morning Emma pondered its meaning.

Who is she? Why am I dreaming about her?

The next day when Emma stopped at the post office to drop the mail, as she did each evening after work, she put down the window of the car at the curbside mailbox. This particular evening her arm could barely reach the mail slot. Pain shot through her shoulder and down the back of her arm, into the wrist. Her hand felt limp and hung tenaciously onto the stack of mail.

Good grief.

Emma moaned lightheartedly.

What in the world have I done to myself now?

146

She dismissed the pain and drove home, enjoying a Brahms symphony on the radio. Her arm and hand felt fine while she made dinner and she did not mention the episode to either her son or her husband. Complaining never cured anything.

The daily mail drop became something of a hassle, with hot pain burning through Emma's shoulder and arm. Occasionally at home, while doing housework, reaching up would recreate what she started calling her post office-itis, yet she never mentioned it to her family. It was only a fleeting annoyance.

The next several weeks the dream repeated over and over, each time more clearly defining the aura, until Emma could finally see the *sweet, beautiful, lady* as she began to call her. Emma also gleaned a personal history of the woman from her dreams, although there was never any dialog that provided this information; it came to Emma intuitively.

Mr. Byrd's companion was a professional person and she wore some sort of suit or uniform to work. She had been married very briefly and desperately wanted children, even though she was already in her early forties. She was beautiful, had a brilliant mind, and Emma adored her.

She's the person I would be, if I could change myself into anyone in the whole world. Maybe Mr. Byrd has recently met her. Maybe that's why I can see her now. That's a nice thought—that he's finally got that lovely lady on his arm. I can't imagine why I dreamed of her before now, though. I wish I could talk to him. At least he seems to be happy. That's what matters. He's happy and they are both okay.

The russet red and golden yellow leaves that colored the Atlanta landscape and beckoned the winter slowly faded and turned crisp brown, drifting lazily through cool autumn air and accumulating in huge piles. Looking out the window wall in her office Emma thought about the wonder of nature, how everything was recycled. In the natural process, unhindered by modern man, the environment was a never-ending cycle. Emma wished she could be one of the oak trees, with deep roots to provide nourishment and branches reaching always toward the heavens, continually glorifying God.

As winter approached, the depression that started almost two years before had not loosened its grip and Emma began to feel disconnected. The son she adored seemed distant and withdrawn, her husband uninterested and non-communicative and her bosses displeased with her job performance. For the first time in her career she found day-to-day routine functions almost impossible to perform, forgetting instructions or overlooking duties she usually did without a second thought.

Emma drifted through the late fall months the way dried, brown leaves floated on the wind, with no idea where she was going or what she was doing. She continued to hold up a facade of cheerfulness to her family, friends and classmates. Although they saw a change in Emma, no one said anything to her directly and occasional references to her weight loss met with Emma's warm appreciation.

Thanksgiving came. This year, Emma's usual feast for twenty-five family members gave her mental and physical anxieties she had never before experienced. After the meal, while washing dishes with Rachel, she tried to make sense of it. Words were inadequate to express her real feelings.

"This is our last family Thanksgiving, Rachel."

Emma's hands were submerged in hot, soapy water, washing the turkey pan.

"What do you mean our last family Thanksgiving?"

"I don't know; it will never be this way again."

"Is someone going to die? What in the world are you saying?"

"No. No one is going to die. Things are changing, Rachel. I know it won't ever be this way again."

Laughter erupted from the living room where the rest of the family was assembled.

"I couldn't have gotten through this dinner without you," Emma said to her twin sister.

"Oh, silly girl; of course you could have. You've fed this many people lots of times without my help."

"No, I couldn't. If you hadn't brought food and organized the menu, there wouldn't have been a Thanksgiving dinner at the St. Claire's this year."

Rachel finished drying the bone china dinner plates and stacked them in the cupboard.

"Now, Emma, you don't feel that bad, do you? I know you're depressed about losing your beautiful home and Jim's bankrupt business and what the bank did to you. Those things are behind you now. Can't you let go and get on with your life?"

"I'm trying, Rachel. Honest to God, I am. I go to work and to school. I'm enjoying my classes. I love going to football games with J.D. and Atlanta Symphony concerts with Bee. I'm grateful for the many good things in my life. I have something hanging over me, something important to do. I feel as if a huge weight is pushing me down and I'm sinking right into the ground. I'm drowning."

Emma rinsed the turkey roasting pan and picked up a dish towel.

"You told me about this a long time ago, Emma. I thought it was something to do with the wedding."

"The wedding? Oh no, not the wedding. It was a pleasure; pure enjoyment; it was a lot of work and I loved every moment. This is different. Almost—foreboding."

The turkey pan was dried and put away and while Emma finished wiping off the counter tops, Rachel sorted and stacked the cleaned, dried silverware.

"Do you think it has anything to do with that teacher, Mr. Byrd?"

"I don't know. I've had nice dreams about him and my sweet, beautiful lady."

"Don't you think that's a bit much? Calling some woman you've never met your sweet beautiful lady?"

"I can't help it, Rachel, I adore her."

"Maybe this feeling has something to do with her."

"What in the world could it be? The first time I saw him I had that vision of the little old lady. She told me to protect him. Sometimes I feel as though she has taken possession of me."

"Emma St. Claire! Don't say such a thing. There's some reasonable explanation why you saw her. We haven't figured it out yet."

"Whenever I think about her my heart beats unbearably fast; I feel it will jump right out of my chest. It's driving me crazy, Rachel."

"You're not crazy! You're not! Quit saying such awful things about my sister!"

"My life has changed since I met that man, Rachel. I don't think it will ever be the same. I'm miserable. I wish I had never met him. I hate myself for the way I feel."

"You're a wonderful, kind person, Emma. Your family loves you."

Emma broke down and started crying.

"I want to get rid of this hideous thing hanging over me, Rachel. If I don't, I would rather die."

The twin's conversation was interrupted when J.D. called from the living room.

"We're ready for a hot game of Trivial Pursuit. Y'all com'in?"

Emma dried her eyes on the dishtowel before she and Rachel went into the living room to play a game with their family.

***

The first Sunday of December, Emma filled the house with the sights, sounds and smells of the Christmas season. A blue spruce tree was trimmed with assorted decorations collected during her marriage and included precious treasures made by her children. Each was hung carefully and proudly by Emma while remembering past holidays.

She decorated the railing up the front staircase and across the porch with garlands of pine boughs and red bows and the fireplace mantle was festooned with a variety of greenery to bring indoors the wonderful smell of pine, holly, cedar and spruce. Glowing candles and a flickering fire added to the visual warmth of the living room and a comfortable homey feeling. Handel's Messiah or Yuletide carols played almost continuously on the stereo and, in spite of her depression, Emma frequently sang along.

For her son's sake, Emma continued her charade of contentment. Emma knew in her mind she needed to adjust to the loss of her home; acknowledging failures and disappointments, however, did nothing to improve her despondent and hopeless feelings.

On New Year's Day, during the marathon of football games she enjoyed watching with her son, Emma St. Claire wrote her resolutions on a legal tablet:

I will be happy.

I will never dream about Mr. Byrd again.

I will be happy.

Emma's hopes for a happy new year abruptly faded in early January when she was awakened by a frightening noise that shook her to the depths of her soul. Getting out of bed she moved slowly to the window and gazed out at the full moon shining on blades of ice-covered grass. The house was quiet; the only sound she heard was the snort of a horse in the yard next door, the yard that had belonged to her.

Why, Dear God? Why did I hear that awful sound again?

Moisture in her eyes made Emma blink. Wet drops trickled down her cheeks; her nose started to run. She was numb and rubbed the back of her hand crudely across her nose.

The dream with the booming sound was a gate to hell. Emma felt herself sliding deeper into the bottomless pit of despair and anguish each time her sleep was bombarded with harrowing nightmares.

What had been a dream of Mr. Byrd kneeling in a field at night, with a looming shadow behind him, became a horrifying, in color, detail of him looking down at a seemingly lifeless body lying in his lap. He would pull his hands out

150

from under the woman he was cradling, look at them, and begin to cry. Each time Emma had the dream another image appeared.

Finally, after suffering from the mental pictures that evolved over two years, the most disturbing detail was added.

When Mr. Byrd looked at his hands, they were dripping with blood and he was surrounded by other lifeless forms lying in a field, with the looming shadow hanging over them.

One Friday night in February, while preparing for bed, Emma sat at the bathroom vanity and surveyed assorted pills she arranged on the counter.

I can't take it anymore, God. I can't. If I go to bed, I'll have that—that—

She picked up one of the pill bottles and read the label.

I can't go on this way. I can't. I've got to end it.

Studying each label, Emma wondered if the combination of drugs would be enough to transport her to another place, a place where she would no longer suffer from nightmares.

She had nothing to live for. Her home was gone; her children were grown. When she lay dying from meningitis, knowing that her children needed her gave Emma the drive to recover. Now her daughter was happily married and Emma was comfortable knowing that Louise would be a wonderful mother for Allison. J.D. was almost seventeen. Emma did not want to leave him but in her current condition she was useless to him as a mother. There was no way out of the bottomless abyss she had fallen into after she met Philip Byrd and the little gray-haired lady.

Her mind was awash in useless, troubling images she could neither control nor eliminate. There was nothing else to do. Emma prayed and prayed, asking God to take the images away; still they came, every one more troubling than the one before. Two years. It had been two, long, long years. Yes, she was crazy. Emma St. Claire was crazy.

Emma picked up the bottle of headache pills, the ones she took for migraines. There were only seven left. That would not be enough. She counted the Flexeril, a muscle relaxant. The old bottle was almost full; would they still have any potency? What about the decongestant? The label said it should not be taken with beta-blockers. She picked up Jim's blood pressure medicine. Didn't the doctor say it was a beta blocker? Emma tried to remember. Remember she could not. Why would she remember anything, anyway? Her mind was gone, wasn't it? She was insane.

Emma poured out a handful of Jim's pain pills.

These are still fresh. They ought to help a lot—

She studied the label—'with codeine.'

No, that won't do. I can't take codeine. It makes me sick to my stomach. I would throw up everything. Damn. What in the world will I do now?

From out of the deep recesses of her weary brain, another ticker tape crossed her mind:

If I die, I can't tell Philip Byrd what I'm supposed to tell him. Tell him? What am I supposed to tell him? How am I supposed to know what these dreams mean? I'm crazy and there's no reason for them. In a few minutes the dreams will be done with forever. I'll be gone. Philip Byrd will have to protect himself.

The door to the adjacent bedroom opened quietly and Jim called out to his wife.

"Baby, are you back there?"

Emma St. Claire was crazy. Crazy people don't hear other people calling them.

"Baby—?"

There was no response to Jim's question; he crossed the room and jerked open the bathroom door.

Emma picked up the headache pills in one hand and a glass of water with the other. The hand with the pills was at her mouth.

"What are you doing?" he yelled.

Jim grabbed her hand away and the pills spewed across the room, falling silently onto the carpet.

The crazy woman looked blankly up at her husband, the man who professed to love her. He lied to her. It didn't matter anymore because she was going away. Forever.

She reached for another bottle of pills just as Jim's huge hand swept the entire assortment onto the floor, then grabbed her up by the arms and enfolded her in a much tighter than comfortable embrace.

"What's the matter with you, Emma? Are you crazy?"

"Yes, of course I'm crazy! You wouldn't know that, though, because you never talk to me. If you would talk to me you'd know I'm crazy. I can't stand your lies, Jim. I can't stand the nightmares. I'm going to end it. You won't have to lie to me and I won't have to have e.s.p... You always said I was a witch—I don't want my son's mother to be a witch. He deserves better than that. A witch! A crazy witch! That's what I am!"

"I don't know what the hell you're talking about, e.s.p. and witches. What's the matter with you?"

He shook her hard.

"I don't know. Let go of me. I want to die."

She broke down, dissolving in his arms, melting slowly toward the floor. She sat there crying amid the multi-colored potions that would have taken her out of hell.

"You can't leave J.D., Emma. What would it do to him? Think about that?"

Sweeping the pink carpet with his wide hand, Jim picked up the pills, threw them angrily into the trashcan and left the room carrying Emma's freedom from hell in the pink wicker basket.

Emma lay on the floor, crying loudly.

There's no escape from hell. None. I'm trapped. I wish I had never met Philip Byrd. I knew I'd regret taking that damn class.

She went upstairs to the bedroom she shared with Jim and picked up her favorite pillow. Then she went downstairs, through the family room and into Allison's bedroom on the far side of the house. The room, decorated in various shades of blue, was comforting to her. She curled up in the middle of the four-poster bed and cried herself to sleep, begging God to help her.

CHAPTER THIRTEEN

**"And although you were formerly alienated...
yet He has now reconciled you."**
-Colossians 2:21, 22

Wonder what this is," Emma mumbled. She picked up a manila envelope Larry laid on her desk along with Joe's other mail. The return address said it was from the County Sanitation Department.

I don't believe this.

It was a bid request from Leo Satterfield. He was asking Joe to give the county a price on the garbage dump—the project she fought. The project that would cover forty-five acres of scenic property rich in endangered species of plants. Emma was flabbergasted.

She laid the mail on Joe's desk and told her boss about the bid request.

"Well, well, they finally sent it out. I need to get working on it."

Emma stammered, not believing what she heard.

"We're, we're—not going to bid on that damn thing, are we? That's the project I tried to stop—it was, it was—one of the reasons I lost my home."

"It will be a good job for us. How 'bout getting my proposal out of the file. I think it was sent sometime last summer."

"Joe, I don't remember sending the county anything on that job."

Her boss was leafing through the bid documents.

"They asked me to write up a set of specifications for them. See this; they copied what I sent them."

Emma leaned forward to look at the page. Sure enough, the typeface matched her typewriter; and the format was identical to Joe's proposals.

"I know I would remember typing that, Joe."

"Look in last year's files."

At the filing cabinets in the conference room Emma looked at the Rolodex cards where quotes were cross-referenced and found the listings for both Leo Satterfield and the county; the specifications had been mailed on July 29, when Emma was on vacation for the wedding.

Emma opened the drawer and pulled out the file. The proposal was typed by Joe's wife the day Emma took off before the wedding. Then she remembered Leo Satterfield's call.

She stood there shaking her head.

How could my boss do such a thing? How could he consort with those bastards? How could he do it?

After laying the file on Joe's desk, Emma returned to her office without saying a word.

It was the last straw! She could not stand to be hurt again. She was numb and weak.

Why, Lord, why? Why do these things keep happening?

Emma went to the kitchen and poured a cup of coffee, then pulled the telephone directory out of the credenza in the conference room. At her desk Emma opened the book and looked up a number.

"Capital City Medical," a cheerful voice said.

"My name is Emma St. Claire. I've seen your television commercials, something about a free consultation. Is that still available?"

"Why yes, it is. May I ask the nature of the problem?"

"Severe depression," Emma said quietly.

"Did you say depression?" the nice voice asked.

"Yes, I've had a lot on me for a long time and I feel I'm losing control. I don't know who to go to. I thought you could help."

"Of course, we can. I'll have one of our counselors call you in a few minutes. Can I have your name and number, please?"

Emma gave the cheerful voice the information and hung up. She had no idea what made her think of calling Capital. Somehow she felt it was a step in the right direction.

Joe and Larry left the office and Emma was alone when the counselor called thirty minutes later. After telling the woman that she was depressed to the point of suicide, she scheduled an appointment for five o'clock the next afternoon.

During her drive to the Capital office Emma went over in her mind everything that had happened the last few years and decided it would be better to stick to the facts and not get into her perplexing e.s.p. episode about Philip Byrd.

My e.s.p. is real and someday I'll understand it. Right now I have to get help to make it through one more day. My son needs a good mother. He deserves a good mother. I want to be a good mother. I've got to get back on track.

There was immediate rapport between Emma and the cute, blond counselor, a woman about Emma's age. She asked Emma questions about her health, her family, religious life, community involvement, and job. Emma thought the woman would be bored with her story but the counselor took prodigious notes and before Emma knew it, two and a half hours had passed.

"No wonder you're depressed, Emma," she said with genuine sincerity. "I suggest you see a psychiatrist."

"A psychiatrist? Do you think I'm mentally ill?"

"No," she almost laughed. "I don't think you're mentally ill. A psychiatrist can prescribe medicine and I think that's what you need. You've been through a lot of emotional trauma in a short period of time. An anti-depressant would help. The doctor could prescribe it and monitor you."

"Okay. That makes sense. Who do you think I should see?"

"We have a referral list. I'll get in touch with someone and call you with an appointment. How's that sound?"

"Sounds great to me. You don't think I'm insane."

"Absolutely not," she laughed.

***

Driving to Dr. Richard Longshore's office a few days later Emma again decided not to mention her e.s.p. The counselor said she didn't think Emma was insane, that she only needed medicine for depression. If the session with Dr. Longshore was easy and open, Emma could always talk to him about it another time.

The receptionist at Dr. Longshore's office gave Emma a cordial greeting and introduced her to the doctor. They were both warm, caring people and Emma felt she had made the right decision by calling Capital.

Dr. Longshore was also interested in Emma's involved story, starting with the death-defying illness and culminating with her boss's plan to build the project she had opposed. While telling her tale, she was relaxed and animated and her not infrequent jokes told the doctor this patient had a very good sense of humor.

After writing a prescription and giving Emma instructions to increase the dosage gradually over the next two weeks, he escorted her to the reception desk to schedule a follow-up appointment.

That night Emma had another dream about Mr. Byrd. He was in Symphony Hall at the Memorial Arts Center on Peachtree with the sweet, beautiful lady; to Emma it appeared they were very much in love. The Atlanta Symphony was playing Emma's favorite piece of music, *Scheherazade* by Rimsky-Korsakov; she dreamed every note.

The medication gave Emma a sound sleep and she awoke on Saturday morning ready to take on the world. Jim was already in the kitchen, working on breakfast, and J.D. was sprawled on the floor in the living room, reading the sports pages.

"Morning, Darlin'," she said cheerfully, stepping cautiously across the wide body in her path.

"Hi, Mom. You feeling better?"

"Yes, I am. Had a good night's sleep. Boy that bacon smells good. Let's eat."

Emma went into the kitchen and put her arms loosely around Jim's rotund middle, hugging him from the back while he flipped pancakes. The back of her arms hurt; they felt weak.

"Morning, Baby."

"Umm, my favorite," she said, eyeing Jim's specialty while he flipped another.

"I miss not having my wife in my bed," he said forlornly.

"I'm sorry, Jim. I'm struggling with a lot right now. Please don't push me."

"Now don't start crying again," he said.

"Dr. Longshore said the medicine will take effect slowly, that it will probably be a couple of weeks before I feel better."

Emma opened the refrigerator door and reached for milk. The gallon jug felt unusually heavy. She strained to lift it.

"Did you tell that doctor you've been losing weight?" Jim asked.

It was typical for Jim to call the psychiatrist *that doctor*. Emma resented the innuendo. She did not respond to her husband's comment. He stacked pancakes and bacon on a platter and set it on the table.

"Breakfast is served."

Emma was still struggling with the milk bottle and when she almost dropped it, Jim came to her rescue, catching it before it hit the floor.

"What's the matter, Baby?"

"I don't know. I must have slept crooked or something. My arms are a little tired."

"Look!" J.D. said, pointing to the long windows.

The outline of a deer could be seen deep in the woods behind the house; the buck moved timidly among the trees until he reached the edge of the lawn. A small doe followed at a distance. Enchanted by the view, Emma, Jim and J.D. ate in silence, not wanting to alarm the beautiful creatures feasting on the tender, young grass.

Emma decided to clean the house before taking a shower; she put on an old sweatshirt and ragged pair of gold sweat pants that J.D. had long ago outgrown. She stripped the beds and put sheets in the washing machine then dusted furniture. When that was done, she went to the laundry room, put the sheets in the dryer, started a load of J.D.'s clothes, and pulled out the vacuum cleaner.

Emma tipped it backwards slightly and rolled it on the two rear wheels. When she got to the blue bedroom she plugged it in. Again, she tried to run it over the thick carpet. It would hardly move.

Geez—must have rollers set too low.

She reset the level of the wheels, turned the machine on. Again, it would hardly move.

What's wrong with this thing?

"J.D., would you come here a minute, Darlin'. Something's wrong with the vacuum."

J.D. got up off the floor, where he had flopped down with the newspaper, and went to the bedroom. He turned on the vacuum and pushed it back and forth.

"Seems fine to me."

"Okay. I don't know why it wouldn't go a minute ago. Thanks, J.D."

Emma stood on her tiptoes and kissed her son on the cheek. He went back to the family room and Emma turned on the vacuum.

Again, it would hardly move.

What the hell's the matter with this thing?

"J.D., the vacuum is still acting funny," she called out.

Her son ambled back into the room, turned on the machine and pushed it easily across the carpet.

"Here, Mom," he instructed, putting her hand next to his on the handle. "See, its running fine."

"Okay, okay, I can handle it."

159

He released his grip and went back to the newspaper. The vacuum would hardly move.

Emma mumbled.

Must be me. Why can't I make this thing go?

The backs of her arms were achy. While rubbing each arm with the opposite hand, Emma thought about the episode with the milk in the kitchen.

Surely, there's nothing wrong with my arms.

Mustering every ounce of strength she could, Emma forced herself to push the vacuum. It was a struggle and she was soon sweating profusely.

Something's wrong. I don't have any strength.

An alarm went off in Emma's head; her heart pounded.

There's something bad wrong, her silent voice said.

A vision of the little old lady flashed through her mind and a cold shiver ran down her spine, shaking Emma violently from head to foot.

No, Dear God. No.

She turned off the vacuum cleaner, crawled into bed, curled into a tight ball and cried herself to sleep.

When Jim came in a few hours later he found his wife moaning with a headache.

"Baby—" he said, gently caressing her shoulder. "Can I get you anything?"

"My head—is killing me—some aspirin and Tylenol—do you mind?"

"Of course I don't mind. I wish you wouldn't say that."

He disappeared and returned with medicine and a small glass of orange juice. Emma gulped it down and handed the empty glass to Jim.

"Thanks, Honey," she said weakly. "I'll get up in a few minutes."

Jim left and Emma lay in bed, trying to collect her wits by giving herself a stern talk.

I've got to get myself together. Weak, sore arms don't have anything to do with Philip Byrd and that little old lady.

Emma staggered into the blue bathroom and took a long shower in water as hot as she could stand. She rolled her head, stretched her arms and tried to limber up. While washing her hair, she sang lustily, "I'm gonna wash that man right outta my hair—"

***

Although Emma was taking antidepressant as prescribed, she continued to have dreams about her teacher and nightmares haunted her in spite of drug-induced sleep. A few days after the incident with the vacuum cleaner, the ghastly dream of Mr. Byrd in the field at night frightened Emma and she awoke crying loudly.

No—No—Not—Not—my—

Her mind's eye moved in closer to Mr. Byrd, akin to a camera zooming in for a close-up shot. Cradled in his arms was Emma's sweet, beautiful lady.

No, Dear God. What's the matter with her? Why isn't she moving? Dear God, in heaven. Help me. Please, please help me.

Emma rolled over and looked at the clock. It was three-thirty in the morning. She lay there until five-thirty, not closing her eyes. Something bad was going to happen.

***

"How are you doing with the medication?" Dr. Longshore asked Emma.

"The first few days it made me drowsy; it's okay now."

"Are you sleeping any better?"

"No, not any significant improvement. Do you think I'm crazy?"

He laughed.

"No, Emma, you're not crazy. I had a long talk with the counselor at Capital. We both feel you've been under a terrific strain for a long, long time. That's why you're depressed. However, depression is not the same as insanity—or being 'crazy' as you put it."

"There is something else that's bothering me that I haven't told you about yet."

The doctor looked incredulous. How could there possibly be more to this woman's story?

"Do you want to tell me about it?"

"Yes; I do. I hesitated to come in here and tell you about it right off, because I—I—thought I was crazy because of the things that have happened to me, that maybe I wasn't in control of my life."

"I would say that you do have your act together, Emma. You work and take care of your family and you're a responsible citizen of your community. Even though you can't control your environment and the things that happen to you, does not mean you are not in control of your life. You are handling your problems properly. Now, if you crawled in a hole and refused to be a viable human being because of adversity, that would be another matter altogether."

Emma nodded her head slowly, satisfied to learn she was not insane. She smiled at the doctor.

"Do you believe in e.s.p.?" she asked.

He looked startled.

"E.S.P.? There are many dimensions of our minds we do not yet understand. As a professional, I would be wrong to say that it does not exist because I have never personally experienced it. Why do you ask?"

"Hmm—"

Could she tell the doctor about the teacher? She did not want to sound idiotic or foolish, or worse yet, an insane person. He said she wasn't insane. Would he change his mind if she told him about the teacher?

"Umm—I have e.s.p.," she stammered. "I had my first episode when I was five years old."

"How interesting."

His positive response encouraged Emma to continue.

"Usually it involves people I know or love—until a couple of years ago when I met a teacher and got a message I was to protect him. Since then I've had a lot of dreams and nightmares which don't make any sense. I'm afraid someone he cares about is going to get hurt real bad. I don't know how."

"My goodness. I wish I could help you. I've never had any experience with the paranormal. I want you to contact Dr. Moody at West Georgia College. He's done a lot of research on paranormal phenomena and has the background to help you with this problem."

"West Georgia College? That's in Carrollton. I don't think that would be very practical for me. I won't be able to take time off from work."

"He'd be the best in this area that I know of. There's also a Dr. J. B. Rhine at the University of North Carolina. Very highly regarded in the field. Of course, that's even further. This isn't something to take lightly. You need to work with someone ethical. That's why I suggest you to call Dr. Moody."

"I'll think about it. Maybe it will go away. Several months ago I started keeping a journal, thinking that would help me sort it out—if I could look at it objectively. I pray about it a lot. God's bound to hear me one of these days," Emma laughed.

The psychiatrist laughed, too, and nodded his head in agreement.

He looked up Dr. Moody's telephone number and gave it to Emma.

"I want to see you to monitor your medication. Continue with the prescription and call Dr. Moody."

"Okay." she nodded and smiled. "I'll think about it. That's a long way to go, though."

"It might be worth it."

They shook hands.

"Thank you, Dr. Longshore. I appreciate everything you've done for me. Glad to know I'm not crazy."

She laughed again and he shook his head.

"Check in with me in two months, Emma. If you need me, you call. Okay?"

"Okay. I'll do that."

***

Yellow daffodils popped up in beds of blue and white pansies, deep pink pyracantha blossoms appeared on prickly bushes and watermelon colored azaleas glowed under the white lace shawls of the Dogwood trees that brought spring to Atlanta. It was time to store the drab, heavy wardrobe of winter and put on new, cheerful garments; it was time to shake off the winter doldrums and put on a fresh coat of optimism. That's what Emma St. Claire wanted to do.

This spring, however, her mind would not cooperate. In spite of medication, dreams and nightmares continued unabated and she only slept a few hours each night before being awakened by either frightening sounds or gruesome visions. She could not take time off work to pursue Dr. Longshore's recommendation to see the para-psychologist at West Georgia and, worse still, her arms continued to lose strength. Even the simplest tasks—putting on makeup and dressing herself—were laborious and time-consuming. The backs of her arms ached almost constantly.

Somehow, she completed the Certified Professional Secretary review course but did not sign up to take the two-day, six-part exam in May with her secretary friends. Although she studied, something told her it would not be possible.

She did sign up for something else—the spring quarter economics class to be taught by Philip Byrd.

"Unless I face him Rachel, I will never get it behind me," she said to her twin one evening on the phone. "I can't afford to work with a top-ranked para-psychologist. Lord only knows what it would cost. I'd never be able to get the time off work, either. How in the world can I tell Joe and Larry that I need a few days off to go to West Georgia to find out why I dream about a teacher?"

"Yes, I see your point, Emma. Maybe it would be a good idea to face him again. He might shed some light on the dreams and then, if you can understand them, they'll go away. What will you say to him?"

"I don't know. I've been praying over that. I know something awful is going to happen to that girl, whoever she is. I can't let it happen, Rachel."

Emma started to cry.

"Please, Emma. Don't cry."

She regained her composure and dried her eyes.

"Agony with no answers. Why? Why, Rachel?"

"Because he's special for some reason. You must talk to him if you want to know what's special about him. Then you'll understand."

"I can't imagine why I feel protective of people I don't even know. I think about that little old lady a lot, Rachel. She's special, too. Why? Why do I have such awful chills when I think about her?"

"This situation is enough to make anyone shudder, Emma."

"I guess. The first time I saw that man, a chill went up and down my spine."

"This has been going on such a long time, I had forgotten about that. What else did you see that night?"

"It was confusing. I almost felt—almost—"

Emma could not choke out the words so Rachel carefully coaxed her.

"Felt what, Emma. What did you feel?"

"I felt a lot of love for him. Not man-woman lustful feelings. It was—it was—"

"What, Emma. What sort of feeling was it?"

"I felt real maternal toward him. Like he was a baby. I wanted to pick him up and tell him everything would be okay. Later, when I'd see him, I'd wonder how he grew up and why I had missed it."

"As I see it, Emma, confronting him again is the only way to resolve it."

"Maybe you're right; but I can't tell him that in my mind he's a baby. I mean, he's a grown man. I don't want to offend him."

"Yes, I know."

"How can I tell him I dream about him in love with a beautiful lady and she's going to get hurt and he's a child?"

***

J.D. was sitting at the table in the breakfast room, surrounded by schoolbooks, when Emma got home from work.

"Hi, Darlin'," Emma said. "Lots of homework?"

"No, not too much."

Although Emma sensed J.D. had something on his mind she didn't push him into conversation. He would say the words when he was ready.

Emma put on her apron, wincing while she struggled to tie it behind her back. Her upper arms were achy.

"I got a question," he finally spurted out. "Please don't get mad at me."

"J.D. why would I get mad at you for asking a question?" Emma asked with a smile. "I've always encouraged you to say what's on your mind."

"Yes, I know. This might upset you."

"No it won't. Go ahead and ask."

She stood next to the table awaiting a response.

"Spring break is coming up."

"Of course I know spring break is coming soon. Why did you think that would upset me?"

"Because I want you to take a trip with me."

"You do! You want your ole Mama to go on spring break with you?!"

Emma was trying to keep the conversation light; she knew her son had something serious on his mind and he was having trouble getting it out.

He paused.

"Will you take me to Texas? I want to meet my grandfather."

Emma was in shock—surprised—and delighted.

"Why, J.D., that's a wonderful idea!"

She glowed with enthusiasm.

"You want to go to Texas? Aren't your friends going to Daytona?"

"Yeah, I guess. I want to go to Texas. I want to meet the grandfather I've never known; and I want to visit Uncle Ed, too."

"I'm thrilled, Darlin'. Absolutely thrilled. I'll call Daddy tonight. Uncle Ed, too. If they are okay with it, I'll call Atlantic Airlines and make reservations."

"You mean we can fly to Dallas?" he asked excitedly.

"Of course; I don't want to spend our time on the road. I haven't seen my dad in almost twenty five years; I want to see him every minute I can."

J.D.'s eyes sparkled. An impish grin lit his face.

He went back to his homework and Emma started dinner.

***

Emma sat in the classroom the first night of spring quarter, awaiting the arrival of Mr. Byrd. Even though she had no idea what she would say to him, it was time to confront her feelings. She wondered if he still slammed his book on the desk.

Students meandered in and gradually every desk was taken.

He's a good teacher; no wonder his class is full.

Fifteen minutes later Philip Byrd had not appeared and Emma knew something was amiss.

Damn. He's not going to teach this class. I bet they changed the schedule.

A moment later a petite woman entered, carrying a briefcase and textbook. Emma was crushed; there was an audible sigh from her fellow students.

"Hello, students. I'm Dr. Ansley. There's been a schedule change and I'll be teaching this class."

My dumb luck, Emma muttered to herself.

It wasn't that she disliked Dr. Ansley; she needed to be in Philip Byrd's class.

"Why, hello, Emma," the perky little woman said to Emma. "I'm glad you're in my class. I haven't seen you in a while. Where have you been?"

"Working on the C.P.S. review course. Now I'm getting back to the regular curriculum."

"Are you going to be a Certified Professional Secretary?"

"I plan to be. I have to pass a two-day exam first."

"You won't have any trouble with it. You'll do great!"

The little woman, who had a Ph.D. in mathematics, was one of Emma's favorite teachers and they enjoyed a good rapport. Dr. Ansley had a way of making her students feel as though they could do anything they set their minds to.

***

Not to be outdone by a change in schedules, Emma went to school the next night. If Philip Byrd was not teaching the Monday-Wednesday class, then he would be there on Tuesdays and Thursdays. She spread out her books on one of the long tables in the accounting room, next door to his class and was writing in her journal when he stuck his head in the door.

"Hi!" he said.

"Huh, hello," she answered. Emma was surprised he was cordial. She had not seen him in almost a year.

"What are you doing in here?" he asked.

"Trying to get some studying done. I can't concentrate at home—too many distractions. I'm keeping a journal, too. I enjoy writing. I'm putting my thoughts on paper."

"Really? I write, too."

"You do?" Emma was surprised he would share something personal. "What do you write?" She smiled at him, trying again to hide her maternal feelings.

"Essays and things."

"Have you been published?"

He laughed.

"No. Never got around to submitting anything for publication."

"Why not?" Emma felt there was something important locked up inside Philip Byrd.

"I don't know. Need to get inspired, I suppose."

"I can relate to that," Emma laughed, nodding her head slowly. "Writers do need inspiration. I was journalism major and I've done a lot of editing. I'd love to read some of your essays."

"Would you? Maybe. I'd have to find them. They're everywhere—at home, at my office. Guess I'm not real organized. I better get to my classroom. Nice to see you again."

"Thank you. It was good to see you, too."

Emma was in a stupor after Philip Byrd left the room.

"He remembered me," she muttered. "He actually remembered me. This is a beginning. If I can talk to him briefly over a period of time, maybe I can sort it out."

A bone-shaking shiver ran down her spine and she went downstairs to the student center to get a cup of coffee.

While she was standing at the vending machine, waiting for it to brew a cup of barely potable coffee, a student from Dr. Ansley's class came up to Emma and asked if she had any change.

"Hi, Tracie," Emma said. "Let me see."

Emma reached into the designer handbag Larry had given her for Christmas and pulled out her wallet. She gave the cute black girl four quarters and Tracie handed her a dollar bill.

"Are you getting a lot out of Dr. Ansley's economics class?" Tracie asked.

"She's a good teacher. To tell you the truth, though, I signed up for Mr. Byrd's class."

167

"You, too! I think a lot of us thought we were getting him. I had him for macro last quarter. He's the best teacher I've ever had."

Tracie's eyes twinkled merrily and a smile lit up her face. It was obvious she adored Mr. Byrd.

"Yes, I know. I feel the same way," Emma said.

The coffee finished brewing. Emma lifted the door on the machine, cautiously picked up the boiling hot cup and went back upstairs. She had to make more entries in her journal.

CHAPTER FOURTEEN

"I wrote to you with many tears"
-2 Corinthians 2:4

Emma was listening to the traffic report while driving to work a few days later. She was distressed because another class had taken over the accounting room next to Mr. Byrd's room and any chance of casual conversations with him had been squashed.

"Interstate two-eighty-five is clean and green; seventy-five southbound is slowing down near the river and backed up to Windy Hill. I-twenty east bound is—"

When the reporter said I-twenty, Emma's heart began beating rapidly and she felt faint. She clasped the steering wheel as tight as her sore arms would allow. Then, out of nowhere, Emma saw a doorway. A sign was hanging over it. On the sign were the numerals 'two' and 'zero.' Mr. Byrd was milling around a group of people. Emma blinked, trying to erase the vision from her mind. In a stupor she drove to work, no longer hearing the radio or the traffic report. A doorway and the number twenty. What in the world was her mind trying to tell her now?

That evening she called Rachel to tell her twin about the new vision.

"I've got to tell him, Rachel," Emma said.

"How are you going to do that? You still don't know what's going to happen. You've tried talking to him. You never got anywhere. A lot of people don't believe in e.s.p. He won't understand your special feelings, Emma. He'll think you're loony."

"I don't care what he thinks of me, Rachel. I don't matter. She does. My sweet, beautiful lady is important to him—or she will be if he ever finds her. I can't let something bad happen to her. I can't; I won't; regardless of what he thinks of me."

"Did it ever occur to you that she may be representative of something dear to him; that she may not be a real person?"

"What do you mean?"

"Even though you think he loves her doesn't mean she is now or ever will be a real person. She might be a symbol for someone he admires—or works for. Or maybe a child."

Emma gasped. His child. Was something bad going to happen to his child?

"He told me he has one child, a daughter. She's a senior in high school."

"There you go. This aura could be anyone he's close to."

"I never thought of it that way. I always thought she was real; that she took up a real void in his life."

"Emma, why do you think there's a void in his life?"

"I have no idea. I do know he needs this person, or whatever it is she represents."

"Why?"

"I don't know how I know; he just does."

Rachel sighed. There was no changing her sister's mind.

"What are you going to do?"

"I'll write him a letter."

"I don't think that will work."

"Why not. I couldn't bring myself to talk to Mr. Durden because I was worried about what he'd think of me. I thought about calling his wife, to warn her. Then I was afraid she'd think I was crazy. I did nothing; absolutely nothing. That was the worst mistake I ever made in my life. I live with it every day."

"Emma St. Claire, listen to me. You weren't responsible for that girl's accident. You didn't cause it! It wasn't your fault."

"I could have stopped it. I didn't. My fear of what the Durden's would think of me kept me from doing what I should have done."

A silence overcame the twins while recalling the agony of that weekend.

Emma was secretary to the regional manager of a multi-national corporation and worked in the local office in Decatur. She admired her boss. They had a beautiful rapport, although other employees thought he was a pompous, stuffed shirt. Emma always felt a depth to him the others did not appreciate. He was devoted to his wife, Katherine, and their two teenagers, a son, Ed, nineteen and a seventeen year old daughter, Sally.

Mr. Durden and Emma often talked about their teenager's school activities and it was during one of these conversations, six weeks before Sally's senior prom, that Emma got a profound and disturbing special feeling.

"Is Allison going to her senior prom?" Mr. Durden asked.

"Yes, she is," Emma beamed. "How about Sally?"

He nodded his head. "She and her mother sure know how to spend money when prom time comes around."

An uneasy feeling came over Emma. Her body felt weak, almost limp. She leaned against a doorframe to steady herself while forcing herself to smile at her boss, seated at his desk.

Emma saw dark water surrounding Sally. A nauseous sensation settled in her stomach. She tried to shake off the vision.

"I know about mothers and prom dresses. They're never too expensive, are they?" she laughed, trying to hide the unusual, unpleasant feeling pulsing through her body. Emma's heart beat like a drum and the vision of Sally and the prom and dark water flowed before her eyes.

Emma returned to her desk, shaking.

What does it mean? The prom. Dark water?

The next few weeks she agonized over the premonition. What should she do? Tell Mr. Durden that Sally should stay away from dark water at the prom? What in the world did that mean, anyway?

Maybe there will be water on a dark street; she should wear her seat belt. Maybe there will be a pool at the prom; she shouldn't go near it. Surely a pool would be lit at night; it wouldn't be dark.

How could Emma explain something both troubling and vague? Her boss might think she had lost her mind and she'd be fired.

As the weeks before the prom passed, Emma became more and more disturbed. Then Allison was injured at a soccer game and Emma was shocked. She had no warning until moments before Allison's face was smashed.

That girl is going to hurt Allison.

Allison jumped up to head the ball. When she came down, the short, stocky player on the other team jumped up—straight into Allison's face. Allison's mouth and cheek took a direct blow from the crown of the rival's head, rupturing the inside of her cheek and tearing her lip open in three places. Blood spurted from Allison's mouth and she doubled over in agony. Teammates ran to Allison, begging her to stay in the game.

"We need you Allison. We're winning—you can't leave now!"

Allison bravely played her sweeper position, defending the goal against an avalanche of kicks on her goalie by the vicious opponents. Emma and Allison could not enjoy the exciting two to one victory over their archrivals; they headed straight to the hospital, where a plastic surgeon was waiting.

The next few weeks Emma chauffeured Allison back and forth to numerous appointments with the plastic surgeon and oral surgeon and pushed to the back of her mind the nagging premonition about Sally and dark water. Doctors worked in tandem to repair damage to Allison's face and Emma was relieved to learn the scars would not be disfiguring.

The morning of Sally's prom, Emma was awakened early by the overwhelming vision of dark water.

"If it starts to rain, I'm going to call Katherine and tell her that Sally needs to wear a seat belt tonight, that the car might be in an accident caused by water on the road."

Emma fought the dreadful premonition and kept herself busy with usual Saturday chores; the unbearable fear would not relinquish its hold on her. Even a long walk with Alex down to the lake did not relieve her anxiety. She shopped for groceries, cleaned the house and ironed clothes. In the afternoon she labored in the yard, mowing grass, pulling weeds and planting dozens of red geraniums and pink impatiens. No amount of activity could ease the mental burden. It was the second weekend in May, the weather was glorious and there was no sensible explanation for her despair about Sally, the prom and dark water.

Late Saturday night, Emma dropped off to sleep, praying for Sally.

Sunday morning Emma arrived at church, worn out from lack of sleep. Walking into a classroom, she noticed a friend's husband sitting near the back wall. He was wearing shorts, as were many others that day; after the church service they would be going to a local park for the annual picnic. The moment Emma saw Bob, she had another alarming vision.

A mental picture of Kristen, Bob and Jane's beautiful two-year old daughter, flashed before Emma's eyes. Kristen was holding out one arm— covered with blood. Blood washed over the vision and Emma could only see red. There were more perceptions, more dark feelings Emma could not acknowledge. She was terrified.

"Where's Jane?" she asked Bob.

"Down stairs, in the three-year old class. Why? Is something wrong?" he asked, noticing the strange look on Emma's face.

"No, I need to talk to Jane."

Emma ran down stairs to the three-year old room and found Jane standing by the doorway, greeting the children.

"Hi, Emma!" the beautiful woman said to Emma. Emma felt that she and Jane were kindred spirits since they were both redheads.

"Jane," Emma said guardedly, knowing she would sound foolish. She had to do something; the vision of precious Kristen and blood was more than she could bear.

"Jane, do you believe in e.s.p.?" she stammered.

Jane was shocked. The look on her face showed she was scared.

"I don't know much about it. Why do you ask?"

"I have e.s.p., Jane. I've had a lot of episodes. Some are good and some are warnings of danger. I don't know exactly what they mean; I've had enough of them to listen to them—sometimes—and I've had one this morning about Kristen."

"What! What was it?"

Jane was disturbed and wanted to know more. She had waited many long years to give birth to the beautiful baby and she was not about to turn a deaf ear toward a friend who may know of some harm coming to her beloved child.

"I don't know what it means. I see her arm and then a lot of blood—It's—it's—awful, Jane. I'm terrified."

Emma reached out and squeezed Jane's hand tightly.

"When? Where?"

"At the picnic. She'll be hurt at the picnic when you're not watching her."

"At the picnic. Then we shouldn't go to the picnic?"

"No. You don't have to miss it. I know your boys were looking forward to it. Don't take your eyes off of Kristen. Not for one moment, Jane. Please. Please don't let anything happen to that adorable little girl. She'll be fine if you watch her. Promise me you'll watch her, Jane," Emma pleaded.

"I promise, Emma. I won't take my eyes off her."

"Thank you, Jane," Emma said, feeling relief from the terrifying vision. Everything would be okay, now; there was no more cause for worry.

"Are you positive it will be okay for us to go?"

"Yes, I am. Now that you are aware of it, you'll watch her and everything will be fine."

Emma left Jane standing in the doorway, surrounded by three year olds, with a very puzzled look on her face.

The church was quiet when Emma entered; everyone else was in Sunday school. She knelt down and prayed a long time, asking God over and over, *Why, Lord? Why do these things come to me?*

She felt weak, almost faint and sat back on the pew.

What about Sally? Why did I have that awful premonition about Sally and dark water?

Emma was busy at her desk on Monday morning when the phone rang; she was surprised to hear Tom Durden's voice.

"I thought you were on your way to Savannah this morning," Emma said. It wasn't typical for her boss to call while in route. He usually called when he arrived at his destination.

"I'm still in Atlanta," he replied flatly.

His voice sounded tired and strained. Emma was scared. Her heart beat wildly, pounding in her ears.

No, no. Not Sally. Not that lovely young woman. No, Lord. Please. No.

"There's been an accident," Tom stammered.

She started to cry.

"What? What happened? Is it Sally? Please tell me she's okay."

"Sunday morning, after the prom—she and some other kids—rafting on the Chattahoochee River—"

"No, please no," Emma pleaded desperately, as if it would do any good now.

Dark water swirled around Emma's head, pulling her into a deep, dark whirlpool; she floated helplessly.

No. Not dark water. Please not dark water.

"What about the Chattahoochee?" she finally asked her boss.

"Sally dove in—"

"No, please don't tell me that—" Emma cried.

"She was rafting with kids she had been to the prom with," he said, slowly and deliberately, having regained his composure for a moment. "She dove into the river, hit her head on a submerged log and broke her neck."

"God, no!" Emma moaned.

"We're at the hospital. She's a quadriplegic. She's barely hanging on—she's strong and we know she's going to make it—she's paralyzed. She'll be paralyzed from her neck down for the rest of her life."

"I'm very sorry," Emma said, dabbing at her eyes. "When can I see her? I need to see her."

"No! Not now. We don't want anyone to see her! Not for a while."

He sounded both mad and defensive. He would not stand for his lovely, vivacious child to go on display in her desperate situation. Not his Sally. His life was perfect. Everything was perfect. At least it had been, until Sally dove into the dark water of the Chattahoochee the morning after the prom.

Emma St. Claire had seen it; she had seen it six weeks before it happened. Had she understood it and known Sally's plans, Emma would have warned her; then things would have been different. Like Kristen. Emma saw Kristen getting hurt at the picnic; she told Jane and that changed fate. Kristen would be okay and Sally would be a quadriplegic for the rest of her life and Emma St. Claire would have to live with that forever.

After Mr. Durden hung up, Emma placed another call.

I'll call Jane. She'll understand. I know she will.

"Jane, this is Emma St. Claire."

"Hi, Emma," she paused. "You sound upset. What's wrong?"

"My e.s.p., Jane—"

"Kristen is fine, Emma. I never took my eyes off her. I never let her out of my sight and the boys had a grand time at the picnic."

"I'm glad to hear that, Jane."

Because Emma had talked to her friend, Jane would never know the agony Emma had seen in the visions of Kristen—the severed arm, the dark oppression of death. If Emma had been able to reach out to her boss, the way she had reached out to Jane, he too could have been spared the agony. Why? Why one and not the other? The guilt consumed Emma. She started to cry.

Between wrenching sobs, Emma told her friend the story of Sally and dark water. Jane was kind and supportive, assuring Emma it was not her fault, she should not blame herself. Her soft voice calmed Emma and the searing pain of Sally's accident slightly abated.

"You're going to have to be strong for your boss, Emma," Jane counseled.

Emma thought about her friend's words; how wise she was. Of course, Emma would have to be strong. Her beloved psychology professor's words echoed:

God is making you strong for a purpose.

***

Sally's accident left an indelible impression on Emma. Now, five years later, she found herself entangled in mind-boggling premonitions about people she did not know and the looming shadow that hung over her teacher in the worst nightmare haunted Emma's every waking hour.

Excessive and obsessive worry took a toll on Emma. She lost so much weight her clothes hung like sacks on a skeleton and dark circles under her eyes added to her haunting appearance. Intractable pain in her arms continued though her doctor could find no cause for the disabling ailment.

Worse still was the apprehension that she had completely lost her mind in spite of the psychiatrist's diagnosis. Why did the dreams torment her if she was not insane? What other plausible explanation could there be?

***

Emma was sitting in the student lounge, drinking coffee, when a message flashed through her mind.

Mr. Byrd is here.

Puzzled, she looked up from her economics book.

Why in the world would I think that? Mr. Byrd is here.

Out of curiosity she got up from the table, walked across the cafeteria to the lobby, and looked out the glass door to the teachers' parking lot. Philip Byrd was getting out of his car.

That's weird.

Emma tried to resume her studies. Her mind wandered. She couldn't concentrate and closed the book, forgetting the economics test.

***

Her sleep was bombarded with loud noises, Mr. Byrd kneeling in the field, blood dripping off his hands, and the party in the Tudor house. It was another sleepless night.

The next evening at school she ran into Tracie at the vending machines.

"You ready for our test?" Tracie teased Emma.

"What? What test?"

"Don't you remember? Dr. Ansley said we'd have a quiz on the first two chapters. Ought to be easy; she said the questions would come from the study guide."

"I forgot about it. The study guide? I haven't even opened mine yet. Is it hard?"

Tracie laughed; her eyes twinkled.

"Are you kidding? You'll breeze through it."

"I don't know about that. I haven't read anything."

"Come on upstairs. I'll give you the answers."

The two women rushed upstairs to the empty classroom and Tracie gave Emma the answers to the multiple-choice questions.

"The answer to number one is A. Two is C. Three is—"

Tracie called out the answers as fast as she could.

"Tracie, this doesn't mean anything to me. I haven't read the material."

"Maybe it will help anyway."

The classroom filled, Dr. Ansley came in, told the students to put away their books and put one sheet of paper and a pencil on their desks. Then she handed out the test questions.

I'm going to flunk this course before it gets started, Mr. Philip Byrd. I'm in a jam because of you. You better get me out of this.

Emma read the first question, analyzed the options for the answer and put a mark on her answer sheet. Then she read the next question.

This is easy.

She read the multiple-choice answers, thoughtfully reviewed each and put another mark on her paper. Before she knew it, she finished. Emma read and answered forty questions on economics, a subject she knew nothing about. She not only understood the questions, she knew why the multiple-choice answers were either right or wrong.

Students exchanged their answer sheets, questions discussed and grades recorded. Then Dr. Ansley returned the tests. Emma was euphoric. She made a ninety-five. She was grinning from ear to ear until she realized what she had done.

Although Emma did not read the text, she made an almost perfect score. She unwittingly invoked her powers of e.s.p. and read Philip Byrd's mind. When she realized what she had done, her excitement over the good grade fizzled.

I can't believe I did that. Why can I read his mind?

***

Emma could take it no longer. The nightmares and dreams; reading Mr. Byrd's mind. Visions painted by traffic reports. It had gone on too long; far too long. The office was quiet and she typed a letter.

"Dear Mr. Byrd—"

"No, Dear Philip would be better."

She snatched it out of the typewriter and started again. Emma had no idea what to say. She only knew she had to get it behind her, once and for all. After she told Jane about Kristen there was immediate relief. Emma needed relief. Her second letter was no better. She wrote it as an analogy to a baseball game; it was humorous. Then she read it over and it sounded as if she wanted to score with Mr. Byrd. No, that was not her intent. She tore it into tiny bits.

After several more tries, Emma had a letter that she thought would do the trick. She said that she needed to explain something to him, that she did not intend to be meddling in his personal life. Then she went on to say that she was empathic.

I can't tell him I have e.s.p. and I surely can't tell him that he's a little child, that I feel motherly toward him. He'd be mortified if he knew I could read his mind; empathy is different. People understand empathy.

Then Emma said she could sense a storm though she had no idea why she wanted to say that. It was as if some sort of dream interpretation was going on subconsciously while she wrote.

She concluded by saying he would survive the storm, that she never had feelings such as these before and was bewildered and dismayed by them and that by writing to him she hoped to rid herself of the feelings.

"—and I'll pray for the sun to shine on you always," she added at the end.

It didn't make any sense to Emma; she had to give it to him. She had to.

That afternoon J.D. was playing soccer at the stadium adjacent to the college. During half time Emma walked over to the Administration building. Without giving it any thought, she knew precisely when Mr. Byrd would be there.

When Emma arrived at the entrance, Philip Byrd burst through the door.

"Hi," he said, smiling down at her. For the first time since she met him, he did not appear as a child to her. He was a full-grown man. It caught her off guard.

Why does he look different?

Give it to him, her silent voice prodded.

She handed him the envelope.

"I've needed to tell you something for a long time," she said, smiling up at him. For the first time in her life she felt petite; and Philip Byrd was a grown up man.

"What about?" He looked amused and befuddled as if to say, "Why didn't you talk to me?"

Was she reading his mind again?

Emma turned and walked away; Philip Byrd was holding a letter from a student with e.s.p. Would he ever understand? Would he ever talk to her?

Emma walked quickly; she could feel Mr. Byrd's eyes staring at her. She rounded the corner of the building and disappeared from his view.

Your life will never be the same, her silent voice said.

What the heck, she said in defiance. *My life hasn't been the same since the day I walked into his classroom.*

She went back to the stadium and cheered loudly for J.D. and his team. The next evening, Emma and her handsome son were flying to Dallas; and Saturday, she would see her father for the first time in more than twenty years. The episode with Philip Byrd was finally behind her.

***

Jim dropped Emma and J.D. at the entrance to the Atlantic Airlines terminal and they raced for the plane. Traffic had tied up the freeway and they would never have made the flight if Jim had not known a back route. When they boarded the plane Emma stopped and stared at the captain. There was something at the back of her mind. They started through the first class section and she stopped again. She stared blankly at empty seats, shook her head and followed her son to the back of the plane.

The flight was uneventful except for J.D.'s excitement at being on an L1011. It was the first time he had flown in one and he read every word on the passenger information card and chatted about the very specific sound of the plane's Rolls Royce engines.

"Engines sound different, Mom," he explained. "Boeing and McDonnell-Douglas both make their own engines. A DC-10 doesn't sound anything like an L1011."

He looked out the window and the glittering lights of Atlanta, fading into the horizon.

"As long as it keeps us in the air and gets us safely from point A to point B that's what I care about, Darlin'."

"Have you ever been scared on a flight, Mom?"

"Nope. Never. If I was, I wouldn't fly. "

"I thought you flew through a hurricane one time."

"I did. When I was pregnant with Allison. We were on vacation in Florida with Janice and David and a hurricane ripped up the west coast. I had to fly because my doctor wouldn't let me sit in a car for ten hours. Grandpa arranged to get me on the last plane out of Tampa a few hours before the main strike of the storm."

"You weren't scared?"

"No, of course not. I knew that me and my baby would be okay."

"How did you know that?"

"I have a special little voice that tells me things I need to know to keep me and my family safe."

"Right on, Mom," he said in a facetious manner. J.D. did not believe in e.s.p.

"I landed in a blizzard in Fort Wayne one time but that didn't scare me either."

"What did your special voice say that time?"

"It said don't be scared."

"Was anyone else on the plane scared?"

"Everyone, I suppose. We had to put our heads down to our knees. The plane almost skidded off the runway. The pilot did a masterful job stopping it. It taxied back to the terminal and when we got there no one wanted to get off."

"They were still scared?"

"No. They were waiting for the pilot. When he finally opened the door from his area—"

"You mean the flight deck, Mom."

"Yes, the flight deck. Anyway, when he came through the door we gave him a standing ovation."

The flight attendants served dinner and before they knew it Emma and J.D. were landing at Dallas-Fort Worth where Emma's Uncle Ed affectionately greeted them.

***

The two-hour trip to Salado the next morning was relaxing. J.D. did the driving and Emma did the viewing. She oohed and aaahed at every new vista, never having seen such open, flat space before. The trees, swept by prevailing winds from the southeast, fascinated her. There was little color, other than occasional green fields of tender young grasses or some sort of purple wildflowers she did not recognize.

"Are you nervous about seeing your dad?" J.D. asked.

180

"No, I'm not. I guess I surprise myself by that. I'm excited, not nervous. We've had a lot of correspondence in the last year and we've already made up for a lot of separation."

"Are you nervous about meeting your grandfather?" Emma asked.

"No—well, maybe a little."

"I think y'all will hit it off great. He loves sports. He played basketball for Tech until he was injured."

"Do you think my knee problem was inherited from him?"

"Possibly. Maybe the tendency to have that sort of problem, anyway. Of course, Allison's back problem is definitely genetic; medical tests proved that."

"I can't imagine how it would be to grow up without a father. Daddy makes a lot of mistakes but at least he tries."

"Yes, I know he does. I think my dad tried, too, even though I never heard his side of the story."

"Do you think he'll tell you?"

"Of course. I think I'll have a lot of questions answered on this trip."

"Such as?"

"Why I always felt he was close to me."

"You lived in different states. How could you think he was close by?"

"No, not close by in proximity—in heart. There was something he did that made him very close; I don't know what it was."

"Did you have fun growing up?"

"We had lots of fun; especially at my grandmother's. We stayed at her big place in Dunwoody every summer and special occasions were just that—special. Bee had a way of making birthdays and Christmas and Thanksgiving quite wonderful even though she was always hard on me because I was my Daddy's twin; Aunt Rachel was her twin."

"I'm glad I have both you and Daddy."

"I am, too, J.D."

She reached over and patted her son gently on the shoulder. They were silent for a while, both of them enjoying the expansive view. After several miles of comfortable quiet, J.D.'s curiosity about his mother's childhood reopened the conversation.

"What's the best thing you remember about your childhood?"

"My goodness, J.D., what a question. Can you be more specific?"

He mulled over his mother's question. "What was your favorite thing?"

"My favorite thing. Oh, that's easy!"

Memories of a little emerald green angora tam flowed through Emma's mind and she smiled.

"Grandmother Browning sent me and Aunt Rachel the most beautiful green tams when we were about six years old—"

"What's a tam?" he interrupted.

"A little hat—a beret—"

"That was your favorite thing?"

He was a little incredulous that a hat would be something special.

"Sure was; and they had matching purses. We wore those tams until we were too big for them—they were little beanies on our heads—Bee finally took them away from us.

"I'll never forget the day they arrived. We were ecstatic when we opened the box; I think it was a birthday present. Anyway, Bee fussed over them and she went on and on about how beautiful they were and about how expensive they must have been because they came from Neiman Marcus."

"Neiman Marcus? Wow! I never had anything from Neiman Marcus."

"Grandmother Browning sent us a lot of things from Neiman's over the years and of course, Bee always made a fuss over them. I never had anything I cared for as much as that green tam."

He cocked his head and gave his mother a lopsided smile.

"A tam. Why would a tam be your favorite thing?"

"I don't know, J.D. It was special. I loved that little green tam."

CHAPTER FIFTEEN

"My help comes from the Lord."
-Psalm 121:2

Emma's father was sitting in a bronze-colored Cadillac where he said he'd be, in front of a quaint country store on the edge of town.

"Here goes, J.D.," Emma said to her son.

She felt neither scared nor timid. Rachel's words echoed through her mind, "You're awfully brave, Emma. I'm glad you're going to see Daddy; I don't think I could do it."

Emma put her hand on the door and slowly emerged. She stood next to the car for a moment, looked up at the cloudless blue sky, took a deep breath, and walked straight across the parking lot.

"Hi, Daddy," she said boldly, as if she had seen her father the day before.

From under the rim of an old straw hat, two deep-set, watery eyes peered up at her.

"Hello, Darlin'," her father said, reaching through the open window for her hand.

His weathered, wrinkled hand still had a strong grip. Looking down at her father's long, tapering, artistic fingers, Emma saw hands that escaped the throes of arthritis that bent and deformed his spine. He was rail thin, and except for a somewhat shabby gray beard, Mr. Browning looked about the way she imagined. His kind melodious voice reflected a deep sense of peace.

I'm delighted I came.

J.D. finally exited the car and came trotting over to the Cadillac.

"Daddy, I want you to meet my son—your grandson—"

The old man's eyes glistened with moisture and he dabbed at them with a linen handkerchief.

"Hello there, young man."

He released his hold on his daughter's hand and reached for his grandson.

"Got ya a big one, didn't you?" he said, looking up at his daughter. "Must have some Browning genes in him."

"That he does, Daddy. That he does."

They drove into Salado, an old town on the Chisholm Trail where the original Stagecoach Inn still stood. Emma could feel the excitement that hailed the arrival of each horse-drawn coach as it came to a jolting stop in a cloud of dust, the shrill of the horses' whinny, ladies in long dresses gracefully exiting the carriage, dainty hankies shielding their delicate noses from blasts of dirty air. The inn was a welcome stopover on their westward journey. Emma sensed it as if it were happening at that moment. She had always loved stories of the Wild West and felt she belonged there.

Mr. Browning gave them a brief tour of town before stopping in front of a restored, picturesque ante-bellum house.

"Thought you'd appreciate this Bed and Breakfast; it will be quieter than the Stagecoach; has more privacy. Lindy, my wife, hasn't been feeling too good lately and we thought you'd enjoy it here. We're not up to entertaining," he said apologetically.

"This is lovely, Dad," Emma said enthusiastically.

She always wanted to stay in a bed and breakfast and couldn't imagine one with more atmosphere. They were greeted in the parlor by a handsome man in his early thirties who obviously knew Mr. Browning.

"I'm putting your daughter and grandson in the General Custer Suite," he said proudly.

"Splendid," the old man said, very pleased that his daughter was getting the finest accommodations.

The General Custer suite was furnished with beautiful Victorian antiques, two comfortable beds covered with hand crocheted comforters and stunning colored quilts. Walls were adorned with oil paintings and daguerreotype photographs; beveled glass windows were trimmed with delicate lace curtains. A window at the back of the room looked out on a slate patio, covered by an arbor from which hung lavender wisteria blossoms. From the double window at the side of the room Emma could see a rose garden.

"This is a dream," she beamed, "a beautiful dream."

The proprietor smiled.

J.D. laid their garment bag on the suitcase rack, kicked off his shoes and flopped onto the chaise lounge, upholstered with a rose-patterned chintz.

"Can we stay here forever, Mom," he teased.

J.D.'s removal of his shoes before crashing onto the antique recliner did not escape Mr. Browning's attention.

"Glad to see you've taught my grandson some manners," he said to Emma, nodding his head approvingly.

***

After picking up Lindy at the Browning's home near a scenic, meandering river adjacent to a golf course, they drove to another town where they ate lunch on the verandah of a charming rustic structure with a breathtaking view of an enormous lake that disappeared into the horizon. Again, they were cordially greeted. It appeared to Emma that her father was known and loved throughout the area.

"What can I get for you today, Mr. Browning?" a cheerful waitress asked.

"My usual," he answered, "and take care of my ladies and my grandson," he instructed before excusing himself.

He was gone for several minutes and drinks were served before he returned. Emma was surprised that a supposedly recovered alcoholic would order a drink when she saw the Scotch on the rocks the waitress put at his place.

"Lindy, can I ask you something?" Emma said haltingly.

The little white haired lady, immaculately groomed and dressed in an expensive suit, forced a smile. It was an uncomfortable situation for her, meeting her husband's grown daughter and grandson for the first time.

"Why, yes, I suppose. What do you want to know?"

Emma was not surprised that the atmosphere was a little strained.

"Is my dad an alcoholic?"

Lindy laughed, "Oh, no, dear. I've never even seen him drunk. Why would you ask such a thing?"

"I was lead to believe he had a drinking problem."

"Sugar, I've known your dad forty years. We've been married thirty-eight. He enjoys his liquor. I've never seen him take more than two drinks."

Emma and J.D. looked at each other with quizzical expressions.

After a scrumptious lunch they drove back to the Browning's home.

"The Lakers are playing this afternoon, J.D. Want to watch the game with me?" Mr. Browning asked.

J.D. plopped down on the sofa and started talking sports with his grandfather, and not wanting to interrupt a good conversation the two were enjoying, Emma quietly slipped away and went to Lindy's room. The elderly woman was stretched out on her bed, resting. Her eyes were open and Emma knocked gently on the open door. Lindy looked in Emma's direction.

"Can we talk?" Emma asked coyly.

Lindy smiled and moved over on the bed.

"Come, sit down," she said, patting the space next to her. Emma sat gingerly on the edge of the bed.

"You can't imagine how much it means to me and my son to have a visit with my dad. I hope you don't feel we are interfering."

The elegant little woman stared at Emma and the corners of her lips turned up.

"Why, no, Dear. Of course not. I think you're very brave to come way out here to see your father after such a long, long time. He's been looking forward to seeing the two of you ever since you called. At our age, with our infirmities, we never know when our time might be up. I think it's good that you came."

"Is dad sick?"

"No. Old age and that damn arthritis."

They talked for a long while with Lindy telling Emma about her career in Washington D.C., where she was the head of a prestigious labor relations law firm. Lindy's credentials were as long as Emma's arm; she was a very impressive woman. Lindy's first husband died shortly after the birth of her third child and she raised her children alone, supporting them with her law practice.

Lindy was several years older than Mr. Browning, and since her children were born when she was a young woman, and his children were born when he was approaching forty, by the time they met her children were out of the nest. Right from the start of their relationship, Lindy knew what Emma's mother faced and she begged him to return to Atlanta, to fix things up with his family, before they married. It never worked out.

Then Lindy told Emma a story about some dolls that she and Mr. Browning bought for the twins.

"They were expensive. Your dad always wanted you to have the best. He was going to give them to you girls when he had a visit but your mother was very bitter. She wouldn't let him see you."

"You mean, Daddy came to visit and Mother wouldn't let him see us?"

"That's right; many, many times. Since he never gave you girls those dolls we finally gave them to a photographer who had a studio on Piedmont Road.

186

He used them in the most beautiful display window. I told him he had to put names on them—one was Rachel and the other was Emma."

Lindy's emotions were genuine and it showed.

"Your dad made every effort to stay close to you children," she said, taking Emma's hand in hers. "It broke his heart not to see you. We finally moved out here and started our lives over."

"When Dad was talking about our infancy and early years at lunch today, I felt a lot of love. A man would not remember the many minute details of his children had he not loved them dearly."

Emma squeezed Lindy's hand, got up and went into the bathroom to get a Kleenex. Then she boldly sat on the bed again. She was comfortable.

"Didn't you miss your law practice when you came to Texas with Daddy?"

"No. By then I was burned out. I did have a very active mind though; hours and hours of driving got boring to me—he was in real estate development—we spent a lot of time on the road—anyway, I took up knitting, to keep my hands busy. Never have been good at doing nothing.

"I used to make things for my children and grandchildren on those trips. Sweaters and mittens and booties. I even made some things for you and Rachel. I never knew if you got them."

"What?" Emma was pleased to know that her father's wife had made something for her and her twin sister.

"We were in this little border town near Mexico one day. While your dad was in meetings I explored the town and came across a shop that had rare imported yarns. I bought up every skein of green angora they had—"

Emma could not believe she was hearing the words 'green angora.'

"—and I knit the prettiest little tams for you and Rachel. I bought green because I thought it would be pretty with your red hair. Then I made purses to match."

Emma wiped her eyes and smiled at the little woman. Her heart beat with excitement.

"When we got back to Dallas your dad said, 'Bee will never let the twins have something from me. Why don't you take labels out of some dresses and I'll get my mother to send the girls these tams for their birthdays. That way, they will have something from me.'"

Emma shook her head slowly, choking back a lifetime of emotions.

"That's exactly what I did. I went into my closet and carefully removed labels from two of my Neiman Marcus suits. Then I sewed them in your tams, wrapped them in birthday paper and took them to your grandmother in Dallas. She mailed them for us."

Emma leaned down and kissed Lindy on the cheek.

"I always knew Daddy tried to be close to me. Rachel and I treasured those tams. Now I know why."

***

On the flight home, Emma opened an old Bible, a gift from her father. It was personalized with underscored passages and notes written in margins, penned in precise script. The trip was more successful than anything Emma could have imagined. A void in her life was filled.

By the first weekend in May of 1989, Emma was deeply stranded in the quagmire of mental despair and physical pain and she could hardly function. Her left arm, almost useless, hung limply at her side and she could not feel typewriter keys with her fingers.

Ever the optimist, Emma tried to see the humor in her predicament by thinking how funny she must look—the Keystone Cop routine she used to open the heavy, unwieldy door on her Pontiac. After unlocking the door and pushing the latch button, she would pry her foot into the narrow opening. Then using her leg, she would push the door open with her knee. Once seated, she would reach across herself with her right arm to close the door.

Dropping things because she had no strength in her hands was a common occurrence. She started drinking out of plastic toddler cups because she broke glasses. Emma laughed at this, too, saying that she would grow up—one day.

The next Saturday morning she awoke with another brutal migraine and except for a few trips to the kitchen to take aspirin, and check on her son, she stayed in bed, curled in a fetal position. She cried; and she prayed.

Later in the afternoon the headache let up, and deciding she was suffering for no sensible reason, Emma pulled herself out of bed and took a hot shower. The water was soothing to her sore neck muscles and she stood there for a long while before shampooing her hair and sudsing down her rail thin body.

With a towel turban around her head, and a bath sheet wrapping her body, she sauntered through the house, pausing briefly to watch a golf tournament on the TV with J.D.

"Are you feeling better, Mom?" he asked in his deep soft-spoken voice.

"Yes, I am, Darlin'. Sorry I've been useless lately—"

Conversation was taxing; Emma fought with her emotions. She abruptly changed the subject.

"What tournament is this?"

"Doral," J.D. answered.

"Where's it being played?"

"Mom, the Doral is played at The Doral Country Club."

"Yeah—it is. My head hurts. I can't think—"

Lost in a maze of pain, Emma went to her closet in the room off the kitchen and dressed. After the ordeal of getting herself into clothes, she took a walk to the lake with Alex. The outing was therapeutic and Emma felt much better when she returned. She thumbed through a stack of mail on the kitchen table and excitedly called her son.

"J.D—Look here, Darlin'."

She held up a letter from Centre College in Kentucky. J.D. was accepted for a Senior Scholars Summer Workshop to begin in June. Emma hugged her son.

"I'm very, very proud of you, J.D. You'll meet other students from all over the country. What a thrill."

In a nonchalant manner J.D. shrugged his shoulders and ambled back into the family room. Emma picked up another envelope and turned it over. The return address was Hampton, Virginia. Here it was. An invitation to her precious Godchild's wedding. She read it three times.

Emma was eager to go to the wedding but in a quandary. She didn't know what to do. After thinking about it a few minutes she called to her son.

"Guess what, J.D.?"

"What, Mom?"

"Patty Reynolds' wedding is the same day you report to Centre. How am I going to be two places at once?"

"Can you wait a sec," he said. "Tom Kite is about to make a long putt."

Emma watched the golfer make the putt, knowing it was pointless to get J.D.'s attention at that moment.

"Now, what?" he said, looking up at his mother from his place on the floor.

"Patty's wedding is the same day you start at Centre."

"And?" he asked.

"How can I be in Kentucky and Virginia at the same time?"

"Don't go to Kentucky," he said in a matter of fact tone.

"J.D., you're going off to college for the summer. I want to go with you and help you get set up."

"Mom, for heaven's sake."

Why are the things that mothers consider important unimportant to their children?

"What am I going to do?"

"Take Allison to the wedding. Daddy can take me to college. No big deal."

Since Emma's dilemma did not seem to bother J.D. she went back into the kitchen and reached for the wall phone.

"Hey, Darlin'," she said when Allison answered. "What do you think about going to a fancy wedding in Virginia?"

***

The next weekend was the holiday Emma dreaded most—Mother's Day. For years she graciously entertained Bee and Janice. When Emma's children were young, she would have welcomed a Sunday away from the kitchen. The longed-for honor never came her way. She finally began to resent the day altogether. At one of the annual events, with the meal prepared by Emma, and the gifts purchased and wrapped by Emma, she presented a poem to Allison and J.D. "What is Mother's Day?" the title asked.

In simple prose she wrote about the special days that made her thankful and proud to be their mother—the triumphs and tragedies that made up the memorable moments in their lives—academic achievements, athletic pursuits, baptisms and confirmations, mementos they gave to her, J.D.'s bravery during the painful treatments for his burned leg and foot, Allison's tenacity playing soccer with facial injuries. Those days were the real Mother's Day—not one day set aside the second Sunday of each May.

This year Emma decided to take her mother to brunch after Sunday services at St. Martin's and she called Bee to make the plans.

"How lovely," Bee said, her brown eyes twinkling. "Where are we going to eat?"

"The Fifty-Seventh Fighter Group," Emma answered.

The theme restaurant, next to Peachtree-DeKalb Airport, was the sight of a dinner party Emma and Jim gave after Allison's wedding. It was also the place Steve proposed. The World War II theme was carried out from the main driveway off Clairmont Road, where vintage Army jeeps and trucks were randomly parked, through the bunker entrance stacked with sand bags, to the vast array of memorabilia adorning walls. In some of the booths, earphones were available for those who wished to listen to the air traffic control tower at the busiest general aviation airport in the country. Behind the restaurant sat a restored P-51 Mustang, one of the great pieces of aviation history.

"What fun," she enthused, recalling happy occasions the family celebrated at the Fifty-Seventh.

"It's gonna be you and me. I told Jim to take care of his own mother this year."

"Good for you, Emma" she answered, rubbing her hands together in the manner of an animated child. It was the first time Emma could ever remember looking forward to Mother's Day.

Early Sunday morning Emma awoke crying loudly, "No, No. God, no!"

A new dream weaseled its way into the random display of nightmares poisoning Emma's mind and the profound visions tortured her in a new and meaner way. She was sitting on the front pew at St. Martin's with the little gray-haired lady. Mr. Byrd followed the processional cross down the aisle and stopped in front of the chancel, looking out at the congregation. A crystal vase of white flowers stood beyond him on a pedestal and Emma thought it was a wedding.

From the left hand door appeared an apparition of Emma's sweet, beautiful lady. It floated across the front of the nave, gently touched Mr. Byrd on the shoulder and disappeared. He looked grief-stricken, putting his hands to his face to shield his eyes from the congregation's view. Mr. Byrd followed a procession of people to a small room on the right side of the chancel. Emma turned to the little woman seated next to her and said, "If only she hadn't taken that trip, everything would have been different."

With those words Emma awoke trembling. Even in the deepest throes of anguish, she realized her beautiful lady appeared as an apparition because she had made a transition—to a different plane of existence. The small room was the columbarium—called the Chapel of the Resurrection because it was the final resting place for the ashes of the departed. Emma's sweet beautiful lady was going to die.

***

The splendid service at St. Martin's on Mother's Day morning was nothing short of agony for Emma. She vainly attempted to hide her swollen, red eyes, emptying again a bottle of Visine into them. They burned throughout the service and her arms ached. It was almost impossible for her to hold the prayer book.

She tried to sing hymns in her usual joyful voice. Words hung in her throat and expired. Emma finally gave up, only mouthing them. Her mother looked at her with concern, then went back to her lusty rendition, "A mighty fortress is our God; a bulwark never failing—"

How can I sing and be joyful when that sweet lady is going to die? I've got to stop it. I have to. I don't care what Philip Byrd thinks of me. He's not the one who is going to die. My lady is. I've got to find out how. I can't let it happen.

At the brunch, Emma and Bee were seated at a window overlooking the runway and ordered coffee before perusing the buffet tables where Bee oohed and aaahed over the tantalizing array of food, taking small portions of everything offered. Emma took only a tiny portion of vegetables and eggs Benedict, one of her favorite dishes.

"You ought to eat more, Emma," her mother said. "You've gotten way too thin."

"I feel fine, Mama. I don't want to get fat."

"You've never been fat. You can splurge. It is Mother's Day. You should enjoy it."

"Mama, I've never enjoyed Mother's Day. I loved making it special for you when I was a child. Jim never made it special for me when Allison and J.D. were little. Raising them made me realize that Mother's Day is not a specific Sunday during a year. Mother's Day is the special times your children give you—when Allison calls me to say she's on the Dean's List again, or J.D. made Honor Roll. My children honor me by being the beautiful, loving people they are, working, studying, playing, helping around the house. Those are the real Mothers' Days."

"You're absolutely right, Emma. I guess I never looked at it that way before," she said, putting another fork full of food into her mouth.

"Rachel and I always tried to show you how much we love you, and honor you, by being good, decent people every day. We always wanted you to be proud of us."

"I am proud of you, Emma. No mother ever had two better daughters."

The conversation shifted to gossip about Bees' friends, who was going where and doing what. While her mother prattled on endlessly about insignificant things, Emma's mind agonized over the sweet, beautiful lady.

She's going to die. My sweet, beautiful lady is going to die. Why can't I talk to my own Mother about my dreams and visions? Why, Lord, why? I'm sitting here eating Mother's Day

Brunch while Mother goes on about her friend's latest trip to New Zealand and someone dear is going to die. Oh, God, will this agony ever end?

***

For the rest of the month Emma was tormented by dreams. Every night; incessantly. The sparkle was gone from her eyes and she lost more weight. Her left arm was limp and lifeless; the right one was not much better. Mentally and physically Emma was a wreck; she drifted in and out of every day, intoxicated by intractable pain. She gave Philip Byrd the letter, trying to warn him in an unthreatening way; it was a futile gesture. She had not seen him since.

Then one evening, a week before exams, he came up to her in the Student Center where she was studying for her economics final.

"Hi," he said cheerfully.

Emma was in a state of shock.

"Hello," she said, looking up into his dark eyes.

"Can we talk a minute?" he asked.

"Yes—" she stammered.

He pulled out a chair and sat down.

"I've been looking for you. I want to talk to you about the letter you gave me."

"Oh, that. I'm sorry. My sister said you wouldn't understand."

"No, I didn't. What were you trying to tell me?"

"I'm—I'm—" she could not make herself say the word 'psychic.'

"I have—I— I—have—e.s.p.—" she finally stammered. "That's why I said in the letter that I'm empathic. I can feel what other people feel."

He was surprised and skeptical. Emma sensed he wanted her to continue.

"When I first met you—

Dear Lord, give me the right words to say. I can't tell him I thought he was a baby when I first saw him.

She shivered.

"—I felt there was a storm around you. That someone you love will hurt you," she blurted out, not meaning for it to sound the way it did.

"How?"

"I don't know. I can feel this pain."

Emma put her hand to her heart. There was a throbbing pang deep in her chest.

"I've been psychic since I was a child, shortly after my parent's divorce. I don't ever want someone to get hurt if I can do anything to prevent it."

"Do you think you can interfere with fate?" he said, somewhat annoyed.

"I don't want to interfere with fate. When I see something happen, something bad, I feel it is my responsibility to prevent it. That's why the information comes to me."

"Tell me how you get this *information*."

"Sometimes in dreams. Sometimes in a vision."

Emma immediately regretted using that word vision. Don't insane people see visions and imagine things that aren't there?

He became more skeptical. She was not advancing her cause in any way.

"One time I saw dark water and my boss's daughter. She dove into the Chattahoochee and broke her neck."

Emma was choking on her words.

"That wasn't your fault."

"I know; but I saw it before it happened; and I've lived with it ever since. Now I feel a storm around you and someone you love hurting you."

Emma could not bring herself to say that someone he loved was going to die. She could only spit out the pain he would feel from a loss. She could not admit the sweet beautiful lady was going to—was going to—

"Are you married?" she stammered.

"No."

Now I know she's not his wife.

"Where are you from?" she blurted out, having no idea why she asked that.

"Thomson."

"Is that right? My daughter married a man from Thomson. I love to visit there, especially the lake."

"I enjoy the lake, too. Went to Clark's Hill a lot as a child. Haven't been back in a long time."

There was something rather sad the way he said it and Emma wondered why he had not gone back.

"Tell me," he asked, smiling, "do you feel any—good feelings?"

"Why, yes," Emma said enthusiastically. "Lots of good feelings."

He was pleased. At last Philip Byrd was pleased.

"Lots of good feelings?" he asked again.

"Yes. Lots of good feelings."

"Thank you," he said, standing up. "See you."

He winked, gave her a smile that warmed her to the depths of her soul and left. He appeared to be happy.

Emma shook her head slowly, watching his departure.

Why would he believe the good things and not the bad?

***

Emma's apprehension over Kristen's safety dissipated when she told Jean of the vision and she thought the talk with Philip Byrd relieved her of any further obligation to protect him, or the woman in the dream. She slept soundly the next several nights, undisturbed by mental processes over which she had no control.

Refreshed and relaxed on Saturday morning, Emma drove into Stone Mountain. The new Home Depot on Highway 78 was having a sale of potted plants and Emma wanted to buy geraniums for the porch and roses for the island turn-around in front of the house. Although she still loathed her in-laws' place she was determined to fix it up since her family had to live there.

Emma was thinking about her son that sunny morning, and the pride he brought to her at the honors ceremony the evening after her talk with Philip Byrd. J.D. received the highest awards in the junior class along with a bar for his academic letter. The school year was over and her baby, the precious child she had given birth to almost eighteen years before, was now a senior. Humming the tune, "Oh what a beautiful morning—" Emma pranced into the store.

She was walking toward the landscaping department when another vision flashed before her. Philip Byrd was standing in a dark opening of some sort, pushing on something with both hands. He gasped and looked at his hands. They were bleeding.

Emma was horrified.

Dear God, not again. Not another one. I told him what I felt. I can't do more than that. Please, Dear Lord.

He's here, her silent voice said. *Philip Byrd is here in the store. No. He's leaving. He's getting in a pick-up truck.*

Emma's heart was pounding in her chest; it hurt. She tried to reason with herself.

If I can find him, I can prove I'm psychic. I'll go to where he is and say, I knew you were here. My e.s.p. told me.

Standing alone in a long aisle, surrounded by cans of paint, Emma felt as though she was rising. She could not feel her feet on the floor and she was looking down on her own head. Her heart was beating rapidly; she felt faint. She reached for a shelf to steady herself. She could not feel it, though she knew her right hand was touching it.

Emma was terrified.

Hang on, Emma. You can figure this out. For some reason you are psychically connected to Philip Byrd. He is here, somewhere; your spirit is trying to find him. You are having an out of body experience. I can't have an out of body experience here. My body will collapse. It might die without my spirit in it. I don't want to leave J.D. Hold on. Hold on tight. Don't leave, Emma. Don't leave.

She closed her eyes; it was dark. She could no longer see the top of her head and her heart quit pounding. Her right hand felt the shelf; her feet were on the floor. Emma took a deep breath, slowly exhaled through her mouth and nodded her head as if awakening from a deep sleep.

Whew, that was close.

Feeling as if she had been drugged, Emma moved sluggishly toward the exit door, walked outside and looked for a blue truck.

He was here. I know he was here. He's out there. I know he is. He's in a truck. I know he's in a truck. Damn you, Philip Byrd. Damn. Go away and leave me alone.

***

That night Emma had another dream. She was reading a story on the front page of a newspaper. The date was May 3, 1990. When she awoke, she could not remember anything except the date on the paper. Emma had no idea what the article said.

***

Knowing that Philip Byrd would be in his classroom awaiting the arrival of his students, Emma marched upstairs determined to have another word with him. She knew she would go completely insane if the visions did not stop and she knew of no other way to bring the interminable ordeal to an end.

"Hi," she said cheerfully, sticking her head into his room.

"Hello."

He almost seemed glad to see her.

"I wanted to thank you for talking to me last week," she said timidly. "I know I've been a bother; I appreciate the time you gave me."

He was embarrassed and shrugged off her thanks.

"I saw you the other day," he said, smiling slightly with a somewhat puzzled look on his face.

Emma was surprised.

"You were coming in the door of the new Home Depot on Seventy-Eight as I was going out."

"My e.s.p. was right again," she said.

"What's that supposed to mean?" he almost snapped.

"When I got to the store it told me you were there, too," she tried to explain.

"I told you I don't believe in that stuff."

"I tried to find you to prove to you it's real."

"You wouldn't have seen me. I was in a blue pick-up truck with a friend."

"I thought you were in a truck—"

"No you didn't. You could not have known I was there and you could not have known I was in a truck. There's no such thing as what you call your e.s.p."

Philip Byrd was mad. Real mad. Emma St. Claire ran from the room.

In spite of acute depression over the encounter with her teacher, Emma sat for the final exam in economics. Of course, she aced it. She only had to think of Philip Byrd and the answers came to her.

That night she was bombarded by the terrifying dream of Philip Byrd in the field at night, holding the body of the sweet, beautiful lady. Emma felt she was on the brink of total insanity. The next morning, having nothing else to do, she called Mr. Byrd at his office and tried again to talk to him.

"You need help," he said angrily and hung up the phone.

CHAPTER SIXTEEN

"Where there is no vision, my people perish"
-Proverbs 29:18

Emma was devastated. Completely devastated. He didn't understand. He didn't even try. He closed his mind and nothing she could say would ever get through to Philip Byrd. What else could she have expected anyway? The first time she looked into his eyes she felt the presence of a three year old and that was the way he acted towards her—like a rebellious child. They never had a decent conversation in spite of her efforts to communicate with him.

Philip Byrd was planted in the materialistic, physical realm, while Emma's e.s.p. had her ensnared somewhere in the spiritual world. Emma was scared; very scared. She shook with fright. Her empty stomach ached and retched as if trying to eliminate a deadly poison from her system the way it did when she had meningitis.

Emma talked quietly to herself between retching and tearful sobs.

I've been living with that dear woman's death for two and a half years. He's right; I do need help. Not for me, though; for that sweet, beautiful lady, whoever she is. Why, Dear Lord, why do I love her? It feels futile. Dreadfully futile, like I've been chasing the wind. What in the world should I do? And the little gray-haired lady; she started all this!! Why? Who is she? Why would she do this to me?

Instinctively she opened the telephone book as if it held the answers to her problems. She called Emory University and asked for the psychology department.

"Do you have anyone doing para-psychological research?" Emma asked, trying to sound sane though she felt completely mad.

"No," came the hasty response, reinforcing Emma's feelings. She called Georgia State University with the same result.

There are two million people in Atlanta and I'm not the only one with e.s.p. Surely there's someone in this city who would understand.

Joe came in and dictated a three-page quote. Concentration was not easy and Emma's mind drifted, though she was glad for the diversion. Somehow she managed to type the quote for Joe and he quickly signed it while talking on the phone.

I'm worried I'm going to screw up a quote. Isn't it bad enough to lose sleep over a stranger? Why must my working life be affected, too? Joe never reads anything. What if I make a mistake? I could type the wrong amount and Joe would never know it until it was too late. Then what? I could get fired. Who would hire a lunatic with e.s.p.? I should die now and get it over with. I'll never figure it out. I told Rachel two years ago. I'll never figure it out by myself.

Emma was working herself into frenzy over the woman lying in the teacher's lap.

I love her and I know she's going to die. How? How is it going to happen? If only I knew how I could stop it. Dear God, please help me.

Joe left the office with the quotation, and Emma picked up the phone book. She turned to the "G" listings.

The Georgia Psychological Association can help me.

How did Emma know about the Georgia Psychological Association? Where had she heard of it? Was her special, silent voice reaching out to her? Emma did not contemplate these questions. She picked up the phone and dialed the number.

"Do you have a listing for a para-psychologist?"

"Why, yes we do," a sweet, sincere voice answered, as if to imply the question was often asked.

I'm on the right track now, I know I am.

Emma felt a slight wave of hope that her ordeal would soon end.

Maybe someone else has asked for a para-psychologist. Maybe I'm not so weird.

"We have a listing for a Dr. David Cooper at Northlake," the sweet voice said.

"That's great!" Emma was ecstatic and carefully noted the phone number. "Thank you, thank you!"

Moments later, Emma was dismayed to get the doctor's answering service rather than making an appointment. Unknown to Emma, however, the answering service taped the doctor's callers; apparently the tone of Emma's voice revealed a troubled emotional state because the doctor called back within an hour.

"This is David Cooper returning your call," he said calmly to Emma after she identified herself.

"Doctor, thank you for calling me." Desperation filled her voice. The doctor did not seem to be in a hurry and engaged Emma in a conversation about e.s.p. and her plague of dreams and nightmares. Emma was confident this unseen man would to help her; she poured out her soul, thinking she must surely sound like a mad woman, beyond any realm of sanity. After listening patiently to her tale for fifteen minutes the doctor told Emma to make a list of the dreams.

"They don't have to be in any order," he told her. His calm, deep voice had an air of authority, as if to say he was in charge now. Emma felt relief listening to him.

"Write down a brief description of each one. Follow your usual bedtime routine, get in bed and relax. Breathe deeply and concentrate on your list."

"I usually drink warm milk when I get in bed."

"That's good. Relax, read your list, concentrate on the dreams, and let's see what happens," he said confidently. "I can see you at four o'clock on Friday afternoon. Is that okay?"

Emma did not even consult her calendar.

"I'll be there," she said, writing down directions to the good doctor's office.

Emma hung up the phone. At last. At long last she would get to the end of the painful journey into her mind that started the night she met Philip Byrd. What would the doctor do? How long would it take to find the answers? Two months? Two years? Was she embarking on another frightful trip? Would the therapy be worse than the dreams and nightmares? Surely not. The doctor's voice was kind and reassuring.

He'll help me. I know he will.

She drove home from work listening to *Scheherazade*, the eerie and inspiring music by Rimsky-Korsakov, telling the tale of a girl who kept herself alive by spinning yarns of thrilling intrigue. If the evil king killed her, he would never hear the end to her stories. Emma suddenly realized that getting to the end of the story was the only thing that had kept her going for a long, long time. Was she finally going to hear the ending? Or was she going to learn that she had indeed lost her mind? What plausible explanation could there be for her feelings? Why did she walk into a classroom and feel that her teacher was only a small child? A child she wanted to love and protect? Why did she shiver violently whenever she saw him? Why did she dearly love a woman she had met only in her dreams? And the little gray-haired lady? Who was she and why did Emma see her standing in front of Mr. Byrd that first night? Why did the little lady seem to know Emma? And why did Emma feel such a strong bond with the old woman who told her Mr. Byrd was special?

Emma stopped at Ingles and bought some groceries.

I'll cook fried chicken for J.D. tonight. His favorite meal. With lots of thick milk gravy and fresh green beans. He's going to Centre College on Friday and Allison and I will be heading up to Hampton. Hampton. Oh, dear. I'm supposed to leave for Hampton at six o'clock on Friday and my appointment with Dr. Cooper is at four. How will I manage that?

Emma's arms were hurting horribly when she turned into the driveway and stopped the car on the turn-around, near the front of the house. When she opened the car door, Alex bounded into her arms, licking her face and wiggling. Emma reprimanded her dog in a playful voice.

"Alex. You bad dog! Why are you out of your pen again? You could get hurt? J.D. fixed you a nice play yard to keep you safe. Come on now. Let's get back inside."

The little animal playfully sulked at his artificial scolding and followed Emma to the back yard. She threw sticks for him to fetch while waiting for fresh water to fill his swimming pool. Boise, the blond shepherd, barked and pranced around and Dobie sat on top of the dog house, yawning in her graceful manner, bored with the black spaniel and his boundless enthusiasm. When the pool was filled, Emma gave each pet a handful of dog biscuits.

"Alex, you stay in the pen. Do you hear Mama? I love you, Alex, and I don't want you to get hurt. Stay!"

She put her hand cautiously on the fence, prepared to wince when shocked by the low voltage charge used to keep the dogs inside their yard. She felt nothing, and grabbed the wire with her fist.

Damn. The power is turned off again.

Emma marched angrily into the garage where she found the cord to the voltage meter unplugged. Hearing the loud rumbling of Jim's Kenworth on the road, Emma waited in the driveway for her husband's arrival.

Jim blew the air horn on the rig when he saw his wife standing at the top of the driveway; he smiled and waved. Emma's red hair shone like polished copper in the late afternoon sun. Her sunken, dark eyes and rail thin body disturbed him.

Her shoulders were drawn up toward her neck, her back arched forward slightly, giving her the appearance of an old woman with osteoporosis of the spine. Emma's smile and return wave belied her irritation; when Jim swung down from the road tractor, she greeted him with an angry barrage of questions, spoken in a soft voice.

"Why did you turn off the voltage meter to the dog's fence again, Jim? They're not safe when they get out. Alex can climb over that fence when the power is off. And he's not ever afraid to try because he's learned it's not always on. I love that little animal, Jim. He's going to get hurt or something even worse. Please, Jim. Please be more careful."

Emma ignored the dumb struck expression on Jim's face, turned around and walked slowly toward the house.

Although Emma had not received any clear e.s.p. messages about her beloved pet, she knew in her heart he was in danger, and she wished she could verbalize her thoughts to her husband. If she did, he would rebuff her with his callous, "You're a witch," remark. Jim never believed in her e.s.p., her special feelings that had saved the lives of her babies and warned her that they would lose everything. Everything they had worked for sat at the top of the gentle hill. Emma glanced toward her house.

We lost it. I knew we would and Jim never believed me. I fought it with every ounce of my being; it's gone. All gone; and he still thinks I'm a witch because I have e.s.p. Friday I'll start walking a new path; maybe then I'll understand.

Emma rinsed the chicken in cold water, laid it on the cutting board, and reached for her sharpest carving knife. Her right hand shook as she cut into the raw meat and when she pressed hard into a joint, pain shot up her arm, into the shoulder.

J.D. had been snapping beans and set them aside to come to his mother's rescue.

"Here, Mom, let me do that."

Emma relinquished her hold on the knife and turned away to hide her pain. J.D. cut up the chicken although the pieces were not identifiable. Emma smiled at her son.

"That's great, J.D."

She dipped the chicken into her seasoned flour mix and dropped it into sizzling Crisco.

"Make the gravy real thick, Mom," J.D. reminded her for the third time.

"It will be, J.D.; it will."

Jim joined them, freshly scrubbed with an Aqua Velva smell, and between the three of them dinner was made. Emma's arms were weak and she could not lift pots or pans but her son and husband were cheerful about following directions. The gravy was creamy and thick, rice was fluffy, chicken was cooked to a golden brown and fresh green beans looked delicious. Jim served fruit salad and they sat down to eat.

Conversation revolved around J.D.'s upcoming experience. He was going off to college and Emma had wonderful feelings about it. In spite of lively table talk, incessant questions rotated through her mind.

Will I get bad news from the neurosurgeon tomorrow? Will my arms become completely useless? Maybe I'm going to die. It would be a relief. I don't know which is worse—nightmares or pain and useless arms and hands.

Jim cleaned up the kitchen while Emma and J.D. checked over his clothes for the trip.

"I wish I could go to Kentucky with you."

"That's okay, Mom. You and Allison will have a good time in Hampton. Don't worry about me and Dad. We'll be fine. Besides, without you we won't have to make twenty potty stops and we'll get there twice as fast."

Grinning at her handsome son, Emma gave him a weak hug with her limp arms. Her bladder was the butt of family jokes and she couldn't help laughing at herself. Emma enjoyed many laughs with her family and she always laughed loudest when the joke was on her.

Jim scrapped chicken leftovers onto an old pan and Emma took them outside to feed the dogs. Alex greeted her enthusiastically while Dobie and Boise sat quietly, watching the black spaniel's antics.

"Alex, you silly little dog. I do love you more than you can imagine."

Emma handed out the juicy tidbits, piece by piece, and let the dogs lick her hands. Her fingertips tingled; she could hardly feel their wet tongues. Alex left momentarily and returned with his favorite stick. He laid it at Emma's feet and wagged the stubby spaniel tail, begging her to play fetch.

"Here ya go, Boy." Emma picked up the twig and gave it a feeble toss. It landed a few feet away and Alex was dismayed. He looked into Emma's eyes. "I know you can't play now, Mama." He picked it up and scurried off.

I'm useless, absolutely useless. I can't even throw a stick for Alex.

Emma went back into the house, washed her hands and sat at the desk to make a list of dreams. Although she was both mentally and physically exhausted, the description of each dream, the good and the bad, flowed onto paper. There was no order and they made no sense whatsoever. When her list was finished she picked up her dad's Bible and read some favorite Psalms. Bible reading was a comfort and Emma asked God again for His guidance.

Jim and J.D. were ensconced on the sofa, laughing at one of the sitcoms on t.v. when Emma breezed through the living room with a cup of hot milk in one hand and her Bible and shorthand pad under the other arm.

"Night, fellas."

She kissed Jim on the check and J.D. on the top of his head.

"Turning in kinda early, aren't you?" Jim asked.

"I'm going to see Dr. Elliott tomorrow about my arms and I want to get a good night's rest."

Emma wished she could talk to Jim about her Friday appointment with Dr. Cooper. However, his many, many years of ridicule about her e.s.p. closed the door on any such conversation.

Thank God for Dr. Cooper. He'll get to the bottom of this, I know he will. I always said I couldn't do it by myself.

Emma knelt by her bed and prayed, asking God for guidance and thanking Him for her many blessings. She climbed into the four-poster, propped herself on a stack of pillows, and sipped warm milk while reading her list over and over. Mental and physical exhaustion overcame her and she nodded off; the light was still on and the shorthand pad lay at her side. A short while later the dreams came again:

Philip Byrd walked in an office, the beautiful woman at his side. A distinguished looking man in his sixties handed Philip an envelope. He opened it, removed a paper of some sort, and stuffed it into his coat pocket. Hand-in-hand the teacher and the lady walked around the Memorial Arts Center. They went into the High Museum and looked at an art exhibition. Still holding hands, they walked into Symphony Hall and listened to a concert.

Emma was in her Pontiac driving down Peachtree Street near the Memorial Arts Center. She turned into a side street and drove around for a long while, looking for a house. When she arrived at the party, she only saw the house from inside; she stood in a hallway with a group of people as the teacher and the beautiful woman passed by with champagne glasses in their hands. Everyone was having a wonderful time. Philip took the woman by the hand and led her into a dark blue bedroom.

Philip and the lady were standing in a crowd of people near a doorway with the number 20 over it. Philip took the envelope out of his pocket and handed it to a woman wearing a blue suit. They walked down a long, narrow hallway and entered an airplane. A pilot was standing at the doorway and greeted Philip. He was not tall, standing about five feet ten. Although he was wearing a hat, Emma knew his hair was sandy colored. His face was appealing in a cute sort of way. The teacher sat in a first class seat; Emma's lady was not there yet.

It was dark outside and the plane took off. Suddenly there was a very loud noise, the teacher's heart was beating fast and he was almost breathless. Philip was kneeling in a muddy field, cradling Emma's lady in his lap. Behind him, in the dark loomed the wreckage of a giant airliner. The teacher looked at his hands, which were covered with blood, and started to cry.

Emma was sitting in the front row of the church and the little gray-haired lady was with her. She knew Emma. The teacher stood in front of a giant arrangement of Queen Anne's lace and an assortment of other white flowers. Emma was crying almost uncontrollably when the apparition of her lady appeared, touched the teacher on the shoulder and disappeared. Emma turned to the little lady and said that fate kept her from her true love and now fate would keep Philip from the one he loves. "If only she had not taken that trip, everything would have been different."

Emma was crying loudly and awakened herself from the dream. For a long while she stared blankly at the ceiling, then painfully rolled toward the lamp and turned out the light. Closing her eyes, she sank into the deepest sleep she had had in many, many months. There were no nightmares.

The next morning Emma stood in her closet in a daze, gazing at the neatly hung clothes. Her body ached from head to toe in spite of a full night's sleep. The pain in her arms was as bad as it had ever been and the left one hung limply at her side while her right hand sorted through the row of blouses. Prevailing depression numbed her mind and incessant mental pictures of the plane crash inundated her every thought.

God. Will it ever end? Will Dr. Cooper be able to help me? And that crash; that awful crash. I never in my wildest imagination would have ever thought that I was seeing scenes from a plane crash. It's like—just like—No. Not again. Not another plane crash. Don't do this to me, Lord. Please don't. Not another one.

Emma collapsed onto the floor, in the middle of the closet, and started to cry. Her mind was transported back to 1962, when she was seventeen years old.

It was a balmy night in March. As usual, the family was gathered around the dinner table, enjoying a delicious meal, and, as usual, the conversation centered on Emma's mother and her activities.

"I'm finally going to Europe," Bee announced.

"That's terrific," the twin's older brother Charlie said. Emma and Rachel looked at each other across the table.

"When are you going? And where?" Charlie asked.

"The Atlanta Art Association is sponsoring a tour to the finest museums in Europe, and I mailed my deposit this afternoon. Can you imagine, in May I'll be visiting—"

It will be a disaster, Emma's silent voice said.

"—London, Amsterdam, Lucerne, Rome, Florence, and Paris," Bee said enthusiastically. "I can hardly wait."

You'll never see her again.

Emma's heart pounded while she forced herself to say something nice to her mother about the trip.

"What a wonderful tour," Momma. "I know you'll have a good time."

It will be a disaster and you'll never see her again.

The remainder of the dinner conversation revolved around the world of fine arts, with Bee discoursing on Rembrandt and Van Gogh, Michelangelo and Botticelli. She knew their life histories as if she had lived them herself and relayed her expansive knowledge to her children in descriptions as colorful as her oil paintings. The troubling premonition was pushed to the back of Emma's mind and she hung on every word her mother said, wondering if she would ever be as smart.

After dinner the twins cleared the table and washed dishes while discussing their mother's plans.

"I don't feel right about it Rachel. I don't. I got two very clear messages that tell me Momma should not go."

"What are you going to do? If you tell her she'll think you're trying to ruin it for her. She'll send you on another guilt trip."

"I don't care. I've got to tell her. I've got to. If I don't, we'll never see her again. Sometimes she's mean to me but she's still my mother—a good mother— I know she can't help herself when she yells at me. That doesn't mean she doesn't love us and it doesn't mean we don't love her either. I can't let something bad happen to her. I can't. I can't. I don't know what to do."

That night in bed, alone with blessed silence, Emma searched her mind for answers to the troubling premonitions: *It will be a disaster. You'll never see her again.*

What was going to happen on that trip? Could it be stopped? If her mother did not go, would it happen anyway? Of course, the most troubling question to the seventeen year old, how in the world would she tell her mother?

Having no answers, she lay in bed and repeated in her mind: *Don't go. Don't go. Please don't go on that trip, Momma.*

For the next several weeks, Emma repeated the mantra, every night, sometimes for hours, while lying in bed.

Don't go, Momma. Please don't go.

The second week in April, Bee made another dinnertime proclamation.

"I'm not going on the arts tour. Charlie's starting graduate school and y'all are going to Georgia State. It would be foolish for me to spend money on a tour right now. I can travel after you've finished college."

Feeling guilty over their mother's decision, Charlie and Rachel protested while Emma sat silently, thanking God. For the next several weeks Emma pondered the cause of the premonition. Was it aimed solely at her mother, or would the trip still be a disaster? Emma had no other clues.

When the tour group left Atlanta on May 9, headed for Europe, the premonition rang loudly in Emma's mind: *It will be a disaster.*

When? Where? Would a bus wreck or a train derail? Would they get food poisoning? What was going to happen?

There were many prominent people from Atlanta's art community on the tour and Emma read every newspaper report of the group's activities. Even though she prayed daily, and asked God to guide them safely, her premonition did not subside. At night Emma tossed and turned in fitful slumber; daytime concentration was almost impossible.

The last day of the tour, when the group was in France, Emma said a prayer and thanked God for bringing them safely to the end of their journey. The next day they would be flying home. For the first time since the tour had left Atlanta, the seventeen-year-old girl had a full night's sleep.

Classical music was playing on the radio while the Browning family was dressing for church on Sunday morning, June 3, 1962, when a special bulletin broke over the airwaves:

"An Air France Boeing 707 jetliner with one hundred and thirty two people on board crashed and burned on takeoff this morning from Orly, France. It appears that the members of the Atlanta Arts Tour group who were on board were killed."

Emma was in shock.

Bee came running into the living room, having heard the news on the radio in her bedroom.

"Momma," Emma cried into her mother's arms. "Your friends—those wonderful people."

Bee was visibly shaken by the news and closely hugged her daughters while composing herself with the inner strength and external hardness often required of a divorced working mother who was the sole support of her family.

"You were going to be on that plane," Rachel exclaimed. "Thank goodness our college expenses kept you home."

They rocked and swayed and swayed and rocked in a tight embrace. There was a long silence before Bee finally spoke.

"I didn't cancel my trip because of your college expenses," she said.

The twins looked puzzled.

"For weeks, at night, I kept having a very bizarre experience—" she paused, trying not to cry.

"What?" Rachel asked.

Bee choked up.

"It was like a ticker-tape message in my mind," she finally blurted out. "It said, 'Don't go.'"

***

Emma sat on the floor crying while visions of the newspaper stories of the Orly disaster processed solemnly through her mind:

106 Atlantans, 24 others die as jetliner crashes in Paris—.

the worst single plane disaster in aviation history—

the greatest tragedy to hit Atlanta since the Civil War—

few were unaffected by the tragedy. The loss could not be measured—

Everywhere, people asked "why?"

The unbearable guilt and pain of the Orly disaster sent the seventeen year old into a depression that lasted several years, eventually leading to a suicide attempt. Now she saw another plane crashing. This time it would be different. Emma St. Claire knew exactly when and where it would be: The first weekend in May, 1990, at Hartsfield International Airport.

Emma crudely wiped her nose on the back of her arm, got up off the floor, and went into the bathroom to wash her face. Looking intently at herself in the mirror she made a vow.

I won't let it happen. I won't. I'll do anything to prevent it. I won't let her die. I won't. I won't.

Then she got dressed and went to work.

***

"I don't know what's wrong with your arms, Emma," the neurosurgeon said after completing his examination. He punched and poked her with a variety of instruments, checking her reflexes and muscle tone. "You seem to have good nerve conduction. For some reason your muscles are exceedingly weak. You may have some atrophy."

"Atrophy?" Emma questioned.

"Yes. When you don't use a muscle, it atrophies," Dr. Elliott explained gently.

"That doesn't sound good."

"That's why I want you to have an MRI immediately. We need to correct this problem before it's permanent."

"Permanent!" she said in a panic. "You mean I might not get better."

"There's a possibility. You have considerable disability now. Hopefully, we've caught it in time and it can be reversed. And you haven't been injured in some way?"

"No. No injuries. I do the usual household chores and I haven't been in any accidents."

"As soon as I see the films I can tell you more."

"I hope to get good news," she said, trying to sound optimistic. Then, almost laughing, Emma told that doctor that she couldn't even open doors.

"When I get to the office in the morning, I stand there until my boss sees me and comes to let me in. When I shop, I wait until someone opens a door, then I slip in behind them."

The doctor was a witness to Emma's plight a few minutes later when she left his office. Because she could not pull the heavy door she stood by with a smile on her face, waiting calmly for the next patient entering. As soon as a stout man cleared, Emma put her foot in the path of the door as it started to swing shut. Then she wedged it open with her shoulder and, bumping it with her fanny, squeezed out before it slammed shut.

The doctor shook his head, turned to the receptionist and laid Emma's chart on the desk.

"Very strange case," he said. "Call my next patient."

On Friday, in her usual daze, Emma drove to the psychologist's office, turning over and over in her mind the visions of the plane crash. Her left arm ached and her hand loosely held the steering wheel. Her mind was consumed with the terrifying sight of the disaster; she never thought about the session she was about to have with the doctor, or the treatment he would use. He was going to help her; that was all she cared about.

The red brick Williamsburg office condo appealed to Emma and she felt comfortable as soon as she entered the building. From behind the closed door to the doctor's consultation room she heard muffled voices. Alone in his lobby, she gazed around and noticed a clipboard on the coffee table. A patient information form was attached to the clipboard. Emma made herself at home, sat on the sofa, and filled out the form. She was reading the patient instruction sheet when the door opened and a slender man stuck his head out.

"Emma St. Claire?" he questioned. He was wearing a dress shirt and tie but no coat. His thick black hair, only slightly combed, covered his fair-skinned forehead and hung almost to his eyebrows. He appeared to be in his mid-thirties.

"Yes."

The doctor's dark eyes sparkled behind horn-rimmed glasses and his almost boyish face greeted Emma with a wide grin. She knew instantly she could trust him.

"Hi. I'm David Cooper. I'll be with you in a minute. Will you please answer the questions on the clipboard?"

He glanced down at the table.

"Here you are," Emma responded, retrieving the page she had laid on the sofa.

"Great," he replied, taking the form. "Be with you in a few minutes."

"Even though I'm crazy I'm still efficient," she laughed.

The door closed and mumbling resumed. A few moments later, a man left the inner office and moved swiftly to the exit door, apparently not wanting to be seen.

Emma was amused.

Why is a psychologist's office different from a dentist's or a doctor's? Why do people act ashamed to be seen at a psychologist office? People talk about root canals, or having babies, or removing warts. They don't talk about their feelings.

Dr. Cooper invited Emma into his office. She eased herself onto soft sofa cushions, cradling her left arm with her right hand, wincing when she leaned back.

"Bad neck," she said nonchalantly to the doctor.

He raised his brows and nodded.

"I have an appointment for an MRI next week. I've been miserable."

"Would you be more comfortable lying down?" he asked.

"No. Thank you, though. I'll be okay this way."

She picked up a throw pillow and rested her limp left arm on it.

"This is fine," she smiled.

Without waiting for a question from the doctor, Emma charged right into her problem.

"I thought I was crazy and I went to see a psychiatrist."

"When was that?"

"February. We talked about everything—" she paused, "except my e.s.p. I didn't tell him about that until I went back for his evaluation. I haven't been the same since I met that teacher and saw that little gray-haired lady. I had to know if I was insane or if the teacher was the cause of—of—"

"The dreams?"

"Yes, the dreams; and this appalling depression. Thanks to you I know why the dreams were disturbing—there's going to be a plane crash, Dr. Cooper."

He winced. "A plane crash?"

"Yes. Terrible."

"We'll get back to that. What was the psychiatrist's opinion?"

"He said what I've had going on in my life would depress any one. He said I was quite sane, that I had my act together. He gave me some medicine."

"Has it helped?"

Emma shook her head slowly.

"No, not much, and I still have nightmares about the teacher. That's why I called you. The psychiatrist told me I should talk to a para-psychologist."

"From what you told me on the phone, you've had quite a few psychic experiences."

"I had the first one when I was five years old—" Emma explained, giving him a ten-minute dissertation on her episodes.

"I never had an episode even similar to the first one with the teacher."

"Why was it different?"

"He was a stranger. My episodes have always involved people I care about; I'd never seen him before in my life."

"When we talked on the phone, you said something about a vision."

"Yes. It was crystal clear. I can still see her. She has been in my dreams, too."

"Who is she?"

"I have no idea."

Emma went on to describe in detail the little gray-haired woman with her arms stretched out in front of the teacher.

"'Protect him; he's special,' she said. You can't imagine what that image has done to me, Dr. Cooper."

"You can call me David."

Emma nodded, "David."

"My life hasn't been the same. I almost feel haunted by her."

"Do you know anything about the teacher? What's his name?"

"Philip. He works for Atlantic Airways and teaches night school; and he's from Thomson."

"Thomson?"

"Yes. Thomson, Georgia. It's such a coincidence. I dearly love that place. My daughter married a man from Thomson and whenever I go to the King's for a visit, I feel I'm at home."

The doctor had a curious expression on his face and nodded.

"I'll never forget the first time we went over there. When we turned off the freeway, I told my husband and son, 'No wonder Allison loves it here. I feel I'm coming home.'"

"When was that?"

"Spring of 1986."

"When did you meet the teacher?"

"January of 1987."

The doctor made some notes on the tablet in his lap.

"Tell me about the plane crash."

While Emma gave the doctor the details of the dream, he made more notes.

Concluding the story she said, "The first time I had that dreadful nightmare, I could see a looming shadow. It never occurred to me it was the wreckage of a jetliner."

Dr. Cooper wrote down the information.

"Have you ever been hypnotized?" he asked.

"Once. By accident," Emma laughed.

"By accident?"

"Yes, at camp. A hypnotist did a show one evening. He got kids from the audience who volunteered to be hypnotized."

"Did you volunteer?"

"No. I was bashful. I didn't want to act foolish in front of the whole camp."

"So how were you hypnotized?"

"The hypnotist had this wheel thing. He spun it around and the kids were supposed to look at it and go into a trance. I was looking at it from the audience and after the show they realized I was in a deep trance."

"Did the hypnotist bring you out of it?"

"No. He tried though. He told them not to worry, that I would sleep it off. I slept it off alright," Emma laughed again. "I slept for eighteen hours."

"Eighteen hours!"

"Yes. I didn't wake up until late the next afternoon. My sister was very worried about me."

"How did you feel?"

"As if I had been drugged or something. Real sluggish. It scared me to realize that I had missed most of an entire day. I never knew what hit me. Ever since then I've had a tremendous respect for the power of the mind."

"Would you mind if I hypnotized you?"

Emma was puzzled. She could not imagine what good it would do but this was the doctor who helped her put the myriad pieces to the nightmare puzzle together. She trusted him.

"I guess not."

The doctor stood up and walked over to the bookcases.

"Do you mind if I make a tape of the session?"

Emma was impressed. He wanted to make a video of her in a trance. She shook her head slowly, and shrugged one shoulder slightly.

"Whatever you want to do is fine with me."

He fiddled with the camera for a moment, gave her a tiny microphone, then sat down again in his rocking chair, facing Emma, and pushed loafers off his feet.

"Try to relax," he said softly, slightly above a whisper. "Take a deep breath, and close your eyes."

Emma took a deep breath, made a concerted effort to relax every muscle in her body, and closed her eyes.

"Everything is very still. Very quiet," he said in a slow monotone.

"You are completely relaxed. Breathe—in—and—out; very slowly. You are relaxed. Completely relaxed."

In a whisper, he said, "Twenty."

Following the doctor's instructions, Emma's achy body began to unwind, taut muscles became smooth.

"You are sleepy. Very—very—sleepy. —Nineteen."

Again, the number was spoken in an indiscernible whisper.

Emma's eyes felt tired. Although her lids had been closed, she no longer had to hold them that way. She started to drift off, her eyes shut in sleep.

"You are in a deep, deep sleep. —Eighteen."

The aches and pains were gone. Emma drifted off in a sleep that was more peaceful than any she had ever known.

"You are completely at ease. —Seventeen."

Emma's breathing was slow and methodical. Her head bobbed slightly with each inhalation.

"You are asleep. —Sixteen."

The doctor's kind and gentle voice was lulling Emma into a dimension where she had never been before. There was no pain. No anxiety. No fears. No tears. Only peace. Blessed peace.

"You are surrounded by a light. A cool light. It is soothing. —Fifteen."

Emma pictured her body surrounded by a white light.

"Your mind is far away. —Fourteen."

"You are going back. Way back. —Thirteen."

Emma felt that her mind was moving; it was no longer a part of her body, going where her physical being could not go. It separated itself from her body and went further into a space where time did not exist.

"You are asleep. Your mind is going back, back. —Twelve."

As Emma's mind moved through this new realm, the light that surrounded her body before moved with her. It was a brilliant light, white in the center, fading to a pleasant, slightly tinted yellow on the edges. The sensation to Emma was very peaceful. She let her mind go further and further, not knowing her destination.

"You are relaxed. —Eleven."

Emma had no concept of her physical body though it continued to breath —in—and—out.

"You are asleep. —Ten."

The white light was moving at a great speed. Emma had no idea where it was headed.

"Your mind is looking for Philip. —Nine."

Emma's moving white light slowed down as if it was scanning the distant recesses of her mind, looking for Philip.

"You are relaxed. You are at peace. You are looking for Philip. —Eight."

The light came to a stop. Emma stared into it.

"You will see Philip. —Seven."

The brilliant white, tinged in yellow, started to open, as if it was the lens of a camera. Slowly—slowly—slowly.

"Where are you? —Six."

The whiteness was fading. The lens began to focus on something.

"What do you see?"

Emma had no awareness of David Cooper, or the sofa on which her body was sitting. She was in another place. The whiteness had completely faded. The lens was focused perfectly. The image was clear.

"Farmhouse—" she responded after a long silence.

The voice was unfamiliar, not even similar to the sound of the Emma St. Claire who had walked into Dr. Cooper's office thirty minutes before. It enunciated each word carefully in a drawn out manner.

Emma saw the little gray-haired lady sitting at a table in the kitchen of a farmhouse. She was wearing an apron.

"Where is the farmhouse?" David asked.

"Thomson."

"What do you see?"

"Kitchen. Little gray-haired lady is sitting at table in farmhouse. In Thomson."

"What is she doing?"

"She's—been—taking—care—of—a—baby."

The little gray-haired woman was holding a tiny child in her lap.

"Does she say anything to the baby?"

"No—one—will—love—him—the—way—I—do.
No—one—will— take—care—of—him—the—way—I—could."

"Who is the baby?"

"Philip—is—the—baby—"

"Is the little lady related to the baby?" David asked.

There was a long, long silence.

"She—takes—care—of—baby—"

216

"Who is she?"

After another long silence, Emma's new voice said, while she was shaking her head, "Can't remember—can't remember."

Emma was aware of the love the old woman had for the infant. She felt it completely. She felt the love the old woman had for the tiny child, lying in her lap, in a farmhouse in Thomson.

"What happened to the old lady?" David asked.

"She died. She died and she left the baby. She did not want to leave him. No one could love him or care for him the way she did."

"You are starting to wake up now," David said.

Emma sat motionless on the sofa, still breathing quietly.

"You will wake up. You will be relaxed and refreshed as if you have had a long nap."

Emma yawned. Her head nodded. Her eyes blinked open one time. Where she had been felt good. Now her mind was back in David's office. She was once again aware of the sofa, the beautiful Oriental rug on the floor, the slender, dark haired man sitting in the rocking chair across from her. She blinked again.

"Am I crazy, Dr. Cooper?"

"No, you're not crazy, Emma. I think you have a wonderful mind."

She blinked in an exaggerated manner to shake off the drowsy feeling and dabbed at her eyes with a Kleenex.

"Who is that little old lady?" Emma finally asked.

"I want you to think about it this week. We'll discuss it when I see you again."

Although Emma was disappointed, she knew the good doctor must have a reason for not telling her what she had wanted to know for more than two years. Surely she could wait one more week.

CHAPTER SEVENTEEN

**"Do no throw away your confidence,
which has a great reward."**
-Hebrews 11:35

E mma drove home as fast as Friday afternoon traffic would allow and found Allison in a full-blown sweat.

"Where in the world have you been, Mama? We should have left for the airport thirty minutes ago."

"We'll make it, Darlin'. I'll tell you about it on the way. Let's get the car loaded. We can stop for a hamburger when we get to Riverdale."

"Have a good time at Centre, Darlin'," Emma said to J.D., giving her son a loose hug with limp arms.

Jim and J.D. threw garment bags into the trunk of Allison's Honda and the two women roared down the driveway. On the way to the airport, Emma gave Allison a blow-by-blow account of the events of the past two plus years, including the most recent revelation—the plane crash.

Allison was neither surprised nor alarmed by Emma's prognostication. She assumed her mother was correct, would sort it out and prevent the foreseen tragedy. Allison's unqualified acceptance gave Emma's spirit a much-needed lift.

She thinks it will work out okay. Only God knows how.

"How do you feel about us flying, Mama?" Allison asked with a hint of emotion.

"Fine, Darlin'. I'm not afraid of flying. I love to fly. The only time I was ever apprehensive was the trip to Dallas with J.D. When I got on that plane, I stopped in the first class section. At the time, I didn't understand I was looking for someone. It didn't make any sense and I was uneasy. Of course, now I know that I was looking for that teacher, sitting in a first class seat. Even then, my psyche was trying to tell me to think about a plane. I never made the connection. My mind has been working rather poorly. Sometimes I feel as though I've completely lost it."

"Mama, for heaven's sake. You haven't lost your mind. To tell you the truth, though, we've been worried about you. You've lost too much weight; you're a shadow of yourself. And I never thought I'd see the day my Mom couldn't cook."

"I'm scared, Darlin'. My arms are pathetically weak. If I can't work, we'll starve. Daddy is never going to seek gainful employment. He wants to drive his wretched old truck. He has no ambition whatsoever. I can't believe I put that man through two years of college and a year of graduate school and he won't even get a decent job."

"Your arms are gonna be fine, Mama. Quit worrying about them."

"You can't imagine how it feels to lose the use of your arms, Allison," Emma said defensively. "It's very frightening. I could have some sort of debilitating disease; I might be this way the rest of my life. You don't understand how embarrassing it is to stand outside a door and wait for someone to come along and open it for me. People look at me as if I'm crazy—I must be."

Allison almost yelled at her mother, "Mama, I told you, you're not crazy. Don't ever say that again, do you hear me?"

Emma cringed. No one understood. The nightmares; the crippled arms; losing everything she had worked for. Would it ever end? Would Emma ever find peace? Would she ever be happy? And her daughter. Her precious daughter. Was Emma estranging herself from her child? Only moments before Emma felt the elation of Allison's acceptance. Now there was friction.

I can't let this situation ruin my relationship with my children. Get a hold of yourself, Emma St. Claire. You can tell Allison what's happened; just don't let yourself get carried away. You're not crazy. The doctor told you that. You have to be objective.

Emma's thoughts were interrupted by Allison's apology.

"I'm sorry I yelled at you, Mama. Honestly, you're not crazy. Everything will work out for the best, you'll see. In time it will work out."

"You sound like your Mama, Darlin'."

"I can't imagine why," Allison said, chuckling. "You must have said that to me a million times when I was growing up, Mama; and guess what? You were right. Things always did work out for the best, even though I couldn't see that when I was upset."

Allison exited the interstate onto the Riverdale Road approach to the airport and stopped at a McDonald's for hamburgers, which they gobbled up while driving. At the airport Emma and Allison made a mad dash to their departure gate, arriving moments before the plane left. Still out of breath, they collapsed into their seats.

"Let's have a good time!" Allison said, patting her mother on the hand.

Emma smiled at her pretty daughter in a silent response. The image of the little gray-haired lady in Thomson, caring for the infant boy, was foremost in her mind.

"I can't imagine who that little lady is," she finally said to Allison.

"Mama," Allison said in a kind yet firm voice, "you have to flow with it."

"Flow with it? How can I flow with it? I don't even know what IT is! I don't even know who that little old lady is! Maybe her soul has taken over my soul. God, you can't imagine how scared I am. Why would her soul be mixed up in me? Why would I feel things she felt when she was alive?"

"Mama," Allison said again in the same tone, "Chill out."

***

Emma was staring blankly out the window and Allison was engrossed in another Danielle Steele novel when the flight attendant came by.

"Would you care for something to drink?"

"Coke," Allison answered without taking her eyes off the book.

Emma blinked slowly, bringing her mind into focus.

"Gin and tonic."

Allison looked at her mother, shook her head slightly, and went back to her reading.

"I need something to help me unwind a little," she explained.

The flight attendant handed Allison a plastic cup of Coca-Cola and set a tiny bottle of Beefeater's gin on Emma's tray next to a cup of ice into which she had poured some tonic. Allison set the book aside and picked up her drink while Emma stirred the Beefeater into the tonic.

"Can't believe my special baby is getting married tomorrow," Emma said.

"Why have you always called Patty your special baby?"

Emma started the story, sipping her drink.

"We were living in temporary quarters after we got to Germany. Another officer's wife befriended me—they lived on the first floor. Her name was Shirley."

"The woman with the kids who tried to do me in?"

"Yes, that's the one. Anyway, she showed up at our door early one morning. She said her husband's battalion was giving a surprise party for their flight surgeon's wife, 'cause they were expecting their first baby and—"

Emma took another sip.

"—she said she needed help getting ready for the party."

"That was sort of presumptuous wasn't it?"

"That's what I thought. We weren't even in the same battalion and I didn't know the guest of honor. I guess because Shirley was sort of abrasive no one wanted to help her even though she was a fantastic cook and loved to entertain. I could think of other things I'd rather do than get ready for a party I couldn't attend."

"What did you say?"

"I stood at the door, sort of in shock that she would make such a request, when I got an e.s.p. message."

"What was it?"

Emma took another sip of her libation.

"This is a 'Special Baby,' it said. 'Do it!'"

"You got a message about somebody's baby being special and you didn't even know them?"

"That's right. Very unusual for me to have special feelings about someone I don't know. Anyway, I started to turn down Shirley's request, sort of stammering my way through it, when the message came again."

"Special baby?" Allison questioned.

"Yep. I thought about it for a few seconds and told Shirley I'd gather up you and your stuff and we'd be down in a few minutes."

"What did you end up doing?"

Emma stared into the plastic cup of gin and tonic as if gazing into a crystal ball.

"The first thing I did was polish silver. That took over an hour. Shirley was dusting and running the vacuum cleaner. Then she came in the kitchen and we started cooking."

"What did you make?"

"Everything you can imagine for a baby shower. Fancy cheese straws, petite fours iced with a delicious white glaze and decorated with pink rose buds Shirley made, fancy sandwiches, and a couple of kinds of cookies. It was quite a spread."

"You didn't get to eat any of it?"

222

"Nope. Not a bite. About three o'clock in the afternoon one of the other wives showed up with the baby carriage. The Germans make the most wonderful trams. Anyway, Shirley and I sort of wrapped it and put a ribbon around it. Then we set out the food. She only had to light the candles when the guests arrived."

"They never asked you to stay?"

"No. When I left a few minutes before four, I was happy that I helped prepare a welcoming party for a special baby."

Emma took another small mouthful of the drink.

Allison raised her eyebrows with a questioning look on her face and Emma resumed the story.

"The next week, we got our permanent quarters. Guess where they were?"

Of course Allison knew where they were. How many times over the years had her parents talked about their Army buddies in Germany?

"In the same building with the couple having the baby."

"Yep. Right across the hall. And after the baby was born, a few weeks later, we got to know the Reynolds. We became best friends and I got to take care of Patty when her parents went on leave and, of course, Catherine took care of you sometimes, too."

"And that's why she's your special baby?"

"That's part of it. When she was eight years old, Catherine called me a few weeks before Easter and said she was having their three children baptized on Easter Eve. They wanted me and Daddy to be Patty's Godparents. That made her special because I feel that every one of my eight Godchildren is special. Each one of them is a treasure. I feel warm and fuzzy when I think about that shower for my special baby. My feelings were right on target."

"For the umpteenth time, huh?" Allison grinned.

"Yes. For the umpteenth time."

***

Emma stood alone under an oak tree in the Reynolds' backyard, thinking about the day's activities. A sumptuous breakfast in honor of Patty and Timothy was held at a fine old resort, overlooking the water of Hampton Roads and the wedding took place at St. John's, the oldest Episcopal parish in the United States.

Now surveying the lavish reception, Emma almost had to pinch herself. It was a Hollywood movie scene.

The lush lawn, at the edge of the bay, was bordered with giant hardwood trees, and sloped very gently toward the water. Under stately oaks on the left side of the yard, white tents stood in a row, each one offering a different type of food. At the first, a chef was stir-frying an assortment of meats with a huge roast beef being carved to order. Gourmet and imported cheeses were presented on silver trays. The next tent sheltered breads and vegetables, and the last offered every type of fruit imaginable. To keep the area cool an ice-carved swan sat in the middle of a huge table decorated with fruits and vegetables cut in the shapes of animals.

A band stand and dance floor were set up near the water, and on the far right side, three bartenders were serving wine, champagne, beer, and mixed drinks. The wedding cake was displayed on a round table near the center of the yard. Baskets of pink begonias decorated the lawn, and gigantic pink bows, with long streamers, hung from the corner of each tent.

Far above Emma's head a mockingbird called to its mate, and she looked up, cautiously moving her head, to see it land on the roof of a tree house nested in the junction of three wide branches. Pink impatiens plants cascaded over the window boxes that adorned each side of the miniature shelter.

"Dear Catherine," Emma said to herself. "No detail overlooked. No expense spared."

She smiled at the view. Then she thought about the little gray-haired lady and wondered what the other guests would think if they knew that Patty's Godmother was psychic. Emma felt estranged. She very much wanted to be a normal person at the gala reception for her beautiful Godchild but she wasn't. She felt as if a mark had been tattooed on her forehead for everyone in the world to see. A tattoo that said, *Look at me. I'm psychic. Some old woman's soul has invaded my body.*

Allison waved to her mother and Emma walked across the lawn to meet some of the guests. It was the most important day in Patty's life and Emma very much wanted to enjoy it—if only that damn repulsive tattoo was not in plain sight.

***

Emma and Allison spent Sunday morning with Catherine and Ed, and were pleasantly surprised when the newlyweds appeared. Tim and Patty opened the present that Emma had brought, and both were thrilled with the silver tea set. Patty sat next to her Godmother and Emma patted her on the knee.

"Patty, you've always been my special baby. Even though I've missed a lot of important events in your life, I want you to know that I've said a prayer for you every day since you became my Godchild. Now that you're married, I'll be saying a prayer for you and Tim."

Patty was pleased and beamed with happiness.

"You're pretty special to us, too. I'm happy you could come to the wedding."

"I wouldn't have missed it for anything, Darlin'," Emma said, wondering if the tattoo still showed.

***

A few hours later Emma and Allison were standing at a departure gate of the Norfolk Airport, awaiting their flight to Atlanta. Allison had a worried look on her face.

"This is Gate Twenty, Mama. Do you think this flight will be safe?"

Emma smiled at her daughter, shaking her head slowly.

"Allison, do you think I'd let you take a flight that wasn't safe?"

"No; but this is a south bound Atlantic Airways flight and it is departing from Gate Twenty."

"Yes. Some coincidence, huh?"

"Are you sure this is a coincidence? This isn't the plane that's going to crash?"

"No. This plane won't crash, Allison. I promise. The one I dreamed about will crash the first weekend in May of next year. Besides, I don't know if twenty is the flight number or the gate number. It could be either one. Dreams have to be interpreted—even precognitive dreams. Don't worry about this flight."

"You're positive?"

"Yes; very. You don't think your Mama would take a chance with your life, do you?"

"No. I guess not.

"Seems strange, though."

"A coincidence, Allison. Just a coincidence."

***

If this MRI turns out normal, I'm going to have myself committed.

225

Emma was lying inside the magnetic imaging tube. Her head was strapped down and she stared at the ceiling of the cylinder only inches above her nose. The machine rattled, banged and made loud gurgling noises as magnetic waves created images of Emma's neck and head on the monitor in the adjoining room. The rattling and banging finally stopped and the technician pulled Emma out of the diagnostic device.

"We'll get these films to your doctor first thing in the morning, Mrs. St. Claire."

"Great. I have an appointment at ten. Can you tell me anything?"

"I can show them to you."

The woman led Emma into a room with an array of monitors and complicated looking equipment.

"Here are your films, now," the technician said. A young man was sitting in front of a monitor, viewing pictures of Emma's neck and head.

"Whoopee. I have a brain," Emma teased.

As bad as her arms hurt, Emma was not as concerned about them as she was about her mental condition. What difference did it make if her arms became useless if her mind was gone? Emma knew that if the MRI was okay that she was mentally disturbed and was immensely relieved when Dr. Elliott told her that she had a bulging disc in her neck.

"We call it C-4, Emma," he said, pointing to film of the fourth cervical disc. Emma could easily see the disc pushing against her spinal cord.

"Where do we go from here?"

"We have a couple of options. Usually, I ask my patients to undergo at least a month of physical therapy before we do anything else. Many cases never need surgery. I don't operate if physical therapy can fix it."

"That's reasonable. I'm to start therapy?"

"Yes, right away. I want you to understand, however, these x-ray findings are inconsistent with your disability."

"I don't understand. I thought I had a C-4 bulge. Isn't that pressure causing the problem?"

"I wish I could say it was. Unfortunately, that's only part of your problem. There's something else going on that I haven't figured out."

"What's that?"

The doctor walked behind Emma and started running his index finger down the back of the limp, left arm. Then he gave her a complicated dissertation on where the nerves ran, which muscles they controlled.

I wish my Mom was here, Emma thought to herself. Bee could have explained it better. She was the medical expert in the family.

"The C-4 bulge is causing the pain here," the doctor continued.

"That's not where it hurts the worst, Dr. Elliott."

"I know Emma. Your pain and extreme weakness seem to be more muscle related. I want you to see a neurologist right away. He can do an EMG."

"EMG?"

"Electro-myelogram—a diagnostic test used to measure nerve conduction. He will be able to tell us if the problem is nerve or muscle related."

"In other words, even though I have a bad disc, there's something else wrong and we still don't know what it is?"

"That's about right," he said, shaking his head. "I'm sorry I can't be more specific. My nurse will set up your physical therapy with the P.T. department downstairs. I'm sending you to the neurologist right now if you can go."

"Anything you say. I want to get to the bottom of this. Do you think my arms will ever get better?" Emma was very concerned now.

"I think therapy will help a lot. I know it will alleviate the C-4 problem. You have a significant disability. The longer it goes on, the less chance there will be for a complete recovery."

Emma trusted the doctor and decided to confide in him about her mental condition.

"I've been under a lot of stress, Dr. Elliott. For a long time. Could that have anything to do with this problem?"

The doctor was a little surprised. Emma acted casual, almost laid back, not anxious or stressed out.

"The mind has a terrific influence on the body, Emma. Stress can take a toll. Can I ask the nature of the stress?"

Emma could hardly believe she was talking to a medical doctor the way she talked to Dr. Cooper. This man unashamedly admitted that he didn't have all the answers and he appeared to be receptive to anything she might say.

"I have e.s.p. and I've been dreaming about a plane crash."

The doctor was surprised and jerked as if jabbed with a hot poker. Composing himself, he nodded his head slowly, mulling over Emma's confession.

"That would undoubtedly create a lot of stress. What are you doing about it?"

This unusual patient, with the undiagnosed medical problem, had obviously piqued his curiosity.

"I'm working with a psychologist."

He nodded his head approvingly and smiled at Emma.

"My wife's a psychologist," he said.

He needed to say no more. There was an unspoken acceptance of Emma's psyche and its possible effect on her body and no condemnation of her e.s.p. She felt a spiritual bond with the good doctor. There were many neurosurgeons in the city of Atlanta; how had it happened that the one she came to was the one who respected her e.s.p.?

***

By the time the neurologist finished his exam, orders for Emma's physical therapy were in the P.T. department. She stopped there to schedule a session and was greeted by a very pretty young woman with enormous black eyes and long, silky black hair.

"Hi!" she said. "My name's Maria. Are you Emma St. Claire?"

"Yes, I am," Emma smiled at the pretty girl. "I want to set up some appointments."

"I'm not busy now. If you want to come on back, we can get started right away."

"That's great."

Emma could hardly believe her good fortune. The neurologist had already scheduled an EMG for the following Monday and Emma was starting physical therapy. Things were starting to look up. Maria gave Emma a hospital gown and put her in one of the treatment rooms to change. A few minutes later she stuck her head in.

"Ready?"

"Whenever you are," Emma said optimistically. "Let's get started."

The session was interesting and informative and Emma realized there was a lot to be learned about the functions of the various muscles in her arms, shoulders and neck and the exercises to strengthen each.

"Take it easy," Maria told Emma. "I don't want you to overdo it."

The exercises were painful and it was not necessary for Maria to caution Emma not to over exert herself.

"Slow and steady does it, Emma," she said, turning Emma's head from one side to the other. There was little mobility in Emma's neck and the left shoulder had drawn up in pain. The disfigurement had been coming on gradually for a long time and Emma did not realize how bad she looked until Maria rolled a full-length mirror into the room.

"This shoulder is more than two inches higher than the right one," she said, pushing down lightly on Emma's left side.

"That's awful," Emma gasped. "No wonder I looked funny in Allison's wedding pictures."

"I have no idea what caused this condition, Emma. You didn't get this way over night."

"Can it be fixed? Will I ever stand up straight again, with even shoulders?"

"Of course you will, Emma. It won't be easy, though, and you'll have to give it time. You'll need to do these exercises at home, twice every day. Remember, slow and steady."

After manipulating Emma's arms and neck she packed Emma in ice for twenty minutes.

"This will ease the discomfort," Maria said. "After you exercise, you should apply ice. No more than twenty minutes, though, okay?"

"Okay. I want to get better. I'll do anything you say."

"I can tell you're going to work at this. That's what it takes. After you get dressed come to my desk. I'll have drawings of these exercises for you and some written instructions."

Emma practically danced to her car.

Oh happy day! I'm going to get better and this awful pain will go away; and tomorrow Dr. Cooper will tell me who that little gray-haired lady is.

***

"Do you know who the little old lady in Thomson is?" David asked Emma.

"I have no idea. She's been on my mind every hour of every day the entire week. I'm terribly scared I'm possessed or something. I don't understand why her feelings would be mixed up in me."

David leaned back in his rocking chair, looking intently at his patient on the sofa, cradling her left arm on the pillow in her lap.

"Do you believe in eternal life?" he asked.

"Of course," Emma quickly responded. "I'm a Christian. I've always believed that when I die, my soul will still live."

"Where did your soul come from?"

"—from God. I mean, we all come from God, don't we?"

"Yes, we do. And God is eternal, right?"

"Right. He always was and always will be. Forever and ever."

"Correct. And if your soul comes from God, your soul is eternal, too."

"Yes. Of course."

"Would you say that if your soul is eternal that it has been around for a long time?"

Emma thought a moment. As a child she used to wonder how her mother had created her soul in her womb.

"I guess. I never looked at it that way. I mean, I never thought about it being here before I was born."

"If your soul was born into the world this time, don't you think it could have been here before?"

Emma contemplated the doctor's question, rolling her eyes toward the ceiling and pursing her lips.

"You mean reincarnation?" she finally asked.

"You told me that you felt Thomson was home. Correct?"

"Correct," Emma said, nodding her head.

"Don't you think it would feel like home if it had been? If you lived there in another life?"

A tiny spark in Emma's soul suddenly erupted into a gigantic flame. She was euphoric.

"You mean that little gray-haired lady was me in another life! That's me, my soul! That's why I felt the things I did? That's why I love Thomson and have such an affinity for my teacher? I took care of him when he was a baby!"

Emma felt as if a weight had been lifted from her shoulders. She wasn't possessed. She wasn't insane. She was merely looking at herself in a past life. She could hardly believe what she was hearing.

It was simple and it made sense. What other explanation could there be?

"Psychologists generally agree that the simplest explanation is the best explanation. I think you have been seeing and feeling yourself in a past life."

Emma was beaming with joy. At long last she had an answer. How many other questions would this Knight in Shining Armor help her answer?

"It feels good to know I'm not possessed. You can't imagine the thoughts I've had. It never occurred to me it was a past life experience I've been feeling."

She sat on the sofa shaking her head in wonder and awe. The old lady was her very own soul in another life. It was incredible!

"I haven't had those nightmares, Dr. Cooper."

"David—"

"David——. I sleep soundly. Every night. It's heavenly. I did have the MRI on my neck and the neurosurgeon still doesn't know what's wrong with my arms. I have to have more tests. You know what's interesting?"

Emma's Knight shook his head, indicating she should continue.

"The MRI showed a bulging C-4 disc. Sally, my former boss's daughter, remember the girl I told you about who broke her neck, she had a C-4 fracture. I thought that was sort of interesting. I mean, such a coincidence that I should have a problem in the same place where she broke her neck. Especially since mine is not related to any sort of trauma."

The doctor concurred, "Yes, that is interesting. If you want to do some more trance work, I can give you some relaxation suggestions. Maybe that would help your neck."

"That would be great. The medical doctors haven't done anything for me yet."

David switched on the camera and gave Emma the tiny microphone. She took a deep breath to unwind. Sitting on the edge of his rocking chair, David leaned slightly toward Emma, speaking in a quiet, monotone voice.

"Your eyelids are very heavy; they are closing. —Twenty."

Emma's eyes closed.

"You are very relaxed. Your head is a balloon. It is floating in the air. —Nineteen."

Emma's shoulders dropped, the tension is her neck eased and her head became buoyant. It gently bobbed up and down. She felt herself drifting off.

"The balloon is floating above your shoulders. Your shoulders are relaxed. —Eighteen."

David continued to give Emma suggestions relaxing her neck and shoulder muscles while inducing the trance. Emma's comforting whiteness again escorted her on the trip into her mind. Exploring a newfound road in a beautiful wilderness, she had no idea where it would take her, or where she was going. Back she went. Further and further. Faster and faster. Unaware of her body, there was no pain. Only the whiteness and the peaceful quiet. The lens of her camera focused on the center of the brightness and she watched as the white light faded.

"Where are you?" David asked.

As in the first session, the voice speaking from the trance was very deep. Each word was spoken slowly and deliberately. It was not the voice of Emma St. Claire.

"I'm standing next to some water. It must be a lake. No, the ocean. I've got on a long dress. A little boy is sitting at my feet. He's playing in the water. He keeps looking up at me. He seems to be having a good time."

"What are you doing there?" David asked Emma.

"A boat. We're going to see the boat."

On the horizon an eighteenth century sailing ship appeared.

"It is a big wooden boat, lots of people. He takes my hand. We walk along the shore."

The boat sailed into the harbor.

"The boat is way off in the distance. People are getting off the boat."

The woman was slight in size. Blond hair piled on her head in a heap of curls was held together with ribbons. A long ecru colored dress covered her fragile body but the small bustle on the back added fullness to her petite form. The boy was wearing a fine blue velvet suit with short pants and a lace trimmed shirt. His tiny hand swished the water, back and forth, back and forth, making small splashes.

"What are you doing there?"

"Going to meet somebody. We're both real happy. The little boy is smiling. My hair is fixed on top of my head. Piled up in curls. My dress is white. There's a lot of people standing around."

"Who are you looking for?"

"A man is coming across the gangplank. A big man. He is wearing a green velvet coat. Real good looking. He has thick, dark hair. He picks up the little boy. He kisses me on the cheek.

"I'm happy to see him. My heart is beating too fast! Been a very long time—overjoyed he's back. Holding my hand. I didn't think I'd ever see him again."

"Why?"

"The little boy was a baby when he left. Can't wait to get home where we can be together."

"How do your surroundings look?"

"Some buildings are wood. Most brick. Signs on them. Everybody stops to talk to him. I want to go home."

"Can you read any of the signs?"

There was a long pause.

"Haberdashery. A shop with bolts of cloth. Pipes in the window of another."

"Can you describe the street?"

"Grey stones. There are carriages with big wheels."

"Where did the boat come from?"

"England."

"Where is it now?"

"Boston harbor."

"What has happened?"

"He left me. I loved him. I took care of his little boy. Yes, my little boy. He grew while his daddy was gone. I'd forgotten how I felt about him. I don't want him to ever leave me again."

"Move forward in time. What do you see?"

"He's taking us on a trip. On a boat. Our little boy is almost grown. He's to go to school in England for a proper education. I go on the trip, too."

"Who is the big man?"

"He's my husband. He never left me again. We were very happy. Our son grew up. We were quite proud of him. He became a famous barrister. He went back to Boston. We stayed in England. We got old."

"What do you see now?"

"He's holding me in his arms. His hair is still thick; now it's white. I have a little cap on my head. Wearing a long nightgown. He kisses me on the cheek. He says we'll always be together in spirit."

"Where are you?"

"I left him."

"Why did you leave?"

"I was lying in bed. I wasn't breathing."

"What have you learned?"

"To always wait for him. That he'll always come back to me. To love my children and let them do what they have to do. I'll always do what he wants. He always wants me to wait for him. He knows how much I love him."

"What lessons are there for Emma?"

"—be faithful, patient, kind."

After a lengthy pause, she resumed.

"He needs good students in his class who appreciate him—to understand him—the way we need him. He doesn't need anyone to look up to him. He's grown up now. I don't have to hold his hand."

"Who is the husband?"

"Philip."

"Who is the son?"

"I don't know."

"Can you tell me more about the son?"

"The son loves his mother. He can talk to her about anything the way J.D. can talk to Emma. They have a special relationship."

"What are the lessons for now?"

"She doesn't want to let him go. It is painful when he is gone. She had to wait for him to come back. You have to go on with your life. You have a baby to take care of. You can't sing to your baby if you're crying. You've got to be happy for other people. Can't pine and pout. He'll come back some day and then you can remember how good it was.

"Don't talk about how much it hurt when he was gone. He is gone because he had important things to do. It is necessary for you to let him do things he has to with his life. If you love him enough, you know in your heart he'll come back. Don't grieve for him while he's gone. Enjoy life now and reflect that happiness when he comes home. Do not allow yourself to be worn out with grief. He wants you to be happy, not sad. He'll love you more if you're happy. He doesn't want to hurt you by going away. He's taking care of business and that will take financial care of his family."

"Is there another lesson for Emma?" David asked.

"I've got to let go. I've got to keep him from being overcome with grief that would keep him from doing the great things he's destined to do. I had to set aside my grief when he was gone to raise our son. I know that he could not do the same if he loses the woman he loves. He may never set aside his grief. I must not let him know that grief. I must protect him from that. I must keep them both safe because he told me we would never part. I know he's right. We'll always be together in spirit."

David brought Emma out of the trance. She blinked her eyes wide open several times.

"Wow," she said. "What a revelation. He's destined to do great things and he needs my sweet beautiful lady, whoever she is. No wonder I've felt protective toward them both."

David nodded, letting Emma draw her own conclusions.

"Seeing him as my husband in another life was a revelation, too. I was feeling—" she hesitated, "aroused, almost. I mean, I never felt that way about Philip Byrd. Maternal, yes; and sort of sisterly, too; but not that way."

"You don't know who the child was, the barrister?"

"No idea whatsoever. I wish it could have been J.D., or even Jim. It wasn't. That's a new soul to me—one I've never met before. That is, I've never met him in this life," she laughed.

"Think about the lessons, about letting go. I'll see you next week."

Emma nodded. This assignment was much better that the last one. She'd be glad to think about this lesson. Emma St. Claire was more than ready to let go of Philip Byrd.

CHAPTER EIGHTEEN

"In much wisdom there is much pain"
-Ecclesiastes 1:18

Emma was lying on the examination table in the EMG room when the neurologist appeared. The medical technician completed her job, preparing Emma for the exam. Electrical wires, electrodes, and cathodes were taped to various areas of Emma's body, including her head, chest, arms, legs, and feet.

"Good morning," he said cheerfully. "How are you?"

"Hi, Dr. Wiley. I think I'd be doing fine if I wasn't a creature from outer space."

He laughed.

"I feel as if I'm being set up for an electrocution, if you want to know the truth," Emma said, feeling somewhat apprehensive about the diagnostic procedure.

"Nah," Dr. Wiley responded. "This will be a piece of cake."

"I have a feeling it will taste nasty."

"Such comments from the lady who said a spinal tap was a breeze."

"It was a breeze. It was the after effects that almost killed me. I'm starting to feel the same way about this."

"Not to worry. Once the test is over, you'll forget about it. It has no side effects."

"Will you swear to that?"

"Scouts honor."

He held up his hand with the Boy Scout sign.

Emma was still apprehensive. When he showed her the probes that would be pushed into her flesh she was horrified. They weren't tiny needles as she had been told. They were blunt ended probes.

"A little prick," he said jovially.

He jammed the probe into the wrist of her left arm. She grimaced in pain.

You're the prick, she said to herself, trying to control tangled emotions of fright, foreboding, and extreme pain. She could not believe how much it hurt.

"A couple more sticks," the prick said again.

Two more probes were rammed into her flesh and she thought he had hit bone. One was at her elbow, another in the muscle on the inside of her arm. She could not believe how awful it hurt. Emma St. Claire had given birth to a nine and a half pound baby without any pain medication and thought she was stoic. The damn probes were hell.

"Now we're set," he said gleefully, reaching for the control knobs on an instrument next to the table.

He flipped a couple of switches, turned some knobs, and said, "Okay, here we go. Ready?"

Emma was not ready for anything except to leave. She wished she had never agreed to the procedure.

"This isn't the Spanish inquisition?" she half-heartedly joked.

A current of electricity ran through wires connected to her arm. It twitched and jerked violently. She was in agony. The doctor was looking at graph paper the nasty machine was spitting out.

"Hmmm—"

Emma was being tortured and the neurologist said "Hmmm—"

"This isn't what I thought it would be," she protested meekly.

There was no sense in trying to escape. Any movement would certainly drive the deadly probes into her arm for a lethal jab. She was trapped.

After ten more minutes of jolting, electrical shocks, and vicious pains searing into her bad arm, the prick turned off the torture machine and pulled out the probes.

"Can you tell me what the graph shows?" she asked, trying to get her mind off the anguish.

"Not yet. Need to study it some. Maybe the other arm will give us more information."

"The other arm. You're not going to torture my good arm are you?"

It was a foolish question for Emma to ask. She had absolutely no intention of letting the sadist near her again.

That night Emma was in agony. The already tender nerves in Emma's left arm had been insulted more than they could stand and they screamed at her the entire night. Propped up on stacks of soft pillows, she laid in angry silence, wondering why she had endured the needless torture. In spite of the pain she did not feel hopeless. The next day she had another appointment with her Knight in Shining Armor.

***

It took Emma longer than usual to shower and dress and she still could not believe her own stupidity.

"I should have known that test would do more harm than good," she cried while washing her hair with only her right hand. If her arm had been in critical condition before, it was now dead.

What's the matter with my e.s.p. anyway? Why didn't it warn me? Philip Byrd is to blame for this. He said there is no such thing as e.s.p. I was a fool to listen to him. Now I'm paying the price. It was hard for me to live with e.s.p. but I don't think I could survive without it. Damn you, Philip Byrd!

Emma's drive to the office was unnerving. A jumbo jet passed over the house and the sound of the engine set her heart to beating wildly. Between the totally disabled arm and echoing sounds of jet engines, she could barely control her car. Emma swerved back and forth in her lane, barely missing other vehicles on the heavily traveled highway.

Safely arriving at the office, she stood at the unwieldy glass door waiting for Joe to see her. He finally looked up from his phone conversation, noticed his secretary's plight, put the phone on hold and came to her rescue.

"I'm sorry I interrupted you," she said apologetically.

"Don't worry about it," he said, hurrying back to his office.

Through her entire ordeal, Joe had always been kind. He never complained about her numerous doctor appointments and when Emma told him about the three-times-a-week physical therapy sessions, he took that in stride, too. It appeared her many years of devoted service were paying off.

Larry laid a stack of invoices on Emma's desk; she cringed at the mound of work and carefully lifted her sore arm to the keyboard. She could not feel the keys.

Dear God, give me the strength. One more day. Please get me through one more day.

By the time Larry returned from the post office with the mail, she had typed two invoices. Emma's faith was getting her through another day. At four o'clock she cleaned off her desk. Her work was finished.

Thank you, Lord. We did it again.

***

"Don't ever have an EMG, David. Unless you're a masochist," Emma said in an upbeat manner.

"That bad, huh?"

"Unbelievable. It kept me awake the entire night. I talked to the neurologist this morning. He said I was having an unusual reaction, that it shouldn't have bothered me in any way."

"What did the test indicate?"

"Nothing. Absolutely nothing. He said there is a problem with my arms. The proper nerve conduction is there but the muscles are too weak to function. I've been tested for every neuromuscular disease you can imagine. They still don't know anything."

David made notes on his yellow legal tablet while Emma prattled on.

"I almost blame Philip Byrd. If my e.s.p. had been working, I never would have subjected myself to that torture."

"Why do you think he has affected your e.s.p.?"

"Because he has given me a complex about it, telling me I'm crazy. Jim calls me a witch but no one has ever accused me of being crazy. You can't imagine how bad it hurts me, David, thinking about the way he said it. Last week you told me to think about letting go. I want to. I've started—but something is still holding me to him. Thank goodness, the dreams are gone. I think about him though. He's always under the edge of my consciousness."

The doctor made more notes on his yellow pad.

"I've been thinking about a couple of other things, too."

"What?"

"I'm not getting anywhere with this arm and neck problem. Physical therapy is helping—though it is painfully slow. Last week, when you did the balloon thing with my head, it helped me feel better and lifted a huge weight. Do you think you could do more along that line?"

"That's an excellent idea. What else have you been thinking about?"

"Remember when we ended up in Boston?"

"Yes," he said, nodding.

240

"I felt as if I was going too far back, too fast. I felt we were missing something?"

"That's interesting. Do you want to see if we did miss something?"

"Yes, I do," she said, nodding her head. "Don't forget my balloon," she laughed.

Emma closed her eyes and took a few deep breaths while David adjusted the video camera. She kicked off her shoes, shrugged her shoulders, relaxed, and he started the induction. In a few minutes Emma was in the deepest trance yet. David started the session with a metaphorical hypnotic suggestion to help her neck.

"There is a very old aqueduct," he said, "and it is corroded."

Emma's mind showed her a picture of an ancient Roman aqueduct, identical to the one she had seen in Italy.

"The water can't flow through it because of the corrosion."

Emma could see the water backed up; it could not move through the chutes.

"We're going to remove the old worn out aqueduct and put in new pipes," David said. "We're going to take out one piece of old stone each time and replace it with new, slick pipe."

One stone near the headwater was lifted out. Emma replaced it with a piece of slick white PVC.

"Now, we're going to take the next piece out."

They continued for several minutes, taking out pieces of corroded aqueduct and inserting Emma's shiny new PVC. At last the project was completed.

"Now water can flow through the new pipes," he said, "the cool water feels soothing as it rushes through the pipes, taking the pain with it."

A refreshing sensation surged through Emma's neck as soothing water flowed down Emma's arms, carrying away the pain.

David's deliberate monotone voice lulled Emma into the deep recesses of her mind and asked her to remember again forgotten memories. His serene manner lulled her as a baby in a cradle; Emma relaxed and slipped further and further away, to another time, another life.

Two beautiful children were walking along a path decorated with a mass of wildflowers next to a narrow, deep, winding river. Behind them in the distance soared huge mountains with steep slopes and pointed peaks. The girl, about eleven, was holding the hand of a small boy. She was wearing a long dress, buttoned down the front. It was made of a floral pattern material that was probably quite stiff when new. Many washings left it slick and soft. On her head was a matching wide-brim bonnet and on her feet were well-worn, brown ankle-high laced boots. The little boy wore dark cinnamon-colored pants held up by suspenders made of the same material. A white shirt was gathered around his neck with a drawstring and the sleeves were long and loose.

The children looked alike, obviously inheriting the best features from each of their parents. Their ash-blond hair was very fine and shimmered in the gleaming sunlight. The girl's long hair hung below her shoulders and cascaded in soft curls around her pretty, square-shaped face. Her skin was very fair and her cheeks were blushed with the healthy glow of a child who was outdoors a lot. His hair was much shorter, making soft ringlets on top of his lovely little head. Their identical mouths had a wide smile outlined by rosy pink thin lips and both children had deep blue eyes.

"He's probably four," she told David. "He's my brother. I love him. I help my Momma take care of him. I always love him. Momma says he's my baby doll."

Again the voice was deep and unfamiliar to Emma. It carefully, slowly annunciated each word as it told the doctor of the image it saw deep within the recesses of Emma's mind.

The little boy looked up into the eyes of his sister and smiled with a look that warmed her soul. Their mutual love enfolded them in a spirit of pure joy.

"What are you doing?" David asked.

"We're picking berries."

The girl removed her bonnet when they started picking berries off small bushes growing beneath the trees near the river. They ate as much as they picked and the girl's wooden bowl was filling very slowly.

"Is your mother there?"

"No. She said we could pick berries and told us not to get near the river. It is early spring. The river is rising. The water is cold. I don't want to go near the water."

"You're picking berries. Then what?"

"He wants to look at the water. I want to pick berries. He runs away from me. He's standing on the bank of the river. The water is full of logs and rubble. Very cold water. Moving real fast. Real loud. I tell him to come back to me. He doesn't. I'm going to go get him. He's standing there. The water is real high."

Emma started to feel very apprehensive. Her heartbeat quickened.

"The embankment is going to cave in! I get to him just as he falls in the water!" she cried out.

Emma was in a panic. Her breath was rapid and shallow. Emma felt the terror of the young girl as she watched her precious little brother fall into the raging river.

"I can't get him," she said tearfully. "He's—I'm crawling down the bank. Try to get him. The water is—cold."

Emma shivered.

"He's holding onto a log. The water is freezing cold—"

Another excruciating shiver shook Emma's body.

"I'm coming, Jason! Please hang on! I'm going to get you."

The terrifying ordeal awakened in Emma St. Claire the terror and panic experienced by the girl. Tears streamed down her face. Ice cold water chilled her to the depths of her soul. Another violent shiver slashed through her body.

The girl was holding onto the root of a tree that hung over the edge of the river where the raging water had washed away the embankment exposing the roots. Her left hand clutched the smooth root, her right hand grasping the hand of the little boy. The torrential flow of the deep water battered her body between the embankment and debris floating in the river. She held onto her little brother, her arms stretching from the root to the child. It seemed as if she hung there for an eternity, her small body being pulled and torn in every conceivable direction. She would not let go.

"I'm cold. He must be cold. He's going to let go. I have his hand—" she said, breathing heavily. "I can't hold him. I'm cold. I'm cold."

She was freezing. She could no longer feel his hand in hers.

"I can't hold him. I can't hold onto him. He's going to let go."

Emma was crying.

The little boy bobbed beneath the water and came up on a passing log. The girl frantically reached out to him again. He was swept away by the river.

A beautiful woman in a long brown skirt, wearing boots similar to the girl's, came running toward the river.

"My Momma's coming, coming to help me," Emma cried out. "She has my hand. He's gone! I can't feel her hand! She's got her hands on me. Cold! Awfully cold! I can't feel her hands! I'm numb."

Emma continued, crying pathetically.

"He's gone. I'm freezing. I can't feel anything. She's wrapping me in a blanket. She's crying."

The beautiful woman, with ash-blond hair tied in a bun on top of her head, was very tall and strong. She gathered the girl into her arms, swaddled the child in a tattered quilt, and ran toward a nearby log cabin.

"A man's coming to help her."

A burly man with a dark beard was right behind the woman. He was followed by several other men wearing hats, boots, and dark pants with suspenders. They lowered a canoe type boat into the river to search for the little boy.

The girl was numb with cold and fright. She was also grief stricken. Her beloved little brother was gone because she could not hold on to him. She was supposed to protect him, to keep him safe from harm. The last time she saw him, his beautiful little face displayed a look of sheer terror.

"I can't feel anything. He's gone—I should have held his hand. I should have taken care of him."

"What was the reaction of others?" David asked Emma.

"I was only a little girl. I tried. Momma said, 'You tried to hang onto him. You did the best you could. We don't blame you.' I loved him. I should have held onto him. He's gone. He was terrified. He thought I was going to get him."

Because Emma was crying uncontrollably, David quickly took her to the end of the girl's life.

"Tell me what you see at her death."

The spirit of the girl was in a bright light. She saw the little boy walking toward her.

"He's very happy to see me. He's smiling at me."

Emma was blissful.

"He's going to give me a hug. He's okay. He's okay. He's happy; smiling. He's not scared the way he was at the river."

"What does he say about drowning?"

"He didn't blame me. He couldn't hold on either. He slipped away. We couldn't hold on to each other."

"What is his reaction to her guilt?"

"He said, 'I didn't hurt.' He told me, 'I didn't hurt. I got real cold. Then I was real happy. I've always been happy. You should be happy, too.' He's taking me by the hand. He's not scared. Not mad. We're together again."

The reunion of the children was peaceful and loving. They held hands and disappeared in a bright light.

"What message is there for Emma in what you have seen today?" David asked.

"She doesn't want him to get hurt again the way he was when he was a little boy—she can't hold on to him, either. He's a big boy, now. She doesn't have to hold him. She can love him from afar. She doesn't need to hold him."

"What about the numbness in Emma's arms? Will there be healing?"

"She doesn't have to feel guilty. She's suffered for a long time. She doesn't have to suffer now. She can always love him. She doesn't have to hold him. He has to be free. He has to be free to be happy. He was always happy when she let go. If she lets go, he'll be happy. She won't be happy unless he's happy."

"Will Emma let go of Philip now?"

"She has to be convinced he won't get hurt and then she can let go. He can be happy, and that will make her happy. She has to tell him one more time. Then she'll let go forever. He'll be free and happy and she will be free and happy."

"Do you have any other comments for Emma?"

"Tell him. She should tell him that she wants him to have a happy life. He must not make that trip."

"The trip on the airplane?"

"Yes."

"What final advice do you have for Emma today?"

"Her neck hurt because Sally was hurt. It was not her fault. It wasn't her fault that Sally got hurt. She didn't want Sally to get hurt. She doesn't want Philip to get hurt."

"You're starting to wake up, now," David said. "Slowly open your eyes."

Emma blinked deliberately, shrugged her shoulders slightly, and shifted her position on the sofa. She stared blankly for a moment, as one does upon waking from a very deep sleep, trying to get a fix on their situation. She wiped her eyes with a Kleenex, blinked again, and rested her chin in the palm of her hand, casting a sideways glance at David.

"Oh, my," she finally said groggily. "That's unbelievable. I never could have imagined that the pain in my arms was associated with a past-life, much less something that tragic. No wonder I've been hurting. And Sally. When the doctor told me there was a problem with the C-4 disc, I immediately thought of her. I never knew that guilt could cause such repercussions."

"The mind is very powerful, Emma. It can do incredible things to our bodies."

"If it made me sick, I know it can heal me, too. The creative visualization helped. I could feel relief almost immediately."

"You can do it whenever you need," David advised. "Relax and go through the same steps."

"I will," Emma said enthusiastically. "Now that I have a reasonable explanation for my mysterious ailment, I can work on getting better."

"And letting go of Philip Byrd, too?"

"Yes. I need to be free of him. Everyone needs to be free, to be themselves. I've always let my children have a lot of freedom. I was stifled as a child. It almost crushed my ego. My children have always been free to spread their wings and soar."

David smiled and gave Emma an approving nod.

"When I saw Philip's future and felt the grief that would come to him if he lost my lady, I felt he would be stifled and crippled emotionally by not having her in his life. It never occurred to me that grief from a past deed of my own was crippling me. No wonder I've been worried about him."

"It doesn't need to cripple you, Emma."

"I know. I feel good, David. The doctors have never been able to come up with any sort of reasonable explanation for my ailment. Guess this would blow their minds."

Raising his eyebrows, David leaned back in the rocking chair and grinned. Then he slowly nodded his head in agreement with Emma.

***

"Guess what happened at David's office today?" Emma excitedly asked Rachel on the phone that evening.

Before Rachel could respond, Emma gave her twin a spellbinding replay of the accident, revealing vivid details of visual images she had seen that she did not give to David. It would have taken hours to describe each scene to him but that was not necessary. Every detail was indelibly impressed on her mind.

"The children were carbon copies their mother," she said, describing the woman in detail. "Her skin was very fair and her long silky ash-blond hair was piled on her head in a bun. She was tall and strong yet still feminine. Very beautiful. She looked Scandinavian."

"What about the father?"

"He was a peace officer of some sort. And a land agent. Highly respected in the settlement."

"How would you know that?"

"Don't know how I know. He did some sort of legal work. He adored his children. It broke his heart to lose his son."

"What happened to the little girl?"

"I don't know. After the accident, I was quite upset; David asked me to go to the end of her life. I guess to get me away from the river. Anyway, I saw her spirit being greeted by the little boy. They were in a bright light. It was very loving. A truly wonderful awareness of total peace."

"I can't imagine how that would feel," Rachel said.

"Amazing, Rachel. I'm sitting in a movie theater, watching a story unwind. Only this story is etched in my mind and soul. It's real. I feel as though I am living through it—again."

"Do you have any idea where you were? Or when?"

"Wyoming, Rachel. I know I was in Wyoming. Sometime in the 1850s."

"How interesting. Do you remember when we were children you read everything in the library on the Old West. You always said you wanted to go to Jackson Hole."

"Golly," Emma gasped, joy glistening in her eyes. "Jackson Hole. A river in Wyoming. It's starting to come together, Rachel. Feelings and thoughts I've had for a lifetime."

"And you have always hated cold water, too," Rachel said.

She shook her head in disbelief and belief. It was real. She had been a child in Wyoming. In another life. Long ago. When she met Philip Byrd, the emotions, love and fear, came flooding back into her mind. No wonder she shivered when she saw him.

"That is astounding, Emma—and inspiring. Makes me wonder what sort of feelings I have because of past life experiences."

"Think of the world-wide repercussions, Rachel. Past hatreds and emotions carried from one lifetime to another by millions of souls. How different the world could be if everyone knew this and forgave one another the way Jesus said and then loved each other and worked in unison to make this planet a better home for all souls."

The twins ended their conversation and Emma hung up the phone. Only a few weeks before their conversations had ended with Emma agonizing over emotions she did not understand. Now, there was an ecstasy in knowing. Feelings of peace and a new kind of love were coming into Emma's life. A new world was opened to her the day she called David Cooper. Bit by bit, the pieces to her puzzle were falling into place. Although she had only filled in a tiny portion of a huge mural, she had made a start. And it was dazzling.

***

Emma arrived early the next morning for her physical therapy session with Maria, determined more than ever to overcome the troubling ailment.

"My, you look chipper this morning," Maria greeted her.

"I'm doing much better. The therapy is starting to work."

How could she possibly tell Maria that it was the therapy of a para-psychologist? Of course, she still needed the physical therapy but the session with David was most revealing. Emma knew she would recover.

"I have someone I want you to meet this morning," Maria said, leading Emma toward whirlpools in the far corner of the room.

"Cybil, this is Emma St. Claire. She's the interesting patient I was telling you about."

"How do you do," Emma said to Cybil, extending her right hand, wondering why Maria would be talking about her case.

The three women crossed the room and entered one of the treatment cubicles. Then Maria began a technical explanation of Emma's ailment.

"She has a bulging C-4 disc," Maria said to Cybil, taking hold of Emma's left arm and holding it up. However, there is considerable atrophy of these muscles with extreme tenderness of the skin. When Maria ran her finger lightly down the arm, Emma cringed.

"She how she flinches?"

"Yes. How interesting. A C-4 should cause pain here," Cybil said, running her finger down a different nerve path. Although this, too, was uncomfortable, it did not bother Emma.

"Doesn't make sense."

"I know," Maria said. "The muscle damage and subsequent atrophy is typical of a trauma, severe trauma in this case. However, Emma insists that there has been no trauma. She's had no accidents, no car wrecks. Nothing."

"Nothing?" Cybil asked Emma.

"Nothing," Emma responded, shaking her head.

After the physical therapists released Emma's arm, Maria told her to change into a loose gown for their morning session.

"It's such a strange case," Maria said to Cybil, glancing at Emma while extending her own arms as far as they would reach in either direction, "this injury looks as if she had been hanging by her arms. For a very long time."

CHAPTER NINETEEN

"Let no unwholesome word proceed from your mouth"
-Ephesians 5:29

Deep in a trance during her next session with David, Emma described the dream of the plane crash, going over many details again and again, giving David new information. It was gruesome for her to look again not only at the lifeless body held in Philip Byrd's arms but also the other victims, either injured or killed. She predicted that there would be twenty-two or twenty-three fatalities. One of them would be a flight attendant who would have a deep laceration on her cheek running diagonally from her ear lobe to her chin. Emma was tormented by the visions and cried in anguish through most of the trance. When she came out of it she felt as though the new facts were worth the mental and emotional agony she endured in order to retrieve them.

She now had precise descriptions of two flight attendants. The first, a ravishing brunette, with long silky henna highlighted hair pulled behind one ear; the other a petite blond, with green eyes. Although Emma's perceptions of the blond were only vague impressions, she had very definite feelings about the brunette.

"This woman has been with the airline a long time," she told Rachel during a conversation that evening.

"How do you know that?"

"I have no idea. That's my perception. She lives alone, too. She's very loving and she was married for a brief period of time."

"Does she have children?"

"No. She has mixed feelings about them. She would have been a wonderful mother though. Very nurturing. She's also a very enlightened soul."

"What do you mean?"

"She's spiritual. She would understand me and my e.s.p. She believes in reincarnation. We'd be very, very close friends. I know we would."

"Why do you think you know these things about her?"

"Philip Byrd won't do anything. I believe my mind is grasping for help by giving me information about other people who will be on that flight next May. That's the only way I can stop it."

"You actually think you can, don't you?"

"I can't live with another Orly, Rachel. I can't. I would rather die. Besides, in a way it's out of my hands now."

"Why's that?"

"David told me today that he has a duty to warn the airline, some sort of professional liability thing. Anyway, he said he was going to call Philip Byrd and talk to him. He also said he was going to call another man at the airline, someone who investigates matters such as this."

"You're kidding? Someone who believes in e.s.p. works for the airline?"

"I only know they have someone who looks into this sort of thing. I don't know if he believes in e.s.p."

"I can't imagine someone in such position would not believe in psychic premonitions."

"Many people think e.s.p. and telepathy and precognition are a bunch of hocus-pocus. I've been reading Dad's Bible a lot and I'm starting to learn how important the prophets were. If they were alive today we would say they were psychic. They used their abilities to help people. That's all I wanted to do. I just wanted to prevent that damn—that damn—"

Emma started to cry when horrific visions flashed through her mind again.

"Don't cry, Emma. You've been doing much better lately."

"It hurts to see those dead and dying people, Rachel. You can't imagine what it does to me. Remember what Isaiah says?"

"No. What does Isaiah say?"

"He says where there is no vision, the people perish. That's true, Rachel; there are few believers in today's world. If it can't be explained scientifically, people don't think it's real. My perceptions are real, Rachel. I know they are. If I don't do something to stop that plane crash, a lot of people will perish."

"Don't think that way, Emma. You've got plenty of time to sort it out. Look at the progress you've made already."

"I'm a snail climbing Mount Everest. I can't even see the top of the mountain yet. I think I'm living on prayer. Somehow, God manages to get me through each day. I pray for my sweet, beautiful lady every day, too."

"Why don't you give her a name, Emma?"

"A name? Such as?"

"I don't know. Think of something. It still bothers me to hear you call her your, your—"

"Yeah. You're right. She should have a name. Help me."

"Describe her. How does she carry herself?"

"She's regal."

"What else?"

"She's graceful."

"Okay. Regal and graceful. What else comes to mind?"

"Fragile as a flower."

"What kind of flower? What's your favorite?"

"Queen Anne's Lace."

"There you go. You should call her Anne."

"That's perfect, Rachel. Anne. Now someone else in this episode has a name."

"What do you mean, someone else?"

"I had a dream the other night. I was in Thomson. I was looking for Margaret."

"Margaret?"

"Yes. The little gray-haired lady. Her name is Margaret. That's what someone told me."

"Who?"

"This woman in the dream. I said, 'that's not what they called her.' I guess she must have gone by a nickname. I also said I was looking for someone named Naomi."

"Who's she!"

"She's supposed to be related to Mr. Byrd."

"How would you know that?"

"That's what I said in the dream. I said that Naomi would know what they called Margaret."

"—more puzzle pieces."

"I don't think my snail will ever get to the top of Everest," Emma said dejectedly.

251

"Yes, he will, Emma. Mark my word. When he gets there, he'll have an unbelievable view."

***

Alex was out of his pen again when Emma left for work the next morning but he came running happily to her when she called.

"You bad boy," she scolded half-heartedly. It was not the little dog's fault that Jim turned off the electricity to the fence.

"Stay here, boy," she admonished, pushing him into the pen. Dobie and Boise enthusiastically grabbed dog biscuits Emma offered. Alex only wanted to play.

"We'll play tonight when Mama gets home from work, Alex."

The drive to the office was again dangerous for Emma. A jumbo jet passed overhead when she entered the perimeter highway. Visions of the plane crash did a wicked dance through her mind and distorted her vision. Emma could barely see the merging lane and swerved in front of a huge tractor-trailer, hit the brakes momentarily for no reason, then slid into the next lane. Trying desperately to get hold of herself, she wiped her blood shot eyes and realized she was surrounded by four road monsters. Ahead and behind her, and on either side, Emma and the four tractor-trailers moved down the freeway in a convoy. Her car swayed back and forth between the lane lines. Emma felt doomed. Her arms ached. The weak left hand rested limply in her lap. The convoy moved down the freeway at increasing speed. Emma swayed and swerved, narrowly missing a giant fender to her left, then a fast-moving road tractor tire on the right. Back and forth, back and forth. The car dodged one way, then another.

"Dear Lord," she prayed aloud, unable to hear her own voice over the roar of the engines surrounding her, "please take care of me."

She cried again.

"Father, in heaven—"

A short while later she was standing at the office door waiting for Joe to see her. Emma's heavenly Father had rescued her again.

That afternoon she was talking to J.D. on the telephone when a storm blew over the office.

"We've got a thunderstorm here, J.D. What's it doing out there?"

"It's starting to drizzle. I better go put up my car windows, Mom. See you in a little while."

"Okay, Darlin'. Love you."

252

J.D. grabbed his keys off the key rack in the kitchen and darted to the car. The temperature dropped to the low seventies when the thunderclouds rolled in, a cooling summer shower not far behind. He opened the car door, turned the key in the ignition, pushed the power window buttons, jumped out of the car, slammed the door and ran back to the house; a bolt of lightning crossed the darkened sky and thunder roared.

An hour later Emma arrived home and parked her car in the garage. A gentle breeze caressed her face when she rounded the corner of the building on her way to the dog pen. While she was reaching over the fence to pat Boise and Dobie, a passenger jet soared through the sky above her. The sound of the engine told Emma it was an L1011.

No. Not that sound. Not that plane.

Visions of the fiery crash and Anne's blood on Mr. Byrd's hands ran through her mind and sent her into the downward spiral of despair and confusion that David labeled a type of traumatic stress syndrome. She sank to her knees, holding onto the fence.

No, Dear God. No. Please get me out of this storm in my mind. Please.

Emma clutched the fence and fell to her knees on the wet, green grass. She was drained. Completely drained. Her mind was on the verge of cracking. Simple mental processes, such as following a chain of thoughts to a logical conclusion, were impossible for Emma when overtaken by these spells. Concrete thoughts, such as math or cooking, could only be accomplished with much effort, and only one at a time. If too many came, she would almost cease to function altogether.

Emma prayed fervently for God not to abandon her when she sank to the lowest depths of her own private hell and somehow, slowly, she would withdraw from the storm as God's comfort surrounded her and shielded her from the anguish. Visions erased from her mind, she regained her composure and God gave her the strength to do what she had to do.

With deliberate effort, Emma haltingly released her hold on the wire, each finger uncurling as she let go of the fence and let go of mental pain. Pulling herself up, she stared ahead at nothing, then walked solemnly to the house. When she got to the front door, Emma received a very strong message from her silent voice: *Check the car.*

She stared blankly at the red front door to the house, her hand resting on the latch. Shaking her head, Emma turned around. J.D.'s car was parked on the far side of the turn-around, not in his usual place near the brick sidewalk next to the steps.

Check the car.

She shook her head more forcefully.

No, I won't give in to it. I won't. Philip Byrd says I make bad things happen. I don't. I know I don't. He's wrong. He thinks I'm crazy because I'm psychic. I'm not. I'm not crazy. I'm not crazy.

She turned back toward the door, pushed the latch, and went inside. Again her e.s.p. spoke out.

Check the car.

J.D. was sprawled out on his bed with the sports pages, the stereo playing loudly. Emma stuck her head in his room.

"Hi, Punk' in'," she called over the high volume of music.

He looked up, "Hi Mom," and returned to his newspaper.

"Alex wasn't in his pen. Have you seen him?" Emma had never been satisfied with the new dog pen and neither had Alex.

Emma went to the kitchen and called Alex from the back door.

"Here, Alex. Mama's home. Heeeere—Alex!"

Alex did not appear.

Emma thought momentarily about cooking and put on her apron. Stress caused by the jetliner lingered; Emma's mind was blank. She took out two pots and a frying pan and stood at the stove trying to remember what she planned to make. For a long while she stared forlornly into the pantry, then she looked in the refrigerator. She went to the back door again.

"Heeere— Alex!"

The black spaniel did not answer her plaintiff voice.

J.D. came into the kitchen.

"What's for dinner, Mom?"

Emma looked at her son with a puzzled expression on her face.

"What's for dinner—" she muttered, talking more to herself than to her son. "Huh—dinner?"

"Yes, Mom. What are we eating tonight? I'm starved."

"Alex. Have you seen him?"

"Mom, we're not eating Alex," J.D. said in a jesting tone. "I haven't seen him."

Emma opened the back door and called again.

"Allll—exxxxx!"

Another jumbo jet flew overhead.

The visions were more than she could stand. J.D. was obviously disturbed.

"I don't know why you hate this kitchen, Mom," he said, thinking she was crying about the room she said she detested when they moved into the house. "You and Dad did a great job fixing it up."

The tall teenager spread his arms, pointing to the remodeling and stylish new decor. How could Emma tell her son, who did not believe in e.s.p., that she was having visions of a plane crash?

Emma took off her apron. Cooking tonight was impossible.

"Let's go to Brick House—" she said half-heartedly.

"Terrif!" J.D. exclaimed.

Jim and J.D. showered while Emma sipped a glass of wine, sitting on the back porch in her rocking chair, waiting for Alex to come home.

At Brick House, Jim and J.D. grazed on the buffet line, each satisfying their ample appetites while Emma leisurely munched on a salad and nibbled on a piece of pizza.

"C'mon, Baby. You have to eat more than rabbit food. You're losing too much weight," Jim begged his wife when he came back to the table with another plate of food.

"I can't eat," she whined. "I'm worried about Alex."

"Don't worry about that stupid mutt. He'll come home."

Calling her dog a stupid mutt did not make Emma feel better. She chewed on lettuce and said no more. Jim never appreciated her feelings.

On the way home Jim stopped at the gas station where he dutifully filled the gas tank, checked oil and water, washed the windshield, and put air in one of the tires. He was responsible and efficient in maintaining their cars and Emma wondered why these skills didn't carry over to his business.

Another light shower started when they pulled into the garage and they dashed to the front door. Emma looked wistfully towards J.D.'s car before going inside.

J.D. and Emma went upstairs to the exercise room where she rode the stationary bike five miles while he worked out with weights. Thirty minutes later Emma found her husband asleep on the sofa in front of the television.

"Honey," she said softly, gently shaking the sleeping hulk. "Why don't you go upstairs and go to bed?"

He snorted, opened his eyes, turned on his side and went back to sleep.

Emma turned on the radio, tuned in the classical music station and listened to the 4th movement of Rimsky-Korsakov's Suite *Scheherazade, Festival, Storm, and Shipwreck*, while doing her physical therapy.

"There's a storm going on in me," she said aloud to the vaulted ceiling. "No one can see it or hear it. The wind is blowing a mighty, silent storm. God, will it ever end? Will that tiny snail ever make it to the top of the mountain?"

Emma lay quietly on her back with her arms resting on bags of frozen turnip greens she used for ice packs after workouts. Though the exercises were painful, Emma did them faithfully, twice each day. After a hot shower she went to the back door and gave another fruitless call for her dog before kissing her sleeping husband goodnight. When Emma got to her room she looked out the front window, across the lawn, to where J.D.'s car was parked.

Check the car.

She closed the blinds while shaking her head.

I'm not crazy. I'm not evil. I'm not. I'm not.

Emma was morose the next morning. Alex was not home yet. She ate breakfast with her husband and son, responding only when spoken to.

"I don't have morning practice today, Mom. Coach has to go to some sort of meeting," J.D. said.

"What about this afternoon? The weatherman said it was going to get hot later today."

"Coach told us to be at the field at four o'clock."

"I don't know how you guys stand it, Darlin', running around in those heavy pads in ninety-five degree heat. Drink plenty of fluids. Too bad you couldn't practice yesterday when it was nice and cool."

Emma finished her coffee, kissed her husband on the cheek, and tousled J.D.'s hair.

"Give me a call, Punkin', when Alex shows up."

"You still worried about that mutt?" Jim asked.

Emma ignored Jim's comment and looked directly at her son.

"Please call me."

"I will, Mom."

Emma went out the front door, down the brick steps, stopped to stare at J.D.'s car before crossing the driveway to the garage. It was not until she reached for the handle on the overhead door that she realized Jim had followed her.

"Here, Baby, I'll do that," her husband said in a kind and solicitous manner.

"Thank you," Emma responded weakly when Jim lifted the door.

She backed the car out and waved limply to Jim before passing J.D.'s car.

Why? Why was I supposed to check J.D.'s car?

Haydn's 84th symphony, one of Emma's favorite pieces of music, was playing on the radio; she turned up the volume to drown out the sound of jet engines soaring above her. Troublesome images charged through her mind; before she knew it, she was parked in front of her office, fighting back the despondency dammed up inside her.

I can't let that plane crash. I can't. I can't. Philip Byrd can say I'm evil or crazy. I know I'm not. I'd never let someone get hurt if I could stop it and I won't let my Anne get hurt. I won't.

Office activities superficially lifted Emma out of her despair. With her mind awash in a sea of gloom she answered the phone, typed a letter, opened mail, and acted the role of a completely normal secretary. A few hours later, when her bosses were gone and morning duties were completed, Emma took her father's Bible out of the desk drawer and opened it randomly.

"Cast your anxieties on him, for he cares about you," she read in I Peter, verse seven of chapter five. Then she read verse ten, which was even more comforting, "And after you have suffered for a little while, the God of grace, who called you to His eternal glory in Christ, will Himself perfect, confirm, strengthen, and establish you."

No matter what happens, I know I'm in God's loving care.

She smiled. The despair had dissipated; Emma St. Claire felt a lot better.

At lunchtime she called J.D.; still no sign of Alex.

"Be careful at practice today," she cautioned her son.

At three thirty, while Emma was in the kitchen making afternoon coffee, the phone rang in the conference room. She answered it cheerfully, "Good afternoon, Smith Construction."

"Mama—"It was J.D. He was crying.

Emma could not remember the last time her son had cried. Her heart pounded; there was a lump in her throat.

"What is it, J.D.?"

"Alex, Mama—"

Emma felt the trembling that overcomes one when they know they are about to hear bad news.

"What, J.D.? What about Alex!"

"He's dead, Mama. Alex is dead—"

Emma cried. "How, Darlin'? How did it happen?"

"He was in the car—"

"No, J.D. He wasn't—he couldn't have been—in the car."

"I'm sorry, Mama."

They both cried for a few moments before J.D. resumed his story. "He must have jumped in the back when I put up the windows yesterday. I didn't see him, Mom. Honestly, I never saw him."

J.D. was crying and apologizing as it if was his fault that Emma's beloved little dog was dead. Of course, Emma knew she could have prevented it. If only she had looked in the car when she got home from work that cool afternoon. Her precious little dog, her companion, her pal, her confidant, her friend, would be alive.

It never occurred to Emma that looking in J.D.'s car had anything to do with Alex. The two thoughts ran on separate tracks that never merged. Now, because of her mental lethargy, and Philip Byrd's admonition, her beloved pet was gone.

"J.D., it is not your fault, Darlin'. Alex loved to hide in cars. How many times have we dragged him out of the back seat because he managed to sneak in? He loved us and he wanted to be with us—"

Emma's heart was broken. She consoled her son again and hung up the phone.

I should have listened to my silent voice. Why didn't I look in the car? Why?

She went to the bathroom to repair her damaged makeup. Mascara ran down her cheeks, her eyes were swollen, her nose was red. She stared into the mirror.

Damn you, Philip Byrd. Damn you! I hate you. You said I was crazy. You said I make bad things happen. I don't. I don't. If I had listened to myself, I would have gone to the car right away. I would have found my precious Alex dog—and he would be alive now. I listened to you, and the awful things you said about me. You were wrong, Teacher. Dead wrong!

***

"I'm sitting at a kitchen table, at a house in the country," Emma said to David in her trance voice. "I'm talking to Margaret. She's fixing us some tea. I— need to talk to her. Why do I have these psychic feelings that I don't understand?"

"What does Margaret tell you?" David asked Emma in his quiet monotone voice used only during trance work.

"She's very religious. She says God has a purpose. That I have to feel these things in order to teach them to other people. It is challenging. They don't want to learn. Margaret says, 'That's why

He chose you, Emma. Because you are strong. You will do the things you are called to do.'

"People think I'm weird when I tell them these things. They don't believe."

"Do you believe these feelings?" David asked.

"Yes, I believe them. I've seen them and felt them. They're very real to me.

"Margaret says, 'Then all you can do is try to tell them and try to show them by example. By living a good Christian life. Someday they will have to believe. If they don't believe now, and they don't listen to you, then what you say will happen, will happen. Then they'll believe.'

"They will get hurt. I don't want the people to get hurt—it feels dreadful," Emma said, a deep frown forming on her forehead.

"Margaret says, 'You've always felt other people's pain. That is part of your gift and part of your burden. You have to believe that God ordained it. He will give you the strength you need.'"

When David brought Emma out of the trance there was a marked improvement in her outlook.

"I never looked at my e.s.p. that way, David. Part blessing and part burden. My psychology professor, the one who goes to my Mom's church, told me that God was making me strong for a purpose. I guess I should sit up and listen, huh?"

"How did you feel when Alex died?"

"That I should have listened to myself. It's not easy, David, to be different. To see visions and dream dreams of the future and then have the people you love ridicule you because of your gift from God."

"You feel that Philip Byrd ridiculed you?"

"Yes, and Jim does, too. He's always called me a witch. My son. J.D. would never say such things to me even though he doesn't believe in spiritual gifts either. David, being psychic, and feeling what others feel, and seeing the future, makes me close to people. It gives me some sort of innate understanding of them—and that very same spiritual connection to others drives them away from me because they are scared of it. That's why it is challenging and exasperating."

David leaned back in his rocking chair and listened. A good counselor helped patients to help themselves, allowing them to draw out the problem and the solution that lay hidden within. Many times a patient is unaware of this concealed wealth, the spiritual abundance that is available to every soul. Through David's skillful and patient guidance, Emma was finding wisdom her soul accumulated through many experiences, in many lives.

"Guess what?" she finally asked.

David shook his head.

"The pain has been worth it— my arms, the nightmares, even the fits of disabling depression when I hear an L1011. This is the price I pay to walk this incredible path with you. I'm changing, David. A lot. I know when I get to the top of my mountain, I'll be a different person. I read a beautiful quote the other day and when things are feeling dark I try to remember it."

"What's the quote?"

"I'm reading a book called *Psychology and Religion* by Seward Hiltner. He's an English theologian. He says only inner light can dispel inner darkness."

David nodded and smiled in agreement.

"He also says that the inner light is the power of God. If God created our souls, doesn't that mean He is in us? And if He is in us, we can get quiet and listen to Him."

A few days later a United Air Lines jet crashed in Sioux City and Emma found herself in a tailspin of depression. There were uncanny similarities between the Sioux City crash and the one Emma dreamed: The plane landed in a field not far from an airport; many survivors walked away unharmed; much of the damage was in the first class section; there was a fire in the tail.

Emma St. Claire wanted to shake Philip Byrd by the shoulders and say to him, "You idiot! Why won't you listen to me? I have to know where you are flying in May! You have to help me!"

Of course, she couldn't do that. She could only listen to the still, small voice within and hope it would tell her what she needed to know to prevent the crash. Being quiet in the midst of a pending tragedy was unbearably difficult to do. How could she be still and listen to the voice within when people lay injured and dying in a field near an airport?

***

Emma left the college library, rounded the corner of the red brick building, and ran right into Tracie, the small Afro-American girl she met in economics class.

"Tracie! How good to see you," Emma exclaimed while trying to catch the stack of books cascading out of her arms.

Tracie laughed and grabbed one of the texts.

"Talk about running into somebody. You mean what you say, don't you?" Tracie teased.

Emma knelt down to retrieve her things. Her journal fell open and papers blew in the warm evening breeze.

"What in the world are you working on here?" Tracie asked while helping Emma.

"This is my journal. These books are for some research I'm doing."

"Research—on what?"

"Oh—hum mm—"

How in the world could Emma tell Tracie she was psychic, that she was doing research on religious and psychological implications of spiritual gifts?

"Hmmm," Tracie purred between her full lips, picking up one of the books and handing it to Emma. "*The Reluctant Prophet*. I ought to read that."

"And why would you want to read it?" Emma quizzed. Although she was reluctant to discuss her e.s.p., for some reason Emma felt Tracie would understand. *Tell her*, Emma's e.s.p. said.

The women gathered the papers, restacked books in Emma's arms and were walking toward the Student Center when a jumbo jet passed overhead. Emma's heart began to flutter the way it always did at the sound of Rolls Royce jet engines. Before Emma could say anything to Tracie about her e.s.p., Tracie stopped in her tracks, put her small hand to her chest, and said to Emma, "Say, tell me what this pain is I feel. You have a trembling type of pain around your heart. It is very uncomfortable and it's hurting me. What is it?"

Emma was astounded. Tracie described exactly the pain in Emma's chest.

"You might say that it is a spiritual vibration—" she couldn't finish.

Tracie reached out and touched Emma on the arm.

"You can trust me. I'm psychic, too. I have e.s.p. I know what you're feeling; I don't understand what's going on."

"It's a long story, Tracie. That's why I'm keeping this journal. I want to understand spiritual life. It—it has something to do with a teacher here at school."

"Mr. Byrd. It is about Mr. Byrd, isn't it?" Tracie was smiling and nodding her head enthusiastically.

It was obvious to Emma that Tracie was more relaxed about her e.s.p. than Emma was. Tracie went with the flow, relaying information as it came to her.

"You handle it beautifully," Emma finally said. "How do you do it?"

"I don't know. I have fun with it. I can tell my friends how many pairs of shoes they have under their beds or whether they left dirty dishes in the sink."

"You're kidding. You can do that?"

"Yep. Sure can."

Tracie went on to relay several of her recent episodes to Emma.

"I wish my e.s.p. was fun, Tracie. I'm working on a major episode now that's about to kill me."

"Is that why you have the pain? Are you doing anything about it?"

"Yes. I'll tell you the whole story when you have the time."

"That's a story I want to hear. No one knows how it feels to be psychic unless they are. I have to be careful about it. My close friends know how I am. Most of the time people just don't understand. They tend to think you're either weird or possessed if you say you have e.s.p."

The women stood in the middle of the sidewalk and talked for thirty minutes. Emma had never known anyone like Tracie and she felt truly blessed to meet a wonderful, vivacious young woman who was completely at ease with her psychic abilities.

"I better get to class," Tracie said reluctantly.

"You can't imagine how much it means to me to talk openly, Tracie."

"I enjoyed it too. We'll have to have more talks. Maybe you can stop by my classroom. I'm here on Tuesdays and Thursdays.

"I will," Emma replied eagerly. "This has been wonderful."

She put her hand on Tracie's, giving a slight squeeze.

"We need to talk about your arms, too," Tracie said.

Emma shook her head slowly.

"You are truly amazing, Tracie. You are a treasure."

There was a bond between the two women that could not be described.

"One more thing I have to tell you real quick before I go," Tracie said, looking up at her new friend.

Emma was curious about Tracie's abilities. What could she possibly say now?

"You have a light blue aura," she said, grinning.

"I do? You can see auras, too? How do you do it? What does light blue mean?"

"I see a lot of auras. I don't know what the colors mean—only how they make me feel. The light blue around you looks nice—a good aura, I know that. Red auras upset me and I avoid people who have them."

"You're remarkable, Tracie."

The newfound friends smiled at each other.

"Maybe one of these books will tell me something about auras."

"If you find out, let me know. That light blue is pretty."

The women parted company and Tracie ran to class. On the way to her car Emma stopped in the Student Center for a cup of vending machine coffee. At long last she could talk to and trust someone besides Rachel or Dr. Cooper. A friend. A real friend. A psychic friend. Emma could only wonder what else Tracie would say.

Tracie says I have a light blue aura. I wonder what that means.

***

During Emma's next session with David he told her he contacted Atlantic Airways and also talked to Philip Byrd.

"He's a very enlightened man," Emma. "He's actually quite knowledgeable of reincarnation."

"I find it hard to believe that Philip Byrd is enlightened about anything spiritual, David."

"We had a long, interesting conversation. I gave him your phone number and asked him to call you. It will be good for you to tell him what has transpired. He said he'd call you."

Emma shook her head, raised her eyebrows, and bit her lip.

"No, David. He'll never call me. He'll never give me the opportunity to explain any of it."

David shrugged his shoulders slightly.

"He said he would."

"Nope. He won't. Mark my word. He'll never call me."

***

"I've decided to leave Jim," Emma said in an unemotional, matter of fact manner to Rachel.

"Emma, I'm sorry."

"I'm not, Rachel. I've been trying to do this for ten years and I'm at peace with it. I'm not going to live with the pain of his lies. There is no trust in our marriage. He does as he pleases with no regard for me or the children. We've suffered from his reckless business deals, his lies, his deceptions. Janice told me the day we were married she would always be first in his life. There was never much place for me in his life and his lies pushed me out of what little space I did have. I still care for him. I can't live with him. At least not for a while. I'm moving out for six months."

263

"Where are you going?"

"There's a new apartment complex in Stone Mountain. J.D. went over there with me this afternoon after work. He made the leasing agent show us ten units before he found one that met his approval. He said it had to be the right one for his mom."

"Did you find one?"

"Yes. It couldn't be better. It's a roommate apartment with a bedroom and a bath on each side connected by the living area. I'll have one and J.D. the other—we'll each have the privacy we're accustomed to. We have a nice little kitchen and laundry room and the view from our patio is magnificent."

"You can see the mountain?"

"Yes. Look right at it. Can't wait for you to see it."

"J.D. is going with you, isn't he?"

"Of course. I could never leave without him."

"When's moving day?"

"September 15."

"Good. I'll be down there to help you move in."

"You will?"

"Of course I will. Haven't I always been there for you when you needed me?"

"Yes, Rachel. Of course you have. I wouldn't be alive if it wasn't for you."

"What are you and Dr. Cooper working on?" Rachel asked, abruptly changing the subject.

"He called Philip Byrd."

"You're kidding!"

"Nope. Said he has a duty to warn. He also talked to that man at the airline I told you about."

"What did he say?"

"He gave David a list of questions for me to answer. In order to do it, I'll have to do more trance work. I'll have to look at the whole disaster again to see if I can come up with anything else. I don't know if I can do it."

"Don't you realize that if you find out more it will help you ward off a tragedy?"

"Yes, but that doesn't take away the terror of seeing it. David said I've lived with it for such a long time that it is entrenched in my emotions. Someday, maybe I can be more objective. Not right now. Besides, I already gave David more info."

"You did? What?"

"After that crash in Sioux City, I dreamed about the one at Hartsfield again. Only this time there was a long crack in the plane. I told David it looked as if it had run into something, or something had hit it."

"Do you have any idea what?"

"No. I hear that loud noise, then see the damage. I don't know what causes it."

"There's still plenty of time between now and next May. I think you're going to get it sorted out, Emma."

"Maybe. If it doesn't kill me first."

"Don't say that!" Rachel snapped.

Emma changed the subject abruptly.

"Guess what I'm taking fall quarter?"

"No telling."

"Reincarnation."

"What! Where in the world can you take a course on reincarnation?"

"The Continuing Education department is offering it in the life enrichment series. I almost fainted when I saw it in the bulletin. I know I'll learn a lot. It will be good to look at this provocative subject from an academic standpoint."

"Did you tell Bee that you're taking it? She believes in reincarnation, too."

"Yes, I know she does. I haven't told her any of this. I'm not up to that yet. I'll tell her when the time is right."

***

That night Emma had another dream about Philip Byrd and Anne. Emma was dangling on the side of a sheer drop-off. In the far distance was a rumbling noise of rushing water. Her left hand desperately clutched the rocky ledge and hanging below her, held only by Emma's right hand, was Anne. Anne was screaming for Philip.

"Get over here and help us," she yelled. "Don't you realize Emma's trying to save us?" When Emma awoke, her arms hurt worse than ever.

In a trance session with David a few days later Emma described the happy home Philip Byrd and Anne could enjoy but would never know if she died in the crash. Then in the deep, old voice that came from somewhere in her soul, Emma said, "He needs to learn about the reality of the unseen. The oneness we all belong to. He's not just one. He's just a part of One."

"There's more to life than what you see and the most important part is the part you can't see. You can only feel it, only reach it through your heart, your mind, and your soul.

"She's aware of these things. She can teach him," the voice said.

"Who is she?" David asked.

"Anne. My Anne. She can teach him what he needs to know. She's the only one who can teach him. She's the only one he'll listen to because he'll let her get close to him. Not that he's incapable of loving. He does not see the necessity for these lessons. She can teach him how important it is to honor these things.

"She wants me to teach him. He doesn't want to learn from me—she says he needs to know what I know."

"What lessons are here for Emma?" David inquired.

"They tell me that I shouldn't feel the pain of others, that it binds me to them. That I can teach those who want to learn. When they are ready to learn the lessons, they will. Many won't learn; and they will be hurt. I feel their pain. Then I try to make them learn the lessons they're not capable of learning. I have to let go of their pain if I'm going to let go of them. I have to bear my own pain; and they will have to bear their own pain. I'm not letting them grow up if I carry it for them. They will grow strong with some adversity.

"If they don't grow strong, they'll never learn the lessons. They'll have to feel their own pain. They have to grow strong in their own time. I've got to get out of their way. I can't do it for them.

"I had to learn my lessons myself. Nobody learned them for me. Nobody made them easy for me.

"Everyone has to walk their own path. Everyone has to learn their own lessons. No path is easy."

***

Emma arose early on the morning of September 15, 1989, and drove to the new apartment complex where she paid rent and picked up keys. Jim and J.D. were loading the few pieces of furniture she was taking and Emma asked them be ready when she returned. Hoping for a reconciliation, she took only the barest essentials and her clothes.

She turned off the paved road and onto the graveled pathway of North Ridge, and rolled down the car window to savor once again the delicious smells of clean country air. Scotch Broom plants decorated shoulders of the narrow lane with clumps of cheerful yellow blossoms surrounded by rare yellow Stone Mountain daisies. A vivid blue sky was dotted with cotton boll shaped clouds and there was a hint of fall in the air. While Emma studied the edges of dogwood leaves already turned a brilliant scarlet, a cool breeze whistled through the forest and brushed her face. Although Emma had driven winding road hundreds of times she relished the view. She would miss her life in the country; she would miss North Ridge Road. Wildflowers blooming from February through November played a symphony with nature, with changes in tone and mood, color and texture, scarcity and surplus. Because the nature show always refreshed her, Emma often stopped at the creek to enjoy the beauty of the seasons.

Emma parked her car at the side of the road and walked to the bridge. The county had replaced rickety old wood railings with substantial iron pipes and she wondered why they planned to use this route for the garbage trucks.

"This old bridge will never hold up to that kind of use," she said aloud to the chirping birds and squirrels playing in the nearby oak tree. "Everything is changing, folks," she continued as if the wild critters could comprehend what she said. "Before long there will be garbage trucks and dump trucks and Lord only knows what else coming up and down our road. Y'all will be moving on, too."

Emma grabbed the rail tightly as if she could squeeze her pain out of it.

No more. I've sowed enough pain. Now I want to reap some joy!

She wiped her eyes with the back of her hand and sniffled. Tears from her eyes fell into the crystal clear brook and mixed for eternity with water flowing under the small bridge. The gentle stream washed across the rocks and gravel, carrying away the by-product of Emma's anguish.

How nice it would be if my e.s.p. could be disposed of as easily as my tears in the water. How nice it would be if we could change effortlessly. Nature changes constantly. If we don't change, we don't grow. I wish Philip Byrd would change his mind about my e.s.p. I know my suffering cannot make him change; it can only change me. He told me three years ago that we get to the point where we have to change. He'll change and grow in his own time, as I have. As we all do—eventually.

Emma threw a pebble in the creek and watched concentric circles spread over the water while thinking about the enormous debt load she had taken on. Jim bailed out of his financial responsibilities via bankruptcy court but to keep her good credit rating, Emma agreed to pay off the accounts held in both their names. Every one of the credit charges had been made by Jim. She could only wonder if he would ever pay her back.

Her arms ached. A jet liner soared overhead, bringing with it the still worrisome visions of the nightmare, sending Emma's mind into another tailspin.

Dear God, in heaven, I can't handle it. None of it. The dreams. The e.s.p. The pain. The plane crash. Now those credit card bills, too. Dear Lord. Help me. I can't handle my life. I can't handle any of it. I'm starting over, God. And I'm putting myself in your hands. Do with me what you will.

Emma returned to her car and drove up the long, steep serpentine hill to the house. As she drove, she felt relief. Her life was in God's hands.

"Ready, fellas?" she called to Jim and J.D. from her car window, waving the apartment keys. "Let's make hay and hit the trail."

J.D. climbed behind the wheel of the truck and Jim checked the rear door of the van before they started down the long driveway. Emma followed them, circling the drive turn-around. She paused to look at Alex's grave beneath the trees.

My precious little Alex—

She turned to look at her rose bushes. Roses that were in full bloom days earlier were now faded and dying; behind them new buds were shooting up from stems Emma had pruned.

We are like a rose bush. Parts of us grow and blossom, then die away. In its place something new comes up and there are new buds on the bush. Our old ideas and beliefs have to die to make room for the new.

Emma followed her men out the driveway, stopping again to look at the tangle of honeysuckle vines and morning glories. Deep purple blooms waved gently in the morning breeze, bowing their heads toward the sun, thanking God for another glorious day.

"Joy cometh in the morning," Emma called to the happy blossoms.

Since the men were out of sight by the time she reached the road Emma decided not to race after them. She drove slowly toward her new home and her new life. Fire red salvia plants and a manicured lawn greeted Emma again when she arrived at the entrance to the apartment. She had no idea what lay ahead. Would her arms recover? Could she prevent the plane crash? How would she ever pay twenty thousand dollars of Jim's bills?

"I'm not going to worry about it," she said, arching her back and looking toward the sky. "I put it in your hands, God. Take me wherever you want me to go."

***

The following Saturday Emma stopped by the house to pick up a few things and almost ran into Janice in the driveway.

"You're the person I want to see," Janice sneered.

"Me? What can I do for you?"

"Here," Janice said, handing Emma an old envelope covered with a long list of penciled notes that started on one side and filled the back, too.

"What's this?" Emma asked innocently.

"That, my dear, is a list of everything I have ever bought for you and your children. Since you are leaving Jim, you must repay me for everything I have ever done for you!" Janice demanded.

Emma was incredulous. Was this not proof that Janice Crymes was an agent of the devil? Who in their right mind would keep a list, for more than twenty years, of everything they had ever purchased?

Emma laughed. "Surely you jest," she said, handing the envelope back to Janice.

She got in her car and left. Had it not been so malicious, it would have been funny.

Emma drove into the village to see her hairdresser, Bob. She was in a new phase of her life and wanted a new hairstyle.

"Morning," she said, entering the shop. People were buzzing around in the usual Saturday hustle.

"Hi, Emma," Bob called out. "Come on back and we'll get started."

Bob escorted Emma to the back of the shop to the dressing room and handed her a smock. Then leaning in close, he whispered, "Hey, tell me about your new honey."

"What?" Emma answered, drawing back. "What in the world are you talking about?"

"You don't have to be shy with me, Emma. Haven't we shared a lot of personal stuff over the years?"

"Yes," Emma stammered. "What are you asking?"

"Hear you have a new honey bun—that's why you're leaving Jim," Bob said with a twinkle in his eyes.

"That's absurd," Emma retorted. "Absolutely absurd. And if you knew what I had been going through, you'd understand why that is an insane accusation. Whatever in the world gave you such an outrageous idea?" Emma was incensed and Bob knew it.

He looked apologetic. "You're not having an affair?" he asked, slowly shaking his head.

"No. I'm not having an affair. I've never had an affair. Why do you think I am?"

He said slowly, "Janice was here this morning. She told me and everyone else in the shop that you were leaving Jim because you had an affair."

It was the last straw. Emma St. Claire had had her fill of Janice Crymes.

"I never want to see that vile woman again, ever. Do you understand, Bob? She is a liar and a vicious woman. If she ever repeats another lie about me, I will sue her for slander. And you can tell her that!"

Emma threw the smock on the floor and left. She would find someone else to do her hair.

***

"My dumb luck," Emma mumbled to herself. Tracie's class was right next door to Mr. Byrd's. It would be impossible for Emma to have a conversation with her friend without seeing him.

While Emma and Tracie were huddled together, deep in conversation, the teacher walked by, glared harshly at Emma, entered his classroom, and firmly shut the door.

"He's upset," Emma said.

"Don't fret yourself over him, Emma," Tracie scolded. "He had every opportunity to be involved in this wonderful story. You must not feel bad for his decision. We each walk on our own path. It's not our place to worry what someone else is doing on their path. You have to let them be. His spirit is learning something, Emma. You can't choose what he is to learn. He might not be ready for your lessons."

"You're right, Tracie. David told me the same thing. You can't teach a first grader how to do calculus when he can't even add and subtract. He'd have no concept of the lesson. It would be totally beyond him."

"And you want to teach Philip Byrd about our type of spirituality and how God has worked in your life. He's still in kindergarten, Emma. You already have your Ph.D."

Tracie's eyes twinkled when she smiled at Emma.

"That's a neat way of looking at it, Tracie. A Ph.D. You think I'm that far along?"

"Yep! Trust your e.s.p., Emma. It will tell you who's ready to learn and who's not. You don't have to feel rejected because another spirit doesn't understand your story. There are many, many souls anxiously awaiting your insights. Share with them, Emma."

"Do you mean that?"

"Yes. Of course. Many do not understand why problems come their way. They believe they are good souls. Maybe they are in this life. Remember, we always reap what we sow, Emma."

"Yes. I know. Losing the use of my arms because of my guilt over the baby brother—"

Tracie squeezed Emma's hand and felt pain surging through her friend's arms.

"I have to go to class now. Remember what I said. Trust your e.s.p. And keep the door to your classroom open, Emma. Pretty soon every desk will be taken."

***

Chats with Tracie were enlightening to Emma. The gifted young woman's insights and advice never ceased to amaze her and their meetings were spiritually enriching.

Several days later Emma was challenged to again trust her e.s.p., the special feelings that Philip Byrd almost bludgeoned into oblivion, with the resulting loss of her beloved pet; the feelings that saved her babies; the feelings that opened her to a wealth of perceptions and visions few could comprehend. Emma was standing in the parking lot, talking to her friend and fellow secretary, Madge Robinson, after the Professional Secretaries meeting, when they heard a loud expletive several cars away.

"Damn!"

"What's wrong?" Emma called out to Gail, another member of the organization.

"I locked my keys in the car!"

Emma and Madge walked over to Gail's car. The keys were lying on the seat.

"Where do you live?" Madge asked.

"Vinings."

"I can take you home," Emma volunteered.

"I can, too!" Madge quickly offered.

"My husband might not be home from work. And if he's not, I'll still be stranded."

"Don't worry," Emma said. "We'll work it out."

Emma and Madge gave each other a farewell hug.

"Call me tomorrow, Madge."

"I will. I promise," she said forlornly, dabbing a Kleenex at the corner of one eye.

"What's wrong with Madge?" Gail asked while buckling the seat belt in Emma's car.

"The teenage daughter of her boss committed suicide last week. Madge has taken it real hard."

"How awful! Do they know why?"

"She left a note. Her family won't reveal the contents. Madge has known the child since she was a toddler."

The two women rode along in silence for a few minutes, each lost in their thoughts of the teenager and the intolerable pain she must have felt that caused her to take her own life.

"What does your husband do?" Emma asked to break the silence.

"He's an aircraft mechanic; works for the airline."

Emma's heartbeat sped up.

Tell her you're psychic, Emma's e.s.p. said.

"Which airline?" Emma asked, ignoring the ticker tape that ran through her mind.

"Atlantic. He doesn't do much of the hands-on work now that he's a supervisor."

"Has he been there a long time?"

"About twenty-five years."

Tell her—

Emma pondered the pros and cons of revealing the psychic side of her psyche to Gail. If she did not believe in such things she might not keep Emma's revelation confidential. On the other hand, if she did know something of psychic abilities, she might be of assistance to Emma.

Tracie said I should trust my e.s.p.. Why was I put in the car with this woman, whose husband is a maintenance supervisor for Atlantic, if no good is to come of this conversation?

Trust your e.s.p. —

She might think I'm crazy.

Tell her —

I'm scared of what she might say. She might think I'm evil or possessed.

You're not evil or possessed, Emma St. Claire. You're not. There's a good reason Gail is alone with you right now. Tell her, damn it!!

"Gail—" Emma stammered, "There's something I want to talk to you about."

"I know something important is on your mind, Emma. You can trust me," Gail said in a kind and caring way.

Emma groped for the right words. Could she trust Gail?

"Gail—"

"It's okay, Emma. You can tell me."

"I'm—I'm—psychic—" she finally blurted out.

"You are!" Gail said excitedly. "I am, too—never get to talk to anyone about it, though. No one believes I see visions and dream dreams. I've been married a long time and my husband is still a skeptic even though he's knows my e.s.p. is usually right on target."

Emma was euphoric. What good fortune had put her with this spiritually enlightened woman? A woman whose husband worked for Atlantic Airways.

"I've been psychic since adolescence," Gail continued. "The messages come to me from nowhere. Usually when I'm not expecting it."

"I'm that way, too. Wouldn't it be wonderful, Gail, if people believed us— that we dream and see visions. Most of the time I'm hurt by this supposed gift. I've found it to be a very painful way to live."

"I couldn't agree more, Emma. No one believes. There are only a few people I can talk to about it. If everyone could realize we are connected spiritually because we come from God, then we could lay aside petty differences and prejudices and get on with making this planet a better place."

"You're absolutely right, Gail. We are connected. Some of us are simply more aware of it. And because of that we're different—and we're rejected because we can feel what others feel or we can see their future. We were given these gifts to help our fellow souls. I've never understood why no one wants to open the package and see what's inside."

"I find that reading about the prophets in the Bible helps, Emma—Miriam and Deborah, and Anna, and the daughters of Philip. Don't forget Jeremiah."

"Why do you suppose there are unbelievers?"

"Many souls have forgotten their divinity. They have forgotten that their very life comes from God. They have alienated themselves from Him and from other souls, too. When we die, we are no longer white people, or black people, or Chinese, or Indian. We are pure spirit. When we are reconnected to our Maker, we realize we wasted our lives here on earth because we spent our time hating others who were different when we could have been working together to make life better for everyone."

"Why are we different, Gail? You and I? Why have we made the connection?"

"I've pondered that question most of my life, Emma. I don't know why God made us this way. Have you ever thought about the contributions a true, gifted psychic could make to the world of science and medicine?"

"No. What do you mean?"

"Take research on disease, for instance. Say a scientist has a multiple number of choices to make during his work. Each decision he makes leads to another round of choices. Think of the time and money he would save if he could ask 'which is the right choice?'"

"Golly, I never thought of it that way, Gail. How interesting. Research is a maze and you have to backtrack a lot because you made the wrong turn."

"Exactly. You ever do puzzle mazes?"

"Yes. I enjoyed them when I was a child."

"And were they hard for you."

"No. I'd ask myself which was the right way to turn and I'd usually get right through it."

"That's what I mean. Knowing which way to turn, and when, can make a lot of difference."

"I'm working on a major episode, Gail—a very frightening and challenging experience. It's also been enlightening. I'm going to a para-psychologist and I've learned a lot even though I still haven't resolved the problem."

"What's it about?" Gail asked. The atmosphere in the car was changed from one of hesitancy induced by fear of rejection to one of true camaraderie between two souls who trusted each other completely.

"An airplane crash—"

Gail gasped. "You don't mean it?"

"Yes, I do. Living with it has been dreadful."

"I can imagine. Can you tell me about it?"

Emma gave Gail a brief summary of Philip Byrd and the two flight attendants. Then she described the crash of the L1011.

"I hear this awful sound—"

"What kind of sound? An explosion?"

"No, not exactly. More mechanical. Then the plane seems to change direction."

"Change direction? Do you mean it veers off course?"

"Yes. I guess."

"It has veered off course. Has it crashed yet?"

274

"No. The plane is at a funny angle."

"—sounds to me—"

"For some reason I keep thinking there is a hydraulic problem. Don't know what significance that would be."

"I do. If the hydraulics fail, the ailerons and rudder could fail. That would throw it off course."

"That makes sense. Are you starting to pick up any specific feelings about it Gail?"

Gail took a deep breath and relaxed. Her eyes closed and her head tipped in a contemplative pose. Emma drove in silence for several miles.

After a while Gail said meekly, "Can you describe the condition of the plane—after the crash?"

"A wing is missing. There's a fire in the tail section and a long crack down one side."

"This crack. Describe it."

"The metal is sharp and jagged. The side of the plane is pushed in from the outside as if someone took a giant screw driver and tore open the metal. That's how Mr. Byrd cuts his hands."

"You're looking at a mid-air collision, Emma," Gail said very confidently.

"What! A mid-air collision? Two planes? You're kidding?"

"No, I'm not. The plane has a hydraulic failure and veers off course into the path of an incoming plane. The wing of the other plane pierces the side and makes a long crack."

No wonder I've had trouble sorting it out. Do you see anything else?"

"Not much. The crash will be at night. The ground is wet. Is it at Hartsfield?"

"Yes," Emma said.

"That's what I thought. Next spring?"

"Yes. How did you know?"

"I don't know. I may be reading your mind, Emma. It might not be my own perception. I wouldn't worry about it though."

"Why? I've got to prevent it Gail! I'm bound and determined that I'll find the crew and warn them. I can't let those three people fly that plane next May, Gail. I can't."

"I know how you feel Emma. Don't worry. There's another way to handle it."

They had reached Vinings and Gail directed Emma to her house. The lights were on, indicating to the women that Gail's husband was already home.

275

"George will take me back to the car, Emma. I appreciate the ride."

"You can't imagine what this has meant to me, Gail. You've given me help and that gives me hope."

"I told you, Emma, don't worry about it. George doesn't usually pay any attention to my e.s.p.—something tells me that he'll be very interested in this. He's got plenty of time between now and next May to check out the hydraulic systems of the L1011s."

***

Emma was huddled in conference with Tracie when Mr. Byrd came by. He glared at Emma and disappeared into his room.

"He hates me, Tracie."

"No he doesn't. He's just a little freaked out."

"There's no reason for him to feel that way. He's not involved. I'm the one who put her integrity on the line. I'm the one David is talking about when he calls the airline. Philip Byrd's name has never been mentioned."

"Have you told him that?"

"No. He never gave me the chance. He never called me and David won't call him again, either. If he wants to know anything about it, he'll have to ask me."

"Okay, then. You shouldn't be upset 'cause Mr. Philip Byrd is hard headed. I keep telling you, you can't change folks."

"I know. You're right, Tracie. People won't change until they want to."

"Your arms haven't changed much, have they?"

"No, even though I'm diligently working on them. I meditate and I do physical therapy. Improvement is very slow. I hate the medicine the neurologist prescribed."

Tracie put her hand on Emma's wrist and squeezed.

"By Christmas, you won't need medicine."

"I won't. Why?" Emma asked excitedly. The thought that she would someday be relieved of the interminable pain was ecstasy.

"Something dramatic will happen. Before Christmas and your arms will heal—a lot. There will be many changes. You will heal."

"What?" Emma asked excitedly. "What will happen?"

"I don't know," Tracie said, with the usual twinkle in her eyes. "It will be something good. Very amazing. You'll get better, Emma. You will get better. Before Christmas. That's a promise."

***

Emma and Jim went to J.D.'s football game together on Friday night and Saturday afternoon both men escorted Emma to the Georgia Tech game. Emma watched proudly as Allison and the other Rambling 'Recks ran onto the field with the football team, followed by Coach Ross.

You wait. Coach Ross will show everyone how great our team is.

It was, for Emma St. Claire, a very happy day.

***

Emma was still euphoric about Tracie's prediction a few days later when she drove to the high school campus where the class on reincarnation was to be taught. The teacher, a handsome man dressed in expensive clothes, was making his introductory remarks when a woman wearing a pink sweat suit bounced into the room.

"Hi," she said, as if she knew everyone. Then she flopped into a desk on the front row, two seats in front of Emma, oblivious of the disruption she caused. Emma heard a low wolf whistle from the male student seated behind her while other students cast a glare at the lady in pink.

There was something vaguely familiar about the woman and Emma tried to watch her but the view was obscured by a student between them. The woman almost monopolized the teacher with her pointed and intelligent questions, and although the other students may have been offended, Emma thought she was fascinating. This student, whoever she was, was obviously educated on the subject.

Class was interesting and informative and Emma took prodigious notes. After the lecture, students surrounded the teacher, asking more questions. Emma did not join in. She sat at her desk, stacking notepapers; she didn't even notice when the lady in pink left. Emma finally looked up and realized the woman was gone.

Darn! I hope she comes back. She seems to know as much as the teacher and she might be bored. If she doesn't return, I'll never know why she looked familiar to me.

***

277

A few days later, at David's office, Emma gave her psychologist the details of another dream.

"I had a dream about another plane crashing, David."

"What! Do you mean another crash, or another plane crashing in the original dream?"

"Another crash. It also takes place at Hartsfield. Only the view I have is near a hangar—there is very definitely a hangar in the background. I see some people wandering around, looking at it the morning after."

"It takes place at night also?" he asked nodding. "Is it also in May?"

"No. The man in the picture is wearing a trench coat. It's chilly. There is water on the runway from rain. The sky is overcast. A big plane hit a little plane. Or maybe vice versa. Anyway, it is definitely a big plane and a little plane. The big plane has a wing knocked off."

"What else? Fatalities?"

"Possibly one. In the small plane."

"Can you identify anyone?"

"No. No one. I don't see any people until the morning after—the inspectors, or whoever they are. They are looking at the wreck."

"Do you think this is a precursor to the other dream—a warning?"

"I don't know, David. I see a little plane and a big plane have crashed. There is one fatality and the big plane is missing a wing. It could be any time in winter or early spring. That's everything I know about it."

David made notes.

"That's not much to go on."

"I know. I'm sorry. I have no feelings about this accident. It was a dream and I'm reporting it to you as I saw it."

***

"Hi, Louise!" Emma said enthusiastically to Steve King's mother. "The books you sent me are great. I'm enjoying them and learning so much."

Allison had told her mother-in-law about Emma's past-life experience and because Louise had a rather extensive library on reincarnation, she sent Emma several books.

"Glad you read them," Louise answered. "They've helped me understand a lot, too."

"I was especially intrigued about auras."

"Why?" Louise asked. "I've never had any experience with them."

"I hadn't either. Tracie told me I have a light blue aura and it's nice."

"Interesting—does she know what it means?"

"No. According to this book, though, light blue means a person is in touch with their inner truth."

"That's comforting. Of course, I always thought that you were in touch with the truth, Emma. Not many souls are, though."

"Can I ask you about something else?" Emma asked. "It has to do with the teacher."

"What is it you need to know?"

"Since he's from Thomson, I was wondering if you ever met him, as a child."

There was a pause while Louise mulled over Emma's question.

"Byrd?—Byrd. No. I never knew a Philip Byrd. I did know a girl named Byrd. She was in my class. Let's see—what was her name?"

Louise was thinking. Emma did not want to break her train of thought and said nothing. Finally Louise spoke again.

"I remember. Naomi. Naomi Byrd. That was her name. I didn't know anything about her or her family although she was in my class. I went to school with Naomi Byrd."

"Thank you, Louise," Emma said, almost euphoric. She told her friend that she loved her and hung up the phone.

It was unbelievable the way God was working in Emma St. Claire's life. Maybe she was in touch with inner truth.

***

Emma was relieved the lady in pink returned for the next class. Unlike Emma, she did not take notes. Because she was sitting diagonally across the room from Emma this time, Emma had an unobstructed view of the interesting gal. She was good looking, what some people would call ravishing, with shoulder length brunette hair. While Emma watched, the woman ran long manicured nails through silky tresses, pulling a swatch of hair behind one ear.

It was all Emma could do to contain an audible gasp when she realized who the woman was. She wiggled anxiously in her seat, unable to concentrate on the lecture. The teacher finally excused the class for a ten-minute break and Emma quickly stood up, dropping her notebook and pencils on the floor. She gathered them in an unordered pile and left them on the desk, then hurried to the door. The woman had already left.

"Gees," Emma moaned.

The woman did not return for the second half of the class. Emma was crushed.

Surely, she'll be back next week. She has to. I have to talk to that woman.

***

"Are you enjoying the class?" Rachel asked Emma during one of their phone conversations.

"The course is fascinating. I'm learning a lot. It makes sense, Rachel. I think the world would be a better place if we believed in reincarnation—if we realized that what we sow is what we reap. You can't hurt someone else and get away with it. Somewhere along the line, you're going to be held accountable for what you did. Don't you think the problem with my arms is proof positive of that? Don't you think I'm suffering now because of my sin in another life? I do.

"Dealing with this pain is more bearable now that I know it is caused by something I did myself, Rachel. God didn't wish this crippling pain on me. And neither did anyone else. I brought it on myself because of my own impatience. In spite of my healing visualizations, and in spite of my prayers, and in spite of the physical therapy, I'm still suffering. I don't know why. Something's not resolved yet. When it is, I will get better. In the meantime, I'm learning what patience is. I've learned to be patient with myself, with this disability, and I'm more patient with everyone else in my life. Something good is coming from the pain. Don't you see that?"

"Yes. I understand now that you put it that way. When we suffer, even if we may not be aware of the cause, there is always something we can learn from it."

"That's right. We learn from our mistakes. Then we grow and hopefully we don't make them again. We continue to learn and to grow with each incarnation we make."

"Doesn't this conflict with Christianity, Emma?"

"No, of course not. The Bible tells us in Philippians that we each have to work out our salvation."

"I think I see what you mean. We're not abandoning our faith in Christ if we believe in reincarnation?"

"No, Rachel! As a matter of fact, Jesus is the way out of the mess the whole world is in. If we are loving and forgiving as He taught we come into a state of grace."

280

"Many Christians believe reincarnation is on the fringe of the occult."

"I have some questions for them."

"What would those be?"

"Number one, do they believe Jesus is coming again—most believe He is, and, number two, how can He come again if there is no such thing as reincarnation?"

***

"Hi, my name is Emma St. Claire," Emma said to the mysterious lady in her class.

"Hi, my name is Connie Mitchell," she replied, batting her long eyelashes.

Emma could hardly believe her good fortune.

"Can we talk a minute?"

"Why, yes," Connie answered in a sweet, girlish voice.

Emma didn't know where to begin. How do you talk to a complete stranger about dreams and visions and past-life therapy and plane crashes? Not being bashful with words, Connie jumped on the stifled conversation when Emma paused.

"What about?" she smiled innocently.

"A dream—" Emma stammered.

"A dream? About me?"

"Yes."

"I have been in your class for the last two weeks. I saw you. Didn't you notice me?"

"Of course, I saw you. This is different. I had this dream a long, long time ago. Before this class started."

"How interesting," Connie said, her lashes fluttering while she slowly closed and opened her eyes again.

She acted innocent and naive but Emma knew from probing comments in class that Connie was spiritually enlightened. Emma's mind was lost in a maze of confusion and she thought about her recent conversation with Gail. After a long pause, she blurted out a question.

"What do you do?"

Connie looked surprised.

"I'm a flight attendant."

Emma could feel her heart beat increasing; it pounded in her ears.

"Who do you work for?"

Another blunt question. Connie looked at Emma apprehensively and drew back.

"Atlantic Airways. Why do you want to know?" she whispered.

"We need to talk. Can you meet me after class for a cup of coffee?"

Connie was skeptical.

"Why? What's it about?"

"A plane crash," Emma squeaked out.

Connie's eyes opened wide, deliberately batting her eyelashes again.

"Whoa—."

The teacher came in and Emma moved quietly across the room to her desk. Another piece of the puzzle was falling into place.

CHAPTER TWENTY

**"Let us not lose heart in doing good,
for in due time we shall reap if we do not grow weary"**
-Galatians 6:9

Emma's information about Connie was accurate. The beautiful brunette was married less than two years, never had children, and worked for Atlantic for almost twenty years; and not only did she believe in reincarnation, she was also psychic.

While drinking coffee at Waffle House, the two women exchanged stories about psychic perceptions and past life experiences and a profound rapport was created. They laughed a lot and commiserated with one another like two old friends united after a long separation.

"I've dreamed about two plane crashes, Emma," Connie said. "One of them woke me in the middle of the night. When I got up later, I turned on the t.v. and learned that a jet went down in Mexico at almost the same time I dreamed it. It was awful."

Emma shook her head slowly and patted Connie's hand.

"I know exactly how you feel," Emma said.

"I felt completely useless. If I had known earlier, I would have done something. Then I realized there was a reason those souls departed together."

"I think you can understand the way I feel and why I'm determined to prevent it."

"Yes, I do. I will give you any information I can to help. You must promise me you will never, never reveal my name to anyone. Ever!" Connie said emphatically.

"I promise, Connie. I would never implicate anyone. Not you, not George, not Mr. Byrd. This burden is on my shoulders and David's. No one else will ever be involved. Of course, since I met you and George, I believe it's preventable. I am truly amazed the way puzzle pieces are coming together."

Emma yawned and looked at her watch.

"Connie, it's one o'clock! We've been talking for three hours."

"You're kidding. I feel we've been here only a few minutes."

"Me, too. I have to get up at five-thirty. We better call it a night. Getting to know you has been wonderful, Connie."

"I've enjoyed it, too, Emma. I feel I've known you forever."

Emma smiled at her new friend.

"Maybe we knew each other before, in another life."

"That would account for our feelings for each other, Emma. Can we get together again? Soon?"

"Why, yes. I'm going to my son's football game on Friday night. How about Saturday for dinner?"

"Sounds great."

They exchanged phone numbers and hugs and thirty minutes later Emma laid her weary body in bed while thanking God for putting Connie in her life.

***

"I'm still hurting over Philip Byrd and Anne," Emma said to David during her next session.

He cocked his head to one side, pondering her words, inviting her to continue.

"I had that dream again about hanging over the cliff and holding onto Anne. When I woke up, my arms were almost useless. I don't think I'll ever get better if I don't let go. Something is still holding me to her. I have this tremendous need to tell him the whole story."

"He never called you? He said he would?"

"No, and he never will. I never had the closure I needed. I still see Margaret and she always says that he's special, to protect him. Apparently, finding Connie and George is not enough. I've still got to locate that pilot."

David raised his eyebrows.

"There are more than two million people in Atlanta, Emma."

"I know. I'm still determined to find him. I have to."

"Do you feel you're ready to let go of Philip Byrd and Anne?"

"Yes. More than ready. I'm tired of hurting."

Deep in a trance a few minutes later, David guided Emma through visualizations of the ancient aqueduct and cool water flowing through new pipes. Soothing sensations moved through Emma's neck and arms, easing the pain.

"Now, let your mind go to a place where you are comfortable," David directed.

Emma's head bobbed and floated effortlessly above her shoulders. A gentle smile curved her lips.

"Where are you?" David asked.

In the deep, deliberate speech of her trance voice, Emma said, "I'm sitting at the kitchen table in Thomson, with Margaret."

"What does Margaret say?"

"It is time for you to let go of past-life feelings, Emma. You need to be about the business of Emma's life now. You can't do that if you are tied to the past."

"Margaret will give you something, Emma. It will be her way of letting go of you."

Margaret stood up from the table where she and Emma were seated and took off her apron. Emma had never seen Margaret without her apron. She carefully folded it and handed it to Emma.

"What did she give you?" David asked.

"Her apron. She gave me her apron. She says I am free of her now and the feelings I've carried from past lives. She says I have tried to protect Philip and Anne and that's enough. That I should take her apron because she no longer uses it."

***

Emma was standing at the vending machine, waiting for her coffee and wondering why Tracie was not at school, when Philip Byrd walked into the Student Center.

"Hello," she said warmly when she saw him.

"Hi," he said flatly.

"Don't suppose I could talk to you for a minute, could I?"

"What's it about?" he snapped, deep furrows on his brow.

Emma immediately regretted starting the conversation.

"Sort of complicated," she babbled. "I'll get my thoughts together and catch you on the break, if that's okay."

He disappeared up the stairs and she wandered forlornly to a table. Emma hoped to engage Philip in a conversation. Of course, that was a half-baked idea.

Absorbed in her writing, she was surprised when he appeared with a cup of coffee two hours later.

"What's it about?" he asked in a very friendly manner. He was an enigma.

She started slowly, pushing her notes toward him. "Since I can't talk to you—"

"What do you mean, you can't talk to me?" he asked. Although he flinched at her hurtful comment, he glanced over her notes about the crash and the house in midtown.

"Next May?" he questioned. "Is that when it is? I thought that had already been settled."

You dummy. Why would you think it was settled when you didn't even bother to talk to me about it?

"I don't know anyone named Naomi in Thomson," he said. "Don't know anyone named Margaret, either."

"I wouldn't expect you to know who Margaret was," Emma tried to explain. Margaret went by a different name and died when Philip was an infant. Naomi was a different matter. Emma thought he'd know her.

In a small town, where everyone knew everyone else, it was hard to believe Philip Byrd did not know who Naomi Byrd was. They would have been close in age. Emma wondered if Philip Byrd was lying.

"You can't control things," he said, bringing Emma out of her thoughts of the conversation with Louise about Naomi.

"I'm not trying to control things. I'm just trying to do what I was told to do. And that means I have to prevent those two planes from crashing."

The conversation shifted to the house. He was very curious about it.

"Where's the house?" he asked.

"I don't know. Somewhere in mid-town."

"How do you get there?"

"I turn off Peachtree, near the Memorial Arts Center."

"Do you think you could find the house?" he asked.

"I guess; I do have an exact description of it."

He raised his eyebrows and asked skeptically, "You do?" vacillating between belief and unbelief.

Emma told him what the house looked like and he was pleased. For the first time since their last run-in, he looked happy.

"I'm planning to move to mid-town next spring," he said. "Maybe I can help you with the house."

Emma was pleased to learn his plans. One more piece was fitting into her puzzle although she could not believe he would *help her with the house.*

"I thought about driving around and looking for it," Emma said.

"That's a huge neighborhood." He rose from the chair. "Will you give me a description of the house," he said.

I don't know why. You'll never use it.

"Okay," she said. "I'll write one up for you."

"I've got to get to class. See ya," he said casually.

Then he smiled at her. Not the same smile from long ago; but he did smile—and he knew. At long last he knew about the plane crash in May.

***

After class get-togethers with Connie became a routine in Emma's life. Connie was a remarkable source of information and being psychic enhanced her insight.

"I had a dream about a plane crash, Emma," she said one November night.

"No! Tell me about it."

"I think it might be the same crash you dreamed about. I was there, with a blond flight attendant. Her name is Jeannie. Would you believe we flew together last week?"

"You're kidding. You actually met her?"

"Yes. I'm convinced she's the same girl you described to me. Jeannie is a super lady. We decided to fly together whenever we can—I'll get to know more about her."

Connie was pleased to reveal this important information to Emma and radiated happiness.

"Guess what else?"

"What?"

"She regularly flies flight twenty. She wants me to fly with her."

Emma gasped.

"Flight twenty. She flies twenty?"

"Yes. And it's always an L1011!"

"No kidding! An L1011 and flight twenty! I never was able to tell if that number was for a flight or a gate."

"I'd be willing to bet it's a flight number, Emma. There is too much information here for it to be a coincidence."

"You think this girl you met and dreamed about is the same one I dreamed about? Tell me what happens."

As in Emma's dream, the jumbo jet crashed a few minutes after taking off. Emma was astounded when Connie told her about the injury to Jeannie's face.

"She has this awful mark on her face, Emma. It looks like Indian war paint, a dark line running from her ear down to her chin."

Emma was speechless. Although she had given Connie most of the details of the tragedy, she never, not one time, ever told her friend of the injury to the pretty blond flight attendant's face.

"What are we going to do, Connie? You've promised me you won't fly L1011s in May. What are you going to say to Jeannie?"

"I'm going to tell her to stay the hell away from Hartsfield the first weekend in May."

"Do you think she'll listen to you? Will she believe you?"

"She'll listen, Emma. She'll believe. She has two children. She won't take a chance. You can count on it."

***

Emma slept an extra thirty minutes since she did not have to be at David's office until eight-thirty. Her arms hurt while she rolled her hair with a curling iron.

Will the pain ever go away?

Slowly, she applied makeup. Mornings were especially bad and her arms and hands often shook. In spite of the physical impairment, she was happy. Emma St. Claire was at peace with herself. She turned her life over to God and incredible things happened.

She put on a pair of winter white slacks, electric blue turtle neck shirt and blue shoes. It was her forty-fifth birthday. Emma fully intended to enjoy the day.

I'm glad I'm starting a new year with David.

She smiled into the mirror and applied ruby red lipstick.

"Good morning," Emma said cheerfully to her therapist and friend, stepping down the stairs behind another patient. The attractive, slim woman had a worried expression on her face and Emma guessed she must be new.

In a few weeks, she will be a different person. David will know what to say, what to do, to help her reach into herself to find solutions to problems. He'll teach her to look through pain and find peace within.

Emma charged into sessions with David as if she were a six year old at a birthday party. Every visit was rewarding and she looked forward to the new insights that would come to her.

"I've been thinking," she said. "Margaret gave me the apron as a token of letting go; since then, I haven't had that disturbing vision of her. I've decided to give Philip a token of my letting go of Anne. Maybe that awful dream, where I'm hanging on the cliff with Anne, will go away, too."

David was pleased his patient had reached this important milestone.

"I'll tell him that he'll have to protect her."

David's smile turned into a frown; Emma was headed in the wrong direction.

"Why not?"

"How can you ask him to do something that you can't do yourself? You can't protect that girl and you can't ask Philip to protect her either."

"I guess not. I see what you mean."

David was right. Emma looked at her list of thoughts, ideas and feelings that she brought to each session and moved to another topic.

"Thanksgiving was not the same this year," she said. "I went to Allison and Steve's. My sister and her family came down and my mom was there. Jim went to his folks and poor J.D. spent half the day with us and half the day with them. It was very hard on him. It was not my choice that he do it that way.

"I don't understand parents who fight over their children. Seems to me, if they truly loved them, they would want them to be happy. That should be their main concern. J.D. had a miserable Thanksgiving holiday because he tried to be with both of his parents. I said last year that Thanksgiving would never be the same. I was prepared. I listened to my inner voice, David. It was right. I was at peace with it. I'm thankful for the many, many delightful happy times I've had with my family. Now there are other things for me to do. I don't want to ruin my future happiness by grieving over my past."

The fifty minute session scooted by too quickly. The next thing Emma knew she was writing a check for David.

"I want to let go of Anne, David. It doesn't matter that Philip won't understand. I will. That's what matters now. He's never been ready for any of it. If he only knew what we have done—George the maintenance supervisor, Connie and Jeannie, the flight attendants. When I think back over what has transpired the last few years, I realize God was always with me. Now I know He will always be with me and that gives me indescribable joy and comfort."

***

Emma bickered with herself over what she should buy.

Whatever in the world should I get him? It has to be something permanent. Of course, the last thing he wants is a memento from a goofy student who bugged him about wild premonitions he couldn't understand—still, I have to give him something. I have to let him know I'm letting go of her. David says I can't tell him to protect her. I'll just tell him I'm letting go. She will be his responsibility. He won't understand; I will. It will be a gift to me. It will be my freedom. They will have to choose their own paths; I can't do it for them. He'll probably think I'm letting go of him. If only he knew the truth.

Emma parked her car behind J.C. Penney's and ran into Allison; she had just taken a break to get some lunch.

"I'll have a cup of coffee with you," she volunteered.

They walked together into the mall and Emma bought her coffee while Allison picked up a gyro. The lamb smelled spicy and delicious and Emma wished she could eat some.

When I quit worrying about my Anne, I'll be able to enjoy food again.

"What are you looking for?" Allison inquired.

"Getting some ideas for Christmas. Can't afford to do much this year, though. Don't have the money."

"No one expects you to do a lot, Mama. We know how tight it is for you right now."

Emma wanted to tell Allison about the letting go token but it was not the right time for an esoteric discussion. Besides, they were both in a hurry. After lunch Emma escorted Allison back to Penney's and scouted the mall for an appropriate gift.

At Macy's she found an exquisite piece of Waterford crystal. The price was out of sight; she couldn't spend that much money. Then she remembered the Crystal Shoppe in Stone Mountain. She drove out Memorial Drive and stopped at the specialty store.

"I need a piece of crystal," she said to a sales lady.

"You chose the right place to shop," the courteous lady laughed, leading Emma around the store.

Emma looked over the assortment of specialty items, picked up one and carried it to the front window where she held it in the sunshine. Multi-colored prisms of light burst forth.

"This is nice," she said to the lady. "I'll take it."

"Do you want it wrapped?"

"No, thank you. This is a gift for someone special. I want to wrap it myself."

Emma was grinning ear to ear when she arrived at the apartment.

A crystal apple. Perfect.

***

During her next session with David, Emma asked why she had to suffer the physical pain.

"Even though there has been some improvement, my arms are still weak, David. They still hurt. Do you think I'll ever get over it?"

"Why don't you ask your Margaret?"

"Could we?" Emma asked. She had come to trust the advice Margaret gave her in trance sessions but she could only extract the valuable information under David's skillful guidance.

Emma took a deep breath and relaxed, kicking off shoes and removing her watch. Her head floated above her shoulders and Margaret appeared in a comforting light. Words came slowly, each one enunciated carefully by the deep voice that had a tendency to ramble on a bit before answering a specific question. Because Margaret's messages contained a lot of simple wisdom, David let her speak freely. He seldom interrupted.

"Margaret says, 'There are many kinds of love. Real love is not for one person. To be part of the universe, you have to love people as they are, without expecting them to love you, because giving love is its own reward.'

"She says I love my daddy even though he left me. I love Jim even though he hurt me in many ways and I love Philip even though he is only a little child who can't understand what I'm trying to tell him. I love Connie; we have the same mindset. Hating people who hurt you is not the way to spiritual growth. If you love those who hurt you, you increase your own dimension.

"I tell Margaret I don't want to come back again. Connie and I have decided there's too much evil on this planet; neither one of us wants to incarnate here again.

"Margaret says if I love my fellow man, I will teach this spiritual message. They want to know there is more to life than what they see. That's the lesson for Philip.

"I tell her the lessons have been painful and she says they were hard lessons, that I have learned them and will never forget them. If they had been easy or painless, I may have cast them off.

"She says I will be happy on the physical plane again. No matter what happens, I will always have peace from knowing that my spirit will never die. That we live forever. That we're here to learn and to teach. Maybe when I come back, even though I don't want to, maybe next time I'll be a teacher instead of a student."

"What does she say about your arms?" David asked.

"She says from now to May won't be as painful. That I will get my strength back. That I must not mourn for the losses of my family life. To be glad for the good times we've shared. My children will be happy at Christmas if I am happy. I must show them the true meaning of love. That it doesn't have to be physical things. I can give them spiritual peace—that is the most important gift I can give them."

***

"My best friend was killed in a car wreck," Tracie said to Emma, "that's why I wasn't here last week."

Emma put her arm around Tracie's shoulder to comfort her.

"Your friend is fine, Tracie. Her soul has gone to be with our eternal Father. There's no happier, more peaceful place to be."

"I keep telling myself that, Emma."

"We've had a lot of talks about walking the spiritual path, Tracie. That's why we are here. We're learning and growing spiritually. When we've completed our lesson plan, we get to go home. You told me yourself, we can't choose someone else's plan for them. We each have our own agenda. Your friend finished her lesson, Tracie, and she got to leave school. You might say she graduated. If she completed her bachelor's degree, you'd be happy for her, wouldn't you, even if she took a job in a distant city?"

"Yes. Of course."

"She finished her work, Tracie. Now she's moved on to a better place. She earned it. We can depart the limitations of the earth plane when our lesson is finished. Haven't you ever wondered why someone walks away from a hideous car crash, completely unscathed, while someone else in the same car dies?"

"Yes."

"Maybe because the one who walks away hasn't finished their work? The one who dies, has. To say that such an occurrence is luck is to demean the power of spirit. Spirit is what we are. Our spirit is the only thing that lasts, along with the thoughts and feelings we etch upon our souls. That's what matters. Everything else eventually comes to naught."

Tracie cocked her head and a furor crossed her brow while she thought about Emma's words.

"I miss her, Emma. We were very close."

"I know you miss her, Tracie. Don't you realize she is always with you now, in spirit? Nothing can ever destroy her spirit. Just let it be with you, Tracie; let it be with you."

Thinking about Emma's advice, Tracie slowly nodded her head.

"We'll be together again, won't we Emma?" Tracie asked.

"Yes, Tracie, you will. Either in heaven or in another life here on earth."

"That's a comforting thought, Emma. Thank you."

"It's the truth, Tracie. Plain, simple truth."

***

During her next session with David, Emma searched for answers to life-long questions: Why was she highly intuitive and why was it difficult for her find peace with the spiritual gift?

As usual, David asked her to go to the source and she found herself in ancient Greece, in the 5th to 4th century B.C. That entity was a seer or oracle, who, although greatly gifted, forsake her duties to devote herself to the love of a man. Failing to protect her home city, she fled Greece and took refuge in Egypt, where she spent the remainder of her life. Although she enjoyed loving devotion from the man who eventually became her husband, at the end of her life she realized she had not fulfilled her destiny.

"You chose this path," Margaret told her. "When you accept that, you will be at peace with it."

***

In her search for truth, Emma St. Claire went on an incredible journey that started one night in economics class when she met a man she had known in another life. Thoughts and emotions she experienced in that existence were so deeply etched upon her soul that she bore them in her memory and brought them into another life—and they almost drove her insane.

Emma's Knight in Shining Armor took her back to the source of those thoughts and feelings and that gave her a distinct and uncommon outlook on life. Although her mind was no longer troubled by old fears and thoughts from her previous life, and her heart was at peace with her former emotions, Emma's body continued to carry the pain of that tragic day at the river. With hope for a final release, she wrapped the crystal apple in plaid paper, tied it with a red bow and gave it to Philip Byrd. At first he did not want to accept it, saying it would incur some obligation on his part.

"The obligation was always mine," Emma said to him.

Of course, he did not understand. He never tried. He told his students to search for truth and that search, though frightening, brought profound peace to Emma. Philip Byrd was left behind while Emma went on her journey; she no longer grieved over his decision. She knew in her heart, her mind and her soul, that someday, when he was ready, he would take the trip himself.

Emma's soul journey, from her first episode of e.s.p. when she was five years old, through the pain of her father's abandonment, her mother's verbal abuse, and losing everything she worked for, including her twenty-four year marriage, made her strong. Her psychic observations were thoroughly honed, giving her the ability to recognize someone from a previous life and learn the lessons her soul had chosen.

After she gave Philip Byrd the apple, Emma no longer dreamed about hanging on the cliff, holding onto Anne, even though the pain in her arms persisted. The left one was still somewhat crippled and she continued with creative visualizations and physical therapy, knowing that in time, when she learned her lessons, the pain would be taken away.

Saturday morning after giving Philip Byrd the crystal apple, she awoke with another silent message: *Go to the Cathedral.* Rachel's oldest son, John, a student at Georgia Tech, asked his aunt several times if she would visit the church in Buckhead with him.

"You'll love it, Aunt Emma," John said.

For one reason or another, Emma and her nephew never got around to visiting the Cathedral together and Emma continued her Sunday habit, attending seven-thirty Holy Eucharist at the Episcopal Church in Stone Mountain and eleven o'clock services at the Presbyterian Church with Jim and J.D. Now, for some reason, Emma was given explicit instructions to go to the Cathedral.

It was a pleasant thought to ponder while she readied herself for another momentous occasion—Allison and Steve's graduation from Georgia Tech. The ceremony was held in the Alexander Coliseum with a celebration party afterwards at Allison and Steve's new home. They both had landed excellent jobs in their chosen careers.

When Emma went to bed Saturday night, she thanked God for the boundless blessings He had bestowed upon her and asked Him to make her receptive to whatever it was He had planned for her. Her life was in His hands.

***

Emma was awake before her alarm rang. She switched on the lamp, turned on the radio and listened to Mozart's Symphony No. 31 in D Major while yawning and stretching in her brass bed.

"I'm going to services at the Cathedral this morning," she said cheerfully to the red cardinal sitting on the bush outside her bedroom window. She moved sluggishly, her arms heavy with pain.

A hot shower will help these arms. How am I going to wash my hair if I can't reach the top of my head?

She brushed her teeth and grinned in the mirror.

I need a spiritual transfusion and God is telling me to go to church at the Cathedral of St. Philip. So I'm going to do exactly what my special feelings are telling me to do.

The shower eased her pain. Afterwards she felt exuberant, although she could only awkwardly handle her hair dryer. Her new haircut was blown partially dry and by the time it finished air-drying, it framed her face in soft ringlets. Emma fussed and teased it for a few minutes before giving up, sweeping curls behind her left ear.

"This will do," she said optimistically, noticing the new hair cut took several years off her age.

Emma ate her usual breakfast and dressed.

"What shall I wear?" she mused while rifling through the closet.

She pulled a red turtleneck shirt off a hanger and put on a black wool skirt and black sweater-jacket with gold buttons. A chunky gold link necklace, with matching earrings, completed her outfit.

"You don't look half bad," Emma said to the image in the mirror.

Picking up black heels, she slipped her feet into driving shoes.

Remember, happiness is not who you are, or what you have, but what you think. Think 'happy' Emma St. Claire and you will be happy!

When she got to her car, she did her usual Keystone Cops routine with the heavy door and started the long drive to the church that sat on top of a hill in Buckhead. When Emma turned onto Stone Mountain Freeway, gray clouds that blanketed the sky began to break up.

That's a good sign. The gray is going away. The sun is starting to shine through. I'm going to the Cathedral and I don't even know why.

Emma entered the Hall of Bishops, remembering sock hops held there when she was a teenager. The curved ceiling soared over her head and arched windows held stained glass shields of the saints and Biblical scenes. At one end a huge stage was covered with royal blue drapes. The opposite end of the hall housed the kitchen from which untold gallons of coffee and meals were dispensed. Eight foot high walnut wainscoting covered the lower walls and added warmth to the expansive space.

The room was almost empty, except for a few scattered groups of people drinking coffee. Several of them smiled as she breezed by.

They are friendly; John said they were.

Emma deposited a quarter in the coffee donation canister, helped herself to a cup and crossed the room to investigate the newcomers' table.

"Don't I know you?" a medium build, sixtyish man said to Emma.

She held out her hand, accepting his warm handshake.

"Yes, you do. I'm Emma St. Claire. I was your secretary twenty-five years ago. You were my first boss."

"My goodness, Emma," Mr. Cox said with a smile on his face.

"How have you been? How is your daughter? Didn't she have a hip problem when she was a baby?"

"You have some memory, Emma. She's fine. She's twenty years old now. Going to college at Georgia State."

"That's wonderful," Emma said, pleased with the good news about Harold's little girl.

"Allison and her husband graduated from Georgia Tech yesterday," she said enthusiastically.

They exchanged niceties for a few more minutes and Emma filled out a visitor's card before walking down the long, narrow, corridor to the neo-gothic cathedral. Being one of the first to arrive for the service, Emma knelt in solitude, lost in prayer. When she looked up a while later the majestic church was almost full.

Because it was Advent season, the time when Christians prepare themselves for the coming of Christ, there was a solemn procession, led by a handsome, dark haired verger. The choir came next, garbed in purple robes with white Elizabethan collars. They were followed by the crucifer, carrying the cross and acolytes with huge church banners. Another verger and an acolyte carrying the clergy cross came next, and then a priest carrying the Bible, followed by the Dean of the Cathedral who was last.

Emma was awe-struck by the spectacle and glorious music from the giant organ and magnificent choir. The Dean preached about opening one's heart to the inflowing of God's divine spirit.

"St. John calls us to empty ourselves of everything; then God can fill us with what we need," the Dean said from the pulpit.

Emma felt as if every word was spoken directly to her.

After receiving communion, Emma knelt in prayer for a long while.

Dear Lord, thank you for bringing me to your loving, spirit filled house to learn this lesson. Now I understand why I had to lose everything. You emptied me—and now You have filled me with something better. You put peace and love and forgiveness in my heart, Dear Lord. Let me never forget that these, indeed, are the greatest treasures in life. Now I have everything.

Emma eased through the crowd of people at the coffee after the service, smiling as she made her way to the serving table. She was happy God directed her to the Cathedral to hear the Dean's sermon and thought the purpose for being there that day was fulfilled.

Eyeing the visitor's nametag she wore, people stopped to introduce themselves and everyone made her feel welcome. Emma was standing at a long table, talking to the Dean's wife, when she felt a presence behind her. Turning around, Emma looked up into the beautiful eyes of a very tall man.

He extended his hand.

"Hi! I'm Paul Sims," he said, grinning at Emma.

"My name's Emma St. Claire," she replied while they shook hands.

They struck up an easy conversation and before Emma realized it, she was going into great details about fighting landfills and garbage dumps and losing everything. She was about to tell him that she had found everything when her e.s.p. spoke up.

This is the man I'm supposed to meet.

What does that mean? I didn't come here to meet a man. I came to this church to hear a message God had for me.

Paul told Emma he was an attorney.

Of course you're an attorney, dear. You've always done legal work.

The message shook Emma and she felt the tremendous surge of a powerful force between herself and the tall stranger.

What in the world does that mean? You've always done legal work?

Then he said he had a master's degree in accounting. Again Emma's silent voice spoke out.

We've always had mutual interests and accounting is my favorite subject.

She felt a magnetic pull toward the man and wondered if he felt it, too. He smiled as if mesmerized by Emma.

"Where did you get your bachelor's?" Emma asked.

"West Point," he replied in a matter of fact manner tone, as if a degree from such a prestigious institution wasn't impressive.

Emma shook, receiving another message from the deep recesses of her mind.

Of course you went to a service academy, dear. You've always gone to the very best schools.

Emma's silent voice was saying one thing while out of her mouth came the words, "My youngest nephew Bobby wants to go to West Point."

The energy surging between Emma and Paul was unbelievably strong. Unlike the vibes from Philip Byrd, these feelings were all positive and all good.

Who is this man? Why is this happening to me?

A kitchen worker appeared with a cart to move coffee urns and Emma realized the Hall of Bishops was empty. Her conversation with Paul Sims was engrossing and neither noticed the time. They strolled toward the door together as casually as two old friends. While walking Emma toward her car, Paul asked about her interests. He was clearly pleased when she told him she enjoyed classical music, theater and sports.

You should know, dear. You know me like your own mother.

Emma's message center transmitted information to her continuously during their forty-five minute conversation and she pondered the source.

I know this man like I know my own children.

They reached her car and the lively dialogue drew to a conclusion, much to Emma's regret.

We have a great deal to catch up on—

Was there no end to the messages she would receive about him?

"Where's your car?" she asked, glancing around the almost empty parking lot.

"Over there; the Porsche."

She should have known he would have an expensive vehicle; he was accustomed to the finer things in life.

Emma didn't want to leave and waited for Paul to turn toward his Porsche. Instead, he walked around behind her, placed his gentle yet masculine hands on the backs of her arms and gave her a kind firm massaging caress with his long fingers covering her sore muscles. Emma was taken aback.

What a strange thing to do.

He said nothing else, seemingly shocked at his forward behavior toward a complete stranger. Obviously embarrassed, Paul turned away and walked swiftly toward his car.

Emma stood transfixed, mentally sorting out the medley of silent voice messages.

Why in the world did he do that? Why did he put his hands on my arms that way?

She put the key in the car door, swung it open effortlessly, sat down, easily closed the heavy door and reached for her seat belt before realizing her arms were free of pain for the first time in almost a year.

Lord, the pain is gone! The pain in my arms is gone! The way Paul touched me—on my arms—exactly where they hurt. Why? How did a man I've never known before know how badly I hurt? Why did he touch me the way he did? Why?

The moisture in Emma's eyes did not burn because these tears were born out of happiness, not grief, and she felt a sense of peace and happiness. The pain and turmoil from almost three years of grief and lingering depression were washed from her body and her soul. Emma St. Claire was a new person.

Paul's car stopped by the red light at the exit from the parking lot onto Peachtree Road and Emma pulled in behind him. Almost three years before Emma met a tall stranger and received the strongest e.s.p. message she ever had. Then he left her alone in the dark and she was launched on a spiritual and mind exploring odyssey that changed her life forever.

Now she had met another stranger from whom she received very significant messages. He reached out to her and took away her pain and left her glowing in the sunshine.

Who is this wonderful man, Lord? And why did you put him in my path?

Winter from Vivaldi's *Four Seasons* played on the radio during Emma's drive back to Stone Mountain. A mellow feeling came over her while she replayed in her mind the conversation with Paul and constant input of her e.s.p. as they talked.

This is the man I'm supposed to meet—why? What's special about this man? Why did my silent voice say he had always gone to the best schools? And 'yes, dear, you've always loved the Anglican Church' when he told me he had divorced his wife but kept the religion she introduced him to? And, 'of course you're a lawyer; you've always done legal work.' And why

299

did he caress my arms the way he did? I'm absolutely ecstatic over meeting this man. Why do I feel as though I've always known him?

Emma drove into the entrance of the apartment complex, parked her car and effortlessly opened the door with her left arm.

The pain is gone, Dear Lord. It's gone!

Emma walked briskly to the staircase, a black purse on long straps swinging gently from her shoulder with each step. It had been a long time since she moved with ease. She was pain free.

She entered her apartment, removed the sweater and swung her arms in circles. No pain. No movement she could conjure up would bring on the weakness. There was no discomfort whatsoever.

"Thank you, God." she said out loud, as if the Lord himself was seated on the sofa. "How did it happen? Why?"

The unusual parting caress Paul gave her played over and over in her mind.

He was trying to tell me something, wasn't he, Lord? What? What was he saying?

She took out a pencil and pad and sat at her tiny breakfast table, then, while sipping a cup of coffee, carefully reconstructed the meeting with Paul, psychic perceptions she received and his farewell gesture.

There must be something to this. There must be. Help me, God. Please help me sort it out.

It never occurred to Emma that she could meet someone else from a past life and recognize them the way she had Philip Byrd. The more she thought about it, the more convinced she was that that was exactly what happened.

This is obviously another past-life experience. Only this time I'm not scared. There's nothing to be afraid of. There's nothing bad between this spirit and me. Who is he? Could he be someone David and I found in one of our sessions? There were many others in my past; people I saw but did not recognize as anyone I knew in this life. I have such good, positive feelings about Paul. He must have been someone close to my spirit. Who? Who was he?

Emma made a list of people she identified in trance sessions with David. Of course, there was Philip. Who else made the most impression on her?

The child on the ship. I told David I wished he was J.D. I didn't recognize that spirit. He was new to me. There was great love and respect between that child and his mother—my spirit. He sailed to England with his parents and went to a fine school. He became a famous barrister. A barrister is a lawyer and Paul is a lawyer. My e.s.p. said, 'Of course, dear; you've always done legal work.'

Emma's feelings exploded into a wild euphoria.

Of course. My child. Paul's spirit is the same spirit as my child. The child who went to fine schools, who became a barrister, who attended Anglican Church services with his devoted parents. That's who he is. My child. Dear Lord. How wonderful! You put this man in my path to show me we do know others from past lives. That it is real. And it happened the way I told it to David. No wonder the vibrations between me and Paul were intense.

What about his caress and taking away the pain in my arms? How does finding the spirit of my child in another life explain my arms and his touch—his beautiful touch?

Everything David and I have worked on revolves around Philip. Surely, he's not the only important person from my past. Paul proves that. We've found Philip in several past lives. Does that mean Paul could have been with me in another past life besides—legal work—'of course, dear, you've always done legal work.' My father at the river—he was a sheriff and land agent. Isn't that a form of legal work? Why didn't I make that connection before?

He would have known about the pain in my arms. He would remember his daughter died from her injuries and he wanted her to stop hurting. He wanted to caress her arms and take away the awful pain.

Emma's eyes glistened with cooling tears.

Dear God, you sent this beautiful spirit from my past to take away the pain. He knew I was hurting. His spirit knew I was hurting. He caressed me; he took away my pain. Dear God in heaven. Paul was my father in another life.

***

The next weekend Emma went to a Christmas party with Jim. Their friend, Lillian Burns, was a psychologist and the three of them were Godparents to the daughter of Emma's cousin, June. Harry, June's husband, was also a psychologist and at one time he and Lillian shared an office.

As usual, Emma and Jim were mostly silent during the drive to Lillian's house. Emma was lost in her thoughts about the probability of a divorce since Jim did not seem inclined to get a job to support his family. The three-month separation was a time of peace and tranquility for Emma. She doubted she would ever return to Jim and the turmoil that life with him entailed. He would never grow up. He would always be a Mama's boy, depending on his mother for his very sustenance. Although she was on a pauper's budget, Emma was making it on her own and paying off Jim's bills.

If Emma divorced Jim, she would be shed of Janice, too. How blessed that would be.

Emma longed to tell Jim the story about Paul.

If Jim had only believed in me and my psychic perceptions we would still be together. Why did he reject me—and my spirituality?

They were enthusiastically greeted at the door by a festively-dressed Lillian, who introduced Emma and Jim to another couple arriving at the same time. The movie-star handsome man had sandy colored hair thinning on the top of his head. He was dressed casually in a pale blue argyle sweater, worn over a white turtleneck shirt. His blue eyes twinkled and he smiled at Emma and Jim when they shook hands. The man's wife said only a polite, "Hello."

"Don't I know you from somewhere?" Emma asked the man, having immediately recognized him.

"No, I don't think so," he answered.

"You look familiar to me," Emma said, cocking her head to one side and shaking it back and forth. "And we've never met?"

"No, we've never met you before," the man's wife said sharply. The little woman, dressed in an expensive red silk pantsuit, obviously misconstrued Emma's motive in questioning her husband. Emma was positive she had seen the man before. He was someone she should know.

"I guess not," Emma said, almost apologetically. She went into the dining room to join her estranged husband who had slipped away from the conversation at the door.

Lillian's Christmas parties were beautiful events and her eggnog was the best in the city of Atlanta. After sipping a cup of Lillian's brew, rich with thick whipped cream blended with beaten egg whites and generous portions of rum, Emma left Jim and made her way through a crowd of people. In the living room, she warmed her hands at the stately fireplace.

Several other guests followed suit and they stood together on the wide hearth, spreading their fingers above flickering flames. Emma was absorbed in her thoughts about the sandy haired man for a long while and did not notice she was alone at the fireplace until she turned around. Everyone else was seated and someone started a conversation about psychological research. It was a reasonable subject of discussion since most of the guests were psychologists.

After listening to the discussion for a few minutes, Emma chimed in, "I've been involved in some psychological research myself."

Emma felt very conspicuous, standing alone at the hearth with a large crackling fire burning behind her. Every one turned toward her and she gazed around the room at the austere group.

"Really?" said one of the women in a patronizing tone. "Why don't you tell us about it?"

Emma felt as if she was a first grader at show and tell.

"It involves e.s.p. I've been having psychic experiences since I was a child and I'm working on a major episode now."

The woman dropped her mantle of aloofness. "Is that right? How fascinating. Do go on."

Emma faltered.

"What's it about?" interjected one of the men.

Emma paused. What had she gotten herself into?

"A plane crash—" Emma finally blurted out.

At that moment the sandy haired man entered the room, holding a cup of eggnog. He stood silently behind the people on the sofa, which was situated near the center of the spacious living room.

"Are you working with anyone on this?" asked another masculine voice.

"Yes. I've been working with a para-psychologist for six months."

"Who?" a different voice asked.

"Dr. David Cooper—"

A wave of oohs and aahs floated around the room.

"He's highly respected for his work—"

"There's no one better in that discipline—"

"He's done some remarkable work—"

The positive comments about her counselor, her mentor, and her friend put Emma at ease. She stood proudly before the gathering and fielded a barrage of questions.

"Where will it happen?"

"Hartsfield."

Gasps.

"When?"

"The first weekend in May."

"What makes you think that?"

"I've dreamed about someone I know being on one of the planes that weekend."

"One of the planes?"

"Yes. Two planes are involved."

"Is it a mid-air collision?"

"No. One plane is taking off."

"Who is the person?"

"A teacher."

"Where's he going?"

"I don't know. He could be on the inbound plane."

"What airline is it?"

"I can't tell you. They could sue me."

"Why?"

"It might hurt their reputation, or their bookings."

"Since you won't tell us the air line, will you tell us the type of plane?"

Emma hesitated.

"Yes, please. Many of us travel a lot. I, myself, fly quite often," said an attractive woman.

A silent tug of war began in Emma's mind.

Tell them, her silent voice said.

If you tell them and it doesn't crash, they will think you were a fake, Emma.

Remember Kristen's arm—

Remember Sally's prom—

You'll regret it—

Will you regret it if the plane crashes—or if it doesn't crash?

Emma struggled with agonizing pros and cons.

These people believe me. They are highly intelligent, educated people. They believe me. If they believe me, I owe it to them—

"One of the planes is an L1011," she finally blurted out.

"Ah ha!" said one of the men. "That means the airline is either Atlantic or International."

"How do you know that?" Emma asked, worried they would be able to pinpoint the exact airline. She'd have to be on guard.

"Because those are the only two airlines that fly L1011s at Hartsfield. Isn't that right, Jay?"

The speaker nodded his head toward the sandy haired man.

"That's absolutely right," Jay replied, nodding his head.

Emma studied Jay's face and stance. He looked familiar. Why? Wasn't he another one of Lillian's psychologist friends?

"Do you have any other information?" asked another voice.

"A number—"

"What?"

"Twenty."

"What does it mean?"

"That is the number of either a flight or a gate. We don't know which. We know that one of the flight attendants will be working flight twenty."

"One of the flight attendants?"

"Yes—"

"How did you locate a flight attendant?"

"I dreamed about her. She suffers an unusual injury."

"What sort of injury?"

"To her face—"

Emma made a motion across her face with her hand.

"How did you find her?"

"Through a friend who is also a flight attendant for—"

Emma stopped. She almost said Atlantic.

"Do you think maybe it was some sort of wild dream because your friend is a flight attendant?"

"No—no," Emma said very assuredly. "For one thing I only dreamed various parts of it for a couple of years—as if taking frames from a movie and mixing them up. It was only after I went to Dr. Cooper that the pieces came together in sequence and made sense."

"You said, 'for one thing.' What was the other thing?"

"My flight attendant friend only became my friend after I dreamed of her."

"What?"

"I dreamed about this girl. I had specific information about her. Months later I took a continuing education class at DeKalb College and this girl came in. At first, I thought I was crazy, but I was convinced she was the same girl."

"What did you do?"

"One day I told her I dreamed about her. I was scared, of course. Very scared. I was also convinced she was the same girl, even though she was dressed differently. I could not ignore her."

"How did she take it?"

"We went out for coffee after class and talked for three hours. She was wonderful. She's has psychic experiences herself; that's why she believed me."

"Exactly what did you say to her?"

"I described clothes she was wearing in the dream and I told her there would be a plane crash."

"What did she say to that?"

"She told me the clothes I described were her uniform, that she was a flight attendant for—"

"How did you feel when she said that?"

"I was shocked. And relieved."

"Relieved?"

"Yes. For the first time I felt as though the disaster could be prevented. I now had a friend who worked for the same airline I dreamed about. She believed me and she said she would help me."

"Did she?"

"Yes. Quite a bit. She explained how the teacher got on the plane without a ticket."

"How?"

"He works full time for—the air line. He only teaches night school. She said he would have written his own ticket, that they don't use ordinary passenger tickets."

"Is that right, Jay?" someone asked the familiar sandy haired man.

"Absolutely."

Why are they asking this man to validate everything I say? Emma wondered.

"Go on, please," Jay said to Emma, obviously interested.

"My friend, the flight attendant—a few days after we talked, she called me. She was quite upset."

"Why?"

"She'd had a dream about a plane crash. She described another flight attendant's injury."

"Is this the flight attendant you were referring to earlier?"

"Yes. She gave me specific information. I never told her about this girl. There's no way she could know I dreamed the exact same thing."

There was an audible gasp from several listeners.

"The collective unconscious—" one voice said.

"Universal mind—" said another.

"What did you do then?" someone asked.

"We decided she had to be warned. Con—I can't tell you her name—was on a flight with her one day and told her the whole story."

"Did the flight attendant believe her?"

"Yes. She did. She also told Con—my friend—that she signed up to start working flight twenty."

"My, goodness—I've never heard of such an episode. I mean, you read about paranormal cases but I've never personally worked with psychics," one of the psychologists said.

"It has been a grueling task," Emma continued. "If it hadn't been for Dr. Cooper, I think I would have gone completely mad."

"That's understandable. Can you tell us how this crash is supposed to happen?" asked a new voice.

"As one of the planes is taking off there's a tremendous noise in the rear, over the tail. A small fire starts, the hydraulic system fails, the pilot loses control without the ailerons or rudder, I'm not sure which, and it veers off course, into the path of an inbound plane. The right wing is knocked off one of the planes."

"Does that sound feasible, Jay?"

"It certainly does."

Again, the sandy hair man. Who was he? Why was this psychologist different from the others in the room?

"How many are killed?"

"Twenty two, maybe twenty three—"

Emma was starting to tire mentally.

"We hear about disaster drills at the airport occasionally. Will there be a good rescue response to this crash?"

"Definitely! You see, there will be a couple of smaller accidents, before this one—if it happens."

"If it happens? I thought you said it would happen next May?"

"I did and it will, if I don't find the pilot. I haven't given up yet. I know if I find him, it won't happen."

"What did you mean by 'smaller accidents?'?"

"A very big plane will run into a very small plane this winter. Maybe early spring. I told Dr. Cooper last summer when I dreamed about it. It will be similar because it will involve a plane landing and a plane taking off. The big plane will lose a wing and there may be a fatality. This accident won't happen at the far end of the runway though. On the news, you'll be able to see a hangar in the background."

"You're not concerned with stopping this accident?"

"It's not that I'm not concerned. I care. I don't have any specific information other than what I've told you. I don't know anyone involved; I don't feel—connected—to it."

"Do you think you can prevent this thing in May?"

"Yes, I do. I've already found two flight attendants. I feel that if I can find the pilot, and warn him, it won't happen. My teacher thinks I'm a nut—warning him is pointless. The man at the airline who handles this sort of situation wants more information than I'm capable of giving—like the i.d. number of the plane. I haven't been able to do that. However, I've seen the pilot in my dreams. I know what he looks like. If he doesn't make that flight—things would be different. Another pilot might leave the gate later, or earlier. It won't be the same without the pilot and two flight attendants."

"Do you think you can find him?"

"I think I could find him, although I worry I might not recognize him."

"Huh? How's that?"

"For instance, my flight attendant friend. In my dreams she was wearing her uniform, but when I met her in person, she was wearing a pink sweat suit. Her hair was longer. She was shorter than I thought because she was wearing different shoes."

"That's understandable. Could you tell us how the pilot looks?"

"Okay. First, he's wearing a hat. I know that would make him look different. I know he has silky looking thin hair."

"How do you know that if he's got on a hat?"

"I don't know how I know. He's got real pretty hair. Sort of blond, with red streaks."

"Sandy colored?"

"Yes. That's a good description."

"What else?"

"He's wearing a pilot's uniform. The color is very dark, navy blue, almost black. He has blue eyes and a friendly smile. He's not too tall; very slender."

"How tall?"

"Maybe five ten or eleven."

Jay in the blue argyle sweater drew back, a quizzical expression on his face. He had set down the empty eggnog cup and stood with his arms crossed. Then the handsome face lit up with his beautiful smile as he said, "I promise you. I'm not flying L1011s in May."

Emma looked at him intently.

"Do you fly a lot doctor—you are a psychologist aren't you?"

"Not me," he said laughing. "I'm not one of Lillian's nutty psychologist friends."

He was obviously teasing the other guests.

"I'm a pilot for Atlantic Airways. I fly L1011s."

Emma's knees went limp. Her heart pounded. She felt light headed, as if she were floating.

"Excuse me," she said, running from the room.

No one followed her.

There was a moment of eerie silence among the guests. Then they resumed their earlier conversation about research.

***

"David!" Emma exclaimed as she rushed into his office, "I found the pilot."

"What?" he asked, somewhat surprised.

"The pilot. The one in the dream and the trance session. I found him. He knows he shouldn't fly L1011s in May. He even said that he wouldn't. He looked at me, right in the eyes. He said, 'I won't fly L1011s in May.'"

David was pleased. He leaned back in the rocking chair and smiled. Emma charged along, ever the thoroughbred in a race.

"I can't believe we did it, David" she said, giving him credit for her good news. "I couldn't have done it without you."

Her closed lips turned up in a smile while she cocked her head to one side and shook it slowly.

"I wouldn't be here today if it wasn't for you."

Emma's eyes felt misty.

"He'll never know, David," she said, her mood changing from elation to deep contemplation.

"Who?"

"Philip Byrd will never know what we did. He'll get on that plane the first weekend of next May and fly off somewhere and then come back and he'll always think I was a fool. A complete fool. I had to do it, David. I had to. I couldn't take a chance that something would happen. I couldn't. If he hasn't found my Anne by now, maybe he will someday in the future. I wish I had the chance to explain it to him, David."

"You're still holding on, Emma."

"I can't help it, David. He never forgave me. I asked for his forgiveness; I never got it. I've tried to make up for past mistakes, David. God knows I've tried. Still, he won't forgive. That hurts."

The mist in Emma's eyes grew heavy. Tears ran down her cheeks. She pulled a Kleenex out of the box on the end table and wiped her face.

"Forgiveness is important, Emma. Unfortunately, some people are not capable of forgiving."

"My mother is not a forgiving person, David, and rarely admits she made a mistake. Why are some people that way?"

"They haven't learned the lesson of forgiveness, Emma, and it binds the other person to them."

"In pain," Emma said, looking up at her doctor. "It hurts the other person not to be forgiven when they have sincerely apologized. I want forgiveness,

David. Then I can let go. I've come such a long way. Even though I'm at peace, I still hurt over this entire ordeal."

"Do you want to ask Margaret if she has something else to say about letting go and forgiveness?"

Emma dabbed at one eye and nodded emphatically, her body moving back and forth in a rocking affirmation to David's suggestion. She pushed off her shoes, took a deep breath, closed her eyes and drifted off, breathing deliberately, watching the bright light in her mind searching for spiritual lessons the way a spotlight scans an expansive, dark night sky.

"Where are you?" David asked.

"Ship. There's a ship on the horizon."

A merchantman sailed toward port, where a fragile, blond woman, with a male child by her side, stood waiting. With the wind behind it, the house flag was blowing in the direction the ship sailed.

"An old lady takes my hand. She says, 'look Missy, the ship is coming.'"

"I know. I know the ship is coming."

"We're not ready. We weren't expecting it," the old woman says.

"I was. I knew he would be here today."

"Who's coming?" David asked.

"John's coming home. He's been gone a long while. I knew he would be here today."

"Move ahead in time. Is the ship at the dock?"

"Late—afternoon," the tired, old trance voice said. "His ship is in the harbor. Men are unloading it. He's standing at the helm. He's telling everyone what to do. He doesn't want anything dropped. The cloth is heavy. He wants the men to be careful."

"What day is it?" David asked, wondering if Emma would come up with any sort of date. After the earlier trance session with these same people she said it was the 1760s.

There was a long, long pause.

"Tuesday. Tuesday. Late spring."

Again, a long pause while the searchlight scanned the recesses of her mind, looking for a more definitive time.

Finally, David asked, "Have you talked to him yet?"

"He is still on the ship."

"Move ahead in time," he gently urged.

A sizeable man, with thick dark hair disembarked. He was wearing a dark green velvet coat.

"He says he missed me. He was faithful to me the whole time he was gone. He's holding me in his arms. I missed him. Now he has come back."

"Move to her death," David instructed in his quiet way. "What lesson is there for Emma?"

"That day he came back was fulfilled, exactly the way she saw it. She cherished that day when they were reunited. When Emma met Philip Byrd she remembered how good it felt and she knew she would never have those good feelings again. She missed those feelings and she mourned for him. She felt empty and alone. She knew that they were never to be together again. Her life and his life will not run the same course again. She must let go of the past and thank God for what she had. She must not cling to those feelings and she must not mourn for their loss. She will repel the love of others who could come to her because she wants it to be the way it was with him. There may be a greater love in her future if she will open herself to it. She can't hang on to the past and be open to the future at the same time."

There. It was finally out. Feelings for Philip Byrd that Emma never consciously remembered, but which, for too long, bound her to him. Now she could let go.

"What lesson have you learned about forgiveness?" David prompted.

Emma was quiet for another long spell.

She started feeling hot and squirmed; she was trying to get more air.

"Hot—"

Her chest heaved.

"Hot—"

"Where are you?"

"Bed. In bed. Next to fire. Holding Momma's hand."

The little girl lay still in her bed.

"What do you see next?"

Emma's spirit was moving through a tunnel at a very great speed. The walls were lined with colorful blinking lights of every shade imaginable. It was impossible to describe the awesome site. Emma said nothing. Her body went limp. Every physical feeling was erased as her mind took her into another realm. A place where she knew total peace. Again, the spirit of the little boy who drowned at the river greeted her. In this trance, however, her mind did not want to let go of the blessed peace. The light of her spirit blended with the light of Philip's spirit and they went through another opening. On the other side was a most intense Brilliance. The spirits of the children merged with those in attendance, in the presence of the Brilliance.

It was beyond description. Total joy. Total peace. Forever. It was always that way. Reunited with her heavenly Father, the blessed peace she longed for was given to Emma again. The spirits of the children moved closer and closer to the loving Brilliance and Emma realized she was in the presence of God and her Lord.

A voice that could not be correctly described as a voice called out to the spirit of the little girl.

"You are forgiven."

Emma St. Claire's breathing slowed. She tried to make it stop altogether. She wanted to stay where she was. She did not want to come back to the sofa in David Cooper's office. Her mind took her on the same trip she had made time after time at the end of each of her spirit's journeys to the place called Earth. She did not want to go back there again. To go back meant that she would forget. She would forget the love, the peace, the infinite, blessed Oneness that spirits can only know when united with their heavenly Father.

Emma could not stay. She had to go back to the sofa, in the office, in the building, that was situated in a place called Atlanta, on the planet Earth. This time Emma would not forget. She would never, not ever again, forget the love she felt in His presence. The infinite love—and the forgiveness.

***

Over the next several weeks, Emma gradually reduced her medication. By Christmas she was pill free. As Tracie predicted, something dramatic happened. The pain in Emma's arms subsided. The fear of the crash faded away.

Tracie was right. Absolutely right. God put another spirit in Emma's path to light the way for her. Emma pondered the spiritual gift that both blessed and burdened her. A peace came over Emma St. Claire as pain and agony, despair and confusion were at long last set aside.

Alone at her apartment that evening, after the incredible session at David's office, Emma picked up her Bible and read a favorite passage.

"Peace," the psalmist wrote. "Peace shall be a path."

"I'm on a peaceful path now," Emma mused. "I wonder where it will take me."

CHAPTER TWENTY-ONE

"Do not be afraid, only believe"
-Mark 5:36

The Christmas holidays were peaceful and pleasant for Emma even though she missed her children. Allison insisted on taking J.D. to Thomson.

"If he goes to Aunt Rachel's with you, Mama, he'll miss Daddy. If he goes to Grandma's to be with Daddy, he'll miss you. I'm taking him to Thomson with me. He'll have a good time."

Much to Allison's surprise, Emma cheerfully went along with the idea. Allison had her brother's best interest at heart and, of course, she was right. Emma loaded up Steve's Bronco with gifts for her children and happily dispatched them to her beloved Thomson for Christmas.

Festivities at Rachel's home in Greenville were beyond compare. The house was beautifully decorated, the Christmas Eve service at Christ Church, complete with brass ensemble, was the most majestic Emma ever experienced. Best of all, Emma did not shed one tear.

While washing the dishes after the feast on Christmas afternoon, Rachel turned to her sister and said, "You're amazing, Emma. Honestly, you are. You're separated from your husband and children for the first time in twenty-four years, yet you are not crying for them and the life you had. How do you manage?"

"It was not easy getting to this point, Rachel. Now I've found peace, no problem seems insurmountable. When you compare a present inconvenience or disappointment to the overall scheme of things—a lot of things we agonize over are not worth it. I mean, what do you gain by tormenting yourself over something you have no control of? You have to let go and get on with your life."

***

A few days after Christmas Emma drove to Connie's house. They had tickets to Tchaikovsky's Nutcracker ballet and Emma volunteered to be the chauffeur.

"Here's something for you," Connie said when she bounced into the car.

"What's this?" Emma said, taking the small paperback book from her friend.

"You need to read this book, Emma."

"I do?"

"This is a biography of Edgar Cayce. Remember, Dr. Franklin talked about him in our reincarnation class."

Emma studied the little book intently.

"This is out of print now, Connie. Do you trust me with it?"

"I'm giving it to you. I hope you'll enjoy it."

"Connie, you're a dear. Thank you. I know I will."

Connie beamed, knowing she had done something very special for her friend.

"Tell me," Connie asked, abruptly changing the subject, "why don't you ever talk about your husband? We've talked for hours and hours and you've scarcely mentioned him."

"I haven't been able to face everything he and his mother Janice have done to me. Denial, I guess. We never had the marriage people thought we had. She ruled my life completely and my thoughts and feelings and opinions didn't matter to either Janice or Jim. Janice not only picked out my wedding ring, she also raised cane about the names I chose for my children. As a result, I didn't name either one of my own children what I wanted.

"God knows I tried, Connie. I went along to get along. I responded to every demand, every harsh word, every lie, with forgiveness and love. I kept thinking that if I showed them how to love that they might love me in return. They never did. Maybe it was some sort of past-life hatred that caused them to treat me the way they have. That does not exonerate them.

"Janice told me at the get-go that I would not be first in our marriage; and she always saw to it that I wasn't. Every woman wants to believe that she is the most important person in the world to her husband. I've never known that feeling. Never."

***

In a session with Dr. Cooper the next day, Emma said, "I told you last summer I couldn't see myself this Christmas. That feeling troubled me. Now I understand it."

"Yes, I believe you said you couldn't see your future, that it was dark?"

"That's right. It was dark, David, because it was dying. My way of looking at life was dying. I saw it from my limited physical perceptions and my emotional experiences. Then, after I went to the end of that little girl's life, my entire perspective changed and that changed me. I wasn't the same person at Christmas that I was last summer when I said that."

"Now you have the Big Picture?"

"Now I have the Big Picture."

"How does it look?"

"Beautiful, David. The Big Picture is beautiful."

***

Emma did a lot of reading about reincarnation and psychic phenomena and the book about Edgar Cayce was a revelation to her. He was not only a gifted psychic who gave more than fourteen thousand readings during his lifetime, he was also a healer who diagnosed ailments and prescribed treatments while deep in a trance. Although Cayce was not a medical doctor, over the course of many years his identification of diseases was proven to be correct time and time again by the physicians who carried out his instructions. Many of his readings were for people suffering from emotional or psychological problems and for these Cayce frequently referred to past life experiences.

"Connie, I've been thinking," Emma said one evening while they were eating dinner at Houston's on Peachtree Street, near mid-town Atlanta. "If Edgar Cayce diagnosed physical problems and recommended treatments that worked, don't you think that gives credence to his theories about reincarnation?"

"Absolutely. If he went into a trance and started spouting off about reincarnation, who would have believed him? But he helped people; thousands of them. It was well documented. Seems to me that if he's right about physical things that can be verified, surely he's right about the spiritual, too."

"This is new to me, Connie. I have a great deal to learn. Today I was reading that Cayce said many souls follow similar paths from one lifetime to another."

"That's why there are prodigies, Emma. They bring their talents with them. After many incarnations, they can play musical instruments or compose music when they are mere children. Look at Mozart. How else could you explain his extraordinary musical talents?"

"Makes sense to me. And Paul Sims. In a trance session with David last summer I told him about my child in Boston. We took him to London to attend a proper school and he became a barrister. Then, in Wyoming, that same soul reincarnated as my father and he was a sheriff and land agent. When I met Paul the first time, my e.s.p. said he always did legal work. When I read what Mr. Cayce said about souls following similar paths, it was an affirmation of my special feelings. I was absolutely elated."

"Do you think that possibly David could have given you leading questions, questions that would make you say the things you did?"

"No, never, Connie. He always asked me questions about what I felt or saw. He would ask me to describe things but he would never say something such as, 'do you see a red brick house,' or 'do you feel scared.' When David put me in a trance, the first time I saw him, I had no idea what was going on. He didn't ask me to go to Thomson and tell him what I saw. He asked me to go back to the source of my feelings. When he explained reincarnation it made sense. It wasn't a weird, complicated explanation. It was simple. I finally realized what was going on and why."

"What about Margaret. Do you know anything about her?" Connie asked.

"Yes, I do. She was born in 1864 and died in the early 1940s. She loved children very much. I keep feeling that she always had children around her but she didn't have a lot of family around her when she died. She was alone, without a mate, for many, many years. She was a teacher or counselor or in some way she was close to education. It meant a great deal to her."

"Have you ever looked for her grave to verify her existence?"

"No, Connie. I'm not up to that yet. When the time is right I'll ask Louise to take me to the grave yard in Thomson and I'll find her."

"There's only one grave yard in Thomson?"

"No, there are several. The first time we went to Thomson we passed by one near a Methodist church on Main Street. I felt very drawn to it. I know that's where Margaret is buried."

"I've thought about doing some past life therapy myself, Emma. I want to know more about that woman in the cave."

"You mean the one you kept seeing when you were a child?"

"Yes. She was either another incarnation of my spirit or someone close to me in another life."

"Did your mother ever scold you for seeing an invisible playmate the way many parents do?"

"No. Maybe that's why I can still see her clearly."

"I didn't tell you what happened the other day!" Emma suddenly burst out.

"What?" Connie asked, batting her long lashes and pulling a loose strand of beautiful hair behind one ear.

"My girlfriend called—the one who is a twin. She was crying about her three year old son."

"What happened?"

"Leslie said Ben started talking about his grandfather—her father. Ben said they went flying together."

"Flying with his grandfather. Is that unusual?"

"Yes, it is. His grandfather died twenty years ago."

"Ohhhh—" Connie was mulling over Emma's story.

"What else did the little boy say?"

"He said they had a plane crash."

"A plane crash?"

"Yes. Leslie's dad was a test pilot. His plane had some sort of mechanical failure. Instead of bailing out he stayed with it to steer it away from a school. He was a real hero."

"Did Ben tell Leslie he was in the crash?"

"Yes. He also told her he died because he fell out of a tree."

Emma took another drink of coffee while Connie urged her to continue with the story.

"And?"

"Leslie's dad died as a result of a broken back. He waited until the last minute to eject and his parachute did not open completely. He fell into some trees, then landed on the ground."

"That's amazing. And her little boy told her this?"

"Yes. It scared her something awful. She called me because she didn't understand what he could possibly know about it. He's only three years old. She swears she never talked to Ben about his grandfather."

"What did you say to her?" Connie asked, picking up her coffee cup.

"First I told her there was nothing to be scared of. I know she believes in eternal life but I asked her again anyway."

"What did she say?"

"Of course I believe in eternal life. Then I asked her when her soul was born if she was eternal."

"And?"

"She didn't have an answer. At first she said God created her soul while she was in her mother's womb. When I asked her again if she was eternal and reminded her that eternity has no beginning and no end she was stumped."

Connie smiled and took a sip of coffee.

"Then I asked her what she was doing here on earth."

"She had the usual answers?" Connie asked. "I was born, grew up, got married and had children."

"Yes."

"In other words she didn't fully understand why she was here."

"No."

"What did you say then?"

"I told her life is a spiritual journey and because our souls are eternal they can incarnate many times."

"Did you tell her what Voltaire said?"

"I did. *It is no more surprising to be born twice than it is to be born once.* That got her thinking about it."

"Did she believe you?"

"Yes, she did. I told her there have been many, many cases of small children recalling experiences from past lives but most of the time parents don't pay any attention to it. They think their children are imagining things. Leslie may have ignored Ben if he hadn't talked very specifically about something that happened when she was a teenager."

"This is great, Emma! What a story!"

"I think it is, too. Guess what?"

Connie shook her head incredulously.

"Because Leslie is listening to Ben, he's starting to tell her about other past lives, too."

"Oh, how exciting!"

"I told her to keep a diary of his comments, to listen to him when he starts talking about these other lives. As a result he has told her about three. Guess what else he said to her?"

Connie shook her head slowly, picking up her coffee cup again.

"Ben told Leslie he had chosen her to be his mother!"

"He did? Dr. Franklin said that souls select their parents."

"That's right. We each choose our parents, for one reason or another. Maybe to resolve some old conflict, or to have a different sort of relationship, or because they will teach us what we need to learn for that incarnation. Obviously Ben came back into this life as Leslie's son because they only had a little time together when his soul incarnated as her father."

"What did she say about that?"

"She said that was a beautiful explanation. She loves the idea of having time with that wonderful soul again."

"Why did you incarnate with your mother, Emma? You said she was verbally abusive. Why would a soul choose that?"

"I believe we had unresolved issues. The good thing is that Momma's verbal abuse made me look into myself for protection. As a child I would ask myself what to do to avoid her wrath. That, of course, enhanced my psychic ability. Looking inside myself for guidance. Because of my e.s.p. I'm walking an incredible path. Even though at one point I thought I was insane and suffered unbelievably with my arms, I've learned and I've grown. I'm at peace with myself.

"Of course, trance sessions with David taught me these things, Connie. It was my e.s.p. that led me to David."

"Which session stands out the most, Emma? Which one was the most helpful?"

"Every single one was important. When you build a house you start with the foundation and then put up the walls and roof, and that's what I did. The foundation was learning about Margaret and reincarnation. Then as other past life experiences came out, the walls went up. I built an entire house and now I feel whole, Connie. I never knew life could feel this good."

"What made the roof of your house, Emma?"

"Seeing myself on the other side. Knowing beyond any doubt that my soul is eternal. When I went to the end of the little girl's life and she was reunited with her brother, the feeling was—was—indescribable and incredibly beautiful."

Connie's eyes lit up.

"Tell me, Emma. Do you think it will be that way when we die?"

"There's no doubt in my mind. The peace was indescribable. Everything I fretted over was irrelevant when I got there. Why in the world did I get mad when Mother spilled chocolate syrup in the refrigerator? Or why was I angry when Jim took the antique Danish phone out of my apartment? Or why did I yell at Allison when she cut the grass too short?

"When I look back at my earthly home, I realize I wasted a lot of energy, Connie. I never had peace because I was worried about making everything perfect. Now I know I can't control things. Each soul is on its own mission. The best way to help it along is to love it, no matter what it does, or doesn't do."

Emma took a long sip of coffee.

"I've also learned you can't be happy if you are depending on other people to make you happy by what they either do or don't do. You have to find it inside yourself."

"You've changed a lot, Emma, just in the short time since I met you."

"You played a part in that Connie. You helped me put lots of pieces in my puzzle."

"Speaking of puzzles, have you decided about Jim yet? What are you going to do?"

"I'm going ahead with the divorce. I'll always love him, Connie, even though I choose not to live with his lies and deceit. He has many good qualities but he'll never change the bad. I can't do it for him. He's walking a troubled path for some reason. It's not my place to say what's right and wrong for him."

"Emma, you've told me that your mother was honest to the core; yet your husband and his mother were deceitful liars. Why did you marry into such a family?"

"That's an interesting question, Connie. Do you think that maybe I was in their lives to teach them something?"

"You probably were supposed to show them the high road—honesty, integrity, and those strong moral standards you hold dear."

"I wish I could have known twenty-four years ago what I know now. I would have done things differently. I can't undo the past. I was young and wanted to have a good marriage. I caved in to Jim's mother to keep the peace and never set boundaries. Then she ran right over me; I was nothing more than a squished bug in the road."

"It was bad, wasn't it?"

"Yes, extremely bad. Would you believe that when I got pregnant with J.D. that Janice said to me, 'How dare you get pregnant and deprive my Allison the privilege of being an only child'? Her Allison. She talked about Allison as if she was her personal possession and told me I didn't have the right to have another child, too. Can you image someone saying such a thing?"

"What gave her such a notion?"

"Janice hated her little brother. Told him for years and years that she wished he had never been born. Of course, he died young and alcoholic. She always thought Allison was her child. She would say to me that Allison was the child she should have had with David."

"But you did have J.D."

"Yes, and we named him after his dad, James, and his step-grandfather, David. It was the only way I could placate Janice into accepting him."

"Oh, Emma. That is sad."

"Sad, but true, Connie. My mom would never in a million years have ever done something that cruel. She adored my child because he was my child and her grandchild, not because of his name. My mom used to yell at me and say mean things but I could always yell back. Janice is insidious; she never raises her voice. She says horrible things in a low, conniving tone. Because it is quiet and painful, you don't fight back. I don't know how to explain it."

"That's the nature of evil, Emma. It always has to have something positive about it to attract others to it."

"Huh? What do you mean? Don't think I follow you."

"If Janice yelled and screamed, then you would have recognized it as wrong, as inappropriate behavior. Right?"

"Yes, I guess."

"Emma, did you ever think of your mother as evil?"

"No. No way. Never. She has a mean streak. Bee is honest and faithful. She would never deceive anyone. "

"Your mother yelled and screamed but she was not evil."

"Yes, that's the way I see her."

"In other words, she kept you at bay with her loud, intolerant voice. She was indirectly saying, don't get too close right now 'cause I'm mad."

"Well—yes."

"Sort of the way a bee buzzes or a rattle snake shakes its tail. Neither of those creatures is evil. They can hurt you but they give you fair warning, right?"

"Yes, that's a good way to look at it."

"Now, Janice on the other hand never did anything to give you a warning. She slid in nice and quiet and stabbed you, right?"

"Yeah."

"She gave you no warning, right? No buzzing? No rattling? No yelling?"

"Connie. I think you're right."

"That's the kind of person you need to stay away from Emma. They strike without warning—their venom is deadly."

321

***

The first week in January of 1990, Emma went to another appointment with David. As usual, she brought a long list of topics to talk about.

"What do you have on your list today?" he asked cheerfully.

"I've decided to divorce Jim. We're walking on separate paths, David. I can't live with his lies. Until he admits he has a problem, he will continue to deceive people. His mother has done it her entire life and I think Jim will, too. I know J.D. is hurting over it, but in time he'll realize there was a reason for what we've been through. Do you think you could talk with my son sometime? Some advice from a professional would be good for him."

"Yes, of course."

Emma charged ahead. In the wink of an eye she closed the door on twenty-four years of marriage and gave David no further details on her painful relationship with Janice St. Claire Crymes. Emma was ready for the next item on her list.

"We found Philip in several past lives with me and I've been wondering if Anne had some past life experience with him, too."

David raised his eyebrows in his questioning expression and Emma continued.

"It seems to me there must be some reason I dream of them being together."

"Let's see what we can find."

Emma pushed off her shoes, going through her relaxation routine and before she knew it, she was deep in a trance. This was a new adventure for Emma. In prior trance sessions, she looked for answers to questions about her own past. This time, she was aiming for a link between two other people. Neither David nor Emma knew if her mind would connect to the past lives of these two people Emma loved but it was worth an attempt.

Emma went to the quiet, restful place, where there was no time, or form, only feelings. Her head bobbed on the balloon string, her mind focusing on her soothing white light, surrounded by a tinge of yellow. She stared at the pleasant brightness, breathing slowly, until her head nodded, as if she was in a deep, deep sleep.

"We're looking for Anne," David said quietly.

The light came closer and closer to Emma; her eyes focused on it. Like the evening sun setting on the horizon, the brightness faded slowly, opening up a pinhole view that gradually increased, allowing Emma's mind a glimpse into the past life of another soul.

"What do you see?" David asked in his trance work monotone.

The woman Emma saw was thin boned and fragile, with deep, dark eyes and pink cheeks. Her facial features were delicate and dark hair was tied in a knot beneath a hat.

"She's walking in a park. She's pretty."

The spirit of Anne was wearing a long, ankle length dress. The high neckline was trimmed with ribbons and lace and long mutton sleeves covered her arms. Her hands wore white kid gloves. On her feet were high-top button shoes with a small heel.

Beside Anne there was a tall, slender man, dressed in a khaki army uniform. His head was adorned with a wide-brimmed felt hat of the same color. Emma knew immediately he was a World War I soldier.

"She's holding his hand. He's a soldier and they are walking to a train station."

A small park where they walked was bordered with a low, black wrought iron fence. The manicured lawn was dotted with blooming plants.

"There are a lot of people. Soldiers are getting on the train."

Emma stared intently at the man in the vision.

"Philip," she said. "Anne's with Philip. He's leaving. He's getting on the train and leaving."

People crowded the station platform, young women seeing their young men off to war.

"The other girls are crying but Anne's smiling and waving to Philip."

"I'll wait for you, she says. The train leaves the station and she's standing there watching it go. He's gone."

David spoke again, asking Emma to move ahead in time to another significant event in Anne's life.

The spirit that Emma called Anne was standing in the parlor of a Victorian house. A man handed her an envelope.

"She's reading a letter from the War Department," Emma said. "He was killed in action in France. He was very brave. She starts crying. The last thing she said to him, 'I'll wait for you.' He's gone, but she's still going to wait for him. She wants to be with him. She knows she will never love anyone the way she loved him."

"Move ahead to Anne's death. What was the outcome of her decision?" David asked.

"She keeps a diary. She never quit missing him. She's not much older. She's in a bed; not in a house; in a building. An elderly lady is holding her hand."

The elderly woman, wearing an ankle length dark dress with tiny pleats across the bodice and a hat with veil partly covering her face, stood next to a bed in a stark room. Sunlight from the adjacent window filled the room with light.

"She's crying," Emma said, referring to the woman standing next to the bed, "the doctor says the lady in the bed won't recover. She's got bandages on her head."

Anne was lying in bed, her head bound with heavy bandages down to her eyebrows. Her eyes were closed.

"She had an accident. She is dying."

"Tell me her about her death," David directed quietly.

"She had much to offer him and she was again denied an opportunity to teach him the things he needs to know. She's looking for him. He's waiting for her, they're together as spirits, they're happy now."

David asked Emma to move to a future time and life the two spirits would share.

"There are lessons for him to learn. There's much she can teach him. She wants to teach him in a kind and gentle way over many years. If she dies and leaves him, he'll still learn the lessons but it will be painful. She could inspire him to do something important with his life. Without her, his life won't be the same. She's held onto me because she trusts me. She knows I love her and I love Philip, too. She wants me to prepare him for what she's going to teach him. She wants me to open his eyes. Then he will be receptive to her ideas, her lessons. I haven't prepared him. He's only closed himself to me and she feels he will be closed to her. She kept holding onto me, urging me to try again to tell him that they shouldn't be on that plane."

"You and Anne will exchange gifts, Emma, as a symbol of letting go of each other."

Emma slowly emerged from the trance under David's guidance. She yawned, stretched and blinked her eyes.

"What gifts did you exchange?" David asked.

"She gave me a comb that was in her hair."

Emma paused.

"Yes," he said, indicating she should continue.

"I gave her Margaret's apron."

David smiled, nodding in gratified agreement with his patient's work. Emma was pleased David approved the exchange of gifts that symbolized her final release from past lives that held her captive more than three years.

"No wonder I felt Anne was holding onto me, David. They were together for a short period of time during the first World War."

The words Emma spoke during the trance, "—she was again denied an opportunity to teach him the things he needs to know—" apparently made no impression on either David or Emma. What did Margaret mean? She was again denied? Again?

***

Several days later Emma was sitting quietly at her desk, contemplating the recent trance session, when the phone rang.

"Hi!" Rachel exclaimed. "Can you talk?"

"You picked a great time. Joe and Larry are both out."

"How's Mother doing today?"

"She sounds a little better. I finally got her to take a shower last night. I had to drag her out of bed. She says she feels worse from this awful flu than from the open heart surgery."

"That bad?"

"Bee's having a rough time with this bug, Rachel. I'm very concerned. Seems to have gone into asthma. The doctor was worried about pneumonia. John took her over to the hospital for me yesterday because it's hard for me to get away from the office. The x-ray was normal."

"Thank goodness. I'm glad John was able to help out."

"He's always been her favorite grandchild. He can handle her better than all the rest of us put together."

"That's true."

"I think it did her good to see him. He hasn't been able to visit her too much this quarter with his work schedule and classes. Putting her in a hot shower last night eased her aches somewhat."

"That's good. Does the doctor have any idea why she's had the flu for four weeks?"

"It's a bad, bad case. I call her every morning, then go by on my way home from work. Makes for a long day. My lease is up in March and I'm thinking about moving back to northeast Atlanta where I'll be closer to her. J.D. spends most of his time with Jim. He just breezes in and out of the apartment."

"He's having trouble dealing with the divorce, isn't he?"

"Yes. I want him to start seeing David. He's extremely depressed. He told me he knows I'll be okay but he's worried about Jim and said he was going to spend as much time with his dad as he could."

"How do you feel about that?"

"There's a reason J.D. has to be with his dad right now, Rachel. I won't discourage him from it. They are only six miles away and J.D. can call whenever he wants. He called me at two o'clock the other morning because he couldn't sleep."

"What did you do?"

"We talked for close to an hour. I think he felt better when we hung up."

"You've got a lot on you right now, Emma. I don't know how you manage."

"God made me strong, remember?" Emma said laughing.

"I'm stuck up here in Greenville and you're there with the problems. I wish we lived in Atlanta again."

"I wish you were here, too, Rachel. It would be great to have my best friend and sister nearby."

"You have friends, Emma. Why don't you go out with some of them and have some fun?"

"I tried that, Rachel. I haven't seen any of my friends since I left Jim. I called Charlotte last week; you remember her, we are in the same circle at church. She was a very aloof."

"Why?"

"It took some persuasion but she finally told me that my friends were appalled to learn that I had an affair."

"What? Are you kidding me? An affair?

"Janice told them I had an affair."

"That lying bitch—"

"She destroyed seventeen years of friendships I made in this community. I can't show my face anywhere without people looking at me is disgust."

"You and I both know she lied, Emma. How can we tell them?"

"You can't. No one would believe it anyway. Janice can persuade anyone to believe anything she wants with her charming lies."

"Good, Lord, Emma. How can you stand it?"

"Because I know that ultimately the truth will prevail. And I know that someday my very best friend Rachel will be here with me and I won't need those people anyway." Emma started to laugh. "We're gonna have our house with a porch and we will sit in our swing and tell our grandchildren stories."

"Oh, the stories we will tell. I think we ought to start writing down some of the things that have happened, Emma. What do you think of that idea?"

"I do have my journal—Rachel—I've been thinking—"

"Yeah, what else is new?" Rachel laughingly asked her twin.

"Come on, now. Don't tease. I've been thinking a lot about Paul—"

"That's not surprising."

"Rachel, listen to me—in my many sessions with David and in my journal writings it never occurred to me I could or would find the spirit that was my child in Boston or my father at the river. Then I met Paul and he fit them both perfectly. My e.s.p. said he was the man I was supposed to meet. Of course, that's why—I would know someone else from a past life. Honestly, Rachel, it never occurred to me it would happen again."

"If it happened once, Emma, it could happen again, couldn't it. I mean, if we do incarnate over and over, why couldn't you meet more than one person from a past life?"

"That's right, we can, even though I never considered the possibility. To know someone in this life and go back and find them in another life is one thing. Paul taught me it also works in reverse."

Rachel thought a moment about Emma's statement before responding.

"That's right! You told me that you did not recognize the spirit of the child, or the father—that you never met that spirit in this life, this incarnation. What are you leading to?"

"I told David about Paul and then I found him. Do you think I could find someone else in this life that I only met in my dreams and trances?"

"I don't know why not. Who?"

"Anne. I would love to find her, Rachel. More importantly, I'd need to know if I have some past life connection with her. I see her with Philip but that doesn't mean she was only important in his past life. I mean, why couldn't she have been someone important to me in a past life, too?"

"That's an interesting question. How are you going to find her in a past life, though? I mean, she's never appeared in a past-life regression, has she?"

"I don't know. Until I met Paul, I never gave it any thought. Meeting him opened a whole new world to me. He confirmed reincarnation for me. Maybe I was still skeptical until I met him. He's a perfect match. His spirit obviously knew about my arms. And I was thinking, Anne must be there, too, in my past."

"You said you adored her, Emma and I always did think that was a little odd. I mean, adoring some woman you dream about? A woman who is about your age? Have you made a list of her traits, the way you did when you found Paul?"

"I can do that right now," Emma said. She laid her shorthand pad in front of her on the desk and started writing.

"First, my Anne is a professional person who wears a uniform."

"Emma!" Rachel exclaimed. "A nurse. Remember three years ago? The feelings you picked up in the coronary care unit? You felt it every time you worked in CCU after that. How could you forget?"

"You're right, Rachel. Even way back then I was getting a sign about her. A nurse. Of course. A nurse. No wonder I told David when I started seeing him that she was a professional person and she wore a uniform. A nurse. My sweet Anne is a nurse!"

"That clears up one open signal. What else do you have on her?"

"She was married briefly."

"How long is brief?"

"Less than a year."

"What else?"

"She loves children and she wants to have a baby. She's never had one."

"What else?"

"I dreamed of her at art shows and symphony concerts; and, of course, her burial—"

Emma was upset. The memory of that premonition was still painful.

"What else?"

"The dream of me hanging onto her at the cliff, trying to save her."

"Who have you seen in past-life regressions who is a nurse, who loves children but doesn't have any? Who did you absolutely adore?"

Emma pondered the question. Her heart started to beat wildly in her chest as a beautiful thought flashed through her mind. She started to laugh and cry at the same time.

"Of course, Rachel. Of course. How could I have been that dumb?"

"What, Emma? What?!"

"My mother, Rachel," Emma said, gasping with the excitement and exhaustion of a marathon runner. "My mother. She was my mother, Rachel. My mother. That's why I adored her when I dreamed of her in this life. That's why I said she wants children. My mother. Of course. My mother!!"

"Emma! What a revelation. I don't know how you've done it."

"Rachel, you can't imagine how good I feel. A thrilling, exciting, wonderful feeling. A wholeness, a light-heartedness. That crushing weight I felt for years is gone."

"Oh, Emma, every piece of the puzzle is finally in place. What an incredible story. I don't think I could believe it if I hadn't lived every single chapter with you."

"This is amazing, Rachel. I can't wait to tell David. It makes sense now I've figured it out. The dreams about her at art shows and concerts and the funeral. Mother. Why didn't I make the connection before now? My mind was trying to tell me long, long ago to think about my mother. I dreamed of Anne, my mother in a past life, doing the things that my mother in this life does—art, and music, and even being interred in the columbarium where we'll put our mother someday."

"It never occurred to me, either, Emma. It's easy to understand now. You see your sweet, beautiful lady with your teacher because they were denied happiness in past lives together. Your mind put her in situations where you'd remember she was your Mother in a past life. That's why you were wonderfully devoted to her; why you put your own integrity on the line when you tried to talk to Philip about her. No wonder your feelings endured the years of tribulation."

"I feel vindicated, Rachel. Now that I know who she is, I know I did the right thing. It was worth the pain and agony. It was. Philip doesn't have to believe. I believe in my own heart. I know in my mind and my soul. God opened up a whole new world to me, Rachel. I've seen things in my mind in my trances with David that I never could have imagined—or dreamed. The world is beautiful from this view, Rachel. My little snail finally made it to the top of Mt. Everest.

"David kept telling me we are spirits, that we come here to learn, to grow spiritually, to redeem ourselves for past wrongs, to be rewarded for our good deeds, and to grow closer to God by being the kind of spirits Jesus Christ taught us to be."

"You've learned your lessons, Emma. Your long ordeal is finally over. I don't think you'll be bothered by nightmares of these people from your past, do you?"

"No, I don't think I will. Three years, Rachel. Three long years. I couldn't have survived without you. I would have gone completely mad without your love and guidance. You never quit believing in me, did you Rachel?"

"No, I never quit believing in you, Emma. I worried about you. In my heart and mind I always knew that somehow, some way, you'd get to the bottom of it; and you did."

"I feel as though the weight of the world has been lifted off my shoulders, Rachel. I am floating. My mother, Rachel. My mother. How could I have overlooked that beautiful woman at the river? She loved her children very much and she lost both of them. She became a nurse in Philadelphia. That's why I dreamed about hanging onto her—the way she hung onto me at the river. Then, in her next incarnation, she found Philip. They would have married and had children but they both died young. Again her desire for children—and in this life she wants the children she was denied before. Maybe she can't carry them because she is punishing herself for what happened at the river. I don't know. It seems unlikely that—"

"Unlikely, what?"

"That there is such a person like her out there, somewhere."

***

"Hi, Darlin'," Bee said when she opened the door and saw Emma standing there on a Sunday afternoon in late January.

Emma gave her mother a kiss on the cheek.

"How are you feeling, Momma?"

"A little better, I guess. You brought me groceries and fresh laundry yesterday, Darlin'. You didn't need to come by today."

"I'm going to a party and thought I'd visit with you while I change my clothes," Emma said, holding up a new outfit.

"Isn't that good looking," Bee chimed.

Emma was glad to see the sparkle returning to her mother's eyes.

"What sort of party?"

"A Superbowl Party, Momma. AESA's having a party and I've decided to go. I know I'm not divorced yet but I need to start mixing with singles. Jim is already dating Patty—you remember Patty don't you, Momma? She was my little sister in the sorority—"

"A Superbowl Party! That's wonderful, Darlin'. What is AESA?" Bee asked, completely glossing over the fact that Jim was not only dating but dating Emma's sorority sister.

"Atlanta Episcopal Singles Alliance."

Bee beamed. Any organization endorsed by the church met with immediate approval.

Emma carried the new outfit back to the dressing room and Bee oohed and aaahed while watching her daughter dress. The bronze colored slacks and over blouse were a great compliment to Emma's hair and the top piece, decorated in the latest fashion with black velvet and various print appliqués, outlined with gold piping, was striking.

"You look gorgeous," Bee said. "The men will surely notice you."

"Momma, I'm only going to have some fun with other singles. Men have never paid me any mind. Why should they now?"

"You were always married before. You've come into your own, Darlin'. You look wonderful. Quite wonderful."

"Thank you, Momma," Emma responded, kissing her mother on the cheek. "You call me if you need anything, okay."

Emma gave Bee the phone number at the church where the party was to be held.

"I'll be by tomorrow after work, Momma. Let me know if you need any groceries. I'll pick them up on my way."

"I don't know what I would have done without you the last few weeks, Emma—"

Moisture glistened in the corners of Bee's eyes.

"Oh, Momma."

Emma was almost embarrassed to be appreciated by her mother. It was a new feeling for Emma to feel accepted and appreciated by her mother. She kissed her mother again and left. Emma was going to a party and she was feeling grand. Very grand.

At the parish hall of St. Anne's church in northwest Atlanta, an attractive man with silver-white hair and short trimmed beard welcomed Emma. He was smoking a pipe and gave the appearance of a college professor.

"Hello!" Emma said to him, trying to ignore a very strong warning.

Stay away from him.

She breezed through the entry, into the spacious room where the singles were gathering. A roaring blaze danced in a fireplace on the opposite wall and three televisions, situated in strategic places around the room, blared the pre-game show.

Emma signed the register, paid the five-dollar fee, put on a nametag and walked across the room to a long table where five or six people were gathered.

"Beer or wine?" one of the men asked.

"Beer," Emma replied.

She was introducing herself to other guests when a partially bald man, wearing an apron, came bursting through the doorway from the kitchen carrying a giant pot of chili.

Emma's face lit up when she saw him.

"Mack! What are you doing here?"

The man set the hot container on the food table and held his arms open for a hug, which Emma readily gave him.

"Emma St. Claire. What a surprise. What are you doing here?"

"Jim and I are separated. I've filed for a divorce and I thought I'd start seeing how the other half lives."

"You picked the right place. We're gonna party!" he said, kissing her on the forehead.

The other singles were amused and baffled by the warm greeting between Emma and Mack.

"I know this fella from work," Emma started to explain, her arm around Mack's waist. "He's an architect and I work for a construction company. He's designed some of our buildings."

Mack recruited Emma for kitchen duty and she followed him through the swinging door. He introduced her to three women working around an island, stirring chili in an oversize pot, chopping salad fixings and grating cheese. Their friendly greetings made Emma feel welcomed and glad she had come to the party. By the time food was prepared and set out, fifty or more people were on hand for the Super Bowl festivities but Emma could tell it was not a serious football crowd. She strolled around the room, greeting people and introducing herself, leading new arrivals to the drink table and generally having a good time.

The beer drinking and talking took a toll on Emma's lipstick, and feeling a little parched around her mouth, she looked for her purse. She was standing near one of the tables, her hands on her hips, trying to remember where she left it, when she heard a deep, male voice.

"Looking for something?" he asked.

Emma turned around and looked right into the eyes of a cute man, perched on the table with young women seated on either side of him. He was boyish and teddy-bear cuddly in spite of his salt and pepper hair.

"My pocketbook—" Emma stammered, slightly embarrassed she couldn't remember where she left it.

"Stop and think for a minute," he instructed. "What did you do when you got here?"

"I signed in, got a beer, went into the kitchen—"

"I bet you set your purse down somewhere in the kitchen," he said before Emma could say anything else.

Emma found her purse sitting near one of the sinks. She put on more lipstick, fluffed her hair and started back to the table where the teddy bear was holding court with several more women.

"He's a real charmer," Emma mumbled.

She decided she wouldn't make a fool of herself and turned her attention to another group across the room. Emma was headed toward them when she heard the teddy bear's voice again.

"Did you find your purse?"

Emma glanced over her shoulder.

"I did. Thanks."

One of the women was obviously annoyed he was talking to Emma and quickly moved to the other side of the room where she took a seat in front of one of the television sets. Mack, who appeared to be the ringleader, announced dinner, said a blessing and Emma found herself in line with the teddy bear, his court having disbanded.

"Are you a manager of some sort?" Emma asked. "You seem to know about organization."

He laughed.

"You might say that. I'm getting my doctorate in operations management."

Emma was impressed. The teddy bear had brains.

They stopped at the end of the serving table to garnish their chili with various offerings of cheeses and sour cream. He followed Emma to an empty table.

"Can I sit with you?" he asked.

Emma was pleased. Moments before he was holding court with the best-looking women, younger than Emma. Now he was sitting with her at dinner.

"I'm delighted," she smiled, trying to see his nametag, partially hidden by his leather flight jacket. "What's your name?"

"Philip Moore," he answered, holding open the jacket and showing Emma his nametag.

"That's an impressive flight jacket, Commander," Emma said, having noticed his rank and initials above the pocket. "Are you on active duty in the Navy?"

"No, not now. Active reserve."

"My boss and my cousin are Navy reserve. Both of them are captains now."

"That's great. I'm on the captain's list."

He was happy talking about his naval career and told Emma he graduated from Annapolis and was a nuclear submarine officer. Philip Moore was an impressive man, but to Emma St. Claire he was a gentle soul carrying a lot of pain in his heart.

Their effortless conversation ran the entire evening. Before Emma knew it, the Super Bowl was over and she had not seen a single down. Philip and Emma were like old friends and easily talked about everything. Between them there was an openness and trust Emma had not experienced before. When they each relayed their stories of estrangement and reconciliation with their fathers, a bond was forged.

Mack supervised clean up and Emma was embarrassed she had not helped. For some reason, conversation with Philip Moore was more important. They walked to the parking lot together and stood in the chilly night air. Feeling an intense pain in Philip, Emma put her hand on his upper arm.

"You're hurting a lot over someone, aren't you," Emma said cautiously.

"You're very perceptive," he said, relieved he didn't have to hide his feelings.

"I've was married for only six months. It didn't work out," he explained almost apologetically, "I was recently divorced."

"Do you want to tell me about her?"

He needed to talk but it was obvious to Emma that it made him uneasy. She decided to draw information about the woman out of him, hoping it would ease his burden.

"What's her name? Tell me about her."

"Her name's Elizabeth, but everyone calls her Liz. She's incredibly beautiful and she has a brilliant mind."

"You adore her, don't you?"

"Yes. I've never loved anyone the way I love her."

"What's the problem? Why can't you two get along?"

"She's insanely jealous. She doesn't trust me. Right after we were married she told me I'm not the man she thought I was. You can't imagine how bad that hurt."

"She's insecure, Philip. That's why she's jealous. It may not have anything to do with you. There's a reason she can't trust."

"You think? I don't know why she can't trust me. I've never done anything to make her feel insecure about us."

"Does her insecurity carry over into other areas of her life? What about her work? Does it affect that, too?"

"No. She's very proficient in her job. She's a very responsible person."

"What does she do?"

"She's a cardiac care nurse. She's kind and nurturing. She's never had children but she adores my girls from my first marriage."

The woman Philip described could have been an ideal mate but her jealousy was destroying their relationship the way Jim's lies destroyed Emma's marriage.

"Trust has to be the foundation for any relationship, Philip. You give the impression of being a very responsible person. I can't understand why she wouldn't trust you."

He was pleased that Emma thought he was trustworthy and grinned.

"She's hurting, too, Philip. For some reason, Liz is hurting real bad."

A cold wind whipped through the parking lot. Emma shivered.

"You better get home," he said. "Can I call you sometime? You seem to understand."

Emma unlocked the door and got into her car.

"Don't forget," she said, "I'll be glad to help you edit that paper we talked about earlier."

"I forgot about that. Do you think you can come over to my house next Sunday? I'll have to get it off my computer."

"I'll stop by after church."

They exchanged phone numbers and Philip told Emma he'd call.

During her long drive back to Stone Mountain, Emma listened to Mozart's Symphony No. 31 in D Major while mulling over the evening with Philip Moore and wondering if he would call.

***

A few days later there was a plane crash at Hartsfield. A jet liner ran into a small private plane as it was taking off, killing the pilot and ripping a wing off the jet. The airline passengers were safely evacuated. The picture in the paper showed a man, wearing a trench coat, inspecting the damage. An aircraft hangar was clearly visible in the background. Emma felt as if someone had walked into her mind and taken a picture of the vision she had six months before the

335

accident. There were still those people who would not, or could not, believe Emma could dream about the future. The entire episode was thoroughly documented. This time, Emma St. Claire had proof.

***

"Do you know how to get to the Emory area from the Cathedral?" Philip asked Emma during their phone conversation.

"I do; I'll come down Peachtree and turn off before I get to the Memorial Arts Center and cut through Ansley Park and Morningside over to Emory. Where is your house?"

"On a corner, on a street right off North Decatur Road."

He gave Emma the address and explicit instructions about parking in the back.

"You'll have to come in through the kitchen door."

As Philip instructed, Emma drove down the side street and parked in the yard behind the house. It was a rainy, dismal day. She was anxious to pick up Philip's paper and get home.

Philip appeared to be disoriented when he got to the kitchen door and showed Emma the way through the cluttered room past a butler's pantry and into the dining room. One computer was sitting on a roll-top desk; a laptop was sitting on the table. Emma stepped around a stack of boxes and seated herself at the table with Philip while he explained the workings of the computer. He brought up the document she agreed to edit, showed her the format he needed, closed it and handed Emma the power cords.

"I'll bring my printer out to your apartment one night and we'll run it off. Let me know if you have any questions."

"Will do. Shouldn't be any problem. I've done a lot of editing. I'll get it fixed up for you."

Philip told Emma how much he appreciated her help. Emma was pleased he asked. She pushed back from the table, stood up, stacked papers and almost tripped over a stack of books lying on the floor.

"You're a little disorganized, aren't you?" she said in a teasing tone.

"Yeah. I moved in here a few weeks ago. Got a lot of work to do."

"Maybe I can give you a hand after we get this paper finished," she said. The place was a mess.

They ran to the car through a heavy drizzle. Emma was glad to be out of the disorganized clutter that did not seem to bother Philip. Something was buzzing in the recesses of Emma's mind. She thought how ironic it was that she had met another man named Philip, who like Philip Byrd, majored in engineering in college and had a master's degree in a business field.

More than that, she also wondered why her e.s.p. told her not to tell him she was psychic.

***

The week after Emma edited Philip's paper he showed up in her Sunday school class. Emma did a double take when she saw him.

"Good morning," she finally said, still surprised he was there.

"I decided to see if this class is as good as you said," he teased.

The teacher, a Robert Redford clone, appeared and the room full of people became quiet when he started his lecture on spirituality of the unconscious.

"We'll be talking about dreams this morning," he said.

Emma started taking notes. In her effort to understand her e.s.p., she read many books about psychic phenomenon, psychology and spirituality, and this class, at the church to which she was drawn by her silent voice, was, to Emma, her religion's affirmation of her unconscious abilities.

"Dreams that wake us are the ones that stir us up the most and we remember the dreams that occur near awakening."

Emma agreed wholeheartedly, remembering the dreams of Philip Byrd.

The teacher continued, "It's important to accept a dream as something that has happened to you. You can awaken from a nightmare experiencing physiological responses that are real."

Emma was amazed at the teacher's comment.

So waking up with a pounding heart and profuse sweating wasn't my imagination.

"Our psychological or our unconscious life is just as important as our outer life," he continued. "We tend to think things that happen outside of us are real and things that happen inside us are not real. Dreams are important but we tend to dismiss them because we have been erroneously taught that they are not real."

"Hmmm—" Emma mused, "Maybe my church wouldn't condemn me because of my dreams."

"Be aware of anyone or any book that says it can tell you what your dreams mean. The first and most important part of understanding the context of your dreams is to realize no one else can enter your world and tell you what they mean.

"The second thing that can be helpful is to write about them, or illustrate them, express them visually. Things will come to you in the form of memories and feelings and this will help you understand them."

To Emma, everything the teacher was saying was an affirmation of what she had already experienced. Time and time again her dream journal writings revealed something she had overlooked.

"Don't press yourself to try to understand your dreams too soon. Turn it over in your mind; talk to someone you trust; someone who won't try to interpret it for you. Picture the dream as a stage. You build the set, you write the script, you are the director and the audience. You put it there for yourself and you don't even have to work hard on it."

Emma never thought her dreams of Philip Byrd were for herself but in the long run they were for her because they transformed her.

"Somehow our dreams are shared—"

When he said that, Emma was momentarily lost in thoughts of the dream she and Connie shared.

"—as the scripture says, there is an element of our dreams in which God participates. The Judeo-Christian heritage is the one in which the importance of dreams grew. They are recognized as a place where prophecy occurs, where God speaks to people."

Emma could hardly believe what she was hearing. This ordained priest was telling her it was okay to have dreams of prophecy.

"The thing about dreams and the unconscious is that they constantly push us to accept the whole of who we are. If we expect others to accept us as who we are, and if we say we expect God to take us into His Kingdom, we can look to God as being that in our lives that accepts all of us. You must come to understand and accept yourself and not reject that which God has made you to be."

To Emma, this was a beautiful way to look at her spirituality—God had made her to be what she was.

After class, Emma and Philip had a quick cup of coffee in the Hall of Bishops before the service.

"Did you ever finish unpacking?"

He shook his head forlornly.

"No, don't have time."

"The offer to help still stands."

His face lit up. "You'd do that for me?"

"What are friends for? Will you be home this afternoon?"

"Yes, I will. Working on my dissertation. You want to?"

"I don't make idle offers, Philip. I'll be there later today."

Emma did not understand why she had such a compulsion to help Philip Moore get settled in his house. It was something she had to do. After another glorious service in the Cathedral she drove to her apartment, changed into working clothes, and went to Philip's house near Emory.

The sun was shining and Emma was glowing with enthusiasm for the self-appointed chores that awaited her when she arrived at Philip's house. He met her at the back door. Seeming somewhat embarrassed she was there, he went back to his work. Emma made herself at home, put on a fresh pot of coffee, and started unpacking dishes while she waited for it to brew.

"How do you take your coffee?" Emma called to Philip.

She put some cream and sweetener in a mug and carried it to him. He was absorbed in his work and did not acknowledge her presence.

"As soon as I finish the kitchen, I'll start unpacking your books. Is there any particular place you want them? Thought I'd start with the shelves in the butler's pantry if that's okay."

Philip stared at the monitor, lost in his thoughts for a moment before he answered, "Huh? Yeah. That's okay."

Emma ambled back to the kitchen, unpacked the rest of the boxes, stacked them next to the back door, and wandered into the small breakfast room adjacent to the pantry. There were stacks of books and boxes scattered across the floor. She gazed in awe at Philip's accumulation of literary works before tackling the job.

She went back to the pantry and analyzed the shelf space, then checked out the cabinet in the dining room. When Emma crossed the threshold between the dining room and the butler's pantry, she noticed the wood floor of the dining room was refinished. It triggered a long lost thought, buried deep in her memory.

That line—along the floor—where it has been partly refinished.

Her heart started pounding; she felt light headed.

No, it couldn't be. It couldn't.

She rushed into the drab kitchen. Sunlight streamed in through the windows. Emma shook her head in disbelief. Then she went to the living room. On the wall adjacent to the dining room stood an antique sideboard. From there she had a clear view of Philip's handsome roll-top desk.

Again, she shook her head.

No. No—.

She slowly walked toward the bedrooms. She wanted to see them; she didn't want to see them. The sound of her heart pulsated in her ears. In amazement, she stood at the door to Philip's bedroom and gazed. The walls were blue. Deep, dark blue.

Extreme anxiety overtook her.

Why. Why is Philip Moore living in this house?

Emma thought the puzzle had been solved, that the pieces were in place. Now, she felt as if someone had thrown another handful at her, saying, "You're not finished yet, Emma St. Claire. You've got some more work to do. Let's see if you can make these pieces fit your picture."

She was crushed. How could it have happened? Why had she dreamed of her teacher, Philip Byrd, living in this house? This house that was occupied by Philip Moore. It was not possible. It wasn't.

The enthusiasm to help Philip Moore faded into confusion and despair and she wandered back to the breakfast room.

Why, Dear Lord, why did this happen?

Emma put her arms on the table and laid her head on them, as if retreating. She did not want to look at Philip Moore's house. She had come there with every good intention of helping him. What could she say to him now? That he was living in a house she dreamed about two years ago? No. She couldn't tell him. He was another Philip Byrd; he didn't believe in e.s.p.

For the first time in many weeks, doubt and despair welled up. She sat at the table for a long while, trying to regain her composure. She had come there to do a job. Agonizingly, deliberately, slowly, Emma picked herself up again and got to work.

She sorted books by subject, arranged them neatly on shelves and the stack of empty boxes in the kitchen grew and grew. When she finally took them outside, to get them out of the way, she walked around the side of the house.

Exactly as she dreamed, the front yard was almost flat, bordered by trees and shrubs on one side and there was no driveway in the front. Because the house was on a corner, the drive emptied onto a side street, which Emma did not see in her dream. She felt unreal; disconnected.

She strolled back into the house trying to feel satisfied she accomplished what she came to do. There was only one more box to be unpacked.

"You're a whiz getting things organized in here," Philip said, pouring another cup of coffee.

Emma opened the numerous cupboard doors, explaining where she put his household goods before returning to the breakfast room to finish.

"Don't worry about that box," Philip said, passing by on his way back to the dining room.

"Just thought I'd finish what I came to do."

"You've done more than enough already," he said timidly.

He sat down at the roll-top desk and lost himself in his work. Emma opened the last box.

"No wonder he told me not to fool with this box," she mused, "photo albums."

"Do you mind if I look at your pictures, Philip?" she called out.

There was a grunt from the other room. Since he didn't say "no" Emma opened the first scrapbook. It was obviously his high school album. Emma thumbed through it, reading about his various activities and awards. She laid it aside and picked up another one with an identical cover. It chronicled his days at Annapolis and his naval career. The third scrapbook had pictures of his children. Emma stared at each one. They were happy, pretty children. She knew she had no business looking at his personal things. She continued anyway. For some reason she had to look at it.

One page held the picture of a beautiful sailboat with Philip at the helm.

"Do you have a sailboat?"

"Yeah. You looking at those old pictures?" he asked in a tone that told Emma he didn't care that she was looking at his scrapbooks.

"Hope you don't mind. You've got some wonderful shots here."

"Help yourself," he said.

Emma was relieved she sort of had Philip's permission. She turned the next page. There, staring out at her was the incredibly beautiful face of Liz. Emma gasped. She stared in disbelief at the picture of Philip's Liz. That face. That beautiful, familiar face. That face that belonged to Emma's sweet beautiful lady. The woman that Emma called Anne.

***

Emma was thankful she had a session with David the next morning. How had it happened? Why had she dreamed of her teacher, Philip Byrd, living in the house now occupied by Philip Moore? Why was Philip Moore married to the woman Emma dreamed of?

"I don't understand it David. I told you before I was worried Philip Byrd didn't know my Anne, that I didn't see them sitting together on that plane, that my mind put them together because that's what Spirit wanted. Why would Philip

341

Moore be in the house? Why would he be married to her? I'm bewildered and confused."

"You told me last week Philip Moore said that Anne, Liz, told him he was not the man she thought he was."

Emma furrowed her brow in thought.

"Yes. That's right. He also told me she is very scared of water. I didn't think anything about it at the time. I mean, I had no idea he was talking about my Anne. He also told me she desperately wants children. She's already lost two and she's not a spring chicken. Then there's the fact that she's a nurse. I don't know what to think. How could it have gotten mixed up this way?"

"Shall we talk to Margaret about it?"

"Yes. That's a good idea. Maybe she can shed some insight on this—this—mess."

Kicking off her shoes, Emma settled into the cushions of the soft sofa and relaxed. She took three deep breathes, closed her eyes and under David's guidance, her mind entered another dimension, away from the constraints of time and space, where only pure spirit existed.

"You're very relaxed," David said.

Bright light, tinged in yellow, surrounded Emma; her body was limp, her head floated and she nodded off in a deep trance. Her breathing was slow and deep.

"You are looking for Philip Moore and Anne."

Emma felt as though she was spinning through space at an immeasurable speed, surrounded by the bright light. Her mind went further and further away from David's office.

Back she went. Way back. Surrounded by the comforting presence of the light, she traveled at ease, going further and further into the past.

"Where are you?" David asked.

"In a town. The streets—are paved—large stones. Very large. Horses—pulling—chariots. Men—in chariots."

"Where is Philip Moore?"

"He's at the—public—bath. He's cavorting—with—women. Beautiful women—at the bathhouse. He's very big—big man. Formidable."

"Is Anne with him?"

"No."

"Where is Anne?"

"She is home—stone house—with babies— small child and infant. She is very plain—homely—she has a good heart—she is faithful to her husband—even though he is cruel to her."

"Who is her husband?"

"The man at the bath—Philip—her husband."

"Move to the next significant time," David instructed.

"Hot—" Emma said, feeling prostrate with extreme heat. "People are running everywhere. It's hot—"

"Why is it hot?"

"The mountain—the mountain explodes. Hot air—hard to breathe—"

Emma choked and coughed.

"What is happening now?"

"People are running from the mountain. She looks for her husband. He does not come—he rides on his horse through the people in the street. He runs down the mountain. He is getting on a boat."

"Where is Anne?"

"She is with her babies. She is trying to protect them. She is in the corner of the house; she—is covering them—with her body. The house is burning. The air—thick with ash. Can't breathe. She can't breathe."

"Where is Philip?"

"He is on a boat. He is sailing away. He did not go back to help her. He abandoned her and their children."

"What happened to them?"

"They perished—with the others—many died. We were poisoned by the fumes from the mountain and buried in its ashes.

"He sailed the waters for many lifetimes. Someday, when their spirits are reunited, she must forgive him. He will have learned compassion and devotion and he will be a good man."

***

"Guess what I found out today?" Emma enthusiastically asked Rachel on the phone that evening.

"Lord only knows—"

"Philip Moore and Anne were in another life together. A long time ago. I was one of their children."

"Do you have any idea when, or where?"

"Pompeii, Rachel. It must have been Pompeii. The streets had giant stepping stones across them and they were spaced wide enough that chariots could cross through. There was a mountain, a volcano. The people were killed by fumes and ashes."

"That's incredible, Emma."

"Yes, my father in that life left me to die in the fumes and in this life after my father left me, I developed asthma and struggled to catch my breath. Kind of interesting, huh?"

"Oh my, Emma," Rachael moaned. "Oh my goodness…"

"And it explains why Philip Moore and Liz have problems. He told me she said he wasn't the man she thought he was."

"That's pretty obvious. She thought she was marrying the spirit that is Philip Byrd."

"That's right. At least, that's what I think. She's also insanely jealous of him. She doesn't trust him, even though he's never done anything, in this life, to deserve that—although in a past life he did. He ran around with other women and then abandoned his family when the volcano erupted."

"That's another lifetime that dear soul was deprived of children, Emma."

"No wonder she almost went insane when she had that last miscarriage. Her soul wants children; for one reason or another she keeps losing them."

"Do you think she'll ever have children?"

"Of course; as soon as she relearns a lesson she taught me a long time ago she can be healed and made whole again."

"What lesson was that?"

"Forgiveness. Until she learns to forgive she will be tied to her past and the pain she knew. She has to let go of the past, and the pain, if she wants to grow spiritually. She can only do that through forgiveness."

"Didn't you say she's scared of water, too?"

"Uh huh," Emma said nodding her head, as if Rachel could see her through the phone lines. "Of course, that fear is probably carried from the accident at the river. Many people have unfounded fears that they carry from one life to another. I was reading the other day about a man who went into counseling because his back hurt most of his life. He was put in a trance and regressed to a past life where he fell off a roof, breaking his back."

"How interesting. What happened after the trance?"

"He came out of it and his back wasn't hurting. He was cured. There are many, many cases of people being cured of phobias and mysterious ailments by tracing the cause to a past life experience."

344

"You'd think you would hear about such things."

"You don't because people don't believe in the power of spirit. There are a lot of people professing belief in eternal life then denying that they've lived before."

"That does seem a bit inconsistent, doesn't it?"

"Yes, it does. I think they deny reincarnation because they're scared of the broader view, Rachel. When you believe in reincarnation, you no longer look outside yourself for blame. You realize you are responsible for yourself. God gave you free will. You will sow what you reap.

"I was reading my notes from Dr. Franklin's class last night. He said our society emphasizes youth, which shows a fear of death. When you believe in eternal life, you are free. You no longer fear death. You are no longer bound to your material possessions. When you live a spiritual life, you have peace, and joy and contentment. The Bible says you will know the truth and the truth will make you free."

CHAPTER TWENTY-TWO

**"May He grant you according to your heart's desire,
and fulfill all your purpose."**
– Psalm 20:4

Guess what I'm doing?" Emma asked her twin sister on the phone one afternoon in early March of 1990.

"No telling!" Rachel answered.

"Writing a poem. A long poem."

"You're kidding. A poem? What's it about?"

"Me and my e.s.p." Emma said proudly, "and my experiences since I met Philip Byrd. It seems to be rolling out of me a few verses at a time."

"How interesting. Have you finished it yet?"

"Almost. From time to time another verse will come to me and I fit it in somewhere. It has been fun and a catharsis, too."

"What are you going to do with it?"

"I don't know. Maybe give a copy to David?"

"What about Mr. Byrd?"

"Maybe. Someday."

"What about Mother? Why don't you give it to her?"

"Gee, that's a good idea, Rachel. I want to tell her the whole entire story, anyway. We've been getting along fine since her illness. For the first time in my life I feel that I can talk to Mother."

"Thank goodness, Emma. It only took you forty-plus years. By the way, how's her asthma?"

"About the same. Good some days, worse on others. She gets out and about now anyway. We went to a concert on Friday. It was terrific."

"What did you hear?"

"The Mahler Symphony No. 2 in C Minor."

"My boss is here," Rachel said dejectedly. "I better get off the phone."

"Okay. I love you Rachel."

"I love you, too, Emma. Give Mother a kiss for me."

"I will. We're going to Piccadilly for supper tonight after I take her to see my new apartment. I signed a lease today and I'll only be three miles from her. Maybe I'll give her the poem tonight."

Emma agonized over the pros and cons of telling her mother the story of Mr. Byrd and Anne. Although Bee mentioned reincarnation from time to time, it wasn't a topic of conversation and Emma worried her mother might in some way resent the feelings Emma had for a mother from another life. Still, it was a fascinating story. A story that changed Emma's life. After weighting the pros and cons, Emma presented her mother with a copy of the sixteen-page poem.

"What's this?" Bee asked, taking the binder.

"A poem, Momma. About an experience I had. I want to share it with you."

Bee leafed through the pages in the binder.

"What's it about?"

"Me and my e.s.p.—." she paused for a while, putting a fork full of rice and gravy in her mouth.

Bee squeezed a piece of lemon into her hot tea and took a sip.

"—and reincarnation."

"Reincarnation?" Bee responded enthusiastically. Her eyes lit up.

"Yes, I met a man I knew in another life—"

"How absolutely fascinating."

In forty-five years, Emma never heard her mother say that anything she did was fascinating. The little woman was eager to know more.

"Go on," she pleaded. "I want to hear about this!"

Emma was relieved and pleased that her mother wanted to hear the story. She still internally agonized over Anne. How in the world would her mother respond to that?

Emma started at the beginning—the first night of the economics class.

Bee was totally absorbed by Emma's tale; at one point she even rubbed her hands together in her child-like manner of enthusiasm, saying, "Emma, this is a thrilling story."

When Emma told Bee about Anne, there was not one trace of jealousy. Emma gave her mother a detailed description of each of the trance sessions that took her back to a past life.

"Remember when I had meningitis, Momma?" Emma asked without pausing for a response. "I thought I was going to die. Then I had a dream while I was curled up in that fetal position. I never felt related to the dream but for some reason it gave me a lot of peace and I no longer worried about dying."

"Why didn't you ever tell me this?" Bee asked.

"We've never talked this way before, Momma."

Bee looked a little hurt.

"No, I don't suppose we have Emma. I'm sorry."

"You have nothing to apologize for, Momma."

Emma reached across the table and patted the hand of a fine artist who used her talents to illustrate medical and scientific textbooks and journals, that drew pictures of every toxic organism known to man, that helped make the world a healthier place.

"What was the dream, Darlin'?" Emma's mother finally asked.

"There was a couple, a man and a woman. The woman was a petite blond and the man was tall. He had a head full of dark, curly hair. There was a little boy with them. They were sailing on a ship. A merchant ship of some sort."

Bee's eyes twinkled while she reflected on Emma's earlier story.

"Do you mean—you had a dream in 1981 about that man and woman on the ship in the 1700's?"

Emma nodded her head slowly.

"That's right, Momma. When I thought I was dying, I dreamed about myself in another life, a long, long time ago. That dream, or memory, or whatever it was, took away my fear of dying. I didn't know why. I felt there was a lot of love between that man and woman and their child. It was beautiful."

Emma took a sip of coffee.

"I forgot about that dream, Momma. Then, when I had that past-life regression, I went back there again. I realized that when I was sick and dying, my mind—no, my spirit—was trying to tell me it was okay. That I wouldn't die. That I'd be back here again, I would have another chance to love the people I cared about."

A drop of moisture formed in each corner of Bee's eyes.

"Many times we don't appreciate what we have, Emma, until we lose it. I've looked at life differently ever since I had my open heart surgery."

"Why is that, Momma?"

"I died."

Emma gasped. Although her mother hemorrhaged and was rushed back into surgery several hours after the operation, she didn't die.

Bee explained what happened that afternoon.

"I wasn't aware of anything after they took me to the operating room until I woke up in a tunnel."

"A tunnel?" Emma asked.

"Yes, Emma. It was magnificent. I've never seen such beautiful lights. I was moving through it at a tremendous speed. I wasn't the least bit scared."

She picked up her teacup and took a long drink.

"Then I came to the end and saw a brilliant white light. I was very cool. The peace was indescribable."

Bee looked down, shaking her head slowly from side to side.

"I didn't want to come back here, Emma. I was ready to stay."

"If you had been ready you would not have come back, Momma."

Bee looked surprised.

"What do you mean, I wasn't ready. I thought I was."

"Your spirit was not ready, Momma. It had some more work to do here, in this life."

A quizzical expression crossed Bee's face.

"What do you suppose it was? I've worked my entire my life. I thought my work was done."

"Everyone knows how you worked, Momma. How you raised the three of us with no help. How many times did you go without and give to us? Your fried chicken is a great example."

"Fried chicken?" Bee asked. The conversation had taken an unusual turn.

"Yes. You always served Charlie the breast pieces 'cause he prefers white meat and you gave me and Rachel the legs and the thighs, 'cause we eat dark meat; that left you with the wings and back, which don't have much meat."

Bee was astounded.

"You noticed that?"

"We noticed, Momma. You cared—you'd do those good things for us, then you'd yell. Especially at me. I never knew what made you do that."

"I never did either, Darlin'. I'm sorry, Emma. I'm sorry."

It was obviously a painful discussion for Bee.

"I know now there was a purpose for it, Momma."

Bee looked slightly relieved. Maybe there was some redeeming grace after all.

"What do you mean?"

"It made me sensitive, Momma. Real sensitive. If you had not treated me the way you did, I would not be the person I am today. I'm glad I'm the person I am, Momma. Thank you."

Bee patted Emma's hand. There was a new understanding between a mother and her daughter, a new awareness of who they were, a new kind of love.

"I want to tell J.D. that I'm sorry we didn't get along better. It was my fault and I'm very, very sorry, Emma. I have missed him more than you can imagine. Do you think he'll ever come see me? I've adored him his entire life."

"J.D. is still hurt over the things you said to him, Momma. Frankly, I've always been at a loss to understand it. You were happy when we moved into Fairfield together. What happened? Why did you turn on him?"

"I said things the wrong way, Emma. I never meant to hurt J.D. I wanted to protect him."

"Protect him. From what?"

"From alcoholism, mainly."

"Alcoholism? Whatever gave you such an absurd idea? We don't have alcoholism in our family."

"It wasn't my idea, Emma. It was Janice's."

"What in the world are you talking about?"

"Right after Janice and David moved in next door, she came up to see me, pay a call. And you know how she gets close to you and talks in that low voice, right in your face, and raises that eyebrow, and glares at you in that penetrating manner that says you better pay attention."

"Yes. I know that intimidating look. What did she say?"

"First, she reminded me that both her father and her brother were alcoholics. Then she said that J.D. had been down at their house and he was drunk, that they didn't keep wine, and that he must have gotten into my wine. She got extremely angry with me. Said if he turned into an alcoholic, it would be my fault."

Bee started crying. For the first time in her life, Emma saw her mother crying uncontrollably.

Emma was dumbstruck. She sat speechless, shaking her head.

"No, no, oh, no—"

After a long silence, Emma asked her mother, "What else did Janice say? What else, Momma."

Bee was sobbing.

351

"Later, Emma. We'll have to talk about it later."

"Momma, don't you see? Janice set it up to alienate you and J.D. I keep a close watch on my child and I assure you he has never been drunk. Why didn't you come to me as soon as she said that to you?"

"I was afraid you wouldn't believe me, Emma."

Emma knew first-hand exactly what Bee meant.

Emma drove Bee to her apartment and made the long drive to Stone Mountain while listening to Dvorak's Symphony No. 9 in E Minor.

"It is a New World, now, Lord," Emma said prayerfully, referring to the subtitle of the musical composition. Puzzling issues had finally come to light. Things were starting to make sense.

Emma could not help but contemplate Bee's comment about not wanting to come back after her open heart surgery. She got down on her knees and prayed.

Thank you, Dear God, for sending my Mom back. She did have some work to finish with me. Now that it is done, I hope you'll let me enjoy her for a while. Please give my son the same gift.

***

The week of final exams Emma ran into Philip Byrd in the hallway.

He looked at her and smiled.

"Where have you been?" he asked, as if he cared. "I've been wondering where you were."

"I have something for you," she said, handing him a black binder.

She had carefully edited the poem and included only the verses pertaining to Anne and the children at the river. There was no need to mention the agonizing pain in her arms, or the past life where they had loved one another in an adult relationship. Nor did she tell him about the flight attendants, the pilot, or the maintenance man she had contacted. In the event the crash did occur, in spite of her efforts, his position with the airline could be jeopardized by any prior knowledge he may have had. In a way, Emma was still protecting Philip Byrd just as Margaret had told her to do.

"I need someone in my life," he said.

Emma could hardly believe her ears. Philip Byrd was talking about something personal.

"I'm looking for someone—special."

"This poem will tell you something about her, Philip. I can't do any more. I don't know where she is now."

He seemed a little disappointed, as if Emma could help him find the woman of his dreams.

"Are you still worried about that plane crash?" he asked in a very matter of fact, completely comfortable tone.

Again, Emma was surprised.

"No," she smiled, touching him on the forearm. Then she shook her head very slowly. "That's been taken care of."

He raised his eyebrows and slightly nodded his head, as if relieved.

"I'm flying to the Kentucky Derby the first weekend in May," he volunteered happily.

Emma was not surprised at this comment. Hadn't she been saying for almost a year that he would be on a plane the first weekend in May?

Students had filed into Philip's classroom during his brief conversation with Emma.

"I've got to go to class," he said, tapping the black binder on his hand.

"That's not the whole story," she quickly explained. "There have been too many misunderstandings. I'm sorry I couldn't give you the whole thing. This version lacks sparkle."

He turned toward his room and opened the cover of the binder, then looked over his shoulder at her.

"See, ya."

Then he smiled.

"Bye," she said cheerfully. "Have fun at the races."

Emma hoped her economics teacher would appreciate the title of the poem, written in typical Emma St. Claire humor: Economics of the Soul - The Effects of Past Debts and Present Depressions on Future Growth in the Spiritual Marketplace.

***

Emma moved into the apartment near her mother the next weekend without the assistance of her husband. Their divorce would be final the end of April. Jim promised Emma she could come to the house any time and retrieve the many things she left in his care during their separation. As usual, he lied. He would not even let her have her cookbooks. Except for a few pieces of furniture, her clothes and some mementos and keepsakes of her children, Emma had nothing. She was happy anyway. She was making new friends at the Cathedral, talked almost daily to Philip Moore and was close to her mom. Best of all, Emma gave and received an abundance of love from Allison and J.D. and Rachel.

After the December encounter with Paul, her arms continued to improve, although there were still frequent bouts of intense pain and weakness. Emma kept up her daily routine of physical therapy and meditations.

"I don't understand why my arms are still suffering," she said to David during a session late one afternoon. I do my exercises and creative visualizations. Do you think I'll ever recover? Completely?"

David shook his head and raised his eyebrows with a quizzical expression on his face.

"I can't say, Emma."

"I'm happy, David. I'm at peace. It would be nice to get rid of this pain though. It lingers and I don't know why. Do you think Margaret could help me understand it?"

"I think it's worth a try," he said, leaning back in his rocking chair.

Emma made herself comfortable and in a few moments she had drifted off, floating as a cloud with no destination.

"Tell me about Emma's arms," David asked, "what is the origin of Emma's physical symptoms?"

The deep, slow trance voice of Margaret spoke.

"The physical pain was terrifying. The thought of losing the use of my arms was anathema to me. My whole life I have tried to serve others. When I saw Philip for the first time, my spirit remembered pain endured in my arms when I tried to save my baby brother. When this memory was placed in my body in this life, it was punishment for what I had not accomplished. Now every day is a struggle and the remembering of that failure. I have worked very hard to overcome this affliction. When Paul touched my arms that day for no reason, he started the healing process. My therapy has been healing and enlightening and when I am emotionally healed, the physical symptoms will diminish. There may be some degree of deterioration that may never be restored but it will only be a minor inconvenience and a daily reminder that this physical life is very brief."

In his trance work monotone, David asked, "What was not accomplished?"

"I didn't protect the baby."

There was a long pause before Margaret spoke again.

"She felt guilty when she lost her baby brother. She died remembering how she tried to save him and the pain had been etched. She should not feel guilty. Her spirit knows there was a purpose for it and much has been learned and much can be taught to those who are ready to listen. If she had not been made to suffer physically, the spiritual manifestations of her past lives may have been misconstrued as a mental illness. The fact that there was a diagnosable but unexplainable physical problem gives her strong substantiation of her past lives."

"Will Emma continue to suffer pain in her arms?"

"It has served its usefulness. Unfortunately, when a physical part is not properly used for an extended period of time, there may be a physical inability to completely restore the body to its former condition."

"Do you have a message for Emma?"

"She needs to get a sense of direction. She should spend more time on her writing. Her friends want to know the story and although Philip could not benefit from her experience, many others will welcome it.

"Margaret said he is special and I was to protect him. I tried to tell him what I thought he should know. He never believed in me or the message I offered. The pain of his rejection was almost unbearable. I regret that I failed. There was more for him to learn about than a plane crash. I wanted him to learn of the spiritual values. He has such a brilliant mind. Armed with the knowledge I offered, he could have done some wonderful work. That work will never get done. If he could have found my Anne, she could have inspired him to do these things. I'm sorry he hasn't found her. He told me he's looking for someone and I told him if he ever saw my Anne he would know right away that she is the right one to love him. He wants to believe these things but I was not the right teacher and I'm truly sorry that I could not present the information in a manner that would be acceptable to him."

"Do you think you were personally responsible for his lessons?"

"They should have been presented by someone he trusted. He always knew there was something different about me the way I knew there was something different about him.

"These feelings scared him the way they scared me. I confronted them and I've grown spiritually. He chose to look the other way. Now he realizes he missed out.

"He has intellectualized my perceptions. Philip has taught me about the intellectual view of precognition and people with a mindset that is closed to spiritual growth. I regret he could not be open to this opportunity because was scared of me."

"How can Emma use this regret and move ahead?"

"We must learn from our mistakes and I've learned that I can only offer what I know. That those spirits who reject my advice and assistance are not rejecting me. They are rejecting the God that lives in each one of us. I hurt for those who do not seek enlightenment. The best way to show them the benefits of spiritual growth is to live and conduct my life in an attitude of spirituality, accepting others for the spirits they are, even though they cannot accept my spirit. Some day they will accept this knowledge; they will then know freedom, and peace, and happiness that can only come when they realize the divinity and the oneness of all souls."

***

Exactly as Emma St. Claire predicted, there were intermittent thundershowers the first weekend in May 1990. Between storms, the sun was shining and the sky was clear blue—and she had seen it, two years before.

***

Adjustment to single life was pleasant for Emma. Between symphony concerts with her mother, church activities, work, an occasional date and preparations for J.D.'s graduation from high school, Emma stayed very busy. She wrote in her journal daily and read her Bible every night before bed.

Long walks by herself on warm evenings brought happy remembrances of Alex, still remorseful feelings over his death and realization there would always be an ache in her heart when she thought of him. Alex was a link in the chain of events that ensnared Emma St. Claire and dragged her out of her circumspect physical view of life, with its pain and suffering, into the spiritual realm, where there was peace.

Allison and Steve held J.D.'s high school graduation party at their house and afterwards he went on a cruise to the Bahamas with his classmates. He was registered for summer quarter at Georgia Tech and Emma felt optimistic about her son's future in spite of his on-going battle with depression. She knew he would eventually learn from and overcome the painful experience in the same way he had finally outgrown the Osgood-Schlatter disease and she wondered why he had chosen such a path. He still had not seen Bee. Emma could not tell him what he needed to hear from her.

Janice continued her depraved attempts to manipulate Emma and her family when she took Emma aside after the graduation party, inviting her into the kitchen to have a chat. Emma optimistically hoped to hear some kind words from her former mother-in-law about raising a fine young man.

Instead, as usual, Janice thrust another knife deep into Emma's soul, saying "you need to get out of J.D.'s life."

"You're a raving lunatic, Janice," Emma retorted. "Why the hell don't you get out of your son's life? Haven't you done enough damage to mine?"

***

The last weekend in July, Emma decided to go on an outing with the Episcopal Singles. They met in the parking lot at St. Martin's and divided into car-pooling groups. Emma was asked to be a driver since she had a full-size car. Bill Manley, the man with silver white hair and beard, was assigned to her car along with two other men. Ignoring the foreboding feelings she had when they met at the Super Bowl party, Emma graciously greeted Bill.

"Wait a minute," one of the other women jokingly protested. "Emma's got three men in her car. That's not fair."

One of the men in the back seat switched places with a woman in another car and they caravanned up the highway to Lake Lanier where one of the members had a summer cottage. Emma was relieved the Kenny Rogers clone did not light his pipe in her car.

The cabin, near the top of a long, steep hill, overlooked the lake. It was a perfect place for the noisy group. There was a ton of food, a generous supply of beer and wine and everyone had a good time. Especially Emma and Bill.

***

Emma enjoyed her relationship with the charming Bill Manley. Although he appeared to be healthy, he occasionally complained of tingling in his hands and feet which he chalked up to age. He had recently turned fifty.

Several weeks after Emma started dating Bill, she dreamed he was in a wheelchair. It was cold, he was bundled up, and she was pushing him down a sidewalk on Peachtree Dunwoody Road. They were going to look at a town house on an adjacent street.

"I don't have the money for a town house," Emma laughed when she told Rachel about the dream. "Can you imagine, me—with a townhouse? It takes

357

every penny I make to pay my rent and utilities and Jim's charges on my credit cards. A townhouse. Isn't that a hoot?"

"What about Bill and the wheelchair? Do you have any idea what that means?"

"It was a foolish dream, Rachel. I shouldn't have mentioned it to you," Emma said apologetically.

"I don't know 'bout that Emma."

"If I can't do anything about it, Rachel, there's no use worrying about it, is there? I have no idea why Bill would be in a wheelchair. And a townhouse. That's absolutely out of the question."

***

Summer slipped by quickly. Emma was having a grand time with Bill and her mother and she enjoyed weekly dinner dates with her son and daily mother-son telephone chats. In August, she ordered a dining room table from Rich's department store at Perimeter Mall, a shopping area on the north side of Atlanta. Delivery was scheduled the first or second week in September. When Emma told her mother of the purchase, Bee insisted on paying for it.

"I bought Rachel a dining room set and I want to do the same for you, Emma. I won't take no for an answer."

After work one evening, Emma drove Bee to the mall where a salesman transferred the purchase from Emma's account to Bee's. Then they walked down the mall to J. C. Penney's. Bee was weak; breathing was labored. It was obvious the asthma had returned with a vengeance.

"I wish you'd call the doctor, Momma," Emma said while escorting her mother to a bench near the mall entrance.

"I'll be alright, Emma."

"You don't look alright to me. There must be something the doctor can do."

"I'm maxed out on cortisone and that's the only thing that helps."

"Maybe a specialist could do something."

Emma held her mother's arm and lowered her to the bench.

"Here, Momma. You sit here while I go get the car."

"Okay, Darlin'. I'll be right here."

Walking swiftly to the other end of the mall, Emma pondered her mother's plight. Surely, there must be some medication that could give her relief from the disabling asthma. Emma drove around the mall to the entrance where she left Bee.

"Do you think we can visit Ellen tomorrow night?" Bee asked while Emma walked her to the car.

Ellen Bourne, Bee's best friend, was in the hospital for spinal surgery. She was one of the elderly women Emma chauffeured to the symphony.

"That's a good idea," Emma responded enthusiastically. "I'll pick you up after work. We can stop for supper on the way. How's that sound?"

Bee smiled.

"You're good to me Emma. I don't know what I would do without you."

Emma was almost embarrassed. Her mother's sincere affection and approval were still new to Emma.

The next evening they stopped at Applebee's for dinner.

"I went to a pulmonary specialist today," Bee announced happily, setting three bottles of pills on the table.

"You did?"

Emma was pleased her mother had taken a step toward getting well.

"What did he say?"

"My heart's okay. He gave me some medicine for the asthma."

Emma picked up the bottles and read the labels.

"I don't recognize any of these medicines. Are they safe for you?"

"Of course!" Bee said defensively.

She opened one of the bottles and swallowed two pills with iced tea.

"I think I'm starting to feel better already."

"Did Dr. Tisdale send you to him, Momma?"

"Yes. He said Rachel called him to complain because I wasn't any better. He told her I couldn't take any more cortisone. Since Rachel insisted he do something, he sent me to this specialist. He's a terrific doctor."

Emma nodded her head.

"Yes, I bet he is. I bet you talked about C.D.C. and weird diseases and he was fascinated when you told him about your work. Right?"

Bee looked a little sheepish.

"I always talk to doctors about the work I did at C.D.C."

"That's fine, Momma. You also need to tell them how you feel. Did you tell him you've had this asthma since December?"

A chagrined expression came across Bee's face. Emma knew her mother did not tell the doctor how bad she felt.

Shaking her head Emma said, "What am I going to do with you, Momma?"

Bee was looking down into the purse sitting in her lap. For a long while she rummaged through the contents, ignoring Emma's intent stares from across the table.

Emma took a drink of coffee, set the cup in the saucer and waited for a response from her mother.

"Momma?"

There was no response from Bee. She sat motionless, still looking into the purse.

"Momma?" Emma said again with growing concern in her voice.

No response.

Emma reached across the table and touched her mother's hand.

Bee looked up, stared blankly at Emma, but said nothing.

"Momma!"

Bee blinked slowly. The blank look started to fade; she rolled her eyes and glanced around the room.

"What's wrong, Momma? How do you feel?"

"I felt a little faint. It's nothing."

"I'm taking you to the doctor, right now."

"No you're not doing any such thing," she snapped. "I want to see Ellen."

Emma protested. She knew her mother should be seen by a doctor.

"I'm fine, Emma. I want to see Ellen. Please take me to see her."

There was no use arguing. Bee was alert and talking and Emma drove her mother to the hospital where the two old friends greeted each other fondly. The three women had a delightful visit and Emma combed Ellen's hair while they talked, then fluffed pillows and straightened sheets.

During the drive home, Bee made a pleasant fuss over Emma's attention to her friend.

"You were very kind to Ellen, Emma. I'm proud of you."

"For heaven's sake, Momma. I combed her hair and tried to make her comfortable."

"You're a wonderful daughter, Emma. I don't know what I'd do without you and Rachel. You've been a blessing."

Emma appreciated the affectionate words even though the comments were out of character for her mother.

During the drive home, they listened to Rimsky-Korsakov's *Scheherazade* on the radio. Emma interrupted the music only one time to say, "I love you, Momma."

"I know you do, Emma."

***

The sun was shining by the time Emma awoke. She yawned and stretched in her brass bed and thought about the day's activities. It was the second Saturday in September. Her new dining room table and six matching chairs were to be delivered that morning; in the evening, she would christen it with a festive birthday dinner for her mother. The doorbell rang. Grabbing a lightweight robe, she ran to the living room and peered through the peephole.

"Goodness, you're early," she exclaimed, opening the door for the deliverymen from Rich's.

Emma was too eager to get the table to be embarrassed by her appearance. While the men attached the legs to the Queen Anne table, Emma unplugged the computer and started moving its various components into J.D.'s room.

"Whatcha working on?" one of the men asked, noticing the stack of three-ring binders Emma had in her arms.

"My journal—and some research I'm doing."

"Is it gonna be a book?" he responded.

Emma laughed.

"Yes, I guess it could be."

"What's it 'bout?" he inquired, turning the screw on one of the table legs.

Emma hesitated. Why should she tell a complete stranger about her journal? He had asked, though, and she did want to tell people her story because she wanted everyone to find the peace God had given to her.

"A girl here in Atlanta," she said haltingly. "A true story."

The man's face lit up; he was genuinely interested.

"Yeah—"

It was obvious he wanted to know more. He moved to the other corner of the table and started to attach another leg while his assistant continued to unwrap chairs, listening to the conversation without comment.

"She's—she's—"

"Yeah?" he asked.

"She's psychic," Emma sputtered.

"Like that Jean Dixon woman?"

Emma laughed.

"Not exactly. She's only psychic about people she knows and loves. Although she did see Kennedy being assassinated several days beforehand."

"No kidding! What else has she seen?"

"A group of people from Atlanta went on a tour to Europe and she knew the trip would be a disaster."

"What happened?" he asked, tightening the screw.

"Their plane crashed."

"Gracious, me—what else?"

Emma thought for a moment, then set her heavy binders on the counter top that divided the kitchen from the dining area.

"She lost everything she had worked for when the county put a landfill and garbage dump near her house in the country and her husband got mixed up with some crooked bankers."

"She lost everything?"

"Yep; and she found everything."

"You mean she got back her stuff that she lost?"

"No. God put peace in her heart. Now, even though she lost her dream home in the country, she feels rich. She has been blessed."

"She found the Lord?"

"She did. Guess what? He was always living in her heart. She found that He was everything she needed."

The delivery man was pleased with Emma's comment.

"That's some kind of story, lady."

The men stood the table on its legs and set it in the solarium, then moved the chairs into position and gathered up packing materials that were scattered around the room. Emma walked them to the door.

"Thank you both," she said, putting a few dollars into his hand.

"You keep up that writing now, you hear?" the friendly man instructed.

"I will. I definitely will," she laughed.

Emma waved to the men and leaned against the closed door. She had talked to a complete stranger about her story and he liked it.

That night she served a fried chicken dinner to her mother and Bill Manley to dedicate the new table and celebrate Bee's birthday. Bee had responded quickly to the medication and pranced around the living room in her new outfit from Emma and Rachel.

"This is beautiful," she prattled, admiring the exquisite blouse and skirt as she carefully folded them and laid them in the box.

Bill Manley was astonished by Bee's extensive knowledge of football. The two of them sat on the sofa and talked about the Atlanta Falcons new running back, Aundray Rison, while Emma washed dishes. When the game was over, Emma walked her mother to her car, carrying the new clothes and leftover birthday cake.

"You make the best fried chicken in Atlanta, Darlin'," Bee boasted.

"Celebrating your birthday was a wonderful way to bless the new table, Momma. We're gonna have lots of fun meals together around that table."

Emma kissed her mother on the forehead and gave her a hug after putting birthday packages in the car.

"I love you, Momma."

"I love you too, Emma."

Bee drove off and Emma ambled back into the apartment.

I shouldn't have said that to her. I shouldn't have said we'll have lots of meals together around the table.

***

Sunday afternoon after church, Emma and Bill were eating brunch at the home of some friends, not far from Bee's apartment. The food was delicious and Emma's closest companions were there. Bill's hands were shaking and he could not even serve his own food so Emma waited on him patiently while chatting happily with other guests. In the back of her mind she kept thinking that she ought to be at home. The feeling nagged at her.

I ought to be home; I ought to be home.

The group disbanded around four o'clock and Emma ushered Bill to the car.

"Want to go to a movie?" Bill asked.

"No," she said shaking her head. "I have to get home for a while."

"How come?"

"I don't know. I have to get home."

The phone was ringing when Emma and Bill arrived. Emma ran to answer it. The caller did not hear her and hung up. Emma was distressed. Then it rang again. It was someone from the church but Emma was not able to concentrate on their conversation, something about a class the Dean was going to teach. Then the call-waiting beep sounded.

"Can you wait a moment?" Emma asked the woman.

Emma hit the flash button that allowed her to talk to the other incoming call. It was J.D.

"Mama," he said. He was extremely upset.

"What is it, J.D.?"

"We're at the hospital with Bee. She's in bad shape, Mama. Real bad."

Emma put him on hold and apologized to the other caller, then went back to her son.

"What hospital, J.D.? Where are you?"

"Shallowford. Do you know where it is?"

"Yes. I'm about five minutes from there. I'll be right over."

"We're at the intensive care unit, Mom."

"Yes. Okay. I'll be right there."

Emma kissed Bill on the cheek, picked up her purse and ran for the door.

"My Momma's real bad. I have to go. Will you please stay here? There are bound to be phone calls. I'll need someone to play central control."

"I'll do anything I can to help, Emma," he said, his beautiful blue eyes staring into hers.

Such a sweet man, she thought.

Emma jumped in the car, roared through the apartment complex not even slowing down for speed bumps. At the hospital she found her son and daughter and son-in-law standing outside the intensive care unit. Rachel's son John arrived moments later.

Allison was pale, as if she were in a light case of shock. Although Steve and John were both composed, their concern was very evident. And J.D., his six feet four inches looming over them all, looked scared.

"Everything will be alright," Emma said.

The foursome appeared relieved that Emma was on the scene.

"The nurse wants to see you right away, Mama," Allison said, pushing open the heavy, wide door to the special care area.

"I'm Emma St. Claire," she said to the only nurse at the station. "Mrs. Browning's daughter."

The nurse was pretty. Her kind eyes expressed concern for both her patient and her patient's family.

"Your mother is very critical, Emma. She collapsed while eating lunch with friends. The paramedics said she had no heartbeat when they got to her and they had to defibrillate to get it started again. She won't recover. She went too long without oxygen."

Emma looked across the nurse's desk, through the sliding glass door of the room where her mother was laid on a bed. The head of the bed was tilted down to keep blood flowing into her mother's brain. A respirator clicked and clacked, hissed and puffed, pushing air in and out of Bee's lungs, the heart monitor beeped occasionally and numerous electronic IVs forced various fluids into the apparently lifeless body of Emma's mother.

She turned to the nurse.

"My mother doesn't want to stay this way. She has a living will and I have a power of attorney. She does not want to be maintained in this condition."

"Are you absolutely certain about that?" the nurse asked.

"Yes. Very. We've had many talks about it. She was on a respirator for three days when she had open-heart surgery nine years ago. She made me promise we would never let her go back on one."

"Alright," the nurse said, nodding her head. "We'll no code her."

Emma learned in her Red Cross days that 'no code' meant no extraordinary measures would be taken if her mother went into cardiac arrest again but she was surprised they did not ask to see a copy of the living will. It would have been easy enough to obtain. Bee had given copies to her daughters, her priest, her attorney and her family doctor.

"Can I see her now?" Emma asked.

"Yes, you can. I want you to know it won't be easy. She's in very, very critical condition."

"I was a volunteer for years at DeKalb General," Emma explained. "I worked in coronary care and intensive care. I've seen situations such as this many times."

"It's not the same when it's your own mother," the kindly nurse explained.

Emma bit her lower lip and nodded. Then she walked boldly into the room.

"I'm here, Momma," she said, walking to the far side of the bed, picking up the limp wrinkled hand of her mother. She ran her finger around her mother's fingers. "I'm here," she said again.

It was evident to Emma her mother's spirit had already left her body but had not left the room. Emma looked up into the far corner, across from the bed, where the television hung near the ceiling. A football game was on.

"You're watching the game, aren't you, Momma?" Emma said to the form that had been her mother. The chest heaved up and then collapsed as the respirator forced air into a lifeless cavity.

"I'm not gonna let them keep you this way, Momma. I know I have to let you go. I know you're ready this time. Aren't you Momma? I'm sad J.D. never came to talk to you. I wish you could have told him how sorry you were about everything. You don't have to stay here, Momma. I know you did your best. We got in a life time of loving in a very short time and I'll always cherish every one of those moments."

Emma fought off tears. Though it was terribly hard, they never got further than the corner of each eye.

"We've had a lot of fun these last six months, Momma. I'm glad you read my poem. I'm very thankful we finally got to talk and talk and talk."

The nurse appeared. Emma looked up.

"I need to check her vital signs again," the nurse said, holding a medical chart in her hand.

"I don't want her to suffer," Emma said. "Please give her something for pain. I want her to have something for pain."

"She can't feel anything, Emma. Her brain is gone."

"I know," Emma said again bravely. "I don't want her body to suffer. Please—give her something for pain."

The nurse left the room and promptly returned with a hypodermic needle. She inserted it into one of the IV tubes.

Emma took a deep breath and sighed. Her mother would never hurt again.

The nurse came around the bed and started to chart the readings on the clicking, clacking, beeping monitors.

"That's interesting," she said, with a puzzled expression on her face.

"What is it?" Emma inquired.

"Her vital signs—her vital signs have improved. Her blood pressure has gone from zero over ten to ten over forty and her pulse is much stronger."

Emma was pleased; the nurse was puzzled.

Emma smiled at her mother and stroked her fine silky hair.

"There is no medical reason why her vital signs should improve," the nurse said, shaking her head in disbelief. "Especially after that pain injection."

"There may be no medical reason," Emma said proudly. "There is a spiritual reason."

The nurse was even more puzzled. "What do you mean?"

"My mom can't talk to me now. The only way she can communicate is through these machines. She told me she knew I was here by making the machines change her vital signs. That's her way of talking to me now."

While Emma patted Bee's hand, the nurse stared at the redheaded woman talking about a patient communicating through machines.

"I know she's gone," Emma went on. "Her spirit has already left her body."

Emma glanced up at the TV screen. She knew without a doubt that the spirit of her mother was floating near the ceiling, watching the football game.

"She's waiting around to say good-bye. She wants to see my brother and sister one more time before she goes."

"When will they be here?" the nurse asked.

"Soon, I hope. She wants to go. She needs to say good bye, first."

Emma kissed her mother's hand and laid it carefully on the bed, then left the room and joined her children on the other side of the door. After they exchanged hugs Allison told her mother what had transpired that beautiful Sunday afternoon.

"We got a call from Betty England," Allison said, starting the story. "She and a few other ladies went to Piccadilly Cafeteria with Bee after church. Right after they sat down Bee clenched her fists, fell forward on the table and then onto the floor. Paramedics arrived real quick and started CPR. Betty said a preacher was there and he led the whole restaurant full of people in prayer until they started her heart and put her in the ambulance.

"Betty took Bee's keys and went to her apartment where she found my number and called me. She didn't tell me how serious it was and since Steve and J.D. were watching the game, I came over here by myself."

Emma watched her daughter fighting the grief she was feeling for her grandmother.

"When I got here and saw how bad it was, I called Steve. He brought J.D. Then I called John and told him to get here."

Allison stopped talking and reached into her pocketbook.

"Here. You take these," she said, placing a plastic pouch in Emma's hand. "I don't want to keep up with this."

"What is it?" Emma asked.

"Her jewelry. She had on her jewelry."

"How did you get it?" Emma asked somewhat surprised. She had not even thought of the diamonds.

"As soon as I saw Bee's condition, I asked for her personal belongings. I know she loves to wear her diamonds."

Emma was proud of her daughter. Bee seldom went to church without wearing the diamond broach and matching ring she inherited from her mother. The two pieces were worth a small fortune.

"Then I called Aunt Rachel and Uncle Jack and Cousin Bobby and told them they better hurry. They should be here pretty soon."

"You did everything perfectly, Darlin'. Do y'all want to see Bee again?"

The next thirty or forty minutes, Emma and the children alternated visits with Bee while her vital signs grew weaker and weaker.

"Are you okay, Mama?" Allison asked while they stood together in the hallway. Steve and J.D. went to get a coke. John was with Bee.

"Yes, Darlin', I'm fine. Why?"

"Steve and I were talking a little while ago. You're not taking this the way we were afraid you would."

"What do you mean?"

"We thought you would go to pieces and be weeping and wailing and carrying on—"

"No, Allison. I've had lots of talks with Bee in the last few months. I told her I love her and she told me over and over how much she loved me, too; and Rachel, and her beautiful grandchildren. We had a reconciliation, a wonderful reconciliation."

Allison acted slightly skeptical that her irascible grandmother could have made peace with her overly sensitive, hyper mother. It was totally out of character for the two of them.

"Allison, I've learned a lot in the last few years. I've changed."

"You sure have, Mama. I never thought I'd ever see my mother this calm in a crisis."

"I have a lot of peace in my life now, Darlin'. It was hard to find. I hope I can keep it forever."

Steve and J.D. returned and John joined them in the hallway while Emma went in for another visit with her mother. She was holding Bee's hand again when Rachel came rushing in. The twins stared into each other's eyes, communicating the way they could without uttering a single word. Rachel took Bee's other hand in hers and talked lovingly to her mother. Then she turned to look up at the television.

"Why's that damn thing on?" Rachel was somewhat annoyed.

"Mother's watching the game."

Rachel gave her twin an agonized smile.

"You were always honest," she said lovingly to her mother, still holding the limp hand. "You saw life through your wonderful artistic eyes. Do you remember when we were little, Momma? You would tell us that purple was red and blue. Or blue was a mix of yellow and green. You never told a lie because you always saw the truth."

"That's beautiful, Rachel," Emma said. "What a legacy Momma left us: she did something with her life to make the world better, she was honest, she loved and served the Lord."

A few minutes later the twins' older brother Charlie arrived, acting somewhat arrogant, as if he was now in charge.

"We don't want this ventilator on her," he said to the nurse.

"I've already taken care of it, Charlie," Emma said calmly. "There's a no code on her."

The nurse came in and took vital signs again.

"She's gone," she said quietly. "I'll have to get a doctor from the emergency room to come up and sign the death certificate."

"Can't that ventilator be turned off?" Emma asked.

"Not until the death certificate is signed," the nurse tried to explain.

The machine was pumping air into the lifeless body, in a sacrilegious offering to modern medicine.

"I want it turned off, please," Emma said again.

Bee's children each said good-bye one more time, then started out the door.

"Don't you think we should turn off the t.v.?" Rachel asked.

"No, of course not," Emma replied with a soft smile on her face, "Mother wants to watch the end of the game."

Rachel and Charlie lead Emma out of the room and back to the hallway where Bee's grandchildren were gathered. They stood there for almost an hour, talking the way a family would in such a situation, while they waited for a doctor to sign the death certificate.

"Why was she hemorrhaging?" Rachel inquired.

"I asked the nurse; she doesn't know" Emma answered.

"Seems sort of unusual to me," Charlie interjected. He had been a medic in the Navy and knew a good bit about medicine.

"She was bleeding from her stomach and her lungs. Her ears and nose. Her kidneys. What medication she was on?" he asked.

Emma reached into Bee's handbag and removed three bottles of pills dated the previous Friday. Each one had the name of the new doctor on the label.

"She saw a pulmonary specialist last week. She was taking these medicines."

She handed the pills to Charlie and his wife, Hazel, who also suffered from asthma and was quite an expert on asthma medications.

"I thought Bee couldn't take cortisone," Hazel said, turning the bottles over in her hands.

"She can't," Rachel quickly responded. "She has a very low tolerance to it."

"I hate to tell you this," Hazel hesitated. "Two of these contain cortisone."

Rachel moaned.

"We ought to sue that doctor," Charlie exclaimed.

"Calm down. All of you," Emma said peacefully. "Nothing will bring mother back. We'll have to have an autopsy done to prove anything, anyway."

Charlie was keyed up. "Let's do it!" he exclaimed.

Emma shook her head and went back through the door where she found the nurse alone at the station.

"Can we have an autopsy?" Emma asked softly.

The nurse looked shocked, almost defensive. Emma could feel the woman's apprehension.

"Don't worry," Emma said calmly. "Everyone here at the hospital has been wonderful. We have reason to believe that my mother may have had a drug reaction."

The nurse's demeanor changed.

"Why is that?"

"Mother had a low tolerance for cortisone yet two of her new medicines, the ones she started taking on Friday, have cortisone in them."

"Are you sure?" the nurse asked, looking relieved.

"Yes. We found it in her purse. Can you arrange the autopsy?"

"I'll have to make some phone calls."

Emma returned to the family group. In a few minutes the nurse reported she had made arrangements for an autopsy and the coroner would call Emma. They huddled together for a while longer, talking over this new development. Finally, thinking the doctor would surely appear soon, Rachel said to the grandchildren, "Y'all can say good-bye one more time if you want."

Allison and Steve went in together. When they returned, John had a turn. The last one, by himself, was J.D. Emma watched her son briefly from the doorway, wondering what he was saying to his grandmother. Her chest continued to rise and fall. He stayed with her much longer than the others, left the room in a hurry and ran down the long corridor. Emma started after him.

"Let him go, Mama," Allison directed.

In a few minutes a doctor charged through the door and J.D. reappeared, looking somewhat pleased with himself.

"J.D., Darlin'. Where have you been?" Emma asked, again trying not to cry while hugging her son.

"I went down to the emergency room."

"What for?" Allison asked.

"I went and found a doctor. I told him that he better get up here quick and sign my grandmother's death certificate and turn off that damn machine."

***

The twins, their brother and his wife left the hospital and drove to Bee's apartment. Charlie and Hazel went into the kitchen to look for something to eat. Emma and Rachel went directly to the den. Their mother's very old yet still sturdy paint-stained drawing board stood solemnly in one corner, next to a window. Fading light from the setting sun cast shadows across the room.

"Look, Rachel," Emma said, peering out the window.

The late evening sky was colored with pink streaks. Little powder-puff clouds drifted through the rapidly changing sunset.

"Wouldn't she have loved to see this sky—" Emma's words faded, moisture dripping from the corners of her eyes.

The sisters turned toward the drawing board. They had no idea why they went to the den together. It felt like the appropriate thing to do. For some reason, Bee had left the usually cluttered place cleared and cleaned. One unfinished painting lay in the middle of the drawing board. Rachel reached for it with care.

"Emma," she oohed quietly.

It was another of Bee's botanical drawings, a single flower stalk, with highly detailed leaves and blossoms. Near the top left side of the picture a small butterfly flirted with a leaf. At the very top, on the right side, was a bigger butterfly. The entire drawing was uncolored, except for the top butterfly, which was painted brilliant yellow.

Emma gasped, putting a hand to her lips.

"What? What, Emma?" Rachel asked. "What is it?"

"The drawing, Rachel. The drawing. She was telling us—"

"What? What was she telling us?"

"She only colored the one butterfly. The rest of the picture is pen and ink."

371

"She didn't finish it."

"No, it's not that. Don't you see? She cleaned off her drawing board. When was the last time you saw this with no work on it?"

Rachel shook her head slowly, "Never."

"That's right. Look. Her water box is empty. Her brushes were put away. She didn't plan to come back."

Rachel started to cry.

"Don't cry, Rachel," Emma said, putting her arm around her sister's shoulder. "Mother's fine. That's why she left this picture for us."

"What do you mean?"

"The butterfly, Rachel. The butterfly was painted yellow—the color of a sunbeam."

"Yes?" Rachel asked, not understanding where Emma was headed.

"Rachel, what does the sun do every morning?"

"It comes up. It rises."

"That's right. I think mother left us this to tell us that her spirit has risen. That she's not dead."

Rachel shook her head slowly.

"I don't know about that, Emma."

"Yes. Of course. Don't you see? The butterfly. The butterfly is a symbol of the resurrection."

***

Emma took the next week off from work and started the long process to settle her mother's estate. Funeral arrangements were easy to make since Bee decreed she would be cremated and her ashes interred in the columbarium at St. Martin's. Emma and Rachel filled the receiving room at the funeral home with their mother's drawings and placed a huge basket of multi-colored flowers on a stand near the center of the room to celebrate the life of an artist.

A writer for the Atlanta Constitution called Emma four times for more details about Bee for the lengthy obituary they were publishing about her gifted mother. Lost in a myriad of activities surrounding final arrangements, Emma forgot her beloved city was nearing the end of its quest to host the 1996 Olympic Games. Her mother's obituary was published in the Atlanta Constitution in the same headlining edition that proclaimed, "It's Atlanta!" How thrilled Bee would have been to know the Olympics would be coming to her beloved Atlanta! Emma knew in her heart her mother was indeed rejoicing with other Atlantans over the momentous undertaking that would keep the city in the forefront of world news for the next four years. She wished secretly, deep within her own soul, that there would be some way she could take part, if only to tell people it was time to lay aside bigotry and war and get on with the job of being loving children of God.

The memorial service for Bee was held two days later. Although it was a beautiful service, Emma could only remember singing her mother's favorite hymn, Fairest Lord Jesus. When they reached to the end of the second stanza, she sang out:

> *Fair are the meadows, fairer still the woodlands,*
> *Robed in the blooming garb of spring;*
> *Jesus is fairer, Jesus is purer,*
> *Who makes the woeful heart to sing.*

***

Bills had to be paid, the apartment emptied and cleaned, and Bee's possessions had to be distributed. Emma worked tirelessly sorting an accumulation of more than a thousand books, hundreds of classical records and a wonderful assortment of household goods. Pots and pans and kitchen utensils were hauled to John's new apartment. He was the closest grandchild and everyone agreed he should receive the bulk of his grandmother's furniture. J.D. would not want it and Allison and Steve were already situated in their own home. Emma's brother and his wife hauled off the valuable Limoges china and much of the fine crystal. Emma and Rachel took the art. Bee stashed away much of it in a small, two-drawer filing cabinet—the drawings she did to make money to feed them as children. For Emma, the real treasure was the botanical drawing, with the yellow butterfly, that now fed her soul.

Final clean-up of her mother's belongings was a time of reflection and soul-searching for Emma. Rather than hire a cleaning team, which she could easily have afforded with the cash Bee left in her checking account, Emma decided to do it herself. John and J.D. came to help but Emma asked them to let her finish the job alone. Somehow it was an appropriate way to say a final good-bye to the mother she loved and admired and finally came to know in the last few months of her life.

There was a chest of drawers full of greeting cards which Emma carefully sifted through. She hummed while she worked, joyfully listening to classical music on her mother's old stereo. A small box contained cards sent to Bee's children. Lifting one off the top, she opened the old envelope and pulled out two identical birthday cards from Grandmother Browning—one for Rachael and the other for Emma. It pictured a little pig-tailed girl, wearing a blue dress, sitting in a red chair, holding a baby doll in its lap. Emma opened her card and read the verse:

You're such a little doll yourself
This birthday card is bringing
A wish for all that you desire
To keep your heart a-singing!

"That's your message for me, isn't it Lord," Emma proclaimed. "No matter what happens or how bad things may seem, if I look for the lesson to be learned and the wisdom to be gained, the compassion to be shared and the love to be given, I can keep my heart singing."

Emma started humming *Ode to Joy* and went back to her chores.

***

Georgia Tech's home opener for the 1990 football season was the following Saturday and Emma went with Bill Stanley. While milling around Fifth Street with other spectators they stopped to inspect a replica of the real Ramblin' Reck that was to be given away at the end of the season.

"Pick the National Champions and Win a Ramblin' Reck" the registration card said.

On the front of the card was a list of teams. Emma studied her card a moment and turned to Bill.

"Who's gonna be the National Champion this year?"

Bill knew a lot about football. Emma was positive he could pick a champion.

"Umm—Florida State," he said.

Emma bent over the table and began to circle her selection.

"FSU," she said happily. "I'll go along with that."

With a bolt out of the blue, her silent voice spoke up.

Make it Tech!

"Tech!" Emma said excitedly to Bill. "Make it Tech!"

He looked at her as if to say she was dim-witted.

"Emma, there's no way on God's green earth Georgia Tech can win the championship this year."

She playfully pouted and stuck out her lower lip.

"Won't be Tech?"

"Nope," Bill answered. "If you want to win that car, go with Florida State."

Emma reluctantly circled Florida State and dropped her card in the box.

Make it Tech! her silent voice said again.

They bought a coke, ate a hot-dog, and trudged up the long hill to the north end of the west stands. Bill was sweating profusely. His knees buckled and he stumbled forward in a drunken stagger though he had no alcohol.

He's ill, Emma thought, wondering what she had gotten herself into. The Ramblin' Reck roared onto the field and Emma laid aside her worry about Bill Manley while watching her Yellow Jackets defeat N.C. State by a score of 21 to 13.

Her silent voice spoke up again at the end of the game: *Make it Tech!*

***

"Our initial exam showed your mother's heart was in good shape, Mrs. St. Claire," the Coroner told Emma a week later. "It may take a while before we know what caused her death. I can send my written report to your family doctor, if you want."

"Yes, that would be fine. Thank you," Emma said.

She hung up the phone and called David Cooper to schedule an appointment. Emma no longer needed regular sessions with Dr. Cooper, though she did see him from time to time. Now she wanted to see him as soon as possible. The next afternoon she was sitting in his comfortable office.

"My mom died three weeks ago, David. I didn't cry for two weeks. Then one day I let loose and cried for an hour. I couldn't cry after her death because I felt she was surrounded by a blessed peace. I didn't want to do anything to diminish her joy."

David was a little surprised.

"She did a number of things to tell us she knew she was leaving. Her desk was cleaned off. In my entire life, I don't ever remember that drawing board being neat. She even emptied the water tray for her brushes. There was one lone picture in the center of her drawing board. It was a stalk of wildflowers with two butterflies near the top."

The doctor rocked back in his chair and listened intently.

"It was a black and white drawing, David. She colored the wings of the one butterfly at the top. It was yellow. While I was admiring it I realized what she was telling me."

"What?"

"The butterfly is one of the symbols for the resurrection, David. It was her way of telling me she wasn't dying—that she was going to a new life."

"That's very interesting," he said, nodding and rocking.

"She told her friends about how good we had been to her, how lucky she was.

"My poem about my experiences with Philip was a tremendous catalyst for healing between us. The pain of the last three years was worth it for the peace and acceptance we finally had. She and I had conversations about eternal life and reincarnation and my experiences were amazing and comforting to her. Whenever grief starts to overtake me, I remember that little boy at the river and what he told his sister when she joined him after her own death. I can't mourn for my Mom when I think of the blessed peace that has come to her even though I do miss her a lot."

Emma's doctor leaned back in his rocking chair. She was calm and at peace, even in the face of her mother's death, and he wondered why she needed to see him.

"Mother's will surprised everyone," she went on.

He raised his eyebrows in a quizzical expression.

"She left her money and stocks to my brother and sister."

"Oh?"

"Yes. She didn't leave me a penny. Her thinking was that she gave me mine earlier because she gave me money when we built the house. They still got the lion's share and I'm fine with that. I do get the diamond broach since I was my grandmother's namesake. Of course, Rachel and I dispersed her household belongings to whomever we chose. Rachel and Charlie get the stocks and cash."

David was slightly shocked.

"Since I'm the executrix of her estate I have to pay it out to them. And mother had a life estate in my grandparents' estate and I'll have to oversee the distribution of that inheritance, too. I will get some money from that."

The good doctor rocked back and forth and nodded his head, still wondering why she needed to see him.